NAVIGATION

FOR

PILOTS

NAVIGATION
FOR
PILOTS

Jim Hitchcock

Airlife
England

First published in 1997 by
Airlife Publishing, an imprint of
The Crowood Press Ltd
Ramsbury, Marlborough
Wiltshire SN8 2HR

www.crowood.com

Paperback edition 2005

© J.E. Hitchcock 1997 and 2005

British Library Cataloguing-in-Publication Data
A catalogue record for this book is available from the British Library.

ISBN 1 86126 797 5

Typeset by Phoenix Typesetting, Auldgirth, Dumfriesshire
Printed and bound in Great Britain by the
Cromwell Press Ltd, Trowbridge, Wiltshire

CONTENTS

	Page
PREFACE	xii
ABOUT THIS BOOK	xiii

SECTION 1   THE EARTH — 1

CHAPTER 1   POSITION — 3

The Cardinal Points – The Earth Graticule – Great Circles – Meridians and Anti-meridians – Small Circles – The Equator – Latitude – Longitude – The Prime Meridian – Difference in Latitude and Longitude – Great Circle Tracks – Rhumb Line Tracks.

CHAPTER 2   DIRECTION — 15

360° Notation – True Direction, Magnetic Direction and Variation – Isogonals – Magnetic Direction, Compass Direction and Deviation – Convergency – Grid Direction and Grivation – Isogrivs.

CHAPTER 3   DISTANCE — 26

Statute Mile – Nautical Mile – Kilometre – Conversion Between Units – The Circular Slide Rule – Departure – Metres and Feet.

CHAPTER 4   SPEED — 34

Units of Speed – Knots – Miles Per Hour – Kilometres Per Hour – Indicated Airspeed – Rectified Airspeed – True Airspeed – Equivalent Airspeed – Ground Speed – Mach Number – Calibrated Airspeed – Correct Outside Air Temperature – Conversion of Rectified Airspeed to True Airspeed – Conversion of Mach Number to True Airspeed – Speed, Distance and Time; Relationships and Calculations.

SECTION 2 BASIC NAVIGATION TECHNIQUES 45

CHAPTER 5 TRIANGLE OF VELOCITIES 47
The Three Basic Velocity Vectors – Drift – The Basic Vector Triangle Problems; Geometrical Solutions and Solutions on the Navigation Computer – Finding the Wind Velocity at a Turning Point – Head and Crosswind Components on a Runway.

CHAPTER 6 FUEL 71
Imperial Gallons and Pounds – United States Gallons – Litres and Kilograms – Conversion Factors – Specific Gravity – Fuel Flow and Fuel Consumption – Selecting the Most Economical Cruising Level.

CHAPTER 7 PILOT NAVIGATION 80
The 1 in 60 Rule – Track Made Good and Track Error – Paralleling the Track – Regaining Track – The Double Track Error Method – Closing Angle – The Standard Closing Angle Method – Altering Heading Directly for Destination – Estimating Track Angles on a Chart – Revising Ground Speed – Revising the Estimated Time of Arrival – Marking up Check Points on a Chart – Distance Marks – Fraction Marks – Time Marks – Use of the Fraction and Time Marks to Revise the Estimated Time of Arrival – Some Practical Pilot Navigation Techniques – Fraction Gone Marks and Closing Angle Lines – Estimating Drift and Ground Speed from True Airspeed and Wind Velocity – Pilot Navigation on Airways – Estimation of Distance on a Chart.

SECTION 3 AERONAUTICAL MAPS AND CHARTS 103

CHAPTER 8 CHART REQUIREMENTS AND SCALE 105
Orthomorphism – Scale – The Reduced Earth

CHAPTER 9 MERCATOR'S PROJECTION 108
Principle and Appearance of the Projection – Scale and Chart Convergency – Measurement of Track Direction – Measurement of Distance – Plotting Radio Bearings – Conversion Angle and its Application – Summary of Properties.

CHAPTER 10 TRANSVERSE AND OBLIQUE MERCATOR'S PROJECTIONS 125
Transverse Mercator's Projection – Principle and Appearance of the Projection – Central Meridian – Limitations of Use – Summary of Properties. – Oblique Mercator's Projection – Principle and Appearance of the Projection – Limitations of Use – Summary of Properties.

CHAPTER 11 LAMBERT'S CONFORMAL CONIC PROJECTION 130
The Simple Conic Projection – Standard Parallel – Appearance of the Chart – Constant of the Cone – Chart Convergency and Scale. – Lambert's Conformal Conic Projection – Parallel of Origin – Two Standard Parallels – Chart Convergency and Scale – $^2/_3$: $^1/_6$ Rule – Appearance of Rhumb Lines and Great Circles – Plotting Radio Bearings – Transferred Meridian – Summary of Properties.

CHAPTER 12 POLAR STEREOGRAPHIC PROJECTION 143
Principle and Appearance of the Projection – Scale and Chart Convergency – Limitations of Use – Summary of Properties.

CHAPTER 13 TOPOGRAPHICAL AND AERONAUTICAL MAPS AND CHARTS 147
The Purpose of Topographical Maps – Detail to be Shown – The 1 : 250,000 and 1 : 500,000 Series of UK Topographical Maps – Display of Natural, Man-made and Aeronautical Features on These Maps – Typical Information Panels Around the Edges of a 1 : 250,000 Series Map – The 1 : 500,000 Series, Minimum Elevation Figures and UK ATS Airspace Classification Chart – Pre-flight Map Preparation – Map Reading in the Air – "Lost Procedure".

SECTION 4 MISCELLANEOUS PROCEDURES 157

CHAPTER 14 RELATIVE VELOCITY 159
Relative Velocity Between Two Aircraft – Uses of Relative Velocity – Overtaking – Adjusting True Airspeed to Achieve a Revised Estimated Time of Arrival – Collision Risk – Line of Constant Bearing – Typical Collision Risk Problems.

CHAPTER 15   NAVIGATIONAL EMERGENCY DATA   170

Critical Point – Single Leg Case – Multi-leg Case – Reduced True Airspeed Case – Point of No Return – Single Leg Case – Multi-leg Case – Alternative Solution – Varying Fuel Flow Case – Point of No Alternate – Concept of a 'Phantom Aircraft'.

CHAPTER 16   TIME AND TIME CONVERSIONS   189

The Julian Calendar – The Gregorian Calendar – Kepler's Laws of Planetary Motion – The Seasons and the Apparent Movement of the Sun – Derivation of Time – The Sidereal Day – The Apparent Solar Day – Mean Solar Time and Civil Time – The Sidereal Year – The Tropical Year – Local Mean Time – Greenwich Mean Time (Co-ordinated Universal Time) – Conversion of Arc to Time – Standard Time and the International Date Line – Standard Times Lists – Conversions Between the Different Time Datum – Sunrise and Sunset – Interpolation of the Tables in the *Air Almanac* – Twilight – Types of Time Related Problems.

CHAPTER 17   PLOTTING   212

The Basic Elements of Plotting – Deduced Reckoning – Plotting Position Lines from Ground Stations – Types of Ground Stations and Types of Bearings Received at the Aircraft – Recap of Plotting Bearings on Lambert and Mercator Charts – Climbing and Descending – Top of Climb – Top of Descent – Factors Required in Calculation of a Climb or Descent – The General Plotting Sequence – The Plotting Chart – The Navigation Log Form – Plotting the Position of an Aircraft – A Visual Pinpoint – A Radar Fix – A Simultaneous Fix – A Running Fix – A "Cocked Hat" Fix – Examination Plots, the Technique – A Demonstration Plot.

SECTION 5   MAGNETISM AND COMPASSES   253

CHAPTER 18   MAGNETISM AND EARTH MAGNETISM   255

Magnetic Polarity – Conventions of Polarity and Lines of Magnetic Force – Repulsion and Attraction – Hard Iron and Soft Iron – Methods of Magnetising and Demagnetising – The Earth's Magnetic Field – Magnetic Variation – Dip – Horizontal and Vertical Components – Isogonals.

CHAPTER 19   DIRECT READING MAGNETIC COMPASSES   265

Types of Direct Reading Compasses – Basic Requirements
– Compass Checks – Acceleration Errors in Level Flight –
Acceleration Errors in a Turn.

CHAPTER 20   CALIBRATION (COMPASS SWINGING)   274

The Reason for Compass Calibration – Deviation –
Coefficients A, B and C – The Deviation Formula – Measuring the
Deviation – Calculating the Coefficients – Correcting for the
Coefficient – Residual Deviation – Heading of Maximum
Deviation.

CHAPTER 21   REMOTE READING COMPASSES   287

Drawbacks of the Direct Reading Compass – How Remote
Reading Compasses Address these Drawbacks – The Flux Valve –
The Detector Unit – The Self-Synchronous Unit – Pre-Flight
Checks – Acceleration and Turning Errors – Compass Calibration
and Correction.

SECTION 6   ADVANCED FLIGHT DECK SYSTEMS   293

CHAPTER 22   INERTIAL NAVIGATION SYSTEMS   295

Requirements of Inertial Navigation Systems –
Accelerometers – The Stable Platform – Rate Integrated Gyro
– Platform Layout – The Integration Process – Correction for
Gyro Errors – Schuler Loop – Bounded and Unbounded errors –
Initial Levelling and Alignment – Mode Selector – Control and
Display Unit – Checks – Strap-Down Systems – The Ring Laser
Gyro – Mode Selector – Inertial System Display Unit – Alignment
Tests.

CHAPTER 23   FLIGHT MANAGEMENT SYSTEMS   314

The Flight Management Computer – The Data Base – Mode
Priorities – The Control and Display Unit – The Function Keys –
The Cathode Ray Tube Display – The Annunciators – Basic Start
Up Checks.

CHAPTER 24   ELECTRONIC FLIGHT INSTRUMENT SYSTEMS   322
The Control Panel – The Attitude Display Indicator Controls
– The Horizontal Situation Indicator Mode Selector – The
Cathode Ray Tube Displays – The Colour Coding – Failure Flags
– Basic Start Up Checks.

CHAPTER 25   GLOBAL POSITIONING SYSTEMS   329
The Global Positioning System – The Space Segment – The
Control Segment – The User Segment – Receiver Displays.

TABLE OF ABBREVIATIONS   333

INDEX   337

ACKNOWLEDGEMENTS

The author wishes to acknowledge the assistance of the following people in the preparation of this book. Mr A du Feu of Flight Crew Licensing 2 at the CAA for his advice on publications relating to Licences for Pilots and sources of related training materials. Mr D P Smith of the Aeronautical Charts section of the CAA for permission to reproduce the plotting chart used in Chapter 17. Mr R Pooley of Pooley's PLC (formerly trading as Airtour International) for permission to use illustrations of the Airtour CRP-5 navigation computer. Except where otherwise credited all illustrations are by the author.

PREFACE

I hope that student pilots who read this book will find it of use when preparing themselves for their written examinations and that some of the practical ideas may be of help as well, even though they do not form part of the examinations.

As someone whose entire working life has been at the sharp end of aviation, (initially as servicing ground crew, then as aircrew and finally for many years as a senior lecturer in navigation subjects at one of Europe's top commercial civil aviation schools), I have at times encountered problems with some text books. One particularly bad trend that appears all too often is text written, supposedly for beginners, where the author has assumed that the reader already has as much background knowledge as he or she! Aviation text books are not the only ones guilty of this sin, quite a few so called basic computer manuals are incomprehensible to the layman, as many of you may have discovered.

In preparing this book I have tried to avoid any assumption of subject knowledge in my readers. As a result, some of you may feel that there is too much 'dotting of i's and crossing of t's'. To you I say, please be patient and remember that not everyone may have the same background as yourself.

Modern education at both primary and secondary level in schools has encouraged the use of pocket calculators and desktop computers to the detriment of mental calculation. This is fine as long as an electronic calculator or computer is available, functioning correctly, and the operator keys in the right information. If any one of these three parameters is missing all that is left is the computer we were all issued with at birth, *brains*. Throughout this book the reader is encouraged to develop an automatic mental checking system *before* programming up any type of computer, i.e. to determine parameters within which the correct answer must lie. This has a twofold benefit:

(1)   It will immediately indicate a nonsense answer from the computer, usually due to faulty information entered by the operator.
(2)   It will in time and with practice develop a mental ability to cope with navigation problems in flight without recourse to any form of computer aid, a great asset during single pilot operations especially in helicopters and light aircraft.

To the aspiring pilot, at whatever level, I would like to say, 'May you be successful in your studies and get as much enjoyment out of flying in the future as I have in the past'.

JE Hitchcock, Abingdon

ABOUT THIS BOOK

The purpose of this manual is to provide a study pack for the subject of Air Navigation as applicable to current Pilot Licences. The introduction of a Joint European Airline Transport Pilot's Licence scheme has led to changes in how items are grouped together for study and examination purposes. As a result, Navigation, which in many European Licences used only to cover the basics as far as plotting, now encompasses items such as Magnetism, Compasses, Inertial Navigation and Flight Management Systems, all of which previously were under different umbrellas. This second edition of *Navigation for Pilots* has been extended to meet these requirements for the Commercial Pilot, ***but it still contains all the navigation basics (and useful tips) for the Private Pilot that were in the first edition***.

The Licence examinations make great use of multiple-choice questions. Here are some words of warning for any candidate thinking that this form of examination is easy! Firstly, most questions have four options from which to choose the answer, and a penalty system is employed that ensures that not only do wrong answers get no marks they also result in a loss of marks. In other words, if you are not sure of the answer, don't guess. Secondly, the examiners have a vast experience of setting multiple-choice questions and many of the wrong answers on offer have been derived from the application of known common errors made by candidates. Ironically, the only time a candidate can be certain that he or she has made a major mistake is when their answer comes nowhere near matching any of those on offer. There are a few, but not many, examples of multiple-choice questions in this book. The main thrust of the book is to give an understanding of the subjects rather than produce a questions and answers manual.

In fact there is now an even greater need for *all pilots* to get a good solid grasp of the basics of navigation. The availability of a variety of automatic navigation aids, even in many modern light aircraft, tends to lead to complacency and over-reliance on electronic boxes. To be fair, the reliability of most modern navigation aids is very high, but they can, and do, go wrong from time to time. It is at these times that a good basic knowledge of navigation can ensure a safe and smooth continuance of the flight. This is not a problem likely to affect the Commercial Pilot who will have had a structured training, but sadly one still comes across the occasional would-be Private Pilot who is only interested in the shortest way to pass the examinations with the least amount of work. If you fall into this last category, try and change your ways and learn the basics properly; it could save you a lot of trouble in the long run and make your flying even more enjoyable knowing that at all times you are on top of the job.

Whilst the whole of this book is relevant to the training of Commercial Pilots, *the following parts are applicable to the training of Private Pilot*:

Chapter 1	All.
Chapter 2	Paragraphs 2.1 to 2.6 inclusive.
Chapter 3	All except paragraph 3.11.
Chapter 4	All except paragraph 4.9.
Chapter 5	All.
Chapter 6	All except paragraph 6.9.
Chapter 7	All.
Chapter 8	All.
Chapter 9	Paragraphs 9.1, 9.2, 9.3, 9.11, 9.12, 9.13 and 9.24 *Uses*.
Chapter 10	Paragraphs 10.1 to 10.6 inclusive and 10.7 *GCs* and *Uses*.
Chapter 11	Paragraphs 11.1 to 11.7 inclusive and 11.6 *Uses*.
Chapter 13	All.

SECTION 1
THE EARTH

Navigation is the art of finding one's way around. Before the subject can be developed it is necessary to explain the standard methods used to identify position, denote direction and measure distance. Since navigation is carried out over, or, in the case of air navigation, above the surface of the earth, the shape and form of our planet is the logical starting point of these studies.

The earth is not quite a perfect sphere, being approximately 42 kilometres smaller at its polar diameter than at its maximum diameter which is at a point not quite half way between its poles, (which means it is also slightly pear shaped). Since the average diameter of the earth is 12,740 km it can be seen that these deformities in the shape of the earth are of the order of 0.33% and can be ignored *for most practical purposes*. Unless stated otherwise, from this point on the earth will be considered to be a perfect sphere.

CHAPTER 1

POSITION

1.1 Identifying position on the surface of a sphere is not easy since a sphere has no obvious natural datum points (such as corners) to which a position can be related. Some form of graticule needs to be constructed on the surface of the sphere along with a system of locating any position on this graticule. Before any such graticule can be constructed, some unique feature of the earth must be identified to which the graticule can be associated.

THE CARDINAL POINTS

1.2 The unique feature that fulfils this requirement is the direction of rotation of the earth. This rotation takes place about two points on the earth diametrically opposite to each other known as **The Poles**, the axis of spin passing through the centre of the earth. The two poles are known as the **North Pole** and the **South Pole**. To distinguish between them it is necessary for an observer to face in the direction of the earth's rotation (towards the rising sun), the North pole will then be on the observer's left hand and the South pole on the observer's right hand. The direction of rotation of the

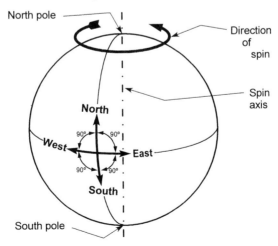

Fig. 1–1. The Cardinal Points.

earth is known as **East** and the opposite direction to East is known as **West**, both of these directions being at a right angle to the North/South spin axis.(see Fig. 1-1). The four basic directions of **North (N), South (S), East (E)** and **West (W)** are collectively termed the **Cardinal Points**.

THE EARTH GRATICULE

1.3 Having established the presence of the poles and the basic direction references of North (N), South (S), East (E) and West (W) these can now be used to construct a graticule on the surface of the earth. If a circle could be drawn on the surface of the earth so that it passed through the position of both the poles, the direction that such a line defined would be N/S. It would also have its centre co-incident with the centre of the earth and a diameter the same as the earth's, such a circle is the largest that can be drawn on the surface of the earth and is known as a **Great Circle (GC)**. Since the poles are diametrically opposite to each other on the earth, it follows that an infinite number of GCs could be drawn to pass through the poles each one defining N/S. Each Semi-GC joining the poles is termed a **Meridian** and forms part of the graticule used in establishing positions. The Semi-GC that shares the other half of GC with a meridian is known as the meridian's **Anti-meridian**.

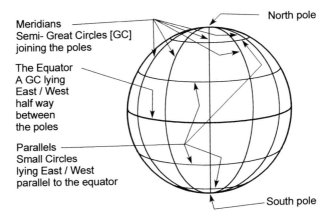

Fig. 1–2   The Earth Graticule.

1.4 With the meridians defining N/S it is necessary to imagine lines running E/W to complete a graticule system on the earth's surface. Such E/W lines would appear as circles around the earth at right angles to the meridians. Only one of these circles (exactly half way between the two poles) is a GC, having the same centre and diameter as the earth. All the other E/W lines are of varying lesser diameters and collectively are known

4

as **Small Circles**. The E/W GC described above is termed the **Equator**; it divides the earth in two. Since all the E/W Small Circles are running parallel to the Equator they are termed **Parallels**. (see Fig. 1-2)

LATITUDE (lat)

1.5 The equator is the only line defining E/W direction that is a GC. This unique property plus the fact that it also divides the earth into two hemispheres provides one of the datums used in establishing position on the earth. The first thing that can be stated is whether or not a position is N or S of the equator, thus eliminating half of the earth from the reckoning.

1.6 The next thing to be specified is the parallel running through a position; this will narrow the search down to all places along that parallel. The centre of the earth is used as the point of origin of the equator and parallels, the equator being described by the rim of a flat disc, the parallels by the rims of the bases of a series of cones and the poles by points at right angles to the equator. The angle between the equatorial flat disc and the cone describing a particular parallel is termed the **Latitude (lat)** of that parallel, (see Fig. 1–3).

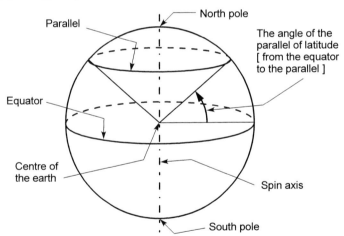

Fig 1–3   *Parallel of Latitude*

1.7 The means of angular measurement used is the established international system whereby a circle is divided into 360 degrees, each degree into 60 minutes and each minute into 60 seconds. Thus the equator becomes 0° of lat, since it is the dividing line between the hemispheres and is neither N nor S. The poles become 90° of lat but must be specified by hemisphere, the N pole being 90° N; similarly the S pole becomes 90° S.

In aviation, intermediate parallels are usually expressed in just degrees and minutes. However, many documents give airfield and ground radio installation positions to a higher degree of accuracy which includes seconds as well. Thus London (Heathrow) is shown as lying on the parallel of 51°28'11"N and Strasbourg (Neuhof) as on the 48°33'16"N parallel (see Fig. 1–4.) Note the use of ° to denote degrees, ' to denote minutes and " to denote seconds. It is common practice to leave these out, thus Neuhof's lat may be written 483316N. This form of notation may be further modified in some documents to conform with the way certain pieces of advanced navigation equipment have their computers programmed. Thus the lat of Strasbourg (Neuhof) could be shown as N4833·27 with no °, ' or " and the 16 seconds being expressed in a decimal form as ·27 of a minute.

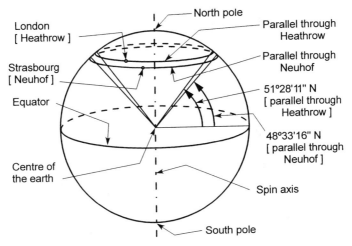

Fig. 1–4   The Parallels through Heathrow and Neuhof.

LONGITUDE (long)

1.8 Having established the parallel on which a position lies, its exact position can be given by identifying the meridian which passes through the position. It has already been stated that there are an infinite number of meridians, so there is no one meridian that is an obvious datum. Nonetheless, one meridian has to be nominated as the datum, or **Prime Meridian**, and here the choice of the meridian passing through **Greenwich** came about as a result of an International Conference held in Washington in 1884 to decide which of several options to adopt as the World standard. The meridian through the observatory set up at Greenwich in 1675 had long been the most likely choice. This was because of the publication in 1766 of a Nautical Almanac, the development of a reliable nautical chronometer by John Harrison (1693–1776) and the establishment of **Greenwich Mean Time (GMT)** (now renamed **Co-ordinated Universal Time (UTC)**). A major factor in the final selection was that the chosen prime meridian would also become the datum for universal time, with the date changing on crossing its anti-meridian which would be known as the **International Date Line**. Obviously such a Date Line needs to be through as much open ocean as possible. Any country having the Date Line running through it would be presented with the administrative problem of always having two different dates operating within its boundaries. Fortunately the choice of Greenwich as the prime meridian does not cause too much of a problem with the Date Line, only a couple of detours in the line being needed to avoid going through countries. There is more of this in Chapter 16.

1.9 Having established Greenwich as the prime or 0° meridian, other meridians can be identified by horizontal angular measurement E or W of the 0° meridian up to a maximum of 180° either way. Again the centre of the earth is the point of origin, the angle being measured horizontally from a line joining this point of origin and the prime meridian at the equator to a similar line joining the same point of origin to the meridian being identified, (see Fig. 1–5). This angle is termed the **Longitude (long)** of the meridian and it must also specify in which 180° arc E or W of Greenwich it is to be found. In paragraph 1.7 it was stated that Strasbourg (Neuhof) is on the 483316N parallel of lat. The meridian that passes through Neuhof is 07°46'41"E of the Greenwich meridian, this normally being written as

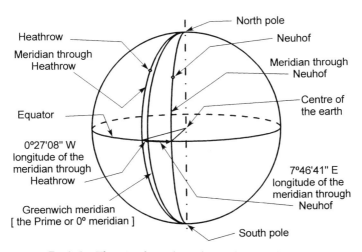

Fig 1–5   The Meridians through Heathrow and Neuhof

074641E. The combination of a position's lat and long are unique to that position, so Neuhof's location is expressed as 483316N 074641E. Note that lat is always given before long and in this case a 0 is written in front of the long to signify that there is no hundred or tens in front of the 7. In a similar way 0 would be use where necessary in quoting minutes and seconds. For instance the long of London (Heathrow) is 002708W, meaning it is zero degrees twenty seven minutes and eight seconds of long W of the Greenwich meridian. In the alternative computer form Neuhof's position is given as N4833·27 E00746·68 the extra 0 in the long being required by the computer which is programmed to expect up to 180° of long, Heathrow's position becomes N5128·18 W00027·13 under this system. Unless otherwise stated the non-computer form of lat and long reporting will be used from here on in this book.

1.10 The speed with which most aircraft change position means that to try and give position reports to within seconds of lat and long is impractical. Apart from documents giving the positions of airfields and various ground located radio aid installations it is common practice, on purely practical grounds, not to give position to an accuracy greater than to the nearest minute of lat and long. Using this system Heathrow's position would be given as 5128N 0027W and Neuhof's position as 4833N 0747E.

DIFFERENCE IN LAT AND LONG BETWEEN PLACES

1.11 It is sometimes required to know the difference in lat and long between two positions. This is termed **d'lat** (short for difference in lat) and **d'long** (short for difference in long) or alternatively **ch'lat** and **ch'long** (for change in lat and long). They both mean exactly the same thing! All levels of Pilot Licences are liable to include questions involving the calculation of d'lat and d'long so here are some ground rules and examples:

d'lat rules:
    If both places are in the *Same* hemisphere *Subtract* the smaller lat from the larger, (remember that one degree has 60 minutes in it).
    If the places are in *Opposite* hemispheres *Add* the lats together.
    The direction of the change will be either North or South *From* the first given place *To* the second place.

d'long rules:
    If both places are on the *Same* side of the Greenwich meridian *Subtract* the smaller long from the larger.
    If the places are on *Opposite* sides of the Greenwich meridian *Add* the

longs together. Now check the answer. If it is 180° or less, that completes the calculation. *If however it is more than 180°, it means that the d'long is less going the other way around the world.* To calculate this lesser value just *Subtract* the answer found from 360°.

The direction of the change will be either East or West *From* the first given place *To* the second place *by the shorter route.*

Example:

Calculate the d'lat and d'long from 'A' 5643N 2716W to 'B' 0552N 6918W.

Answer:

Both 'A' and 'B' are in the same hemisphere and West of the Greenwich meridian, so subtract the smaller from the larger in both cases.

Latitude 5643N 'A'	Longitude 6918W 'B'
-0552N 'B'	-2716W 'A'
d'lat 5051 Southward	**d'long 4202 Westward**

d'long <180°, so is the correct answer (see Fig 1–6a).

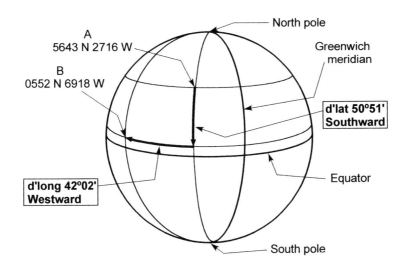

Fig.1–6a   D'lat and D'long

Example:

Calculate the d'lat and d'long from 'A' 1435S 12754E to 'B' 7149N 16628W.

Answer:

'A' and 'B' are in opposite hemispheres and on opposite sides of the Greenwich meridian, so add the values in both cases.

Latitude 1435S 'A' Longitude 12754E 'A'
+7149N 'B' +16628W 'B'
d'lat 8624 Northward **d'long 29422 Westward**
d'long > 180° , so subtract from 360° and reverse direction of change.

36000
-29422 Westward
d'long 6538 Eastward

(See Fig. 1–6b)

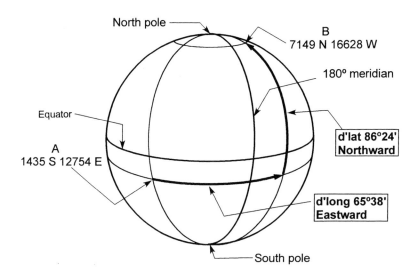

Fig. 1–6b   D'lat and D'long

Example:
Calculate the d'lat and d'long from 'A' 2128S 5619W to 'B' 4952S 2103E.

Answer:
'A' and 'B' are in the same hemisphere but on opposite sides of the Greenwich meridian, so subtract the smaller latitude from the larger and add the longitudes together.

Latitude 4952S 'B' Longitude 5619W 'A'
-2128S 'A' +2103E 'B'
d'lat 2824 Southward **d'long 7722 Eastward**
d'long < 180° , so the answer is correct. (See Fig. 1–6c)

10

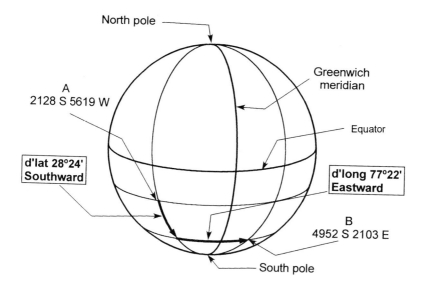

Fig. 1–6c   D'lat and D'long

MORE GREAT CIRCLES

1.12 Meridians and the equator are not the only GCs that can be drawn on the earth. GCs can be drawn at any angle to the latitude and longitude graticule and there is only one particular GC that can be drawn to pass through any two selected positions on the earth (the one exception to this being places, like the Poles, that are geographically opposite each other where the number of possible GCs joining them is infinite). The shorter arc of the GC passing through any two places will represent the most direct route between them. This gives rise to the rule that:

'The shortest distance between two points on the earth is along the shorter arc of the GC passing through them.'

Since radio waves travel by the most direct route from transmitter to receiver it can be seen that they will be following a GC route. As will be shown later this can influence the choice of chart projections for some tasks.

1.13 Fig. 1–7 shows the earth with the GC drawn on it passing through New York and Paris. Also indicated are the angles that this GC makes relative to the meridians it is crossing, in this case the angles get larger as movement is made from New York to Paris.

The only cases where GC directions remain constant along their length are up or down any meridian (due N or S), or along the equator (due E or

*Fig. 1–7   GC passing through New York and Paris showing the
change in the (T) direction along it.*

W). To summarise, the shorter arc of a GC joining two places on the earth gives the shortest distance between them but, apart from up or down a meridian or along the equator, the direction will not be constant. The reason for this is because the meridians which are parallel to each other at the equator converge to meet at the poles thus changing their direction *relative to one another*, this is dealt with in detail in Chapter 2.

RHUMB LINES

1.14 Fig. 1–8 shows the same GC joining New York and Paris as in Fig. 1–7. Also shown drawn between New York and Paris is a curved line which maintains a constant direction relative to the meridians it crosses. Such a constant direction line is called a **Rhumb Line (RL)**.

Meridians and the equator, which are GCs, also have constant direction so by definition they are RLs as well as GCs, (in fact they are the only GCs that are also RLs). In all other cases, such as in Fig. 1–8, the RL does not coincide with the GC joining two places on the earth and, since the GC arc is the shortest distance between the points, it follows that the RL distance between the points *must* be greater.

12

*Fig. 1–8   The Constant (T) direction Rhumb Line (RL)
between New York and Paris*

1.15 Apart from the meridians and equator cases where GC and RL coincide:

Flying along a GC between two places has the disadvantage of changing direction but the advantage of the shortest distance.

Flying along a RL between two places has the advantage of constant direction but the disadvantage of greater distance.

Over short distances these differences are not of any great significance. For instance a GC drawn from W to E across southern England only changes direction over its length by about 4° and a similarly drawn RL is less than 1% greater in length. Over great distances the differences can be considerable and influence the choice of route to be flown. For instance from New York to Paris (see Fig. 1–8) the GC changes direction by some 54° and the RL is around 10% longer than the GC . With modern airliners equipped with navigation aids capable of automatically flying along GC routes the saving in fuel and time by selecting the GC route for such a journey is obvious.

1.16 It is of interest that when Charles Lindbergh (1902–1974) flew from New York to Paris solo in 33 hours back in 1927 the route he chose approximated to the GC. A study of the GC route (see Fig. 1–8) shows that it follows the North American and Canadian coast up to Newfoundland and this he flew in a series of short RLs. He then crossed the Atlantic to southern Eire using a pre-calculated sequence of timed single headings to keep him approximately on the GC until landfall when it was back to a further series of rhumb lines across the Celtic Sea, Cornwall, Plymouth, the English Channel and France to Paris. Had he chosen the single RL route he would have been over open ocean for most of the way and have needed at least three more hours of flying time!

CHAPTER 2

DIRECTION

360° NOTATION

2.1 In Chapter 1 the four cardinal points of N, E, S and W were introduced. Using the same 360° notation for direction as is used for lat and long and going in a clockwise direction starting from N, the angular values of the cardinal point are:

North	=	000° (or alternatively 360°)
East	=	090°
South	=	180°
West	=	270°
North	=	360° (or alternatively 000°) (see Fig. 2–1).

Note how three figure groups are used throughout, 0 signifying no hundreds or no tens as appropriate. This is to reduce the chance of errors

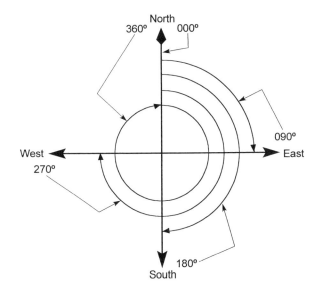

Fig. 2–1   The 360° notation

15

being made when transmitting information by whatever means, particularly in the case of Radio Telephony (R/T) transmissions if reception conditions are poor. For example, if a pilot is instructed to steer 026° but only hears 26 there could be a 0,1,2 or 3 in front of the 26 or any number from 0 to 9 after it. So three figure groups are *always* used for directions and if less than three figures are clearly received a repeat of the message *must be requested and confirmed to clarify the situation.*

TRUE DIRECTION, MAGNETIC DIRECTION AND VARIATION

2.2 The directions so far mentioned are relative to the geographical cardinal directions on the earth. These directions are said to be **True Directions** and are suffixed **(T)**. Unless an aircraft is fitted with sophisticated navigation equipment, such as an Inertial Navigation System (INS), it will not normally have immediate means of finding (T) direction and recourse to a magnetic compass is necessary. The earth has a weak magnetic field which can be sensed in the horizontal plane by a suitably designed compass system (see Chapter 19). Navigationally the main problem with **Magnetic Direction (M)** is that the axis of the earth's magnetic field is not in line with the earth's spin axis, the N (M) pole being situated in the vicinity of Victoria Island, Northern Canada and the S (M) pole on the edge of Antarctica not quite geographically opposite the N (M) pole. As a result the lines of the magnetic field vary in direction when compared to the meridians (which define N (T)). This difference between the (T) direction and the (M) direction at any point on the earth is known as **Magnetic Variation** or **Variation (varn)**. The value of varn is different from place to place (anything from 0° to 180°) depending on the relative directions of the (T) and (M) poles from the observer's position on the earth, the direction of N (M) as defined by the magnetic lines of force may be either E or W of the N (T) direction.

2.3 If (T) direction is to be derived from (M) direction, or vice versa, the value of the local varn has to be applied in the correct sense. The values of local varns are displayed on topographical, plotting and radio navigation charts by lines joining all places having the same value of varn; these lines are called **Isogonals**. Isogonals are currently portrayed by broken lines made up of a series of dashes and labelled at intervals with their value (quoted in whole degrees plus a half degree) and whether it is E or W of (T). To extract the value of local varn from a chart, first make sure the chart is up to date. The chart validity date can be found in one of the information panels around the edges of the chart (explained in detail in Chapter 13), the chart validity date is also the validity date of the varn shown on the chart. Unfortunately, due to the movement of the magnetic poles varn values are not constant, and this movement, although very slow, means that charts need updating every few years, the value of change being different from place to place. The annual rate of change (quoted in minutes E or W) for a particular chart can also be found in the information panels usually alongside the validity date of the chart. Fig. 2–2a shows isogonals with values of $5\frac{1}{2}°$ W , $4\frac{1}{2}°$ W and $3\frac{1}{2}°$ W.

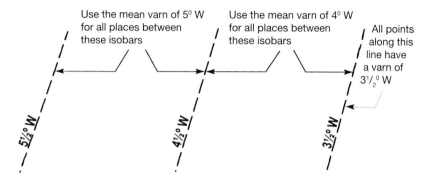

Fig. 2–2a   Isogonals.

2.4   Fig. 2–2b shows in plan view the relative directions of N(T) and N(M) at a place on the earth where variation is 19E. Also shown is a line representing the direction an aircraft is pointing in (known as its **HEADING (hdg)**). From the Figure it can be seen that the aircraft hdg when measured

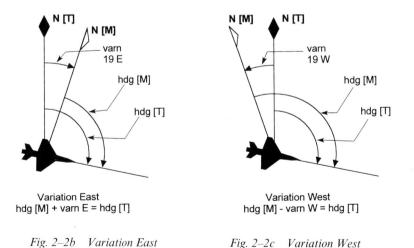

Variation East
hdg [M] + varn E = hdg [T]

Variation West
hdg [M] - varn W = hdg [T]

Fig. 2–2b   Variation East   *Fig. 2–2c   Variation West*

from N (M) will be 19° less than when measured from N (T). When variation is E, (M) direction is always *Less* than (T) direction and conversely when variation is W, (M) direction is always *More* than (T) direction (see Fig. 2–2c).

MAGNETIC DIRECTION, COMPASS DIRECTION AND DEVIATION

2.5 It would seem that all that has to be done is to install a magnetic compass in the aircraft and read hdg (M) from it, extract the variation from the chart and apply it in the correct sense to get hdg (T). Unfortunately it is not quite as simple as that, because magnetic fields within the aircraft structure also affect magnetic compasses causing the reading to be deflected from the hdg (M), the resultant indications being known as **Compass Headings (hdg (C))**. The difference between the hdg (C) and the hdg (M) is called **Deviation (dev)** and its value varies with the hdg of the aircraft. Like varn, the dev is given in degrees E or W, only in this case it is the number of degrees the hdg (C) is lying to the E or W of the hdg (M). Similar rules for converting hdg (C) to hdg (M) and vice versa apply as were used between hdg (M) and hdg (T), (see Fig. 2–3.)

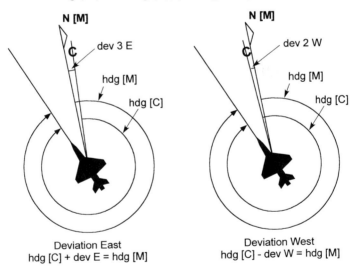

Deviation East
hdg [C] + dev E = hdg [M]

Deviation West
hdg [C] - dev W = hdg [M]

Fig. 2–3   Rules for applying dev to hdg (C).

The derivation of compass dev and methods of correction are dealt with in Chapter 20 and will not be dwelt on here. Amounts of dev present once a compass has been corrected should normally be no more than 3° though in practice slightly larger values are sometimes encountered.

Uncorrected compasses have been known to display very large amounts of dev due to such things as the fitting of extra fuel tanks in the rear fuselage for ferry purposes. Because no two aircraft have precisely the same amount or disposition of magnetism in their structure and no two compasses will be precisely identical in performance, it follows that values of dev will be different for every individual magnetic compass installation as well as varying with the hdg of the aircraft. Dev cards are displayed beside magnetic compass indicators giving the necessary correction to convert hdgs (C) to hdgs (M).

2.6 Conversions between (C), (M) and (T) in both mathematical and diagram form are given in the following examples:

Example:
hdg 097 (C), dev 3E, varn 17W. Calculate hdgs (M) and (T).

Answer:
dev 3E means hdg (C) < hdg (M) by 3°.
varn 17W means hdg (M)> hdg (T) by 17°.
hdg 097 (C), + dev 3E = hdg **100 (M)**,– varn 17W = hdg **083 (T)**
(see Fig. 2–4a).

Example:
hdg 342 (T), varn 21E, dev 2E. Calculate hdgs (M) and (C).

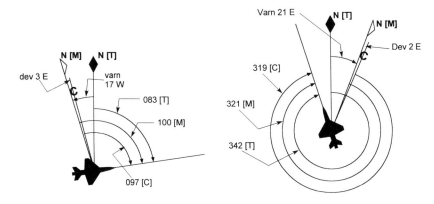

Fig. 2-4a
hdg 097 (C), dev 3E, varn 17W.

Fig. 2–4b
hdg 342 (T), dev 2E, varn 21E.

Answer:
varn 21E means hdg (M) < hdg (T) by 21°.
dev 2E means hdg (C) < hdg (M) by 2°.
hdg 342 (T), – varn 21E = hdg **321 (M)**, – dev 2E = hdg **319 (C)**
(see Fig. 2–4b).

Example:
hdg 006 (M), dev 1W, varn 8W. Calculate hdgs (T) and (C).

Answer:
dev 1W means hdg (C) > hdg (M) by 1°.
varn 8W means hdg (M) > hdg (T) by 8°.
hdg 006 (M), + dev 1W = hdg **007 (C)**.
hdg 006 (M), – varn 8W = hdg **358 (T)**.*
*(006° – 8° = – 2° from 000 / 360° = 358°) (see Fig. 2–4c).

Example:
hdg 053 (T), varn 49W, dev 3E. Calculate hdgs (M) and (C).

Answer:
varn 49W means hdg (M) > hdg (T) by 49°.
dev 3E means hdg (C) < hdg (M) by 3°.
hdg 053 (T), + varn 49W = hdg **102 (M)**, – dev 3E = hdg **099 (C)**
(see Fig. 2–4d).

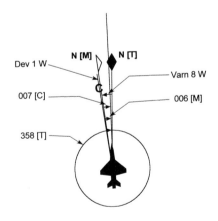

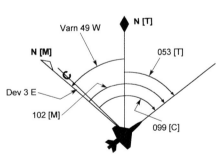

Fig. 2–4c
hdg 006 (M), dv 1W, varn 8W.

Fig. 2–4d
hdg 053 (T), dev 3E, varn 49W

Note: Figs. 2–4a, b, c and d highlight the point that there is only one aircraft but its heading can be measured from more than one datum. It is therefore essential always to annotate a direction with its applicable datum.

CONVERGENCY

2.7 A look back at Fig. 1.7 shows that the meridians start off parallel to each other along the equator but converge towards each other to meet at the poles. This leads to a problem with N (T) for apart from along the equator or up/down a meridian the *relative direction* of N (T) varies from place to place. This change in direction is known as **Convergency (conv)** and is a factor that affects many aspects of navigation.

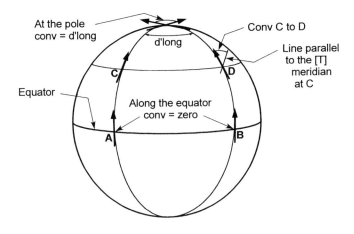

Fig. 2–5   Convergency.

2.8 Fig. 2–5 compares the direction of N (T) at various places on the earth:

At 'A' and 'B' on the equator N (T) is in the same direction although there is a considerable d'long between them, (conv at the equator is 0°).

If the meridians through 'A' and 'B' are followed up to the N pole it can be seen that they converge by the amount of d'long between the meridians, (conv at the poles is maximum = d'long).

'C' and 'D' are on the same meridians as 'A' and 'B' but they are at a lat some way from the equator and the value of conv is somewhere between 0° and d'long.

To summarise, conv is zero at 0° lat and maximum (d'long) at 90° lat. Since sine 0° is zero and sine 90° is 1 (maximum) it follows that conv varies as the sine of the lat and is equal to its maximum value × sine of the lat. In navigation the value of conv is often required between places at different lats and the formula used is:

Convergency = d'long (in degrees) × Sine of mean lat

By *mean* lat is meant the lat half way between the two places *in the same hemisphere*. This can be calculated by either one of two methods:

Either Work out the d'lat, halve it and add to the lower lat (or subtract from the higher lat).

Or Add the two lats together and halve the result.

2.9 As will be shown later the sense in which conv is applied in the southern hemisphere is the opposite to that in the northern hemisphere. Calculation of conv between places on either side of the equator has to be carried out in two steps, from one place to where the equator is crossed and from that point on to the second place in the other hemisphere. Calculations of this nature are not usually found in the licence examinations but if set would give the candidate the long of crossing the equator to enable the two separate parts to be resolved, the final answer being the algebraic sum of the two parts.

2.10 In Chapter 1 the route New York to Paris was discussed with regard to GC and RL differences and it was stated that the direction of the GC changed by some 54° along this route. This is due entirely to the conv between New York and Paris. In round terms their positions are New York 4100N 7400W and Paris 4900N 0200E; this gives a mean lat of 4500N and

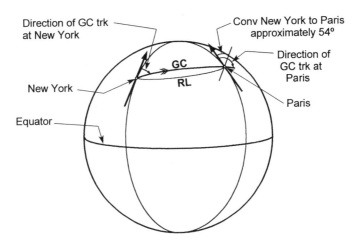

Fig. 2–6   GC direction change from New York to Paris.

a d'long of 76°, (apply the rules from paragraphs 2.8 and 1.11). Putting these facts into the conv formula gives:

Conv New York to Paris = 76° × Sine 45°
                        = 76° × 0·7071
                        = 53·7396° or approximately **54°**.

Fig. 2–6 illustrates this example and shows a line parallel to the meridian through New York drawn through Paris. The angular difference between this line and the meridian through Paris is the conv between New York and Paris i.e. 54°. It is apparent from Fig. 2–6 that direction of the GC measure from the (T) meridian at Paris is greater than the direction of the GC measured from the (T) meridian at New York by the amount of conv between the two places. In the northern hemisphere going Easterly along a GC the (T) direction increases by conv from the departure point, going Westerly it will decrease. Fig. 2–7 shows the southern hemisphere case where the (T) direction decreases with Easterly movement and increases with Westerly movement, (also shown is the RL appropriate to the GC illustrated).

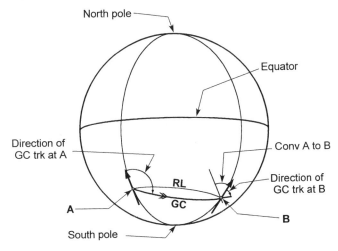

Fig. 2–7 Convergency in the Southern Hemisphere.

Figs. 2–6 and 2–7 highlight another fact. Apart from the equator and the meridians (where GC and RL coincide) the RL *always* lies on the equatorial side of the GC, or conversely the GC path between two places *always* lies on the polar side of the RL path.

23

GRID DIRECTION AND GRIVATION

2.11 For long distance flying, particularly in high lats, a technique known as **Grid Navigation** is sometimes employed, the idea being to draw a squared grid over the top of the lat and long grid with one axis of the squared grid being denoted as the **Grid North (N (G))**. In some cases the grid may be aligned with N (T) at the point of departure, at other times it may be offset so that the planned route will in general stay close to N (G) (see Fig. 2–8).

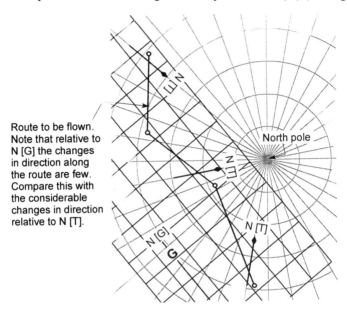

Route to be flown. Note that relative to N [G] the changes in direction along the route are few. Compare this with the considerable changes in direction relative to N [T].

Fig.2–8   A Grid Overlay on a Polar region chart showing Grid North (N(G)).

Navigation is now carried out with reference to the squared grid and N (G), the effect of conv between N (G) and the local N (T) is combined with local varn to give a correction known as **Grivation (griv)** which is applied in a similar way as varn but in this case it is used to convert hdg (G) to hdg (M) and vice versa.

2.12 On grid navigation charts all points having the same griv are joined by lines known as **Isogrivs**. These are annotated in the same way as the isogonals are for denoting lines of common varn. An example of how griv is calculated is given in Fig. 2–9.

At position 'X' the conv between N (G) and N (T) is 28W (*always* measured *from* N (G) *to* the local N (T)), local varn (*always* measured *from*

24

N (T) *to* N (M)) from the isogonal is 7E, therefore griv at 'X' is conv (between N (G) and N (T)) plus varn = 28W + 7E = 21W. As already stated griv is applied in the same sense as varn, so at position 'X' the 21W griv is added to hdg (G) to give hdg (M) or subtracted from hdg (M) to give hdg (G).

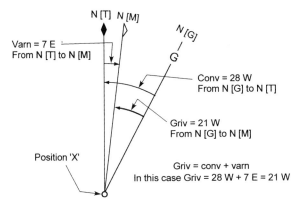

Fig. 2–9   Calculation of Grivation (griv).

CHAPTER 3

DISTANCE

3.1 Through the ages there have been many units used for measuring distance, most of which have long been forgotten. Currently there are three predominant standard units of measurement in use in the world and all have found their way into aviation. Until such time as some universal standard is agreed it is necessary for aviators to know something about the origins of these three units of measurement and, most important of all, how to convert from one to another.

THE STATUTE MILE

3.2 The first of these units of measurement is the **Statute Mile (st m)**. The name 'statute' gives the origin away, it derives from a Royal statute, or law, of Queen Elizabeth the First of England (1535–1603). This law was introduced standardising weights and measures throughout the country, the units being developments and modifications of existing empirical units. The st m is 5280 feet (ft) = 1609 metres (m) long.

THE NAUTICAL MILE

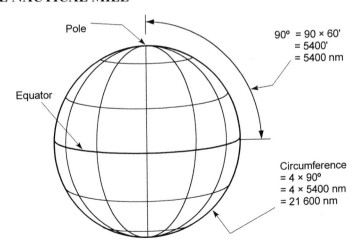

Fig. 3–1   *Nautical Miles on the Earth.*

26

3.3   The next unit of measurement is the **Nautical Mile (nm)**. As the name implies the origin is a nautical one, this being a unit of measurement origi- nally derived for navigation at sea. It was evolved as a unit of measurement to tie in directly with the latitude graticule. The nm is the *average* length of the arc of 1 minute of latitude at the earth's surface measured up, or down, a meridian. Since a meridian encompasses 90 degrees from the equator to a pole and each degree has 60 minutes in it, it follows that there are 90×60 = 5400 minutes of arc from equator to pole which gives 5400 nm, so the full circumference of the earth is four times this distance i.e. 21 600 nm, (see Fig. 3–1). The nm is 6080 ft = 1852 m long.

THE KILOMETRE

3.4   The final unit of measurement is the **Kilometre (km)**. This unit has its origin in the metric system initiated by Napoleon Bonaparte (1769–1821) and like the rest of that system has 10 as its root. Metrification intended to replace the 360 degrees in a circle with 400 metric degrees, giving 100 metric degrees in a right angle. Furthermore each metric degree was to have 100 metric minutes in it thus giving 10,000 metric minutes in a right angle. The km is the *average* length of the arc of 1 metric minute at the earth's surface measured up, or down, the meridian through Paris. Since there are 10,000 metric minutes in a right angle there must be 40,000 in a full circle, which means that the circumference of the earth is 40,000 km. The km is 1000 m = 3280 ft long. Metric degrees were never universally accepted because of a fundamental flaw; figures like isosceles triangles that occur naturally in trigonometry do not have a straightforward number of metric degrees to their internal angles. For example 60 standard degrees converts to 66.66666 (recurring) metric degrees turning quite simple trignometrical problems into number crunching nightmares.

CONVERSION BETWEEN STANDARD UNITS

3.5   Because of the direct relationship between the nm and a minute of lati- tude the nm is the favoured unit of measurement for navigation with many countries, but not universally so. It is therefore a requirement of pilots to be able to convert from one standard to another. This may be achieved by straight mathematics using the following conversion factors:

$$1 \text{ nm} = 6080 / 5280 = 1 \cdot 152 \text{ st m}$$
$$1 \text{ nm} = 6080 / 3280 = 1 \cdot 854 \text{ km}$$
$$1 \text{ st m} = 5280 / 6080 = 0 \cdot 868 \text{ nm}$$
$$1 \text{ st m} = 5280 / 3280 = 1 \cdot 61 \text{ km}$$
$$1 \text{ km} = 3280 / 6080 = 0 \cdot 539 \text{ nm}$$
$$1 \text{ km} = 3280 / 5280 = 0 \cdot 621 \text{ st m}$$

This can be a rather tedious chore and there are many electronic navigation calculators on the market that are pre-programmed to do these conversions, *unfortunately the use of such calculators is not allowed in the licence examinations!* A close study of the rules governing the use of electronic calculators in all examinations is strongly advised. At the time of writing they are not allowed at all for the navigation paper and only non-programmed or nonprogrammable electronic calculators are allowed for other papers. Since the rules governing examinations can change, candidates should check the current rules pertaining prior to sitting any examinations.

THE CIRCULAR SLIDE RULE

3.6 The use of a navigation computer such as the Airtour CRP–5 Computer is allowed in all the examinations. The circular slide rule side on such computers has index marks for the full range of measurement, weight, and volume conversions that a pilot may have to make. Circular slide rules, or straight slide rules come to that, are not often taught in schools these days, the electronic calculator having taken over the number crunching role

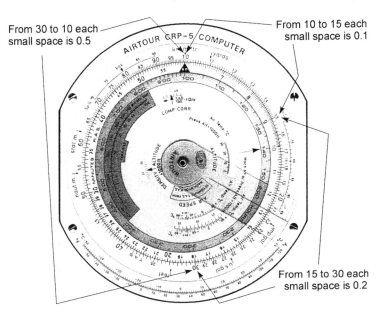

From 10 to 30 each whole number is marked but from 30
on as the scale contracts only each fifth number is marked

*Fig. 3–2   The CRP-5 Circular Slide rule showing the spacing
and numbering of the scale.*

in most cases. For anyone unfamiliar with slide rules a few points regarding layout and procedures now follow, even the experts may like to refresh their memories!

3.7　The circular slide rule is basically a device for solving ratio problems. In fact it is a scalar form of logarithms but no knowledge of the theory and use of logarithms is required in its use. There are however two aspects of the scale that need to be clearly understood; these are the way in which the scale is spaced out and how it is numbered. Reference to Fig. 3–2 shows:

Spacing. This is not constant, closing up as the numbers get larger.

Numbering. The actual numbers printed go from 10 to 95, with some omissions due to compression of the scale. Computers like the Airtour CRP – 5 have a rotatable cursor and by moving this around the graduated scale it is possible to select any value from 10 to 99·9. Since only whole numbers are printed on the scale any decimal point has to be mentally inserted. This may seem to be a drawback when compared to an electronic calculator but in fact it gives the circular slide rule great flexibility. By mentally moving the decimal point to the right or the left a selected number on the scale can be used to represent any one of a whole range of numbers. For instance half way between the third and fourth small division to the right of 22 can be used to represent 22·7; 2·27; 22700; 0·227; 0·00227 etc.

3.8　When carrying out calculations on the circular slide rule particular care has to be taken when positioning the decimal point in the *final* answer. To ensure the correct positioning of the decimal point when reading off answers on the scale *carry out a rough check of the expected answer **before** programming the computer.* This is one of the golden rules when using *any* computing device from abacus through to a main-frame computer and reduces the chance of a nonsense answer being accepted as gospel. Nonsense answers are invariably the result of incorrect inputs to the computer by the human user. Examples of the rough checking procedure will be found throughout this book.

3.9　Reverting to distance conversions on the computer: On the outer scale of the circular slide rule at 10 will be seen **km – m – ltr** with a small vertical index line under the **m**, this being the index mark used for km input or readout during conversions involving km, nm and/or st m. The index marks for **naut m** and **stat m** will be seen at approximately 54 and 62 respectively, (see Fig. 3–3).

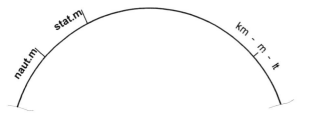

Fig. 3–3
Computer distance
conversion datums.

3.10 Suppose it is required to convert 972 nm into st m and km. First carry out a rough check of the expected answers. These do not have to be very precise, the aim being to make sure the decimal point goes in the correct place in the final answer. Referring back to paragraph 3.5, the conversion factors show 1 nm = 1·152 st m = 1·854 km, for the rough check the use of 1·1 and 2 respectively is good enough and in the example given 972 can be rounded up to 1000. Thus the rough check for 972 nm is 1000 × 1·1 = approximately 1100 st m and 1000 × 2 = approximately 2000 km. The computer is now programmed by turning the inner scale round until the known number (972) of nm is lined up with the **naut m** index on the outer scale. Use of the rotatable cursor can be of great assistance in both lining up with and reading off from index marks. Fig. 3–4 shows the computer set up.

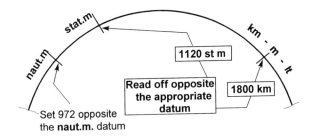

Fig. 3–4   Example of distance conversions.

Reading off opposite the **stat m** index gives 112, since the rough answer expected was 1100 the correct answer is therefore **1120 st m.** Opposite the **km** index is 18, rough answer 2000, therefore the correct answer is **1800 km.** *For rough working of distance conversions the following factors will give answers close enough for the correct positioning of the decimal point in the final answer:*

1 nm	= 1·1 st m	= 2 km
1 st m	= 0·9 nm	= 1·5 km
1 km	= 0·5 nm	= 0·6 st m

DEPARTURE

3.11 From the definition of a nm it follows that any N or S movement up or down a meridian will give a change of 1' of latitude for every nm moved. Conversely every minute of d'lat results in 1 nm of movement N or S. Movement due E or W is not quite so straightforward. Along the equator, which is a GC, a similar relationship exists as for up and down the meridians, that is to say 1' of d'long = 1 nm (of E/W movement). Due to the meridians converging towards the poles, at all lats other than the equator 1' of d'long < 1 nm (of E/W movement), becoming 0 nm at either pole (see Fig. 3–5). This is a Cosine relationship, being 1 (maximum) at 0° latitude and 0 at 90° latitude. E/W distance is given the title **Departure (Dept)** and it is derived from the formula:

Dept (nm E/W) = d'long (in minutes) × Cosine lat

Provided two of the elements are known the third can easily be resolved. This formula has several applications in navigation and will appear from time to time in this and other text books. It should be learnt by all licence candidates.

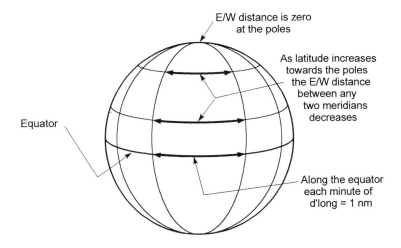

Fig. 3–5   E/W Distance between Meridians.

Example:

An aircraft sets out from 5347N 0928W. It is flown 275 nm due S followed by a further 124 nm due E. Calculate its position at the end of this flight.

Answer:

275 nm due S = 275' d'lat = 4° 35' d'lat S.

lat at end of first leg = 5347 N – 4° 35' = **4912 N.**

Dept = 124 nautical miles E at 4912 N.

124 = d'long (in minutes) E × Cosine 49° 12'.

124 / Cosine 49° 12' = d'long (in minutes) E.

124 / 0·6534 = 190' d'long = 3° 10' E d'long.

long at end of second leg = 0928 W – 3° 10' = **0618 W.**

 Position at end of flight = **4912N 0618W** (see Fig. 3–6)

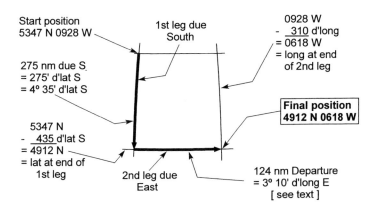

Start position
5347 N 0928 W

1st leg due
South

0928 W
-   310 d'long
= 0618 W
= long at end
of 2nd leg

275 nm due S
= 275' d'lat S
= 4° 35' d'lat S

5347 N
-   435 d'lat S
= 4912 N
= lat at end of
1st leg

Final position
4912 N 0618 W

2nd leg due
East

124 nm Departure
= 3° 10' d'long E
[see text]

Fig. 3–6   Change of position using d'lat and departure.

CONVERSION BETWEEN METRES AND FEET

3.12 Calculations to convert **Metres (m)** to **Feet (ft)** and vice versa mostly arise in problems concerned with altimetry and the selection of safe cruising levels, such problems are common in the meteorology and instrument papers. From time to time the navigation paper also comes up with a problem needing conversion between m and ft and candidates are advised

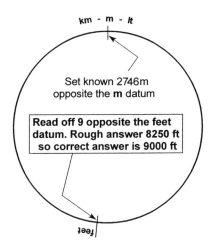

km - m - ft

Set known 2746m
opposite the m datum

Read off 9 opposite the feet
datum. Rough answer 8250 ft
so correct answer is 9000 ft

feet

Fig. 3–7   Conversion between Metres and Feet.

32

to be on the lookout for the need to convert from one to the other as needed. Conversion is carried out on the circular slide rule in the same way as the nm, st m and km conversions, the **m** at the 10 on the outer scale and the **feet** datum line near 33 on the outer scale being the appropriate index marks. There are 3·2808333 ft in a m so for the initial rough check multiply the number of m by 3 to approximate the answer in ft, similarly divide the number of ft by 3 to approximate the answer in m.

Example:
Convert 2746 m to ft.
Answer:
Rough check 2750 × 3 = approximately 8250 + ft.
Set 2746 on the inner scale of the circular slide rule opposite the **m** index on the outer scale.
Opposite the **feet** index on the outer scale read off 9 on the inner scale.
Rough check 8250 + ft therefore the correct answer is **9000 ft** (and not 900 ft or 90,000 ft), (see Fig. 3–7)

CHAPTER 4

SPEED

4.1 Speed is rate of movement. It can be expressed in many ways and different units of measurement. This chapter will only be dealing with those aspects of speed applicable to aircraft navigation.

AERONAUTICAL UNITS OF SPEED

4.2 Rate of movement is how much distance is being covered in a specified time. In aviation it is most commonly expressed in units of distance per hour. Chapter 3 introduced the distance units of nm, st m and km. Speeds expressed in these units per hour have their own names:

Nm per hour are known as **Knots (kn)**, a nautical derivative from the days of sailing ships when a rope with knots along its length was trailed behind the ship. The faster the ship went more of the rope was visible from the stern and the number of knots revealed indicated the speed of the ship through the water.

St m per hour are known as **Miles per hour (mph)**.

Km per hour are known as **Kilometres per hour (kph)**.

Since these units of speed are based on the standard units of distance, the ratios for conversion are the same. The same index marks on the navigation computer used for conversion of distances are used for speed conversions. Just imagine each index mark has 'per hour' added to turn it into a speed index. The same rules of rough checking before setting up the computer apply.

SPEEDS USED IN AVIATION

4.3 In aviation the measurement of speed can be expressed in several different ways. These are:

Indicated airspeed (IAS)
Rectified airspeed (RAS)
True airspeed (TAS)
Equivalent airspeed (EAS)
Ground speed (GS)
Mach number (M No)

Apart from GS all of these are explained in detail in the instruments syllabus, nonetheless some level of clarification is needed before proceeding with navigation proper. Note: In American aviation the equivalent of RAS is known as Calibrated Airspeed (CAS).

4.4 The Air Speed Indicator (ASI) measures the difference between the Pitot (or Total) pressure and the Static pressure, this difference being the Dynamic pressure due to forward movement of the aircraft. Dynamic pressure is generated by the number of air molecules that collide with the forward faces of the aircraft as it moves through the air and will therefore vary with air density and the true speed of the aircraft through the air (its TAS). The ASI is calibrated to indicate speed on the assumption that air density has a fixed value of 1225 grams/cubic metre. This causes it to give the same readout for a given amount of dynamic pressure no matter what combination of air density and TAS has produced it. Since the control of an aircraft is directly related to dynamic pressure, this means the ASI reading required for any manoeuvre will be the same at any altitude. Although this makes for ease of control it means that the TAS is rarely the same as the speed shown on the ASI. Since the density of air decreases with the decrease in pressure as an aircraft climbs to altitude, it follows that in the majority of flight conditions the TAS will be greater than the IAS displayed on the ASI. TAS is fundamental to navigational and fuel requirement problems and the procedures for calculation of TAS on the navigation computer are given in the following paragraphs. Note: 1225 grams/cubic metre (g/cub m) is the *assumed* **mean sea level (msl)** air density in the **International Standard Atmosphere (ISA)** which is used in the calibration of pressure instruments.

4.5 The 'raw' reading on the face of the ASI is the IAS and has first to be corrected for any errors in sensing of the Pitot and Static pressures (position error) as well as any anomalies in the individual instrument (instrument error). These two errors are usually calibrated together and a correction table produced over the operating speed range and for various flap and landing gear configurations. These corrections are usually quite small and when applied to the IAS give the corrected speed known as RAS. RAS is used in conjunction with the **Correct Outside Air Temperature (COAT)** and the pressure altitude to solve for TAS on the Navigation computer. Note: Differences in inputs and procedures found on many American Navigation computers are briefly covered in paragraph 4.8.

CONVERSION OF RAS TO TAS (TAS < 300 kn)

4.6 Rotate the inner disc of the circular slide rule to align the **COAT** on the outer edge of the **AIR SPEED** window with the pressure altitude (altitude with 1013 mb set on the altimeter sub-scale) inside the window.

Opposite the value of the RAS on the inner circular slide rule scale read off the value of the TAS on the outer slide rule scale. Use of the rotating cursor, where available, will make for easier alignment and read off.

Example:
Pressure altitude 21,000 ft. COAT -32 C. RAS 174 kn. What is the TAS?
Answer:
In the **AIR SPEED** window set 21 (pressure altitude × 1000 ft) opposite -32 C on the **COAT** scale. Position the cursor through the RAS of 174 kn on the inner scale and read off the **TAS of 238 kn** on the outer scale (see Fig. 4–1).

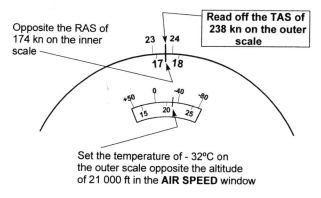

Fig. 4–1   RAS to TAS (TAS>300kn).

Note:- As an aide memoir the AIRTOUR CRP-5 computer has a **red RAS** on the inner slide rule scale between 35 and 40 and a **red TAS** in the same position on the outer scale. Most makes of navigation computer have some similar form of reminder on them.

CONVERSION OF RAS TO TAS (TAS > 300 kn)

4.7   At high TAS air becomes compressed causing an extra pressure over and above normal Pitot pressure to be sensed by the ASI. In the ASI a modification to the calibration formula eliminates this error at the calibration density of 1225 g/cub m, but this correction does not hold good above 300 kn TAS when flying at levels where the air density is less than 1225 g/cub m. The uncorrected residual error is non-linear and gets larger the higher and faster the aircraft is being flown. This uncorrected compressibility factor results in the TAS found on the computer coming out at a higher value that the correct TAS. Any time the conversion of RAS to TAS on the computer results in an initial TAS in excess of 300 kn a *subtractive* correction has to be made using the

COMP.CORR. (compressibility correction) window on the computer as follows:

Having calculated RAS to TAS (as described in paragraph 4.6) and arrived at an initial TAS in excess of 300 kn, apply the TAS found into the formula printed by the **COMP.CORR.** window, i.e. **TAS/100 – 3 Div.**

The answer this gives is the number of divisions that the arrow pointing at the **COMP.CORR.** window has to be moved to the *left* against the scale visible in the window. This scale varies and has large spacing at high altitudes and very close spacing at low altitudes, in fact at msl it is at infinity.

Rotating the inner scale to the left to reposition the pointer will align the RAS opposite a lower value of TAS on the outer scale, this being the correct TAS to use for navigation purposes.

Example:

Pressure altitude 33 000 ft, COAT -50 C, RAS 266 kn. Calculate the correct TAS.

Answer:

In the **AIR SPEED** window set 33 (pressure altitude × 1000 ft) opposite -50 C on the **COAT** scale. Opposite the RAS of 266 kn on the inner slide rule scale read off the initial TAS of 450 kn on the outer scale. Since this is over 300 kn enter the 450 kn initial TAS into the formula giving 450/100 – 3 Div = 1·5 Divisions. Moving the inner disc to the left 1·5 divisions in the **COMP.CORR.** window repositions the RAS of 266 kn opposite the correct **TAS** of **435 kn** (see Fig. 4–2).

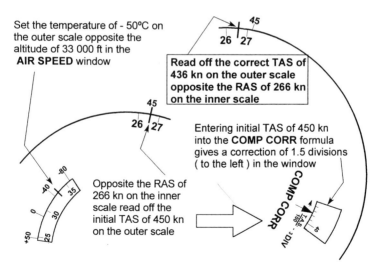

Fig. 4–2   RAS to TAS (TAS >300kn)

4.8   Most American navigation computers are labelled **CAS** as opposed to RAS (see paragraph 4.2) and programmed to use **Indicated Air Temperature (IAT)** instead of COAT. COAT is, as its name implies, the actual temperature of the air surrounding the aircraft. COAT is also known as the **Static Air Temperature (SAT)** and IAT as the **Total Air Temperature (TAT)**. As the aircraft moves through the air its forward faces are striking air molecules which release kinetic energy in the form of heat. This leads to temperature rises on, amongst other things, the external air temperature probe feeding the Air Temperature Gauge. The IAT shown on the gauge will therefore be warmer than the COAT, the actual amount of heating varies with the TAS, a fairly accurate rule of thumb goes:

$$\text{Kinetic heating temperature rise} = (TAS / 100)^2 \, °C$$

An accurate scale of Temperature Rise v TAS is to be found on many navigation computers. A check against such a scale shows only small discrepancies in this rule of thumb. The use of IAT on a computer means that in flight the IAT reading of the temperature gauge can be used to input the computer directly. It does mean however that pre-flight planning require the meteorology forecast temperatures (which are expected COAT) to be modified for expected temperature rise to give an IAT for planning purposes. Another difference often found is in the way compressibility is corrected. Instead of a **COMP.CORR.** window a correction factor table is supplied. This may be printed on the slide of the computer or within the computer handbook. The table is entered with the pressure altitude and the CAS and a correction factor (of less than one) extracted. The initial TAS is then multiplied by this factor to give the correct TAS.

MACH NUMBER (M No.)

4.9   This is the ratio of the aircraft's TAS to the local speed of sound (the local speed of sound at msl is in the region of 660 kn, varying with changes in the COAT). The significance of M No on the handling of the aircraft at high speed and high altitude is covered in detail in the Instrument syllabus. The Navigation examination is only concerned with the conversion of M No to TAS on the navigation computer. The previous examples of RAS to TAS problems employed the **AIR SPEED** window of the circular slide rule. M No to TAS uses the same window but it has to be rotated clockwise until the highest pressure altitude indicated on the scale in the window has been passed (on the CRP-5 this is 75,000 ft) to reveal an arrow head labelled **Mach No. Index** pointing at the **COAT** scale. To convert M No to TAS align the **Mach No. Index** with the COAT at the level being flown, locate the M No on the inner scale of the circular rule and read off the TAS opposite it on the outer scale. (see Fig. 4–3.)

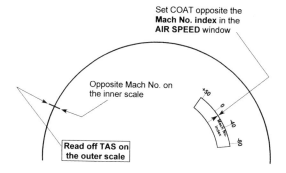

Fig. 4–3   COAT, Mach No. and TAS set up on the Navigation Computer.

Setting the **Mach No. Index** opposite COAT + 50 and reading off against Mach 1·0 the TAS is seen to be 700 kn whereas at COAT – 80 the TAS opposite Mach 1·0 is only 541 kn. At Mach 1·0 the TAS = local speed of sound and the above two calculations show how the local speed of sound varies with the COAT. If the same two settings are repeated it will be seen that the **COMP. CORR.** window is empty in both cases, the inference being that no correction is required for compressibility effects even though the TAS is greater than 300 kn. This is in fact correct as compressibility error is calibrated out in the mechanism of the Machmeter itself. With a fixed index and three variables if any two of the variables are known the computer will solve for the unknown third variable.

Example:
COAT – 46 C, M 0·8. What is the TAS?
Answer:
Align the **Mach No. Index** opposite the COAT of – 46 C. Opposite M 0·8 on the inner circular slide rule scale read off the **TAS of 468 kn** on the outer scale. (see Fig. 4–4a.)

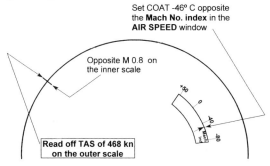

Fig. 4–4a   Finding the TAS from Mach No and COAT.

Example:
COAT – 20 C, TAS 390 kn. What is the Mach no?
Answer:
Align the **Mach No. Index** opposite the COAT of – 20 C. Opposite the TAS of 390 kn on the outer scale of the circular slide rule read off **M 0·63** on the inner scale (see Fig 4–4b).

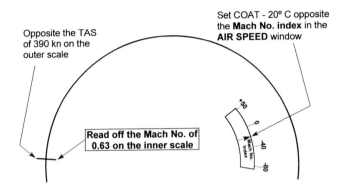

Fig 4–4b Finding the Mach No from COAT and TAS.

Example:
If M 0·78 gives a TAS of 445 kn what is the COAT?
Answer:
Align M 0·78 on the inner scale of the circular slide rule with the TAS of 445 kn on the outer scale. Read off the **COAT** of – **57 C** opposite the **Mach No. Index** (see Fig. 4–4c.)

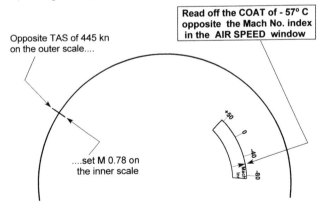

Fig.4–4c Finding the COAT from Mach No and TAS.

40

GROUND SPEED (GS)

4.10 This is, as its name implies, the speed of the aircraft relative to the ground surface over which it is flying. GS and the actual track of the aircraft are the end results of the wind effect on the hdg and TAS of the aircraft. This is covered in depth in Chapter 5.

SPEED, DISTANCE AND TIME

4.11 The relationship between speed, distance and time is a major factor in both the planning and execution of any flight:

If an expected GS is calculated, how long will it take to cover a known distance?
If a known GS is flown for a given time, how far will the aircraft fly over the ground?
If a known distance is covered in a measured time interval, what is the GS?

All are questions that can arise many times in planning or in flight. It was stated in Chapter 3, paragraph 3.7 that the circular slide rule of the navigation computer is basically a device for solving ratios. Any relationship that can be expressed in the form A / B = C / D can be set up on the circular slide rule in the way shown in Fig. 4–5 and provided the value of any three of the variables is known the value of the fourth can be read off.

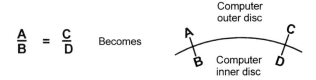

Fig. 4–5   Setting up a ratio on the Navigation Computer.

4.12 The relationship between speed, distance and time is one that lends itself to solving for unknowns by this method. GS is the distance travelled over the earth's surface in 60 minutes (mins), or 1 hour (hr), so in 30 mins (half the time) it will cover half the distance it would have covered in 60 mins (i.e. half the GS). That is to say the distance covered is in the same ratio to the GS as the time gone is to 60 mins. This can be written in the ratio form:

$$\frac{\text{Speed}}{60 \text{ (min)}} = \frac{\text{distance}}{\text{time (min)}}$$

If the speed used is GS then the distance will be ground distance. Similarly if the speed used is TAS then the distance will be air distance and if the speed used is wind speed the distance will be wind distance. It is also important to remember that speed in kn goes with distance in nm, speed in mph goes with distance in st m and speed in kph goes with distance in km.

Avoid mixing units, *always* compare like with like! In the same way note that the times in this ratio are quoted in mins. This is because on a slide rule the use of hrs would require mins to be converted to a decimal part of an hr (i.e. 1 hr 47 min would have to be entered as 1·783333 hrs!) it is quicker and more accurate to work in mins (1 hr 47 mins = 107 mins).

4·13 In the ratio mentioned in paragraph 4.12 the number 60 is a constant, it is also a constant for other navigational calculations as will be seen in later Chapters. Because it is such an important constant it is highlighted on the inner scale of the circular slide rule of all navigation computers, usually by a triangular pointer as on the AIRTOUR CRP-5 COMPUTER. Many computers also have an hrs and mins scale inset on the inner scale to help with quick conversion into mins (see Fig. 4–6.)

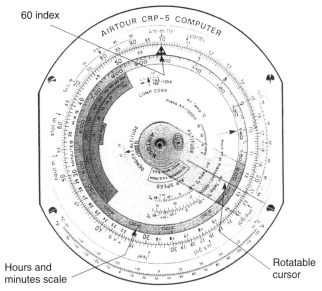

Fig. 4–6   The CRP-5 Circular Slide Rule showing the 60 Index and Hours and Minute Scale.

4.14 The ratio in paragraph 4.12 is set up on the circular slide rule as shown in Fig. 4–7. Provided any two of the variables is known the third can be solved.

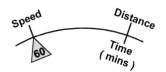

Fig. 4–7   Distance, Speed and Time ratio set up.

42

Example:

GS = 285 kn, distance to go 346 nm. How long will it take?

Answer:

Rough check. Calling it 350 nm at 300 kn; 350 nm at 5 nm / min gives a rough answer of 70 mins.

Rotate the inner scale to align **60** with the GS of 28(5) kn on the outer scale. Locate the distance of 34(6) nm on the outer scale and read off 7(3) opposite it on the inner scale. The rough check puts the answer in the region of 70 mins, therefore the correct answer is **73 mins** = 1 hour 13 mins (see Fig. 4–8.)

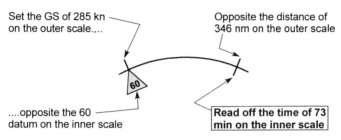

Fig. 4–8   Computer set up to solve for Time

Example:

GS 196 kn, what distance will be covered in 17 mins?

Answer:

Rough check. Calling it 15 mins (0·25 hour) at 200 kn gives a rough answer of 50 nm.

Rotate the inner scale to align **60** with the GS of 19(6) kn on the outer scale. Locate the time of 17 mins on the inner scale and read off 55(5) opposite it on the outer scale. The rough check puts the answer in the region of 50 nm therefore the correct answer is **55·5 nm.** (see Fig. 4–9.)

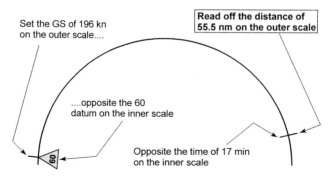

Fig. 4–9   Computer set up to solve for Distance.

Example:
An aircraft covers 154 nm over the ground in 21 mins. What is its GS?
Answer:
Rough check. Calling it 150 nm in 20 mins (a third of an hour) gives a rough answer of 450 nm in 60 mins or 450 kn.

Rotate the inner scale to align the known time of 21 mins on the inner scale with the known distance of 15(4) nm on the outer scale. Opposite the 60 (mins) datum on the inner scale read off 44(0) on the outer scale. The rough check put the answer in the region of 450 kn therefore the correct answer is **440 kn GS.** (see Fig. 4–10.)

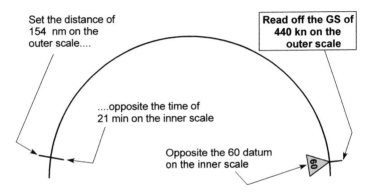

Set the distance of 154 nm on the outer scale....

Read off the GS of 440 kn on the outer scale

....opposite the time of 21 min on the inner scale

Opposite the 60 datum on the inner scale

Fig. 4–10 Computer set up to solve for GS.

4.15 One mistake that can be made, especially by newcomers to the circular slide rule, is that of reading the answer off in the wrong direction. For example if, in the first of the three examples above, having set **60** on the inner scale opposite 285 on the outer scale the distance of 346 nm had been erroneously located on the inner scale a very wrong answer of 16(4) would have been obtained on the outer scale! Such an error should be instantly detected *provided the rough check had been carried out first.* As a further help most computers have mind joggers on them. For instance the CRP – 5 has the word **minutes** printed in red between 30 and 35 on the inner scale to remind users that the inner scale is for time entries, leaving the outer scale for (in this case) distances and speeds.

SECTION 2

BASIC NAVIGATION TECHNIQUES

Aircraft fly in air which is itself moving relative to the earth. Movement of the air, better known as wind, is variable in both direction and speed depending on the weather situation. The path and speed of an aircraft relative to the ground over which it is flying (known as the track and groundspeed) is the end product of the vector generated by the heading and true airspeed of the aircraft and the local wind velocity vector. Knowing how to use these vectors during both the planning of a flight and the conduct of the flight itself are fundamental to navigation and flight safety.

Unless an aircraft is equipped with means of in-flight refuelling (mainly a military requirement) it has to be operated within the available fuel in the tanks at start up. Knowledge of the fuel load carried and the monitoring of its consumption are vital cockpit functions.

In some circumstances cockpit workload and lack of space call for simplified navigation techniques, this is especially true of single pilot operations in light aircraft or helicopters. This leads to a form of navigation known as Pilot Navigation which requires careful preparation of maps before flight and uses visual map reading and rules of thumb (based on logic) when in flight. Professional pilots also employ many of these techniques on the flight deck of large aircraft using information from sources other than visual ones.

This section is concerned with the basics of these techniques.

CHAPTER 5

THE TRIANGLE OF VELOCITIES

THE THREE BASIC VELOCITY VECTORS

5.1 In the introduction to this section three vectors were briefly mentioned. These constitute what is known as the triangle of velocities. They are:

Aircraft Heading and True Airspeed (hdg / TAS) relative to the air.
Aircraft Track and Groundspeed (trk / GS) relative to the earth.
Wind Velocity (WV), the wind direction and speed of the air relative to the earth.

Unlike the hdg and trk of an aircraft, which are always expressed as the direction *towards* which movement is taking place, wind directions are always given as the direction *from* which the wind is blowing (another inheritance from the days of sailing ships). This sometimes confuses newcomers to navigation but with usage it soon becomes second nature. The vector of WV is added to the vector of hdg / TAS to give the resultant vector of trk/GS. Fig. 5–1 shows an example of a vector triangle.

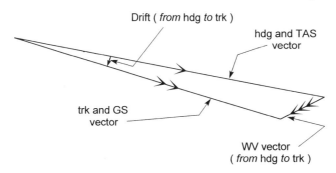

Fig.5–1 The Vector Triangle

This Figure also introduces the conventional symbols used for the three vectors:

47

A single arrow-head for hdg/TAS.
Two arrow-heads for trk/GS.
Three arrow-heads for WV.

The point of the arrows indicates the direction of movement in each case, the length of each vector represents the speed (all to a common scale).

DRIFT

5.2   Also illustrated in Fig. 5–1 is **Drift**, this is the angle between the hdg of the aircraft and its trk over the earth. Drift is *always* measured *from* hdg *to* trk and *never* the other way round! Fig. 5–2a shows a hdg of 049 (T) and a trk of 045 (T) giving a drift of 4° to the left or **Port**. Fig. 5–2b shows a hdg of 284 (T) and a trk of 295 (T) the drift in this case being 11° to the right or **Starboard**.

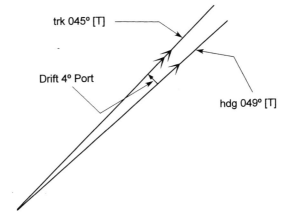

Fig. 5–2a   Port Drift.

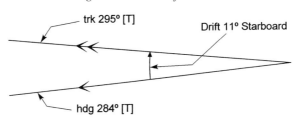

Fig.5–2b   Starboard Drift.

Once again the nautical origins of navigation arise with the use of the terms Port and Starboard, terms which unfortunately must be mastered. A useful mnemonic is the one about the customer enquiring of the wine merchant:

'Have you any RED PORT LEFT ?'

Red being the navigation light which is carried on the **Port** or **Left** wing of an aircraft. Drift angle is often expressed by a number followed by P or S, thus in the two cases already cited drifts are 4P and 11S respectively, the use of the degree sign in the case of drift angles seems to have become optional. It is of interest to note that electronic computers on equipment such as Inertial Navigation Systems have adopted **L** and **R** for Left and Right drift in place of P and S.

5.3 There are three situations when the drift angle will be 0° and the trk will be the same as the hdg:

When there is no wind at all, i.e. flat calm. In such a case the GS will be the same as the TAS. (see Fig. 5–3a).

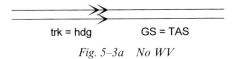

Fig. 5–3a   No WV

When the aircraft is heading directly into the wind, i.e. a headwind. In such a case the GS = TAS – Windspeed.(see Fig. 5–3b).

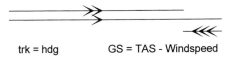

Fig. 5–3b   Headwind.

When the aircraft is heading directly downwind, i.e. a tailwind. In such a case the GS = TAS + Windspeed. (see Fig. 5–3c).

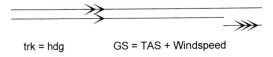

Fig. 5–3c   Tailwind.

It follows that the GS must *always* fall somewhere within the range of TAS – or + Windspeed. Any time there is a tailwind element GS > TAS and with a headwind element GS < TAS. These basic facts should always be used to check for possible errors in GS due to programming mistakes on the slide side of the navigation computer (how this is done is explained later in this Chapter). Another point that Figs. 5–1 & 5–2 highlight is that apart from the 0° drift cases the *trk always lies downwind of the hdg.*

5.4   In Fig. 5–4a an aircraft is shown flying on a hdg of 269 (T) at a TAS of 170 kn, the WV is 150 (T) / 30 kn giving a trk of 277 (T) at a GS of 187 kn the drift being 8S. Although the diagram shows all the vectors of the triangle of velocities the actual movement of the aircraft is along the trk / GS vector with its nose pointing towards 269 (T). Fig 5–4b illustrates this showing the 8S drift *from* hdg *to* trk and the trk lying downwind of hdg.

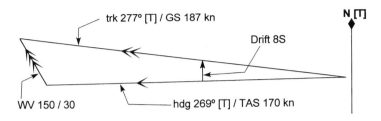

Fig. 5–4a   Vector Triangle with values.

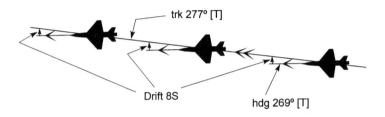

Fig. 5–4 b   Aircraft flying down the trk showing drift angle.

THE BASIC VECTOR TRIANGLE PROBLEMS

5.5   In any vector triangle there are six elements, three directions and three speeds. Provided any four of these elements are known it is possible to solve for the other two. Considering the navigation vector triangle the elements are:

hdg / TAS (signified by a single arrow-head).
Trk / GS (signified by two arrow-heads).
WV (signified by three arrow-heads).

In practical navigation terms there are only three cases of solving for two unknowns that need to be considered, these are:

Finding WV from known hdg / TAS and trk / GS.
Finding trk / GS from known hdg / TAS and WV.
Finding hdg and GS from known WV, TAS and desired trk.

How these problems are solved will first be illustrated in the rather long (and in one case cumbersome) method of drawing out the complete vector triangle of velocities. The slide side of the navigation computer will then be introduced to show how the same problems are solved on this instrument in simpler and faster ways.

GEOMETRICAL SOLUTIONS

5.6   Finding the WV. WV varies with altitude, time and place and it is these continual changes that generate the majority of navigation problems. A pilot knows from his instruments what the hdg/TAS is. If the current trk/GS is also known the WV can be solved by the vector triangle. Many aircraft still carry equipment known as 'Doppler'. Doppler is a radio aid that measures and indicates the drift and GS. The drift readout enables the trk to be calculated from the present hdg so the pilot of an aircraft fitted with Doppler has continual access to all the elements needed to find the WV. Any time an examination question quotes a Doppler drift and GS, candidates are in effect in a position to solve for trk/GS plus WV. Other techniques for finding current trk/GS are given in later Chapters.

Example:
hdg 157 (T) / TAS 145 kn ; trk 151 (T) / GS 130 kn. What is the WV?
Answer:
Fig. 5–5a shows the hdg/TAS and trk/GS vectors plotted to scale from a common start point. Drift from hdg to trk is 6P and since GS < TAS there is an element of headwind. Fig. 5–5b shows the same two vector with the WV vector drawn in blowing *from* hdg *to* trk. Using the same scale the length of the WV vector gives 21 kn as the windspeed and measurement of the angle shows the wind to be blowing *from* 198 (T). Answer: **WV is 198/21**.

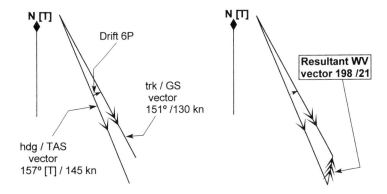

Fig. 5–5a   hdg/TAS and trk/GS vectors   Fig. 5–5b   Resultant WV Vector.

Note: Since wind speeds given by the Meteorological Office are in degrees (T) it is common practice to ignore quoting the (T) for winds based on (T) direction. Some navigation techniques employ winds based on (M) directions. In such cases (M) is written in after the direction to avoid possible errors. In the same way wind speeds are assumed to be in kn unless otherwise stated. These practices will be used throughout the rest of this book.

5 7   Finding trk/GS. Trk/GS are the end product of the hdg/TAS and WV vectors.

Example:
hdg 293 (T), TAS 210 kn, WV 165/30. What is the resultant trk / GS?
Answer:
Fig. 5–6a shows the hdg/TAS vector.
Fig. 5–6b has the WV vector added with the arrows following on from the end of the hdg/TAS vector.
The resultant vector of trk / GS is now drawn in from the start of the hdg/TAS to the end of the WV vector as in Fig. 5–6c. Measurement of this vector gives a trk of **299 (T)** and a **GS of 230 kn**. It also shows the drift to be **6S**.

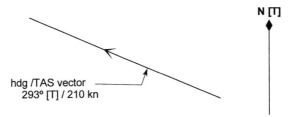

Fig. 5–6a   hdg/TAS vector.

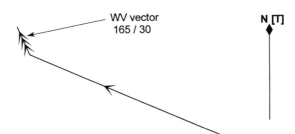

Fig. 5–6b   Added WV vector

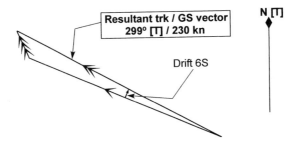

Fig. 5–6c   Resultant trk/GS vector

5.8 Finding hdg to steer and GS. Finding hdg to make good a desired trk (using the aircraft's TAS and a known, or forecast WV) is both a basic pre-flight planning requirement and an in-flight navigation technique. The solution of hdg will complete the vector triangle enabling the expected GS to be measured. Because the unknowns are from different vectors the procedure for drawing the diagram has to be changed. This is illustrated in the following example.

Example:

Required trk 018 (T), TAS 300 kn, WV 150/80. Calculate the hdg (T) to steer and the resultant GS.

Answer:

Draw a line in the direction of the desired trk and mark with two arrows. GS is not known, it cannot be greater than TAS plus wind speed 300 + 80 = 380 kn, or less than TAS minus wind speed 300 – 80 = 220 kn (see paragraph 5.3). Make the length of the vector slightly longer than the greatest possible GS (see Fig. 5–7a).

At the end of the trk vector draw the WV vector blowing in towards the trk (see Fig. 5–7b).

From the beginning of the WV vector strike off an arc with a radius equal to the TAS so as to cut the trk vector near its beginning (see Fig. 5–7c).

Join the point where this arc cuts the trk to the beginning of the WV vector with a straight line to form the hdg/TAS vector and mark it with a single arrow-head pointing to the beginning of the WV vector (see Fig. 5–7d).

Measuring the direction of the hdg vector gives a **hdg of 029 (T)** and the length of the trk vector gives a **GS of 350 kn**. The drift works out as **11P**.

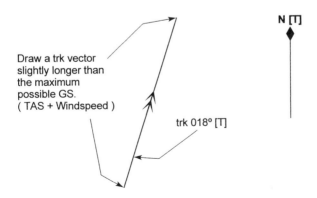

Fig. 5–7a   *Vectorial solution to find hdg and GS. Step 1.*

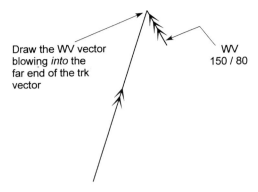

Draw the WV vector blowing *into* the far end of the trk vector

WV
150 / 80

Fig. 5–7b   Vectorial solution to find hdg and GS. Step 2.

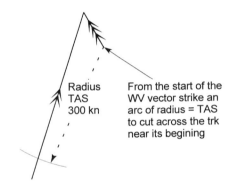

Radius
TAS
300 kn

From the start of the WV vector strike an arc of radius = TAS to cut across the trk near its begining

Fig. 5–7c   Vectorial solution to find hdg and GS. Step 3

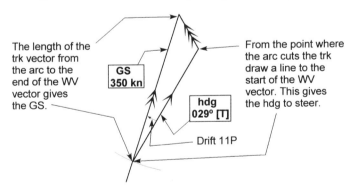

The length of the trk vector from the arc to the end of the WV vector gives the GS.

GS
350 kn

hdg
029° [T]

Drift 11P

From the point where the arc cuts the trk draw a line to the start of the WV vector. This gives the hdg to steer.

Fig. 5–7d   Vectorial solution to find hdg and GS. Step 4.

5.9   The above geometrical solutions of vector triangle problems are tedious and for the number of calculations involved in the preparation and execution of a flight would consume large quantities of paper and time.

Navigation computers have been developed in a variety of ways to speed up this calculation process. The simplest and most widely used system is a transparent direction plate backed by a speed and drift angle slide (see Fig. 5–8).

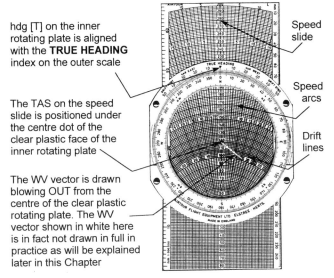

hdg [T] on the inner rotating plate is aligned with the **TRUE HEADING** index on the outer scale

Speed slide

The TAS on the speed slide is positioned under the centre dot of the clear plastic face of the inner rotating plate

Speed arcs

Drift lines

The WV vector is drawn blowing OUT from the centre of the clear plastic rotating plate. The WV vector shown in white here is in fact not drawn in full in practice as will be explained later in this Chapter

Fig. 5–8   A Typical navigation computer showing the rotating transparent direction plate and Speed and Drift Slide.

The navigation computer solution of the triangle of velocities concentrates on that part of the triangle where the WV vector is. Since the pilot is directly in control of hdg and TAS, computers are designed to have this vector displayed running up to the centre of the transparent disc, the triangle being correctly set up when:

The disc is rotated to have the hdg aligned with the **TRUE HEADING** index.
The slide is moved to set the TAS under the centre dot of the disc.
The WV vector is drawn blowing **Out** from the centre of the disc.

Under the end of the WV vector the GS can be read off against the speed arcs and the drift angle read off against the drift lines, hdg + S drift or – P drift giving the trk.

5.10 Reworking on the computer of the three previous examples is given below but beforehand a *word of warning* . There are a number of well meaning, but misguided, people around who advocate a different 'short cut' method for solving the hdg and GS problem which involves reversing the WV and switching the other vectors around. In the case of inexperienced students this frequently leads to confusion. In over a quarter of a century of teaching professional pilots, the author has had to spend a lot of time curing problems that have emanated as a result of trainees being introduced to this and other 'short cuts' before they had a sound grasp of the basics. Remember 'short cuts' are for the experts. Until you are an expert leave them alone!

5.11 Before demonstrating the computer techniques for solving the vector triangle problems take a look at the speed and drift angle slide. Most computers have a double sided slide, these may vary slightly in detail, the AIRTOUR CRP-5 COMPUTER being typical of the majority in its layout. The CRP-5 slide has a low speed side (marked **L** at the top right) with speed arcs 40 to 300 and a high speed side (marked **H** at the top right) with speed arcs from 150 to 1050. The **L** side has a squared section at the bottom which is used to calculate head and cross wind components on runways (covered in paragraph 5.16). Both sides of the slide have drift lines. Below the 100 speed arc on the **L** side and below the 300 speed arc on the **H** the lines are 2° of drift apart. At the higher speeds on each side the drift lines are 1° apart. Care must be taken not to read the 2° lines as 1° and vice versa. Fig. 5–9 illustrates both sides of the CRP-5 slide and highlights another feature common to most computer slides – the speed scale on the **L** side is more than double the speed scale on the **H** side.

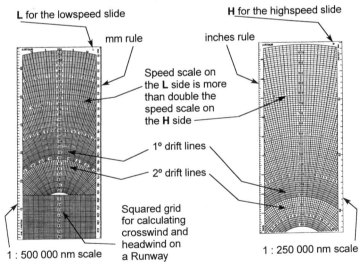

Fig. 5–9   The Low and High speed sides of the Navigation Computer Speed Slide.

This means that a WV vector marked on against the scale on one side of the computer will have to be remarked against the new scale if the slide is reversed during a calculation. This of course should not happen if the procedures for selecting the correct side of the slide are carried out as in the reworked examples that follow.

SOLUTIONS ON THE NAVIGATION COMPUTER

5.12 Finding the WV. Paragraph 5.6 had the example: hdg 157 (T) / TAS 145 kn, trk 151 (T) / GS 130 kn. What is the WV?

TAS is 145 kn and GS is 130 kn so select the **L** side of the slide and with the **L** on the slide and the **TRUE HEADING** index both uppermost move the slide up until the speed arc 145 kn (the TAS) is lying under the centre dot of the disc.

Now rotate the transparent disc to align the hdg of 157 (T) with the **TRUE HEADING** index. The hdg/TAS vector is now in place.

With hdg 157 (T) and trk 151 (T) the drift (*from* hdg *to* trk) is 6P. The trk of 151 (T) will be seen to be to the left of the **TRUE HEADING** index opposite the 6 division on the scale labelled **DRIFT PORT**, this confirms the drift already calculated.

Making certain not to move the hdg/TAS settings, take a soft lead pencil and mark a cross on the transparent disc over the point where the 6P drift line intersects the speed arc of the 130 kn GS (see Fig. 5–10a). The centre dot is the start of the WV vector and the pencil cross the end of it.

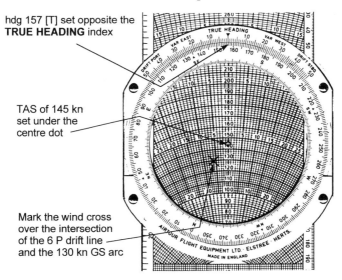

hdg 157 [T] set opposite the **TRUE HEADING** index

TAS of 145 kn set under the centre dot

Mark the wind cross over the intersection of the 6 P drift line and the 130 kn GS arc

Fig. 5–10a   Finding the WV from hdg/TAS and trk/GS. Step 1.

To measure this WV vector rotate the disc to place the pencil cross on the centre (0° drift) line *below* the centre dot of the disc, The direction under the **TRUE HEADING** index is the direction from which the wind is blowing and the length of the vector measured along the speed scale gives the wind speed (Fig. 5–10b.) In this case the **WV** read out is **198/21** the same as the answer found previously in paragraph 5.6.

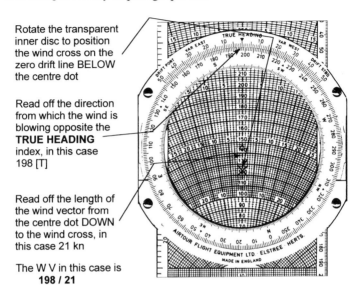

Rotate the transparent inner disc to position the wind cross on the zero drift line BELOW the centre dot

Read off the direction from which the wind is blowing opposite the **TRUE HEADING** index, in this case 198 [T]

Read off the length of the wind vector from the centre dot DOWN to the wind cross, in this case 21 kn

The W V in this case is **198 / 21**

Fig. 5–10b   Finding the WV from hdg/TAS and trk/GS. Step 2.

5.13 Finding trk/GS. Reworking the example from paragraph 5.7 on the computer requires the WV vector to be marked on first once the correct side of the slide has been selected. Here is the problem again: hdg 293 (T), TAS 210 kn, WV 165/30. What is the resultant trk/GS?

Checking the limits of the GS gives 210 – or + 30 kn, a range of 180 to 240 kn which could go on either the **L** or the **H** side of the slide. In such a case it is advisable to use the **L** side as its larger scale makes for greater accuracy. Insert the **L** slide into the computer but do not set the TAS under the centre dot just yet.

To set the WV vector, rotate the disc to align the wind direction of 165 (T) under the **TRUE HEADING** index and with a soft pencil mark in the end of the WV vector with a cross the appropriate number of speed units *below* the centre dot. The speed arcs can be used as a guide here; for instance in this case a vector of 30 units is required, if the 130 speed arc is positioned under the centre dot the cross is drawn over the point where the 100 speed arc intersects the centre line (see Fig. 5–11a).

With the wind cross marked now move the slide to position the speed arc of 210 kn (the TAS) under the centre dot and rotate the disc to align the hdg of 293 (T) under the **TRUE HEADING** index, the hdg/TAS vector is now set with the WV vector blowing *out* from its end (see Fig. 5–11b).

The wind direction of 165 [T] is set opposite the **TRUE HEADING** index

The wind cross is marked in on the zero drift line 30 kn BELOW the centre dot. In this case the 130 kn and 100 kn speed arcs are used as a means of ensuring that the vector length is correct

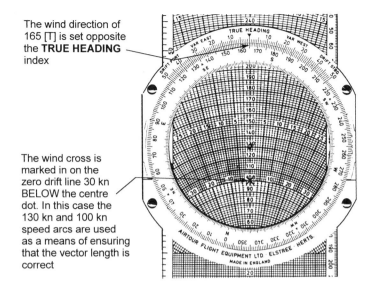

Fig.5–11a   Finding trk/GS from hdg/TAS and WV. Step 1.

The wind cross is seen to be lying over the intersection of the 6S drift line and the 230 speed arc. Going to the **DRIFT STBD** scale to the right of the **TRUE HEADING** index opposite the 6S mark read off the trk (T) of 299 (T) on the disc scale. Answer **trk 299 (T)**, **GS 230 kn**, the same as found in paragraph 5.7.

hdg 293 [T] set opposite the **TRUE HEADING** index

TAS 210 kn set under centre dot

Under the wind cross read off the **GS 230 kn** and the drift 6° S

Opposite the 6° mark on the **DRIFT STBD** scale to the right of the **TRUE HEADING** index read off **trk 299 [T]**

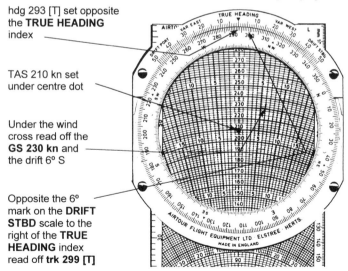

Fig.5–11b   Finding trk/GS from hdg/TAS and WV. Step 2.

5.14 The worked examples in paragraphs 5.11 and 5.12 illustrate the way the computer appears with all the vectors set on correctly as mentioned in paragraph 5.9:

The TAS is under the centre dot with the hdg opposite the **TRUE HEADING** index.

The WV vector is blowing **out** from the centre of the disc. (The whole vector is not needed, a cross marking the end of the vector being sufficient).

The GS lies under the end of the wind vector as indicated by the cross with trk lying along the drift line under the cross.

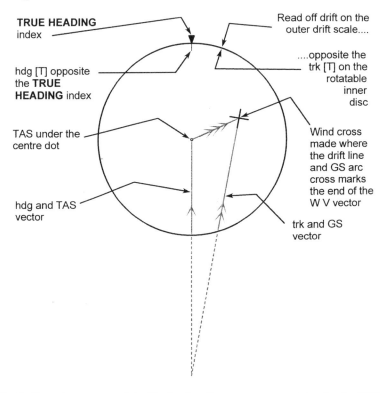

Fig. 5–12a   Appearance of the Navigation Computer set up solving for the WV.

Figs. 5–12a and b show, in a simplified form, this standard method of setting up the computer to solve triangle of velocity problems. In the two examples so far given two complete vectors were used to solve the third vector. The third problem is not so straightforward and requires a simple piece of logical drift balancing to achieve the standard set-up. It is at this point that an alternative 'short cut' method is sometimes advocated which involves plotting the WV vector in reverse, it also involves switching the other two vectors around and is altogether non-standard! Unlike the standard layout which can be used to solve *all* known vector triangle problems this alternative layout is limited in its uses and has been proven time and time again to be the prime cause of many pilots having problems, with basic navigation. This book will only deal with standard methods as used by professionally trained pilots. Readers are advised to learn the basics properly and not to get seduced into trying 'quick fix' methods.

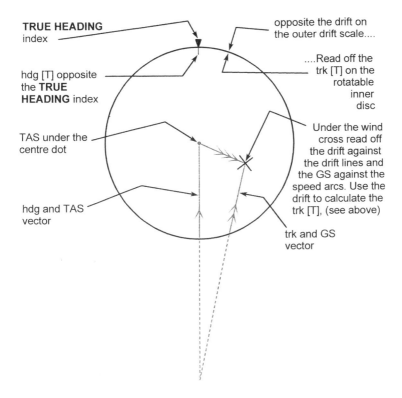

*Fig. 5–12b   Appearance of the Navigation Computer set up solving
for trk (T) and GS.*

5.15 Finding hdg to steer and GS. Here is the problem from paragraph 5.8 again:

Required trk 018 (T), TAS 300 kn, WV 150 / 80. Calculate the hdg (T) to steer and the resultant GS obtained.

GS range is from 300 – 80 kn to 300 + 80 kn = from 220 to 380 kn therefore select the **H** side of the speed slide.

With the wind direction of 150 (T) aligned under the **TRUE HEADING** index mark the wind cross 80 speed units **below** the centre dot.

Move the slide to position the 300 speed arc under the centre dot. The WV vector and TAS are now set.

The logic now goes like this, 'If drift were 0° the hdg would be the same as trk. So set trk direction opposite the **TRUE HEADING** index and see if drift is 0°. If it is not, rotate the disc *towards* the cross until the drift line under the cross is the same value as drift reading opposite the trk direction on the disc scale'. This is best illustrated by following the problem through.

Rotate the disc to align the desired trk direction of 018 (T) with the **TRUE HEADING** index (see Fig. 5–13a.) It is clear that drift is not 0° but 10P and if 018 (T) were steered it would result in a track of 008 (T)!

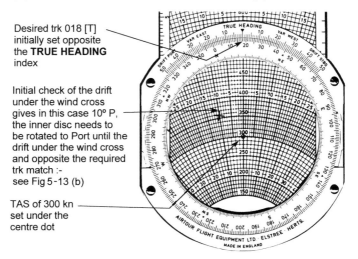

Desired trk 018 [T] initially set opposite the **TRUE HEADING** index

Initial check of the drift under the wind cross gives in this case 10° P, the inner disc needs to be rotated to Port until the drift under the wind cross and opposite the required trk match :-
see Fig 5-13 (b)

TAS of 300 kn set under the centre dot

Fig. 5–13a   Finding hdg and GS from required trk WV and TAS. Step 1.

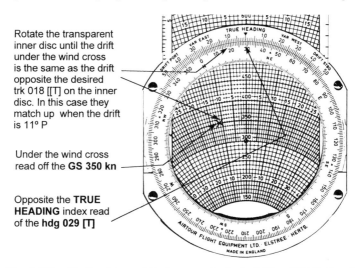

Rotate the transparent inner disc until the drift under the wind cross is the same as the drift opposite the desired trk 018 [[T] on the inner disc. In this case they match up when the drift is 11° P

Under the wind cross read off the **GS 350 kn**

Opposite the **TRUE HEADING** index read of the **hdg 029 [T]**

Fig. 5–13b   Finding hdg and Gs from required trk, WV and TAS. Step 2.

62

By rotating the disc towards the cross (anticlockwise for P drift) bring the trk direction under the 10P mark on the scale to the left of the **TRUE HEADING** index.

Check to see if the drift angle under the cross is still 10P. If it has changed, move the disc until the drifts under the cross and opposite the trk direction are identical. In this case they match up at 11P, the computer is now set-up in the standard way and the problem is solved (see Fig. 5–13b).

The **hdg** under the **TRUE HEADING** index is **029 (T)** with the 11P drift giving the desired trk of 018 (T). At the same time the **GS of 350 kn** can be read off the speed arc under the cross. This is the same answer as in paragraph 5.8.

This explanation may seem longwinded but with very little practice this routine can be completed in seconds.

5.16 Finding the WV at a turning point. The slide side of the computer has other things to offer. It is possible to find the WV from a series of drifts found on different widely spaced headings, with no knowledge of the GS being available. This was a technique in common use before the advent of today's sophisticated aids. Although no longer considered a prime navigation technique it is still employed as a back-up check and occasionally the solution of a plotting question on the examination paper requires the candidate to exhibit knowledge of this technique.

Example:

An aircraft is approaching a turning point on a hdg of 327 (T) at a TAS of 156 kn with a drift of 7S (drift can be assessed in several ways, both visually and from various radio aids, the actual method is not relevant to this

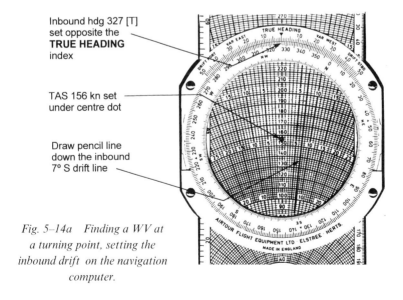

Inbound hdg 327 [T] set opposite the **TRUE HEADING** index

TAS 156 kn set under centre dot

Draw pencil line down the inbound 7° S drift line

Fig. 5–14a   Finding a WV at a turning point, setting the inbound drift on the navigation computer.

example). At the turning point hdg is altered to 044 (T) with TAS unchanged. Once settled down on the new hdg the drift is checked and now found to be 3P. What is the WV in the vicinity of the turning point?

Answer:

With a TAS of 156 kn select the **L** side of the speed slide and position the speed arc for the TAS under the centre dot.

Rotate the disc to position the inbound hdg of 327 (T) opposite the **TRUE HEADING** index and with a soft pencil draw a line down the 7S drift line (see Fig. 5–14 a).

Now rotate the disc to position the outbound hdg of 044 (T) under the **TRUE HEADING** index, the TAS being unchanged leave the speed arc of 156 under the centre dot. (Had there been a change in the TAS on altering hdg the new TAS should be set at this point).

The outbound drift is now drawn in down the 3P drift line so as to cross the inbound drift line (see Fig. 5–14b).

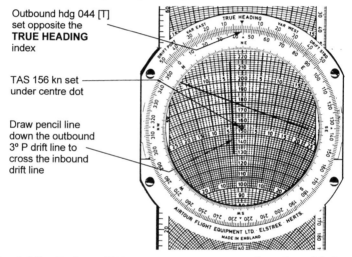

Outbound hdg 044 [T] set opposite the **TRUE HEADING** index

TAS 156 kn set under centre dot

Draw pencil line down the outbound 3° P drift line to cross the inbound drift line

Fig. 5–14b   Finding a WV at a turning point, setting the outbound drift on the navigation computer.

The intersection of the two drift lines is the wind cross marking the end of the wind vector. Rotating the disc to put this cross on the centre line *below* the centre dot enables the wind direction to be read off opposite the **TRUE HEADING** index and the wind speed to be assessed from the speed scale, the answer being a **WV of 202 / 26** (see Fig 5–14c).

The use of only two drifts to find a WV requires the hdg change to be large enough to give drift lines that cut at 90° + or – 20°, accuracy falling off rapidly with shallower cutting angles. The classic multi-drift wind finding method was to fly a 60° / 120° / 60° dog-leg (see Fig. 5–15). taking visual drifts on each leg, and adding time to the **Estimated Time of Arrive (ETA)** at the next turning point to correct for time lost on the diversion. All right at low level over the open sea but not practical over land in today's crowded and restricted airspace.

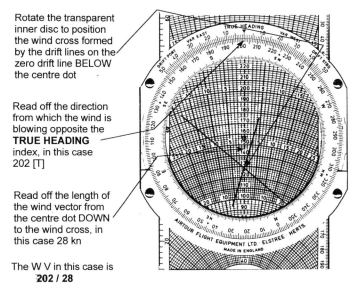

Rotate the transparent inner disc to position the wind cross formed by the drift lines on the zero drift line BELOW the centre dot

Read off the direction from which the wind is blowing opposite the **TRUE HEADING** index, in this case 202 [T]

Read off the length of the wind vector from the centre dot DOWN to the wind cross, in this case 28 kn

The W V in this case is **202 / 28**

Fig. 5–14c   Finding a WV at a turning point, reading off the WV.

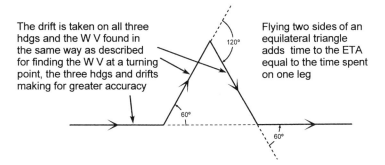

The drift is taken on all three hdgs and the W V found in the same way as described for finding the W V at a turning point, the three hdgs and drifts making for greater accuracy

Flying two sides of an equilateral triangle adds time to the ETA equal to the time spent on one leg

120°

60°

60°

Fig. 5–15   The classic dog-leg method of finding a WV by multiple drifts.

HEAD AND CROSS-WIND COMPONENTS ON A RUNWAY

5.17 The squared grid (found at the bottom of the **L** side on the speed slide of most navigation computers) is used to calculate the headwind and cross-wind components for take off and landing to check that these are within the limits for the type of aircraft being operated. Because **Runway (RW)** directions are given to the nearest 10° (M) the aerodrome air traffic control always pass surface WV for take-off and landing in degrees (M) and kn. This is the only WV passed in degrees (M), WVs at all other levels are passed in degrees (T). Since RW direction and surface WV direction are both in (M) they can be directly compared with one another to check the head and cross-wind components (this can be achieved by using the **TRUE HEADING** index as if it were a **MAGNETIC HEADING** index). If the surface WV were passed in (T) it would be necessary either to convert it to (M) or the RW to (T) before they could be compared. (This is a non-standard element that is sometimes introduced in examination questions – so beware!)

To calculate the wind components start by moving the slide to position the centre dot over the top horizontal line of the squared grid and rotate the disc to align the surface wind direction opposite the **TRUE HEADING** index.

Mark in a wind cross below the centre dot using the scale of the squared grid.

Rotate the disc to align the RW direction opposite the **TRUE HEADING** index.

Using the squared grid read off the wind components from the top and centre lines.

Example:

RW 22 (i.e. 220 (M)), surface WV 260/25. What are the wind components on the RW?

Answer:

With centre dot over the top line of the grid, rotate the disc to align the wind direction of 260 with the **TRUE HEADING** index and mark in the wind cross 25 unit below the centre dot (see Fig. 5–16a).

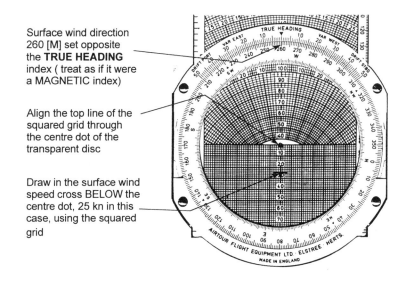

Surface wind direction 260 [M] set opposite the **TRUE HEADING** index (treat as if it were a MAGNETIC index)

Align the top line of the squared grid through the centre dot of the transparent disc

Draw in the surface wind speed cross BELOW the centre dot, 25 kn in this case, using the squared grid

Fig. 5–16a   Finding the wind components on a RW. Step 1.

RW direction 220 [M] set opposite the **TRUE HEADING** index (treat as if it were a MAGNETIC index)

The surface wind cross is displaced to one side showing there are both head and cross wind components in this case

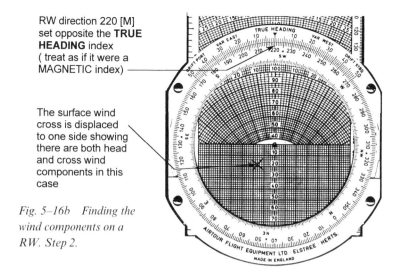

Fig. 5–16b   Finding the wind components on a RW. Step 2.

Now rotate the disc to align the RW direction of 220 with the **TRUE HEADING** index (see Fig. 5–16b).

Reading vertically down from the top line to the cross gives the **headwind** as **18 kn** and reading horizontally from the centre line to the cross gives the **crosswind** as **16 kn** from S (right) to P (left) (see Fig. 5–16c).

Reading across from the centre line to a vertical through the wind cross shows the cross wind component on the RW in this case to be 16 kn blowing from S to P

Reading down from the top of the squared grid to a horizontal through the wind cross shows the head wind component on the RW to be 18 kn in this case

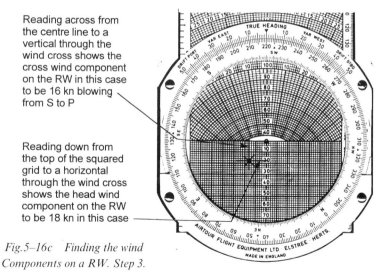

Fig.5–16c   Finding the wind Components on a RW. Step 3.

If a surface WV is marked on using the squared grid and the RW direction set results in the wind cross appearing above the squared grid (on the drift lines and speed circles) it means that there is a tail-wind on that particular

RW direction. The drift and speed circle readings in such a case have no validity and a more suitable RW giving a head-wind should be selected.

MAXIMUM ACCEPTABLE SURFACE WV ON A RUNWAY

5.18 Questions are sometimes set asking what is the maximum surface wind speed that could be blowing from a given direction without exceeding the given crosswind limits on a particular RW

To answer this type of question start as before by positioning the top line of the grid under the centre dot and rotating the disc to align the wind direction with the **TRUE HEADING** index.

Draw a vertical line down from the centre dot to the edge of the disc and then rotate the disc to align the RW direction with the **TRUE HEADING** index.

Horizontally across the top line of the grid mark off the crosswind limit from the centre dot on the side where the drawn wind direction line now lies. Draw a line vertically down from this mark to cut the wind direction line making a wind cross.

Rotating the disc to put the wind cross on the centre line below the centre dot enables the value of the maximum acceptable wind speed to be read off the grid.

Example:
RW 07, maximum allowable crosswind 18 kn. What is the maximum acceptable surface wind speed from a direction of 030 (M)?
Answer:
With the top line of the grid under the centre dot and the wind direction of 030 opposite the **TRUE HEADING** index draw the vertical down from the centre dot (see Fig. 5–17a).

Surface wind direction 030 [M] set opposite the **TRUE HEADING** index (treat as if it were a MAGNETIC index)

Align the top line of the squared grid through the centre dot of the transparent disc

Draw a vertical line down from the centre dot to the edge of the transparent disc to mark on the wind direction

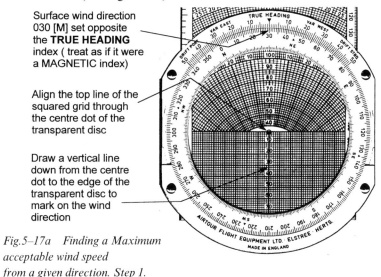

Fig.5–17a   Finding a Maximum acceptable wind speed from a given direction. Step 1.

Rotate the disc to align the RW direction of 070 under the **TRUE HEADING** index which, in this case, puts the wind line to the right of the centre line (see Fig. 5–17b).

RW direction 070 [M] set opposite the **TRUE HEADING** index (treat as if it were a MAGNETIC index)

The surface wind direction is now displaced to the right side of the centre line

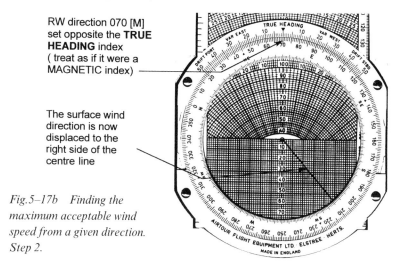

Fig.5–17b Finding the maximum acceptable wind speed from a given direction. Step 2.

Measure the 18 kn cross-wind limit horizontally to the right from the centre dot and draw a vertical down to cut the wind direction line forming the wind cross (see Fig. 5–17c).

Measure the maximum acceptable cross wind component, 18 kn in this case, horizontally from the centre line to the side where the wind direction line lies

Draw a line vertically down from this point to cut the wind direction line making a wind cross

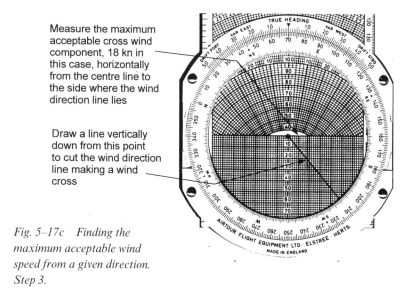

Fig. 5–17c Finding the maximum acceptable wind speed from a given direction. Step 3.

Rotating the disc to place the wind cross on the centre line below the centre dot enables the value of the maximum acceptable wind speed from 030 (M) to be read off as **28 kn** (see Fig. 5–17d).

Reset the surface wind direction 030 [M] opposite the **TRUE HEADING** index

Measure the maximum acceptable wind speed vertically down from the centre dot to the wind cross, in this case 28 kn

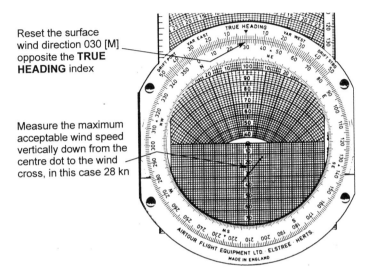

Fig. 5–17d   Finding the maximum acceptable wind speed from a given direction. Step 4.

CHAPTER 6

FUEL

6.1 Calculation of the fuel requirements for any flight and the monitoring of fuel consumption in flight are paramount to flight safety. At all times pilots must ensure that sufficient fuel is uplifted to cover the planned flight plus contingency fuel for possible air traffic delays or diversions. Detailed fuel planning for commercial flights is covered in the Flight Planning syllabus, the Navigation syllabus being restricted to dealing with the various different ways of measuring the volume and/or weight of fuel and the solution of basic fuel problems.

STANDARD UNITS OF VOLUME AND WEIGHT USED IN AVIATION

6.2 **Imperial Gallons and Pounds**. As the previous paragraph implied there is more than one standard used in aviation for the measurement of fuel volumes and weights. One system, which stems from the same Royal Statute that gave rise to the st m, has the **Imperial Gallon (Imp Gal)** as its measure for volume and the **Pound (lb)** as its measure for weight. 1 Imp Gal of water weighs 10 lb, or at least that was the original idea; the later adoption of more precise conditions of temperature and pressure under which such comparisons are carried out has modified this to a minute fraction over 10 lb of water to the Imp Gal (for practical problems in navigation the use of '1 Imp Gal of water weighs 10 lb' is an accurate enough starting point for calculating the weight of various fuel and oil loads).

6.3 **United States (US) Gallons**. The American system uses the same lb as in the Imperial system, the **US Gallon (US Gal)** however is smaller than the Imp Gal there being 1·2 US Gal to the Imp Gal.

6.4 **Litres and Kilogram**. As might be expected the third system in use is metric based, the unit of volume is the **Litre (lt)** which is 1000 cubic centimetres (cc) or 0·001 cubic metre. The weight of 1 lt of water giving rise to the metric unit of the **Kilogram (kg).**

CONVERSION FACTORS

6.5 In commercial aviation there is a definite trend towards standardisation onto the metric system of volumes and weights. However general aviation manufacturers in some countries seem loath to change to this common standard. Add to this the fact that there are still many aircraft of earlier vintages around with gauges and load sheets in gals (either Imp or US) and lbs means that pilots may be faced with the need to convert from one system to another. The conversion relationships are listed below:

1 Imp Gal = 1·2 US Gal = 4·546 lt
1 US Gal = 0·833 Imp Gal = 3·78833 lt
1 lt = 0·22 Imp Gal = 0·1833 US Gal
1 Imp Gal of water weighs 10 lb
1 US Gal of water weighs 8·33 lb
1 lt of water weighs 1 kg
1 kg = 2·205 lb
1 lb = 0·4546 kg

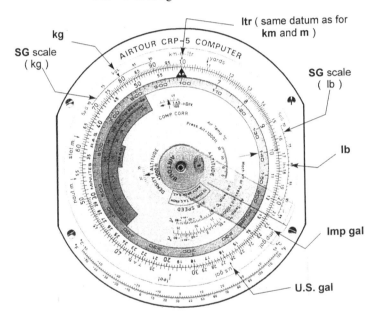

Fig. 6–1   The CRP–5 circular slide rule showing the fuel weight, volume and SG Datums.

The relationships are further complicated by the fact that aviation fuels and oils weigh less than water volume for volume, the amount varying from fuel to fuel and oil to oil. For a given volume the ratio of the weight of a fuel/oil to the weight of water is termed its **Specific Gravity (SG)** (referred to as 'relative density' in some physics text books). For instance if an Imp Gal of fuel weighed 7·4 lb as against 10 lb for an Imp Gal of water, the fuel would be said to have an SG of 0·74 (the ratio of 7·4 lb to 10 lb). In general terms the aviation fuels used in piston engines have an SG in the region of

0·72, gas turbine fuels have an SG in the region of 0·74 and most engine oils have an SG of around 0·8. Actual values for a specific fuel or oil are obtainable from the fuel suppliers. The SG of a fuel may be amended if large ambient temperature and pressure changes occur since this could affect the overall weight of fuel on board an aircraft possibly influencing its weight and balance calculations.

6.6 The circular slide rule of most navigation computers has index marks for carrying out all the conversions for fuel volumes and weights. The circular slide rule of the AIRTOUR CRP-5 is particularly well laid out, for once the known factors are correctly set on, all the possibly required answers can be read off from the one set-up. Fig. 6–1 shows the CRP-5 slide rule and its various fuel related indexes. Fig. 6–2 illustrates the various rough check calculations that should *always* be carried out *before* setting up the computer to solve fuel problems. Without such checks it is very easy to get the decimal point in the wrong place, especially when very large fuel loads are involved.

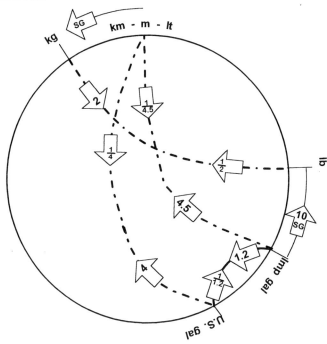

Fig. 6–2   Rough check fuel conversion factors.

6.7 Problems vary in that the fuel values may be given in Imp Gal, US Gal, lt, kg (with SG) or lb (with SG) and the solution may be required in any of the other forms:

Example:
2750 Imp Gal of fuel has an SG of 0·72, what is its volume in US Gal and
lt and its weight in kg and lb?
Answer:
Rough checks. Round up to 2800 Imp Gal and call SG 0·7.
2800 Imp Gal × 4·5 = Approximately 12 600 lt
2800 Imp Gal × 1·2 = Approximately 3360 US Gal
2800 Imp Gal × SG 0·7 × 10 lb = Approximately 19,600 lb
12,600 lt × SG 0·7 × 1 kg = Approximately 8820 kg
Or 19,600 lb / 2 = Approximately 9800 kg
Setting the given value of 2750 Imp Gal on the inner scale opposite the **Imp
Gal** index mark on the outer scale read off (on the inner scale):
12(5) opposite the **lt** index, rough check was 12,600 lt so the correct answer
is **12,500 lt.**
33 opposite the **US Gal** index, rough check was 3360 US Gal so the correct
answer is **3300 US Gal.**
19(82) opposite 0·72 on the **Sp.G** scale by the **lb** index, rough check was
19600 lb so the correct answer is **19,820 lb.**
9 opposite 0·72 on the **Sp.G** scale by the **lt** index, rough check was 8820 to
9800 kg so the correct answer is **9000 kg.** (see Fig. 6–3).

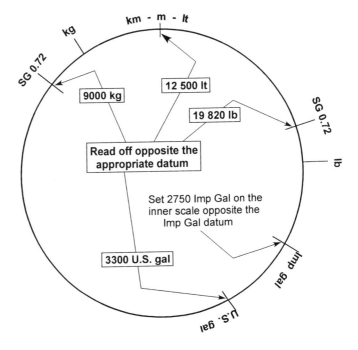

Fig. 6–3   2750 Imp Gal of fuel with SG of 0·72.

Example:

A volume of fuel with an SG of 0·74 weighs 24,600 kg. What is its weight in lb and its volume in lt, Imp Gal and US Gal?

Answer:

Rough checks. Round up to 25,000 kg and call SG 0·75

25,000 kg × 2 = Approximately 50,000 lb

25,000 kg / 0·75 = Approximately 33,000 lt

33,000 lt / 4·5 = Approximately 7000 Imp Gal

33,000 lt / 4 = Approximately 8000 US Gal

Setting the given value of 24,600 kg on the inner scale opposite 0·74 of the **Sp.G** scale by the kg index on the outer scale read off (on the inner scale) 54(4) opposite 0·74 on the **Sp.G** scale by the **lb** index, rough check was 50,000 lb so the correct answer is **54,400 lb**.

33(25) opposite the **lt** index, rough check 33,000 lt, so the correct answer is **33,250 lt**.

73(25) opposite the **Imp Gal** index, rough check was 7000 Imp Gal so the correct answer is **7325 Imp Gal**.

87(9) opposite the **US Gal** index, rough check was 8000 US Gal so the correct answer is **8790 US Gal**. (see Fig. 6–4).

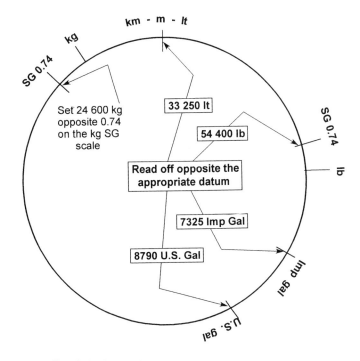

Fig. 6–4   24,600 kg of fuel with SG of 0·74.

FUEL FLOW AND FUEL CONSUMPTION

6.8 The fuel required for any flight depends on how long the flight is planned to last (this to include time on route plus diversion and holding time) and the rate of fuel consumption of the aircraft known as its fuel flow. Fuel flow can vary with changes in altitude, COAT, MNO/RAS and decreasing all-up-weight as fuel is burned off. Calculation of the fuel flow taking these factors into account does not form part of the Navigation syllabus but will be needed by candidates sitting the Flight Planning examinations. Flight Planning text books explain how to use the appropriate data sheets and graphs to extract the correct fuel flow for each situation. The *basic* rules of fuel calculation are common to all types of aircraft and are very similar to the GS/distance/time problems (see Chapter 4, paragraphs 4.11 to 4.14) in their solution. Substitution of fuel flow for GS and fuel for distance gives the ratio:

$$\frac{fuel\ flow}{60} = \frac{fuel\ required\ (or\ used)}{time\ (mins)}$$

The fuel units must of course be in the same units as the fuel flow (do not mix lb with kg, or Imp Gal with US Gal or lt in the same equation). In the same way as with the GS/distance/time problems if any two of the three variables are known the third can be solved on the circular slide rule of the navigation computer:

Example:
Flight time for a leg of a flight is 43 mins. If the fuel flow on the leg is 2350 kg / hr how much fuel will be consumed flying the leg?
Answer:
Rough check. Calling it 45 mins and 2400 kg / hr gives a rough answer of 1800 kg.
Rotate the inner scale to align the **60** (mins) datum with the fuel flow of

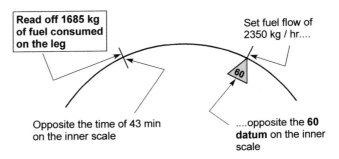

Fig. 6–5   Computer set up to solve for fuel consumed.

2350 kg on the outer scale. Locate the time of 43 mins on the inner scale and read off 16(85) opposite it on the outer scale. The rough check put the answer in the region of 1800 kg therefore the correct answer is **1685 kg** (see Fig. 6–5).

Example:

An aircraft consumes 73 US Gal in 107 mins, calculate its fuel flow in US Gal/hr.

Answer:

Rough check. Calling it 70 US Gal in 110 mins gives a rough answer of 40 US Gal in 60 mins.

Rotate the inner scale to align the time of 107 mins on the inner scale with the 73 US Gal of fuel consumed on the outer scale. Opposite the **60** (mins) datum on the inner scale read off 40(9). The rough check put the answer in the region of 40 US Gal therefore the correct answer is **40·9 US Gal/hr** (see Fig. 6–6).

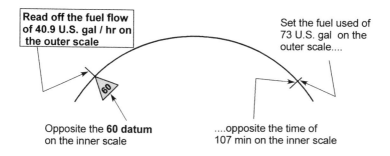

Read off the fuel flow of 40.9 U.S. gal / hr on the outer scale

Set the fuel used of 73 U.S. gal on the outer scale....

Opposite the **60 datum** on the inner scale

....opposite the time of 107 min on the inner scale

Fig. 6–6   Computer set up to solve for fuel flow.

Example:

An aircraft has 9700 Imp Gal of usable fuel in its tanks. How many mins could it fly until its tanks were down to 800 Imp Gal of usable fuel if its mean fuel flow is 1450 Imp Gal/hr?

Answer:

Available fuel 9700 – 800 = 8900 Imp Gal. Rough check. Calling it 9000 Imp Gal and 1500 Imp Gal/hr gives a rough answer of 6 hr or 360 mins.

Rotate the inner scale to align the **60** (mins) datum on the inner scale with the fuel flow of 1450 Imp Gal/hr on the outer scale. Locate the 8900 Imp Gal of fuel available on the outer scale and read off 36(8) opposite it on the inner scale. The rough check put the answer in the region of 360 mins, therefore the correct answer is **368 mins** (see Fig.6–7).

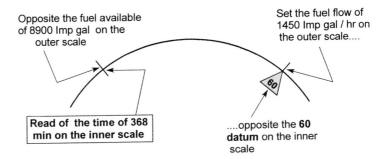

Opposite the fuel available of 8900 Imp gal on the outer scale

Set the fuel flow of 1450 Imp gal / hr on the outer scale....

Read of the time of 368 min on the inner scale

....opposite the **60 datum** on the inner scale

Fig. 6–7   Computer set up to solve for endurance.

SELECTING THE MOST ECONOMICAL CRUISING LEVEL

6.9   If the GS on a leg is divided into the fuel flow it will give the fuel required per unit of ground distance flown. If a choice of altitudes is available to the pilot this ratio can be used to select the most economical altitude for a particular flight. At different altitudes:
A given MNo or RAS will give a different TAS.
The WV will probably be different.
The fuel flow may be different.

It does not always follow that the level having the lowest fuel flow will be the most economical, changes in the TAS and WV may be such that the GS plays the most significant part in the calculation:

Example:
Select the most economical altitude to fly at from the following:
13,000 ft, -13 C, RAS 297 kn, WV 250 / 40, trk 012 (T), fuel flow 1250 kg / hr.
17,000 ft, -22 C, RAS 297 kn, WV 280 / 55, trk 012 (T), fuel flow 1170 kg / hr.
21,000 ft, -38 C, RAS 297 kn, WV 320 / 80, trk 012 (T), fuel flow 1090 kg / hr.
Answer:
13,000 ft, -13 C and RAS 297 kn gives a TAS of 356 kn.
TAS 356 kn, WV 250 / 40 and trk 012 (T) gives a GS of 382 kn.
GS 382 kn and fuel flow 1250 kg / hr gives **3.27 kg / gnm.**
17,000 ft, -22 C and RAS 297 kn gives a TAS of 377 kn.
TAS 377 kn, WV 280 / 55 and trk 012 (T) gives a GS of 372 kn.
GS 372 kn and fuel flow 1170 kg / hr gives **3.15 kg / gnm.**
21,000 ft, -38 C and RAS 297 kn gives a TAS of 395 kn.
TAS 395 kn, WV 320 / 80 and trk 012 (T) gives a GS of 340 kn.
GS 340 kn and fuel flow 1090 kg / hr gives **3.20 kg / gnm.**

Comparing the results at each level show that, in this example, the most economical level to fly at would be **17,000 ft** since it has the lowest fuel requirement for each gnm to be covered. Note: Detailed workings for the above example have deliberately not been given but readers may care to check them out for themselves. Each level has three steps:

RAS to TAS (in this case TAS > 300 kn) ... (see Chapter 4, paragraph 4.7).
Finding hdg to steer and GS (only GS is applicable to the fuel problem) . . . (see Chapter 5, paragraph 5.15).
Dividing fuel flow / hr by GS (gnm/hr) to give fuel used / gnm.

6.10 In the example above the fuel was given in kg and the distance in gnm, the consumption being in *fuel used per unit of distance*. Fuel consumption can also be quoted in terms of *distance covered per unit of fuel* in which case the greatest distance covered per unit of fuel will be the most economical. As well as ground distance (relating to GS) the distance may be given in air distance (relating to TAS). Similarly the fuel units may be given by either weight or volume. This may sound rather daunting but the golden rule is the old one of:

'Do not mix units within a calculation.'

If confronted with a problem containing a mixture of units such as Imp Gal, US Gal, lt, lb and kg make converting them all into a common base unit the first task and work from that. The same applies to distances which may be a mix of nm, st m, km, air distance or ground distance. Which common unit to work with in each case is a matter of personal preference and may well be dictated by the way the problem presents itself.

CHAPTER 7

PILOT NAVIGATION

7.1 Pilot navigation is airborne navigation carried out mainly in the pilot's head. To be successful it requires practice in the estimation of both distances and direction on a chart and the ability to work out simple ratios without the aid of a navigation computer. Another secret of good pilot navigation is careful preparation and study of the chart(s) during pre-flight planning. The main application of pilot navigation is in cross country flying by visual map reading techniques but, as will be demonstrated, aspects of pilot navigation can be used when flying on airways.

7.2 A pilot sets out to fly an aircraft along a desired trk by maintaining the pre-planned altitude, hdg and RAS. Provided the forecast WV was accurate, the aircraft should stay on trk and arrive at the far end of the trk at the planned **Estimated Time of Arrival (ETA)**. Any change in the WV from that forecast, or slight errors in hdg or RAS, will result in deviation from the planned trk or a change in the arrival time, or more likely both. Because WV is such a variable factor it means that deviations from the planned route are a common occurrence. The object of pilot navigation is to assess any such deviations and calculate hdg changes to reach the destination and revise the ETA if necessary. Calculation of hdg change will be dealt with before considering the revision of ETA.

THE 1 IN 60 RULE

7.3 At the heart of pilot navigation is what is known as the 1 in 60 rule, a method of estimating angles which gives answers that are close enough for practical navigation purposes provided the angles involved are not too large. The rule is based on the premise that if a right angle triangle has a base line 60 units long the value in degrees of the smaller enclosed angle is

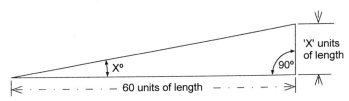

Fig. 7–1   The 1 in 60 rule for estimating angles.

the same as the number of units in the shorter side of the triangle (see Fig. 7–1).

A comparison of the result given by this rule against the actual value of the angle being assessed shows errors of less that half a degree for angles from 1° to 9° and only one degree of error at 16°. By 20° the error is one and a half degrees but increases rapidly as angles get larger. In pilot navigation the 1 in 60 rule is considered to be acceptably accurate for estimating angles up to 20°. Since most practical problems involve angles smaller than 20° the errors incurred are less than the accuracy to which most pilots can manually fly a hdg.

TRACK MADE GOOD AND TRACK ERROR

7.4   Once it is established (by whatever means) that the aircraft is not flying along the desired trk, the obvious conclusion is that if the present hdg is maintained the aircraft will continue along its present incorrect trk taking it further and further from the desired trk and its destination (see Fig. 7–2).

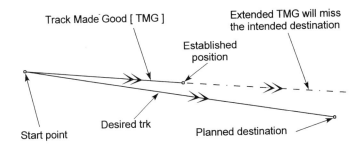

Fig. 7–2   Track Made Good (TMG).

The trk that the aircraft is actually flying along is known as the **Track Made Good (TMG)**. The angle between the desired trk and the TMG is known as **Track Error (TE)** and is measured *from* desired trk *to* TMG (see Fig. 7–3).

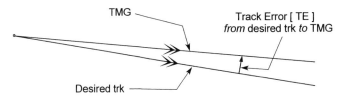

Fig. 7–3   Track Error (TE).

81

TE *is not the same as drift* and care must be taken not to mix these two up. For example Fig. 7–4 shows an aircraft being flown on a hdg of 074 (T) which was calculated to fly the aircraft along a desired trk of 077 (T) but is actually achieving a TMG of 079 (T).

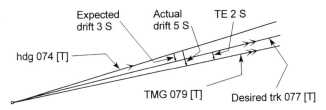

*Fig. 7–4   Track Error (TE), **from** desired trk **to** TMG.*

In this case:-
The TE (*from* desired trk *to* TMG) is **2S**.
The original expected drift (*from* hdg *to* desired trk) was **3S**.
The actual drift experienced (*from* hdg *to* TMG) is **5S**.

PARALLELING THE TRACK

7.5   If the hdg of the aircraft is altered towards the desired trk by the amount of TE this will alter the TMG by the same amount. The new TMG will have the same direction as the desired trk but will be parallel to it. This is known as **Paralleling the trk** (see Fig. 7–5).

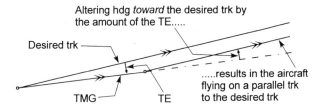

Fig. 7–5   Paralleling trk.

Paralleling the trk is used in some navigation situations to prevent the aircraft getting further off the desired trk while more fixing information is being sought. Paralleling the trk is seldom used in pilot navigation. In pilot navigation the aim, when a TE has been detected, is either to alter hdg to intercept the desired trk and then make a further hdg change to fly along it, or to alter hdg directly for the destination point at the end of the desired trk.

REGAINING DESIRED TRACK

7.6 The Double Track Error method   There are two methods of inter-
cepting the desired trk. The one that is frequently included in the written
examinations will be dealt with first. This first method can only be carried
out provided the aircraft has *not* passed the half way point along the leg
being flown. It requires the value of the TE to be resolved before applying
a simple set of rules.

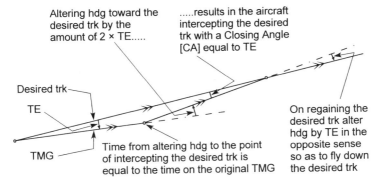

Fig. 7–6   Regaining the desired trk by the Double TE method.

From Fig. 7–6 it can be seen that by altering hdg towards the desired trk
by 2 × TE the new TMG will converge onto the desired trk with a **Closing
Angle (CE)** having the same value as the TE. At the point where the new
TMG intercepts the desired trk a second alteration of hdg, equal to TE but
in the opposite sense to the first alteration of hdg, is required to fly the
aircraft down the regained desired trk. Since the TE and CA are identical,
the distance from the start of the leg to the point of first altering hdg is the
same as from there to the point of regaining the desired trk and the time to
fly each will be the same. The drill for this technique, known as 'Regaining
trk by the **Double Track Error** method' is:

Establish TE (calculation of TE is dealt with later in this Chapter).
Note the time elapsed from the start of the leg and alter towards the desired trk by
  2 × TE.
Hold this new hdg for the same amount of time as the elapsed time observed at
  moment of altering hdg.
When the time is up, alter hdg by TE in the opposite sense to the first alteration of
  hdg. The aircraft should be back on, and flying down, the desired trk.

Example:
Fig. 7–7 shows a situation where an aircraft has departed from 'A' at 1015
on a hdg of 117 (T) intending to fly down the desired trk of 120 (T) to
point 'B'.

83

At 1024 the position of the aircraft is established at point 'x' showing that the actual TMG is 123 (T). The TE from desired trk 120 (T) to the TMG of 123 (T) is **3S** and the elapse time from point 'A' is **9 mins**.
At 1024 hdg is altered to intercept the desired trk by 2 × TE.
New hdg = 117 (T) – (2 × 3) = 117 (T) – 6 = **111 (T)**.
9 minutes later at **1033** the aircraft has intercepted the desired trk from 'A' to 'B' and hdg is altered by TE to S so as to maintain the desired trk. **At 1033 new hdg** = 111(T) + 3 = **114 (T)**.

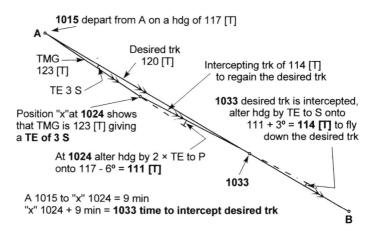

Fig. 7–7   Demonstration of Double TE method of regaining trk.

7.7   Standard Closing Angle method   The second method of regaining the desired trk is known as the Standard Closing Angle method, which is used by high speed low-flying aircraft and is of particular use when flying over areas with few navigational features. From this it can be gathered that it has more military than civilian application and as such does not at the time of writing feature in the CAA examination syllabus. However the method is based on the 1 in 60 rule and is worth looking at for its interest value. With this method for every GS there is a Standard CA which is equal to

$$\frac{60}{\text{The number of nm covered / min}}$$

From this a simple table – presented in graphical form in Fig. 7–8 – can be drawn up:-

GS 180 kn = 3 nm / min Gives Standard CA of 20°
GS 240 kn = 4 nm / min Gives Standard CA of 15°
GS 300 kn = 5 nm / min Gives Standard CA of 12°

GS 360 kn = 6 nm / min Gives Standard CA of 10°
GS 400 kn = 6·66nm / min Gives Standard CA of 9°
GS 600 kn = 10 nm / min Gives Standard CA of 6°

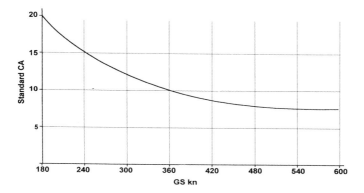

Fig. 7–8   The Standard CA graph.

During the pre-flight planning stage the GS for each leg is computed. The Standard CA for each leg is extracted from the table or graph and noted on the pilot's cockpit flight plan. In flight if position is fixed showing the aircraft to be off the desired trk the hdg is altered towards the desired trk by the Standard CA for the leg being flown. This new hdg is held for a number of minutes equal to the number of nm the fix had shown the aircraft to be displaced from the desired trk. At the end of this time the desired trk will be intercepted and hdg altered for destination at the end of the desired trk, this hdg will be the original hdg for the leg corrected for TE (which has to be calculated by the 1 in 60 rule during the closing manoeuvre).

Example:
At 1147 a pilot sets out to fly an aircraft from 'P' to 'Q' at a GS of 355 kn on an initial hdg of 067 (T). At 1155 a fix shows the aircraft to be 3 nm S of the desired trk 46 nm from the 'P'.
What is the hdg to intercept the desired trk?
At what time will the desired trk be intercepted?
What is the TE?
What is the hdg to be flown on regaining the desired trk?
Answer:
For GS 355 kn the Standard CA is 10°, so at 1155 the hdg to steer to inter-cept the desired trk is 067 – 10° = **057 (T)** (the 10° alteration being made to P to correct for being off trk to S).
3 nm off trk so hold hdg 057 (T) for 3 min. Desired trk will be intercepted at 1155 + 3 = **1158**.
3 nm off trk in 46 nm along = 4 nm off in 60 nm so TE = **4°**.

Hdg to steer on regaining the desired trk = initial hdg of 067 (T) corrected for TE of 4°, = 067 (T) – 4 = **063 (T)** (see Fig. 7–9).

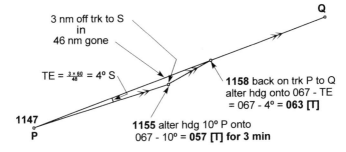

Fig. 7–9   Demonstration of the use of the standard CA.

ALTERING HEADING DIRECTLY FOR DESTINATION

7.8   This pilot navigation technique requires the assessment of both the TE (from desired trk to TMG) and the CA (between the desired trk and the direct trk required to close destination) to be carried by the pilot. From Fig. 7-10 it can be seen that an alteration of hdg towards the desired trk by the amount of TE would only cause the aircraft to fly parallel to the desired trk. To fly down the direct trk to the destination point at the end of the leg requires a further hdg change equal to the CA. The total alteration of hdg to fly directly to destination is **TE + CA.**

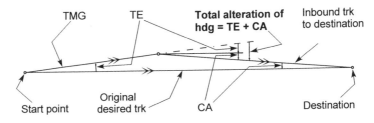

Fig. 7–10   Altering hdg directly for destination.

This method can, in theory, be carried out at any point along a leg but for practical reasons should not be left too late. The later a correction is left, the closer to destination, and the necessary corrections become larger (even for quite small distances off trk). A large hdg change often results in a change of drift angle which simple pilot navigation techniques cannot take into account. Pilots should try and detect any deviation from the desired trk during the first part of the trk before the corrections needed become too large.

7.9   Assessment of TE and CA by the 1 in 60 rule is based on ratios. For instance if an aircraft is found to be 2 nm P off the desired trk at 30 nm along trk, then:

2 nm off in 30 nm = 4 nm off in 60 nm = **4P TE** (see Fig. 7–11).

In the same way the CA can be assessed from the distance off trk and the distance to go to destination. In Fig. 7.11 this is 2 nm off the desired trk with 20 nm to go:

2 nm off in 20 nm = 6 nm off in 60 nm = **6P CA**.

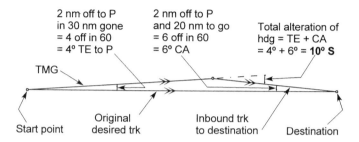

2 nm off to P
in 30 nm gone
= 4 off in 60
= 4° TE to P

2 nm off to P
and 20 nm to go
= 6 off in 60
= 6° CA

Total alteration of
hdg = TE + CA
= 4° + 6° = **10° S**

TMG

Start point   Original
desired trk

Inbound trk
to destination   Destination

Fig. 7–11   Demonstration TE + CA method of altering hdg directly for destination.

So in Fig. 7–11 the alteration of hdg from the fix directly to destination is TE + CA = 4 + 6 = **10 S** (correcting for being off trk to P). Real situations seldom give rise to such straightforward figures and some rounding up or down of distances is common practice in pilot navigation. Bearing in mind the small inaccuracies of most compasses and the degree of accuracy to which the average pilot can fly a hdg manually, answers to within 2° are acceptable when carrying out pilot navigation. It is of course possible to get the answers within 1° by working the ratios out on the circular slide rule of the navigation computer. However in flight a pilot (particularly if flying solo) may have his or her hands full in which case all calculations will have to be carried out in the head. Only study and a lot of practice will achieve the necessary degree of skill needed.

Example:

An aircraft is being flown from 'A' to 'B' a distance of 136 nm. After 43 nm the aircraft's position is found to be 2·75 nm to the right of the desired trk. What is the TE?

What is the CA?

By how many degrees and in which direction should the pilot alter hdg to fly direct to 'B'?

Answer:

TE. 2·75 nm S in 43 nm gone, say 3 in 45 = 4 in 60 = **4S**.

CA. 2·75 nm S with 136 – 43 = 93 nm to go, say 3 in 90 = 2 in 60 = **2S.**
Alter hdg by TE + CA = 4° + 2° = **6° to P** (see Fig. 7–12).

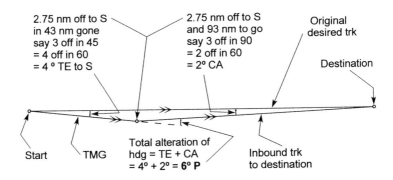

Fig. 7–12 Rounding figures up and down.

Checking the TE on the navigation computer the ratio of 2·75 in 43 gives a ratio of 3.·83 in 60 = **TE of 3·83° S.** Similarly the CA ratio of 2·75 in 93 gives a ratio of 1·77 in 60 = **CA of 1·77° S.** Total alteration of hdg = TE + CA = 3·83° + 1·77° = **5.6° to P,** indicating that the 1 in 60 rule approximation is well within acceptable limits. This method of pilot navigation frequently appears in examination papers and candidates should be familiar with it. When doing practice questions, *ab initio* students in particular should test their ability to carry out estimations in their head by cross checking their answers on the navigation computer.

ESTIMATING TRACK ANGLES ON A CHART

7.10 The 1 in 60 rule can also be applied to the estimation of track angles on a chart. This is not a skill that is formally examined but all pilots should aim to become proficient at estimating angles to a fairly high degree of accuracy. Such an ability can save precious time in the event of an airborne emergency requiring a rapid unplanned diversion. The Cardinal Points were introduced in Chapter 2, these being N 000°/360°, E 090°, S 180° and W 270° (see Fig. 7–13). Half way between each Cardinal Point are the 45° lines of NE 045°, SE 135°, SW 225° and NW 315°. Most people can estimate these 45° steps by eye, for anyone having trouble remember that a 45° right angle triangle has 1 × 1 sides (see Fig. 7–14). Estimation of 15° either side of these eight major compass points will add a further sixteen directions to the compass rose (based on the 1 in 60 rule 15° gives 15 across for 60 along, or a triangle with right angle sides of 1 to 4) (see Fig. 7–15). From the twenty-four 15° radials the 1 in 60 rule can be used to assess intermediate angles.

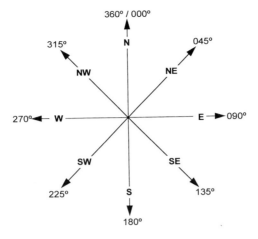

Fig. 7–13   Estimating direction, the 45° steps of the compass.

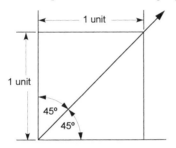

Fig. 7–14   Estimating 45°, 1:1 ratio.

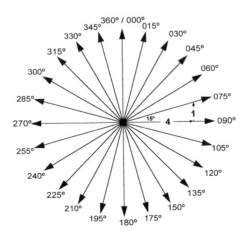

Fig.7–15   Estimating direction, the 15° steps of the compass.

Example:
Estimate the direction of the trk in Fig. 7–16 below.

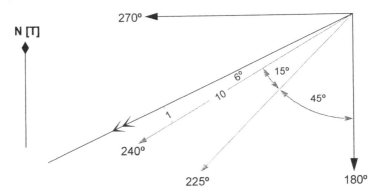

Fig 7–16   Estimation of trk direction.

Answer:
Using 1:1 and 1: 4 ratios puts the direction between 240 (T) and 255 (T). The direction is 1 across to 10 along (6 in 60) or 6° beyond 240 (T) = 246 (T). Protractor measurement gives the actual direction as being 245 (T) showing the estimate to only be 1° out.

Like all skills the estimation of direction can only be achieved with practice. A way to enhance this skill is always to estimate the trks drawn on a chart before measuring them with a protractor. Drawing straight lines at random on an old chart will provide more practice if required. Most people find they quickly reach a level of accuracy of within 5° (or less) and after a while can get the same degree of accuracy by eye alone, without recourse to the 1 in 60 rule.

AMENDING THE ESTIMATED TIME OF ARRIVAL (ETA)

7.11 Amending the ETA can be solved by:
Either Working out a revised GS and using this GS to calculate the time needed to fly the remainder of the leg.
Or Using one of the ratio methods employing time checks at pre-selected check points along the route.

CALCULATION OF REVISED GS AND ETA

7.12 **Revising GS.** Use of the navigation computer to solve the GS from distance covered in time gone was covered in Chapter 4. In pilot navigation the aim is to carry out the calculations in one's head. Consider the case where 30 nm has been covered in 11 min, applying the navigation computer ratio this would be:

$$\frac{30 \text{ nm}}{11 \text{ min}} = \frac{GS}{60 \text{ min}}$$

Transposed this becomes:

$$\frac{30 \times 60}{11} = \frac{1800}{11} = \mathbf{164 \text{ kn GS}}$$

Or

$$\frac{\text{Distance gone} \times 60}{\text{Time gone}} = \mathbf{GS}$$

From this the pilot navigation rule for the calculation of GS is:

'multiply the distance gone by 60 and divide by the time gone in mins'.

7.13 Revising ETA. Having revised the GS the time to go for the remainder of the leg can be solved using the same basic ratios:

$$\frac{GS}{60 \text{ min}} = \frac{\text{Distance to go}}{\text{Time to go}}$$

Transposed this becomes:

$$\frac{\text{Distance to go} \times 60}{GS} = \mathbf{Time\ to\ go}$$

Suppose that in the example in paragraph 7.12 that there were 54 nm to go to the end of the leg. This would give:

$$\frac{54 \times 60}{164} = \text{Time to go}$$

Working this out in one's head, say 54 goes into 164 three times (ignore the 2 over as not being significant) and 3 goes into 60 twenty times. Time to go to the end of the leg is 20 min. In the above example the solution on the navigation computer gives a GS of 163·75 kn and a time to go of 19·8 min. Rounded to the nearest whole number these are the same as the pilot navigation answers. It is often the case that the GS as such is not needed, only the time to go being required. The 'time to go' can be solved in one step by substituting the 'GS formula' in the 'time to go formula'. The 60s cancel out and the formula tidies up to give:

$$\frac{\text{Distance to go} \times \text{Time gone}}{\text{Distance gone}} = \mathbf{Time\ to\ go}$$

This is a far simpler ratio to deal with in one's head, as substitution of the figures already used shows:

$$\frac{54 \text{ nm to go} \times 11 \text{ min gone}}{30 \text{ min gone}} \quad = \quad \frac{594}{30} \quad \text{say} \quad \frac{600}{30} \quad = \quad \textbf{20 min to go}$$

MARKING UP CHECK POINTS ON THE CHART

7.14 Amending the ETA can also be done by other ratio methods which use pre-planned check points along a leg. These methods require the chart to be marked up during the pre-flight planning stage, there being several different options available to pilots. Which to use at any one time will depend on circumstances and, in some cases, personal preference

7.15 The marking up options are:

Distance marks, say every 10 nm for a slow aircraft and increasingly larger intervals (preferably in 10 nm increments) for faster aircraft. Whatever intervals are used each should be clearly annotated but at the same time care must be taken not to obscure features on the chart. Such marks are useful for assessing distances to use in the formulae discussed in paragraphs 7.12 and 7.13. For a route that is being flown regularly these marks will not need changing from one flight to the next (see Fig. 7–17).

The actual marking of the distances is
a personal choice. However care should be taken
not to write over map details that may be needed in flight

Fig. 7–17   Regular distance marks.

Fraction or Ratio marks. These are marks along the leg indicating the fraction of the leg travelled from the start of the leg. The most common fraction markings are at the quarter, half and three-quarter points of a leg. In some cases marking

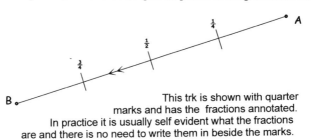

This trk is shown with quarter
marks and has the fractions annotated.
In practice it is usually self evident what the fractions
are and there is no need to write them in beside the marks.

Fig. 7–18   Fraction Marking of a trk.

the leg into thirds or even fifths may be more suitable so as to tie up with navigation features on the ground. Like the distance marks these fraction marks will not need changing for a route that is being flown regularly (see Fig. 7–18).

Regular Time marks. These are marked in after the flight plan has been worked out and the GS for each leg calculated. The GS so deduced is known as the **Deduced Reckoning (DR) GS** (also known as **Dead Reckoning**). The DR GS is used to calculate the distance the aircraft is expected to travel in a particular time interval. This distance is then stepped off down the leg each mark being annotated with its expected elapsed time from the start of the leg. This method has the drawback that the marks are good for just the one flight and only then provided it is flown during the valid period of the winds and temperatures used in preparing the flight plan (see Fig. 7–19).

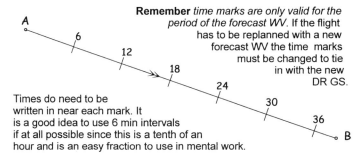

Remember *time marks are only valid for the period of the forecast WV. If the flight has to be replanned with a new forecast WV the time marks must be changed to tie in with the new DR GS.*

Times do need to be written in near each mark. It is a good idea to use 6 min intervals if at all possible since this is a tenth of an hour and is an easy fraction to use in mental work.

Fig. 7–19   Time Marking of a trk.

Time marks at prominent navigation features. These are used when flying a route that has few prominent navigation features none of which tie in with any of the above marking systems. The time to reach each feature from the start of the leg is calculated using the DR GS for the leg. These DR times are then noted on the chart beside the appropriate feature. Like the regular time marks these time marks are only valid for the one flight and the period of the forecast winds and temperatures (see Fig. 7–20).

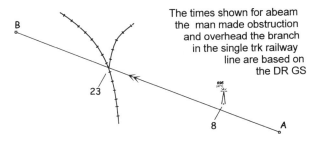

The times shown for abeam the man made obstruction and overhead the branch in the single trk railway line are based on the DR GS

Fig. 7–20   Time Marks at Prominent navigation features.

USE OF FRACTION MARKS TO REVISE ETA

7.16 Fraction marks are not normally encountered in examination questions. However their use in actual flight conditions is very popular with pilots because of the way they help simplify pilot navigation problems. For example if the elapsed time to a fraction mark is multiplied by the inverted fraction gone it will give the 'total flight time' for the leg (Note that it does not give 'time to go'). Fig. 7–21 illustrates this type of calculation for different fraction marks along a leg.

Elapsed time from A to the ¾ mark = 1444 - 1417 = 27 min

Revised time for the whole leg = 27 × $\frac{4}{3}$ = **36 min**

Fig. 7–21   Revising the total time for a leg using fraction marks.

An alternative way of using fraction marks is to use the DR GS to calculate the expected time to reach each fraction mark and annotate them accordingly. The actual time taken to reach a fraction mark is noted and compared with the DR time written on the chart. If they agree the original flight plan ETA is confirmed. If they do not agree the amount of time 'early' or 'late' on the DR time is multiplied by the inverted fraction gone to give the total amendment to be applied to the original flight plan ETA. Fig. 7–22 shows a leg marked in fifths with the DR time at each fifth marked in.

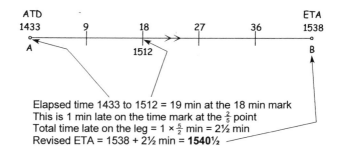

Elapsed time 1433 to 1512 = 19 min at the 18 min mark
This is 1 min late on the time mark at the $\frac{2}{5}$ point
Total time late on the leg = 1 × $\frac{5}{2}$ min = 2½ min
Revised ETA = 1538 + 2½ min = **1540½**

Fig. 7–22   Amending ETA by the time early / late at fraction marks.

If the **Actual Time of Departure (ATD)** is 1433 then the ETA would be 1433 + 45 min = 1538.

If the second mark were actually reached at 1512 this would be an elapsed time of 19 min instead of the DR time of 18 min.

This is 1 min late in ²⁄₅ so the total time late on the flight plan ETA will be:

$$1 \times \frac{5}{2} = \textbf{2·5 min}$$

Revised ETA = Flight plan ETA + time late = 1538 + 2·5 min. = **1540·5**

USE OF TIME MARKS TO REVISE ETA

7.17 Regular time marks are used to amend the ETA by time 'early' or 'late' at a mark multiplied by the ratio:

DR time for the whole leg: DR time to the mark.

Fig. 7–23 shows a leg with 6 min time marks and a total DR time for the leg of 32 min.

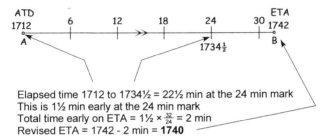

Elapsed time 1712 to 1734½ = 22½ min at the 24 min mark
This is 1½ min early at the 24 min mark
Total time early on ETA = 1½ × $\frac{32}{24}$ = 2 min
Revised ETA = 1742 - 2 min = **1740**

Fig.7–23   Amending ETA by the time early / late at time marks.

If ATD is 1712 then the ETA would be 1712 + 32 min = 1742.
If the fourth (24 min) mark is reached at 1734·5 this would give an elapsed time of 22·5 min instead of the DR time 24 min.
This is 1·5 min early at the 24 min time mark.
Total time early will be:

$$1·5 \times \frac{32}{24} = \textbf{2 min.}$$

Revised ETA = Flight plan ETA – time early.
1742 – 2 min. = **1740**

7.18 Time marks at prominent navigation features are used to amend the ETA in exactly the same way as regular time marks. Where unique navigation features are sparse along a leg it makes sense to mark the DR times against those features most likely to be identified even though it may make for more awkward pilot navigation calculations in some cases.

SOME PRACTICAL PILOT NAVIGATION TECHNIQUES

7.19 Some of the more practical forms of pilot navigation do not lend themselves to written examination. By their very nature written examinations usually place more emphasis on the theoretical aspects and as a result pilot navigation questions about hdg changes and ETA revision usually require candidates to employ the formulae given in paragraphs 7.12 and 7.13. The remainder of this chapter deals with some pilot navigation techniques of a more practical nature which (apart from the use of radio aids on an airway which sometimes feature in plotting) are unlikely to appear on question papers.

FRACTION GONE AND CLOSING ANGLE LINES

7.20 Fractional marking of a leg and the use of the inverted fraction gone is generally accepted as being the simplest and most practical method for revision of the ETA. The calculation of the hdg change direct to the end of a leg is also greatly simplified by fraction marks and what are known as **Closing Angle Lines**. Fig. 7–24 illustrates the pre-flight markings that prepare a topographical chart for this method of pilot navigation.

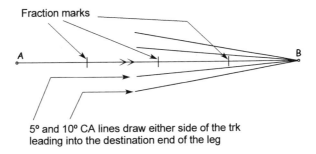

Fraction marks

5° and 10° CA lines draw either side of the trk
leading into the destination end of the leg

Fig. 7–24   Fraction marks and 5° and 10° CA lines.

The leg is divided into fractions and is marked accordingly (quarters are shown but other fractions could be used). At the destination end of the leg 5° and 10° closing angle lines are drawn extending back either side of the leg to about the half way point. If the aircraft's position is established as being off the desired trk the calculation of the hdg change required to fly direct to the destination end of the leg is as follows:

Use the 5° and 10° closing angle lines to estimate (by eye) the CA from the aircraft's position to the end of the leg. At the same time note the fraction gone along the trk.

Multiply the CA by the inverted fraction gone to give the total hdg change required.

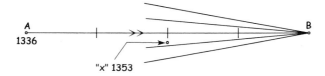

Estimated CA 4° S, fraction gone ½
Alter hdg by 4 × $\frac{2}{1}$ = **8° P**

Time gone 1353 - 1336 = 17 min at ½ fraction mark
Revised time for the whole leg = 17 × $\frac{2}{1}$ = **34 min**

Fig. 7–25   Demonstation of the use of fraction marks and 5° and 10° CA lines.

Example:
In Fig. 7–25 the aircraft left 'A' at 1336 and was fixed as being off the desired trk at position 'x' at 1353.
Time gone is 17 min, fraction gone is ½ and from the closing angle lines the CA can be estimated by eye as 4° S.

Hdg change	= CA × inverted fraction gone.
	= 4° × ²/₁
	= **8° P** (correcting for being S of desired trk).

Total time for leg   = time gone × inverted fraction gone.
 = 17 min × ²/₁
 = **34 min.**

Revised ETA   = ATD + total time for leg.
 = 1336 + 34 min.
 = **1410.**

This was a simple example since at the half way point the TE and CA will be the same, and TE + CA = 2 × CA.

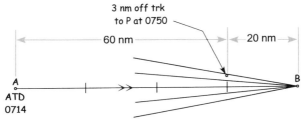

See the text for the comparative methods of working out the hdg change and ETA for the above situation

Fig. 7–26   Solution of hdg change and ETA revision. Comparison between the 1 in 60 method and the fraction marks and CA lines method.

7.21 Fig. 7–26 illustrates a situation of an aircraft off trk to P at the ¾ fraction mark. Some distances have been included on the diagram to enable the closing angle line method to be compared with the basic 1 in 60 method.

From the 1 in 60 rules:
TE = 3 nm off in 60 nm gone = 3°
CA = 3 nm off with 20 nm to go = 9°
Total alteration of hdg = TE + CA = 3° + 9° = **12° S**
From ATD 'A' to the fix is 36 min.

Time to go	$= \dfrac{\text{Distance to go} \times \text{time gone}}{\text{Distance gone}}$
	$= \dfrac{20 \text{ nm} \times 36 \text{ min}}{60 \text{ nm}}$ = **12 min.**

Revised ETA = Fix time + time to go.
= 0750 + 12 min.
= **0802.**

From the closing angle lines:
Estimated CA (by eye) = 9°
Alteration of hdg = CA × inverted fraction gone.
= 9° × ⁴⁄₃
= **12° S.**
From ATD to the fix is 36 min
Total time for the leg = Time gone 5 inverted fraction gone.
= 36 × ⁴⁄₃
= **48 min.**
Revised ETA = ATD + total time for leg.
= 0714 + 48 min.
= **0802.**

7.22 When using pilot navigation techniques *always make the hdg change calculations first*. The revision of the ETA can be carried out at a more leisurely tempo once the hdg change has been implemented. Things can be speeded up in some cases. For instance, if the aircraft can be seen to be off the desired trk and on a TMG that will carry it over an identifiable feature the required change of hdg can be worked out before reaching the feature. On altering hdg when over the feature, a note of the time should be taken for revision of the ETA.

7.23 A pilot navigation calculation that is not often used these days is one for estimating drift and GS. Its particular use is in carrying out an unscheduled diversion, enabling a reasonably accurate hdg and ETA to be calculated from TAS, forecast WV and estimated trk and distance to point of diversion. In paragraph 5.3 it was shown how the GS could never be less than (TAS – Windspeed) or greater than (TAS + Windspeed) and that in these limit cases the drift would be 0°. Equally it can be said that if the WV is at 90° or 270° to trk GS = TAS and the drift angle will be maximum. Fig. 7–27 shows these limits of GS and drift.

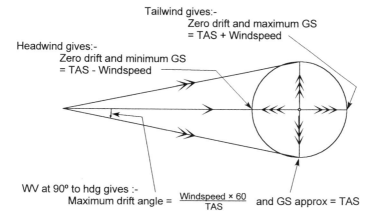

Tailwind gives:-
Zero drift and maximum GS
= TAS + Windspeed

Headwind gives:-
Zero drift and minimum GS
= TAS - Windspeed

WV at 90° to hdg gives :-
Maximum drift angle = $\dfrac{\text{Windspeed} \times 60}{\text{TAS}}$ and GS approx = TAS

Fig. 7–27   The limits of GS and drift.

The 1 in 60 rule can be used to work out the maximum drift angle: treating the TAS as distance gone and the Windspeed as distance off gives:

Maximum drift angle $= \dfrac{\text{Windspeed} \times 60}{\text{TAS}}$

Fig. 7–28 shows the effect on GS and drift for WVs at 30° , 45° and 60° to trk. In all cases the effect on wind components and drift is to reduce them from their maximum values by rule of thumb factors of 0·5, 0·7 or 0·9 depending on the angle of the WV to the trk.

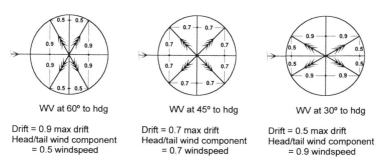

WV at 60° to hdg

WV at 45° to hdg

WV at 30° to hdg

Drift = 0.9 max drift
Head/tail wind component
= 0.5 windspeed

Drift = 0.7 max drift
Head/tail wind component
= 0.7 windspeed

Drift = 0.5 max drift
Head/tail wind component
= 0.9 windspeed

Fig. 7–28   Effect of WV at an angle to hdg.

It may seem a lot of extra information to carry in one's head but it could pay to keep in mind what the maximum possible drift and GSs are for the speeds that are flown on a day to day basis. For instance a pilot who regularly flies at 240 kn the maximum drift is 1° for every 4 kn of Windspeed and GS limits are 240 kn + or – Windspeed.

PILOT NAVIGATION ON AIRWAYS

7.24 Although pilot navigation is associated in many pilot's minds with visual map reading and topographical charts the principles are equally applicable to Airways flying using radio navigation aids. For instance, most overland Airways legs are designated between ground based radio aids from which brgs and/or ranges are obtainable on the appropriate (mandatory) radio receivers carried on board commercial aircraft. Flying along such an Airway and tuned to receive brgs from radio aids at either end of the leg in effect gives a pictorial presentation of TMG and the required inbound trk when shown on a multi-pointer display such as a **Radio Magnetic Indicator (RMI).** The information is displayed as follows:

If the aircraft is flying down the centre line of the Airway the two brgs will be in line (see Fig. 7–29a). Any drift being experienced will show on the RMI as an offset of the forward needle from the aircraft (M) hdg index at the top of the display.

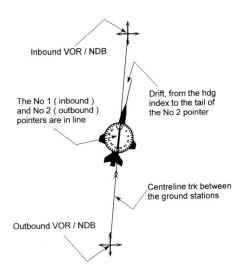

Fig. 7–29a   Use of the RMI for pilot navigation between VOR/NDB ground stations. On the Centreline.

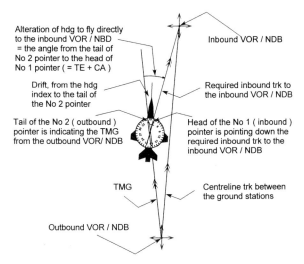

Fig.7–29b   Use of the RMI for pilot navigation between VOR/NDB ground stations. P of the centreline.

If the aircraft is going off the Airway centreline the two needles will form a shallow V, one needle pointing back down the TMG and the other forward along the inbound trk needed to reach the radio aid at the end of the leg. Fig. 7–29b shows an RMI display where an aircraft is tracking to Port of the Airway

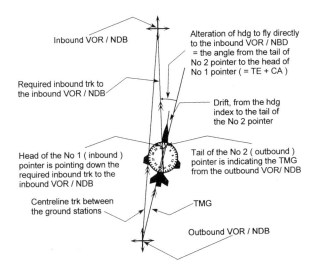

Fig. 7–29c   Use of the RMI for pilot navigation between VOR/NDB ground stations. S of the centreline.

centreline. The extended 'tail' of the back brg needle is indicating the TMG and the pointer of the other needle is indicating the required inbound trk. The total hdg change to fly down the required inbound trk (equal to TE + CA) can be read off from the 'tail' of the back brg needle to the pointer of the inbound needle, the direction from 'tail' to pointer being the required direction of the hdg change (Starboard in this case). For an aircraft tracking to Starboard of an Airway centreline the display would look something like Fig. 7–29c.

It can be seen that such a display is in effect giving a plan view of the TMG and the required inbound trk, with the aircraft at the centre of the dial. A single hdg change to reach the end of the leg being a simple reading from the 'tail' of the back brg needle to the pointer of the other needle. In the case of an aircraft that has not tracked down the centreline of the Airway drift assessment is from the present hdg to the current TMG. Along Airways, amendment of the ETA is simplified by obtaining ranges from **Distance Measuring Equipment (DME)** located at the ends of a leg or using pre-planned brgs from off-trk radio aids to check the rate of progress at fraction marks along each leg.

ESTIMATION OF DISTANCES

7.25 The ability to estimate distance on any chart is a skill all pilots should try to acquire. Since the scale of charts (see Section 3) can vary according to their intended use, pilots should always make certain that they are aware of the scale of the charts they are currently using. Estimation of distance can be carried out with a simple rule (such as a pencil with notches cut to match distance on the chart). The trouble with such a device is that it can never be found when most wanted. A good tip for all pilots is to know the chart distances covered by their handspan and top joint of their thumb. Like the estimation of direction, the estimation of distance on a chart is a matter of practice, so when pre-flight planning try estimating trk lengths before carrying out an accurate measurement.

SECTION 3

AERONAUTICAL MAPS AND CHARTS

The origin of the use of pictorial representation of features on the surface of the earth as an aid to travellers is lost in the distant past. Primitive man probably used simple directions scratched on the ground to indicate to his companions where a source of food or shelter could be found. He would have used symbols such as wiggly lines to show rivers and inverted 'V's for tops of prominent hills to help his explanation.

As man began to extend his field of exploration the pictures of the earth he produced became more detailed. With the invention of more sophisticated ways of measuring distances, direction and time the information portrayed on maps and charts improved until today the majority of the earth's surface has been surveyed and plotted to a degree of accuracy that is more than adequate for aeronautical purposes.

This section deals with the basic principles of producing maps and charts and also an in depth look at the specific projections that are currently used in air navigation

CHAPTER 8

CHART REQUIREMENTS AND SCALE

CHART REQUIREMENTS

8.1 A chart is a pictorial representation on a flat piece of paper of the earth's surface. Since the earth is for all practical purposes a sphere, it follows that in translating its surface onto a flat sheet of paper some distortions are bound to occur. It is physically impossible to produce a flat chart upon which *all* features on the earth's spherical surface are correctly reproduced at the same time.

8.2 Different methods of projection can produce charts for specific tasks. Such charts accurately represent selected earth features whilst allowing other earth features to become distorted. It is a matter of considering what earth features *must* be accurately displayed that decides whether a particular projection is suitable for navigation purposes or not. The main features on the surface of the earth are:

Direction (between places)
Distance (between places)
Shape (of land masses)
Area (of land masses)

For navigation it is essential to be able to measure **direction** *and* **distance** *between places and these two features have to take precedence on any navigation chart.*

ORTHOMORPHISM

8.3 The chart property of correctly showing direction is known as **Orthomorphism** or **Conformality** and is a prerequisite for any aeronautical navigation chart. The measurement of distance varies depending on the chart projection and the area of its coverage. Some charts can be considered as having a constant scale (the ratio of chart length to distance on the earth) and on such charts distances are easily measured by means of a suitably graduated straight-edge. Other charts have varying scale and distances and

105

these have to be measured using the scale at the mid lat of each leg. How, and at what point, direction and distance are measured on different chart projections is discussed later.

8.4 In achieving orthomorphism, shapes and areas get distorted by varying amounts. Whilst area is not important for navigation purposes shape can be, particularly for map reading. Fortunately distortions in shape are gradual and relative to one another so that the overall shapes of the small area visible beneath an aircraft will not appear to be distorted when map reading in flight. Shape distortions are most noticeable when large areas of chart are compared with the same areas on a globe of the world.

SCALE

8.5 Direction has already been covered in Chapter 2, along with convergency (conv) which also has to be considered when looking at various chart projections. Another factor of any chart is its **Scale**, this was mentioned briefly in paragraph 8.3 and needs to be explained in more detail before looking at the various aeronautical charts.

> **Scale is the ratio of chart length to the**
> **distance it represents on the earth's surface.**

Scale of a chart can be given in different ways:

As a ratio such as 1 : 250 000, meaning that 1 unit of measurement on the chart represents 250,000 of the *same* unit of measurement on the earth's surface. i.e. 1 cm on the chart = 250,000 cm (2·5 km) on the earth.

As a graduated scale, Fig. 8–1 shows a typical triple scale covering the three universal units of measurement often found on constant scale charts. When using such a scale pilots must take care to use the correct scale for the units in which they are working and it is a good idea to cross out the unwanted scales to prevent their inadvertent use.

Fig. 8–1   A triple graduated Scale.

As a statement such as '1 inch equals 4 nm', such a statement is self explanatory. Such statements are no longer common on aeronautical charts.

On charts that do not have a constant scale the scale is quoted for a specified lat. To find the scale at any other lat it is necessary to know how the scale varies on the particular projection and this is one of the aspects that will be discussed later.

8.6   Different scales of charts are used for different purposes. A so-called 'large scale chart' is one that covers a relatively small area in considerable detail. This sort of chart might be used for low-level visual map reading from a helicopter or light aircraft, it would be of little use for high level map reading as most of the detail on the chart would not be discernible and if the flight was of any length, dozens of charts would be required. 'Large scale charts' used in aeronautics range from aerodrome plates with scales in the region of 1 : 40,000 up to the 1 : 250,000 UK Topographical series which is for use when map reading *below* 5000 ft.

8.7   'Small scale charts' are the exact opposite, covering much larger areas per chart but with far less detail shown. The range of 'small scale charts' could be considered as starting with the 1 : 500,000 Topographical charts (where an area approximately 280 nm × 210 nm appears on each chart) up to scales of around 1 : 6,000,000 used for oceanic or trans-continental flights.

8.8   Note that the larger the figure to the right in the scale ratio, the smaller the scale and vice versa. Anyone who has difficulty with this concept should think about scale model aircraft. An aircraft having a length of 36 ft (10.58 m) and a wingspan of 48 ft (14.11 m) modelled to a scale of $1/24$ would produce a model of 18 inches (45.72 cm) length and 24 inches (60.96 cm) span. The same aircraft modelled to a scale of $1/72$ would come out at 6 inches (15.24 cm) long and 8 inches (20.32 cm) span. A box 18 inches × 24 inches could hold only one model of $1/24$ scale but it could hold nine of the $1/72$ scale models. By virtue of its size it is obvious that the larger $1/24$ scale model can show much more detail than its smaller $1/72$ scale equivalent.

THE REDUCED EARTH

8.9   The basis of all chart projections is what is termed the **Reduced Earth (RE)**. This is a hypothetical transparent model of the earth made to the required scale for the chart. This RE is assumed to have a latitude and longitude grid on its surface and a light source at its centre or, alternatively, at one of the poles. The light source is assumed to project the graticule onto a sheet of paper which, depending on the navigation projection required, may be in the form of a cylinder wrapped around the RE in contact with its surface, a cone with its apex above one of the poles or a flat sheet of paper tangential to one of the poles. Once the graticule has been projected onto the sheet, and after any mathematical correction needed to achieve orthomorphism, geographical and man-made features are added as deemed necessary for the intended use of the chart.

CHAPTER 9

MERCATOR'S PROJECTION

9.1 This projection is based on a cylinder wrapped around the RE (see Chapter 8, paragraph 8.9) with its point of contact along the equator and the imaginary light source at the centre of the RE. The scale at the equator will be that of the RE but as Fig. 9–1 shows, the scale expands increasingly with movement N or S from the equator and neither pole can be shown on this projection. Another point to note is that the parallels of lat, which on the earth are small circles progressively reducing in diameter towards the poles, are all projected as being the same size as the equator.

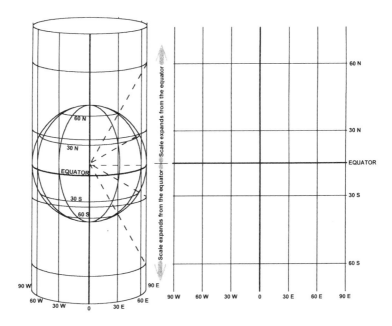

Fig. 9–1   The Basis of Mercator's projection, a cylinder wrapped around the RE along the equator.

9.2   To achieve orthomorphism on a chart it is essential that at any point on the chart the scale changes N/S and E/W are identical . Figs. 9–2 (a), (b) and c illustrate this requirement and show how direction is distorted if scale changes N/S and E/W are different.

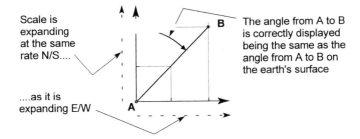

Fig. 9–2a   Orthomorphic Chart.

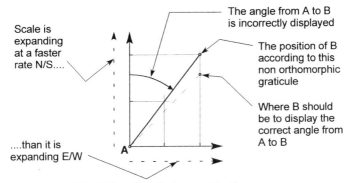

Fig. 9–2b   Non Orthomorphic Chart.

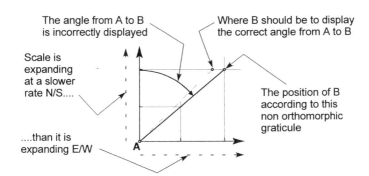

Fig. 9–2c   Non Orthomorphic Chart.

Unfortunately the straight projection from the RE onto the cylinder as shown in Fig. 9–1 produces a different rate of scale change N/S to that E/W and a small mathematical correction has to be incorporated to make the projection orthomorphic. It is interesting to note that this projection was perfected by Gerhardus Kramer (1512–94) a Flemish mathematician and cartographer who used the *nom de plume* 'Mercator' (hence the title of the projection) and to date none of his original calculations have come to light. It seems trade secrets and industrial espionage are nothing new and 'Mercator' protected his corner of the chart-making market very efficiently.

9.3 When the mathematically corrected cylinder is cut along one of the meridians and flattened out the projection appears as in Fig. 9–3 with meridians appearing as equally spaced N/S parallel lines and the parallels of lat as parallel E/W lines increasing in spacing with increase in latitude.

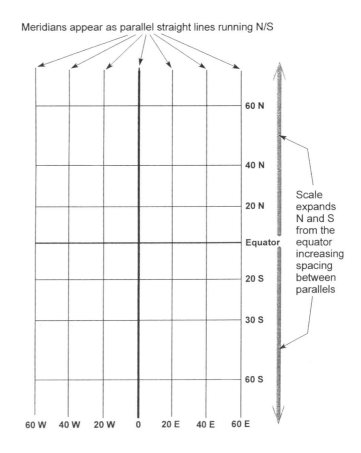

Fig. 9–3   The opened out Mercator's projection showing the appearance of the meridians and parallels.

SCALE ON MERCATOR'S PROJECTION

9.4   As just stated the parallels of lat are shown as parallel straight lines running E/W but because of the expanding scale away from the equator the chart spacing gets larger with increasing lat. The scale on Mercator's projection actually expands from the equator by the Secant (sec) of the latitude, thus:

Scale at latitude 'x' = Scale at the equator × sec 'x'

Since sec = 1/cosine (cos) it is more convenient to use 1/cos if required to convert from scale at the equator to scale at some other lat, this amends the formula to read:

Scale at lat 'x' = Scale at the equator × 1/cos 'x'

Example:
On a Mercator chart scale at the equator is 1 : 2 000 000, what is the scale at 60° N?
Answer:
Scale at 60° N = Scale at equator × 1/ cos 60°

$$\frac{1}{2,000,000} \quad \times \quad \frac{1}{0.5} \quad = \quad \frac{1}{1,000,000}$$

Scale at 60° N = **1 : 1,000,000** (see Fig. 9–4).

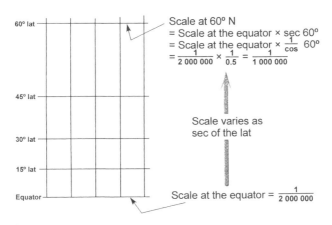

Fig. 9–4   Converting scale at the equator to scale at a lat.

9.5   Similarly if the scale is known at a particular lat the scale at the equator can be found by multiplying by the cos of that lat. Since cos = 1/sec the formula for finding the scale at the equator is:

Scale at the equator = Scale at lat 'y' × 1/sec 'y'

Example:
On a Mercator chart the scale is given as 1 : 500 000 at 44° 30'N. What is the scale at the equator on this chart?

Answer:
Scale at the equator = Scale at 44° 30' × 1/sec 44° 30'

$$\frac{1}{500\ 000} \quad \times \quad \frac{1}{1.402} \quad = \quad \frac{1}{701\ 000}$$

Scale at the equator = **1 : 701,000** (see Fig. 9–5)

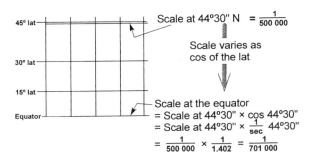

Fig. 9–5   *Converting scale at a lat to scale at the equator.*

9.6   Given the scale at one lat and asked to find the scale at a different lat on the same Mercator chart the process is to find the scale at the equator first and then use that to find the required scale. This of course can be achieved by combining the two formulae thus:

Scale at lat 'x' = Scale at lat 'y' × 1/sec 'y' × 1/cos 'x'

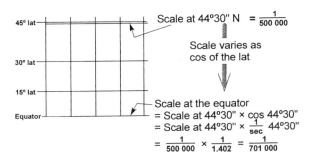

Fig. 9–6   *Converting scale at one lat to scale at another lat.*

Example:
On a Mercator chart the scale is given as 1 : 1,000,000 at 55° N. What is the scale at 38° N on this chart?
Answer:
Scale at 38° N = Scale at 55° N × 1/ sec 55° × 1/cos 38°

$$= \quad \frac{1}{1,000,000} \quad \times \quad \frac{1}{1\cdot7434} \quad = \quad \frac{1}{0\cdot788}$$

$$= \quad \frac{1}{1,360,000}$$

Scale at 38 00 N = **1 : 1,360,000** (see Fig. 9–6)

CONVERGENCY ON MERCATOR'S PROJECTION

9.7   On the Mercator projection the meridians appear as parallel straight lines running N/S. This means that the value of conv is zero over the whole of this chart. On the earth the only place where conv is zero is along the equator, elsewhere conv equals d'long × sine mean lat (see Chapter 2, paragraphs 2.7 to 2.10). So on Mercator's projection the chart conv is *only* correct along the equator (which was also the point where the cylinder was in contact with the RE). With a chart conv of zero if a straight line is drawn across the chart it will cut all meridians at the same angle thus producing a RL (see Chapter 1, paragraphs 1.14 and 1.15). Apart from along the equator or up and down any meridian GCs would appear as curved lines concave to the equator. Since curvature of any GC varies with its latitude, overall direction and length, it is generally not practical to draw GCs on a Mercator chart, (see Fig. 9–7).

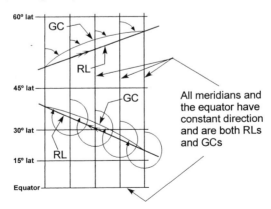

Fig. 9–7   Straight lines represents RLs on Mercator's projection. GCs are curves that vary with trk, distance and lat.

9.8 Having said that, in the vicinity of the equator earth conv is not far removed from zero and the scale expansion on this projection is small, such that in a band 600 nm either side of the equator (latitudes 10°N to 10°S) Mercator's projection can, *for all practical purposes*, be assumed to have constant scale and any straight line will approximate to a GC. Although once widely used for plotting up to latitudes as high as 70° N or S the airborne use of the Mercator chart is now confined almost exclusively to this band 600 nm either side of the equator. In this equatorial band it is used for topographical charts, radio navigation charts, plotting charts and meteorological forecast charts.

9.9 Mercator's projection is sometimes used for high lat aeronautical information charts that are not intended for use in the air. One such is the UK Danger Area Chart. Any reader who has access to this chart, or any similar high lat Mercator's chart, will easily see the effect of the expanding scale. At 60° N (where sec = 2) the parallel spacing on the chart is double the equivalent meridian spacing.

9.10 Despite the decline of the Mercator chart it is required that candidates for the UK ATPL examinations are able to demonstrate the correct basic procedures for high lat plotting on this projection. This is partly academic and partly as a back-up to cover the remote event of no other chart being available for a particular flight. The basic requirements are the measurement of direction and distance and how to convert radio bearings (which follow GCs) into their equivalent RLs for plotting as straight lines.

MEASUREMENT OF TRK DIRECTION ON MERCATOR'S PROJECTION

9.11 Since on this projection all straight lines are RLs (i.e. constant direction) the measurement of trk direction can be made from any point along the trk, however it is best to measure from a point near the start of the trk as this reduces the risk of accidentally measuring 180° out (see Fig. 9–8).

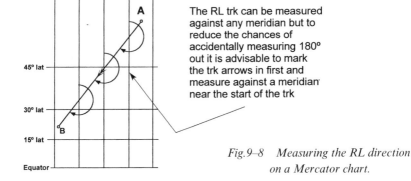

The RL trk can be measured against any meridian but to reduce the chances of accidentally measuring 180° out it is advisable to mark the trk arrows in first and measure against a meridian near the start of the trk

Fig.9–8   Measuring the RL direction on a Mercator chart.

MEASUREMENT OF DISTANCES ON MERCATOR'S PROJECTION

9.12 Measurement of distances is not so straightforward. As already stated the scale expands with sec of lat, so at 48° lat the scale is almost 1·5 × the scale at the equator and at 60° lat it is 2 × the scale at the equator. Now 1° of lat = 60' of lat = 60 nm (see Chapter 3, paragraph 3.3) so, due to the expanding scale, at 60° lat the chart length equal to 60 nm will be ⅓ longer than the chart length equal to 60 nm at 48° lat on the same chart (see Fig. 9–9).

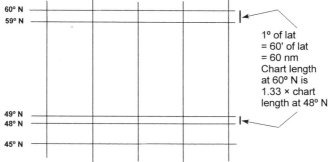

Fig. 9–9   Difference in chart length at different lats.

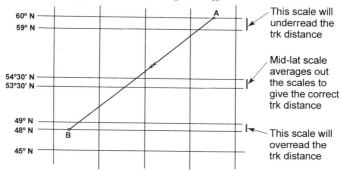

Fig. 9–10   Measurement of distance on a Mercator chart.

9.13 For a track as drawn in Fig. 9–10, if the chart length between 48° and 49° were used to step off 60 nm lengths along this track, the total length of the track would come out ⅓ longer than if the chart length between 59° and 60° had been used – and both answers would be wrong! The scale at the mid-lat of the trk should always be used on the Mercator projection as it cancels out the differences in the scales at the lower and higher lats so giving the correct distance overall. In the example in Fig. 9–10 the mid-lat point is at 54° and the chart length up the meridian from 53° 30' to 54° 30' will give the average length of 60 nm for this particular track.

9.14 In Chapter 2, paragraphs 2.7 to 2.10 conv was introduced and it was shown how the directional change of a GC equalled the conv between the meridians against which the bearings were being measured. Consider Fig. 9–11 which shows the RL route from New York to Paris as plotted on Mercator's projection. This RL trk is an easy to plot straight line. The appearance of the GC trk has also been sketched in although, as mentioned in paragraph 9.7, due to variations in the curvature at different lats and values of d'long this is totally impractical for accurate plotting purposes and is only shown here for academic reasons.

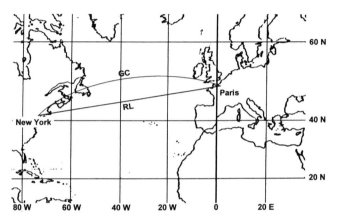

Fig. 9–11   RL from New York to Paris on a Mercator projection.

9.15 Compare the appearance of these trks with the same routes as shown in Chapter 1, Fig. 1–8. The same change of direction of the GC is obvious as is the constant direction of the RL but on Mercator's projection the RL *appears* to be shorter than the GC! This illusion is brought about by the expanding scale on Mercator's projection. The distance along the RL trk should be measured using the scale at the mid-lat of the RL trk which is, in this case, at around 45° 30' N whereas the distance along the GC trk should be measured using the scale at the mid-point of the GC trk, in this case, at about 51° 30' N. This means that a unit of chart length equal to 100 nm along the RL track only equals 88·8 nm along the GC trk, resulting in the RL earth distance coming out greater than the GC earth distance even though the RL *chart length* is shorter. The ratio of 100 nm to 88·8 nm can be verified by comparing the departure at 51° 30' N against departure for the same d'long at 45° 30' N, which due to the parallel line presentation of meridians on Mercator's projection will have a common chart length (see Fig. 9–12).

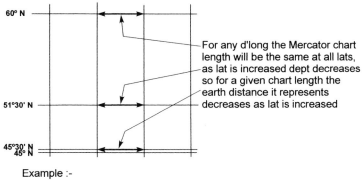

Example :-

For a d'long of 143' at 45°30' N and 51°30' N the depts are :-

Dept at 45°30'	Dept at 51°30'
= d'lat ' × cos 45°30'	= d'lat ' × cos 51°30'
= 143 × 0.70091	= 143 × 0.62252
= 100 nm	= 88.8 nm

Fig. 9–12   Change of dept with lat for a given Mercator chart length.

PLOTTING RADIO BRGS ON MERCATOR'S PROJECTION

9.16   Brgs obtained from any radio aid to navigation will be GC brgs since radio waves always follow the shortest path from transmitter to receiver. Apart from the 600 nm band either side of the equator and brgs due N/S (which are also RLs) GC brgs cannot be plotted directly onto Mercator's projection and have to be converted to RL equivalents. Fig. 9–13 shows a ground-based radio station and the position of an aircraft at 1743 hrs. If at 1743 hrs the ground station took a brg on a transmission from the aircraft which measured 271 (T) at the station, by the time this radio brg was tracked back to the aircraft along the GC it would have changed its (T) direction by the amount of conv on the earth between the aircraft and the ground station.

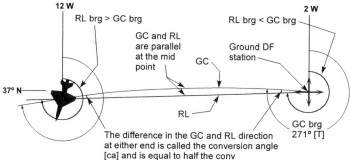

Fig. 9–13   Difference between GC and RL brgs on a
Mercator chart (N Hemisphere).

117

9.17 In this example the aircraft and ground station are in the N hemisphere with the aircraft to the W of the ground station, the straight RL is drawn in from ground station to aircraft and if this is compared to the GC which has also been sketched in (concave to the equator) it can be seen that the RL brg at the ground station is *less* than the GC brg of 271 (T) but *more* than the direction of the GC as it passes through the aircraft. Further inspection of the two lines shows the RL and GC to have the same direction at a point mid-way between the ground station and the aircraft. Since the RL direction is constant and the GC direction changes with conv it follows that the direction of the GC at the mid-way must have changed by:

½ × Conv between the ground station and the aircraft.

= ½ × d'long (in degrees) × sine mean lat.

This is also the angular difference between the RL and the GC directions at both the ground station and the aircraft and is known as the **conversion angle (ca).**

9.18 To plot the brg from the ground station on a Mercator chart it is first essential to convert the GC radio brg into a RL brg which can be plotted with a straight edge. This will require the ca to be calculated and then applied *in the correct sense* to the GC brg *at the measuring station.* Calculation of ca will need knowledge of the estimated, or DR, position of the aircraft for the time of the brg to enable d'long and mean lat between the ground station and the aircraft to be established. In the example in Fig. 9–13 the d'long is 10° and the mean lat is 37° N. This gives:

$$ca = \frac{1}{2} \times 10° \times \text{sine } 37°$$
$$= \frac{1}{2} \times 10° \times 0{\cdot}6018$$
$$= 3{\cdot}009°$$
$$= 3° \text{ in practical terms.}$$

In the example the RL direction from the ground station is less than the GC direction by the amount of the ca so the straight line (RL) to be plotted from the ground station is:

$$GC - ca = 271 \text{ (T)} - 3° = \mathbf{268 \text{ (T)}}$$

9.19 The above example showed a N hemisphere case with the aircraft W of the ground station with the ground station taking a brg of a radio transmission by the aircraft.

From Fig. 9–14 it can be seen that had it been the aircraft that was taking a brg on a transmission from the ground station (i.e. a **Non Directional Beacon (NDB)** it would have registered a brg of 085 (T) along the GC transmission *at the aircraft's longitude.* It will also be obvious that in this particular case the ca would have to be added to the GC brg to find the RL brg *from* the aircraft *to* the ground station. Since the object is to calculate the RL brg to be plotted *from* the known position of the ground station 180° must now be applied to the RL brg at the aircraft.

GC brg aircraft to ground station	= 085 (T)
ca	= + 3°
RL brg aircraft to ground station	= 088 (T)
+ or – 180°	= 180°
RL brg ground station to aircraft	= **268 (T)** Plot

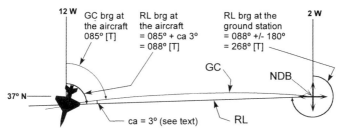

Fig. 9–14   Calculation of RL brg to plot from a GC brg taken from an aircraft West of an NDB (N hemisphere).

9.20 This confirms that, in the example given, the RL brg to plot from the ground station (the position of which can be found from charts or published lists) is the same whether the brg is measured at the ground station or at the aircraft. Application of the ca in the correct sense and the need to apply + or – 180° to the RL brg in the case of brgs taken by the aircraft are the points to watch. Also remember that the value of the ca will have to be recalculated with each change in d'long or mean lat.

9.21 Figs. 9–15a, b, c and d illustrate the four possible variations.

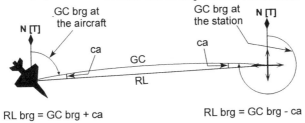

Fig.9–15a   Converting GC brgs to RL brgs. Aircraft West of the ground radio station in the Northern hemisphere.

In Fig.9–15a is repeated the situation used in the last example with the aircraft W of the ground station in the N hemisphere, where the RL to plot from the ground station:

= GC brg at ground station – ca **or** GC brg at aircraft + ca + or – 180°

119

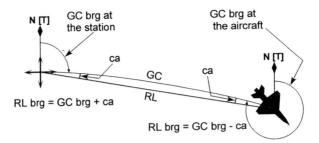

Fig. 9–15b Converting GC brgs to RL brgs. Aircraft East of the ground radio
station in the Northern hemisphere.

In Fig. 9–15b the aircraft is E of the ground station in the N hemisphere. Inspection of the figure shows that in this situation the RL to plot from the ground station:

= GC brg at ground station + ca *or* GC brg at aircraft – ca + or – 180°

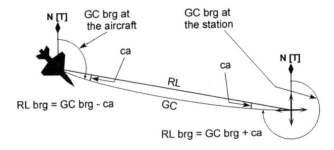

Fig.9–15c Converting GC brgs to RL brgs. Aircraft West of the ground radio
station in the Southern hemisphere.

In Fig. 9–15c the aircraft is W of the ground station in the S hemisphere. Inspection of the figure shows that in this situation the RL to plot from the ground station:

= GC brg at ground station + ca *or* GC brg at aircraft – ca + or – 180°

In Fig. 9–15d the aircraft is E of the ground station in the S hemisphere. Inspection of the figure shows that in this situation the RL to plot from the ground station:

= GC brg at ground station – ca *or* GC brg at aircraft + ca + or – 180°

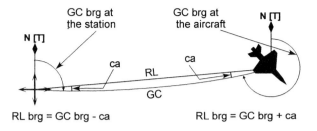

*Fig. 9–15d   Converting GC brgs to RL brgs. Aircraft East of the ground radio
station in the Southern hemisphere.*

9.22 Further analysis of the above figures and application rules show that
the ***ca is always applied to the brg at point of measurement and always
towards the equator.*** Candidates for the Licence examinations confronted with a problem on plotting radio brgs on a Mercator chart
may find it of help to employ a sketch of the situation given in the
question:

Example:
An aircraft whose DR position is 5248N 0307W obtains a brg of 115(T)
from an NDB situated at 5134N 0041E. What is the brg to be plotted from
the NDB on a Mercator chart?

Answer:
First find the mean lat and the d'long between the NDB and the aircraft's
DR position. Use these to calculate the ca.

5134N		00041E		
5248N	+	00307W	+	(crossing 0° meridian)
10422N / 2		00348	=	d'long
5211N = mean lat		3° 48"	=	**3·8 d'long**

$$ca = \text{d'long} \times \text{sine mean lat.}$$
$$= 3\cdot8° \times \sin 52° \ 11"$$
$$= 3\cdot8° \times 0.79$$
$$= 3\cdot002 \text{ or } 3° \text{ in practical terms.}$$

Now do a rough sketch marking in the known facts and indicate the RL
brg to be plotted from the NDB (see Fig. 9–16).

121

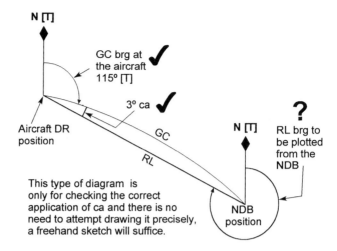

Fig. 9–16   Sketch of 'Known' and 'To be found' factors.

From the sketch it is apparent the 3° ca has to be added to the GC brg of 115 (T) at the aircraft to give the RL brg of 118 (T) at the aircraft. A further + or – 180° has to be applied to give the RL brg of **298 (T)** to be plotted from the NDB.

9.23 The use of such sketches is probably the best way of tackling one type of question related to plotting on a Mercator chart. For instance:

Question:
An aircraft and an NDB are in the same hemisphere. The aircraft takes a brg of 245 (T) on the NDB. The brg to be plotted from the NDB on a Mercator chart is 069 (T). Which hemisphere are they in and what is the value of the ca?

Answer:
From the brgs given the aircraft's position must be somewhere to the East and slightly North of the NDB. With this knowledge freehand sketches of the possible North and South hemisphere cases can be made and the known brgs at the aircraft and the NDB marked in (see Fig. 9–17a and b). It is then a matter of inspection and simple calculation to resolve which is the only feasible case and the value of the ca.

In both cases the reciprocal of the RL brg from the NDB is 069 (T) + or – 180° = 249 (T), this being the direction of the RL at the aircraft. The question gives the GC brg of the radio signal received at the aircraft as 245 (T). The ca, being the difference between the RL and GC measured at a common point, must be 4° and by inspection it can be seen that in Fig. 9–17a (N hemisphere case) the ca would have to be subtracted from the GC bearing giving a RL bearing of 241 (T) which eliminates the N hemisphere case. Inspection of the S hemisphere case, Fig. 9–17b, shows that the ca has to be added to the GC bearing giving the RL brg at the aircraft as 249 (T). Thus the correct answer is:

Southern hemisphere and the ca is 4°.

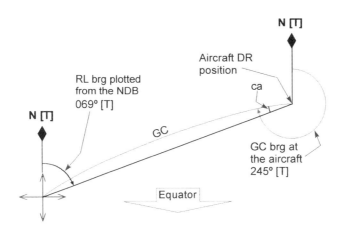

Fig. 9–17a. Sketch for assessing hemisphere and ca. Northern hemisphere situation.

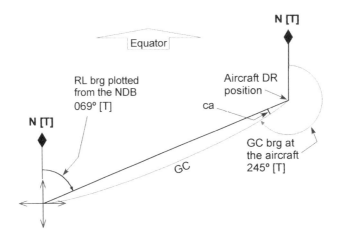

Fig. 9–17b. sketch for assessing hemisphere and ca. Southern hemisphere situation.

9.24 Summary of the properties of Mercator's projection:

Scale:

Correct (same as the RE scale) only along the equator.

Expands away from the equator as the sec of the lat.

Conv:

Only correct at the equator.

Has a constant value of zero over the chart.

Meridians:

Appear as parallel straight lines running N / S.

Parallels of lat:

Appear as parallel straight lines running E / W.

Spacing between parallels increases as scale expands with lat.

RLs:

Are straight lines (having constant direction).

GCs:

Appear as curves concave to the equator. The exceptions to this are the equator and all meridians, these are both GCs and RLs and appear as straight lines.

Uses:

Plotting, topographical and meteorology charts in a band 600 nm either side of the equator. Some aeronautical information charts at lats above 10° (i.e. UK Danger Areas Chart).

CHAPTER 10

TRANSVERSE AND OBLIQUE MERCATOR'S PROJECTIONS

TRANSVERSE MERCATOR'S

10.1 This is another cylindrical projection with the assumed light source at the centre of the RE. Instead of the cylinder being wrapped around the equator it is turned through 90° to lie along a meridian and its anti-meridian (see Fig. 10–1).

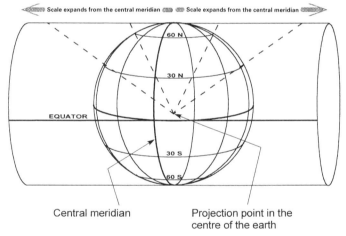

Fig. 10–1   The basis of the Transverse Mercator's projection, a cylinder wrapped around the RE along a chosen central meridian and its anti-meridian.

10.2 Like the ordinary Mercator's projection, the graticule projected has to have a small mathematical correction applied to make it orthomorphic. Furthermore since the point of contact of the cylinder with the RE passes over both poles these can be projected, but by the same token it follows that not all of the equator can be shown. The datum, or central, meridian will be chosen depending on the intended use of the chart. The scale will be correct along the central meridian and will expand with the secant of the

125

GC distance due E or W from this meridian, (1 nm = 1' of arc). Like the ordinary Mercator's this means that *for all practical purposes* scale can be considered constant up to 600 nm either side of the chosen central meridian. **10.3** If the cylinder is now cut at right angles to the central meridian along the two equator lines and unrolled the projection would look like Fig. 10–2, which shows one hemisphere only (the other hemisphere being identical in appearance).

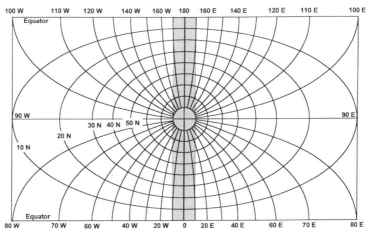

Northern hemisphere Transverse Mercator projection with the 0° Greenwich meridian shown as the central meridian of the projection. The shaded area extended 600 nm either side of the central meridian is the only part of the projection that is of practical navigation use.

Fig. 10–2   The Transverse Mercator's projection.

10.4 Inspection of the projection produced shows that the expansion of the scale at right angles to the central meridian (in Fig. 10–2 the Greenwich 0° meridian has been chosen as the central meridian) results in increasing distortion along the two meridians at 90° to the central meridian. The characteristics of this projectioin are:

Parallels of lat which are small circles on the earth's surface become portrayed as ever increasing ellipses with movement away from the pole.

The only meridians which are projected as straight lines are the central meridian, its anti-meridian and the two meridians at right angles to it. All other meridians project as curves concave to the central meridian.

The equator projects as a straight line but as stated in paragraph 10.2 not all of it can be portrayed.

From this it can be deduced that GCs are only straight lines on this projection when they are directly up or down the central meridian (or its anti-meridian) or at right angles to it. Having said that, within the band 600 nm either side of the central meridian *for all practical purposes* GCs can be considered to be straight lines.

10.5 Since the only part of this projection that is not grossly distorted is the band 600 nm either side of the central meridian, its uses are restricted to within this band. Navigation in the polar regions can be achieved on this projection but at lower lats movement E/W is limited. Apart from the polar case this projection is mainly used to map areas of considerable N/S extent that do not have a large E/W extent. Unfortunately not many natural or national land masses do this.

10.6 One of the few areas that fulfil the criterion is the UK and the Ordnance Survey (OS) maps and 1 : 250,000 Topographical maps (which are based on the OS maps) of these isles are plotted out on a Transverse Mercator's projection whose central meridian is 2° W. The choice of a meridian W of the 0° Greenwich meridian is because the 0° meridian is not central enough to the land mass to be covered. The 1 : 250,000 Topographical map features in more detail in Chapter 13.

10.7 Summary of the properties of the Transverse Mercator's projection:

Scale:
  Correct (same as the RE scale) along the datum (central) meridian.
  Expands as the sec of the GC distance E / W of the datum meridian. At 300 nm error is 0.38% and at 600 nm error is 1.54%.
Meridians:
  Datum meridian and meridians at 90° to it appear as straight lines. All other meridians are complex curves.
Parallels of lat:
  Appear as ellipses with their shorter axis along the datum meridian.
RLs:
  Datum meridian, meridians at 90° to the datum meridian and the equator appear as straight lines. All other RLs are complex curves.
GCs:
  Datum meridian, meridians at 90° to the datum meridian, the equator and all GCs at 90° to the datum meridian appear as straight lines. All other GCs are complex curves. However within a 600 nm band GCs can be assumed to be straight lines *for all practical purposes*.
Uses:
  Plotting in the polar regions only (because of the curvature of both the meridians and the parallels plotting of positions at lower lats is difficult). Topographical maps of land masses with large N/S extent and small E/W extent (such as the UK).

OBLIQUE MERCATOR'S

10.8 As its name implies this projection is not aligned with the equator or a particular meridian. It is still based on a cylinder wrapped around the

RE but the point of tangency is a chosen obliquely aligned GC. Choice of the alignment of the GC will depend on the use to which the particular map or chart is to be put. Long and relatively narrow land masses whose alignment precluded them from fitting onto a Transverse Mercator's projection can be fitted onto an Oblique Mercator's aligned to a GC which bisects it longer axis. Malaysia is one such country to be mapped onto an Oblique Mercator's projection. Another use of the Oblique Mercator's is in the production of strip maps for long distance flights following a GC.

10.9 Like the Mercator's and Transverse Mercator's the Oblique Mercator's projection requires a mathematical correction to make it orthomorphic. Fig. 10–3 shows just one typical example of how the lat and long grid looks for an Oblique Mercator's. The only GCs that appear as straight lines are the ones that the cylinder is touching when wrapped around the RE and the meridian at 90° away from the point where that GC crosses the equator.

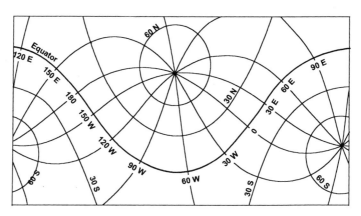

Fig. 10–3   The appearance of a typical Oblique Mercator's projection.

10.10   Use of the Oblique Mercator's is confined to the band just either side of the GC of tangency where, *for all practical purposes*, scale can be considered as constant and GCs approximate to straight lines. Because this projection is quite complex and expensive to produce plus the fact that each sheet is limited to a specific 'corridor' it is not widely used. Apart from mapping countries like Malaysia it is only used to make strip maps for long GC routes that are in regular use and therefore merit the production of special charts.

10.11   Summary of the properties of the Oblique Mercator's projection:
Scale:

Correct (same as the RE scale) along the GC of tangency. Expands as the sec of the GC distance at right angles to the GC of tangency.

Meridians and parallels:

Appear as complex curves.

RLs:

Appear as complex curves.

GCs:

The GC of tangency and all GCs at 90° to the GC of tangency appear as straight lines. All other GCs are complex curves. However within a 600 nm 'corridor' either side of the GC of tangency GCs can be assumed to be straight lines for all practical purposes (most Oblique Mercator charts do not extend to anything like 600 nm either side of the GC of tangency).

Uses:

Topographical maps of long and narrow land masses (such as Malaysia or Italy).

Strip maps of regular used GC routes.

CHAPTER 11

LAMBERT'S CONFORMAL CONICAL PROJECTION

THE SIMPLE CONIC PROJECTION

11.1 As its name implies, Lambert's projection is based on a cone. Consider a cone, like an old fashioned dunce's cap, placed over the RE so that its apex is directly above one of the Poles and the light source at the centre of the RE (Fig 11–1a). Since the apex of the cone is directly above one of the poles it can be seen that the point of contact with the RE is along a parallel of lat. Which parallel a particular cone touches will depend on the steepness of the cone, a shallow cone will contact a high parallel of lat (Fig. 11–1b) and a steep cone a lower parallel of lat (Fig. 11–1c). On conical projections the parallel that the cone is tangential with will have the same length on the chart as length on the RE, it will therefore have correct scale along that parallel of lat. Such a parallel is given the name of **Standard Parallel (SP)**.

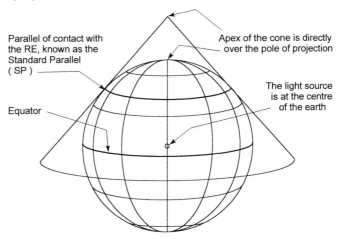

Fig. 11–1a The basis of a simple conic projection showing the Standard Parallel (SP) and light source.

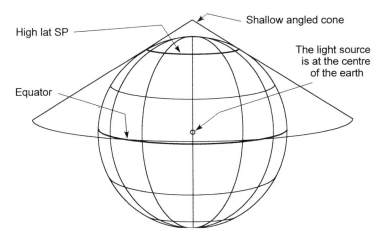

Fig. 11–1b   A shallow angled cone giving a SP with a high lat.

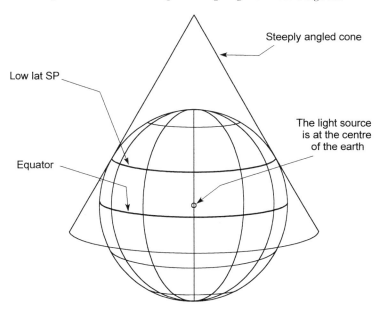

Fig. 11–1c   A steeply angled cone giving a SP with a low lat.

11.2 No matter what the angle of the cone only one Pole, the Pole it is placed over, can be projected, but the entire Equator can be projected if required. Fig. 11–2a shows the lat and long grid projected onto a cone whose SP is 55° N. If this cone is now cut along the 180° meridian and flattened out it will look like Fig.11–2b.

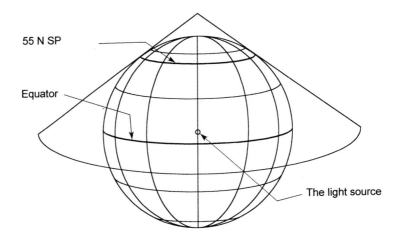

Fig. 11–2a   A Conical projection with SP at 55N.

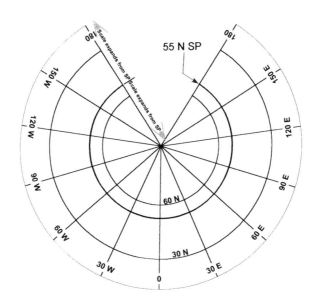

Fig. 11–2b   The Cone opened out flat to show the appearance of the graticule. The 'pie' is 360° × sine SP.

11.3 Inspection of Fig.11–2b reveals certain properties of this simple conic projection:

132

The SP is the same length on the chart as it is on the RE, therefore scale along the SP is correct. However, the flattening out of the cone results in the SP being shown as an arc of a circle instead of a full circle, the size of this arc being 360° × sine of the lat of the SP. The sine of the lat of the SP is known as the **Constant of the Cone** and is sometimes given the symbol of a lower case letter '**n**'.

The other parallels and the equator also appear as arcs of 360° × 'n'.

All the meridians appear as straight lines radiating out from the Pole of projection.

Meridians and parallels cross each other at 90°.

The conv of the meridians is the same over all the chart = d'long × 'n'. The only place on the earth where conv = d'long × 'n' is along the SP. Earth conv is less towards the Equator and greater towards the Pole.

So on this projection:
Chart conv is:
    Constant.
    Correct along the SP.
    > Earth conv between Equator and the SP.
    < Earth conv between the SP and the Pole.
Scale expands N and S from the SP.

Such a simple conic chart needs mathematical adjustments to make it orthomorphic and would be limited in use to a narrow band either side of the SP.

LAMBERT'S CONICAL ORTHOMORPHIC PROJECTION

11.4 Lambert's projection is a more sophisticated mathematical treatment of this basic conic projection:

An initial SP is selected and the value of 'n' for the chart is established.

The chart scale along the initial SP is them mathematically reduced so that it no longer fits the definition of a SP and it is renamed the **parallel of origin (p/o)**.

The reduction in scale at the p/o also affects the scale either side of the p/o and works in opposition to the scale expansion that took place on either side of the initial SP. The end result is that there are now two parallels, one either side of the p/o, where scale along them is the same as on the RE, thus creating **two SPs**. Mathematical fine tuning is then carried out to ensure that the projection is orthomorphic.

11.5 The effect of all this mathematics is the same as if it had been possible to push the cone down into the RE as in Fig. 11–3a. When cut along a meridian and flattened out the Lambert's projection looks like Fig. 11–3b.

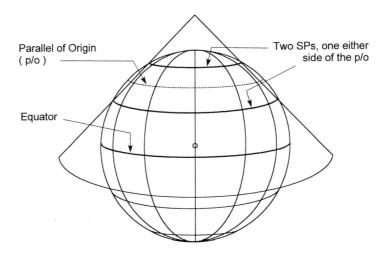

Fig. 11–3a   The apparent geometry of Lambert's projection, as if the cone had been pushed into the RE.

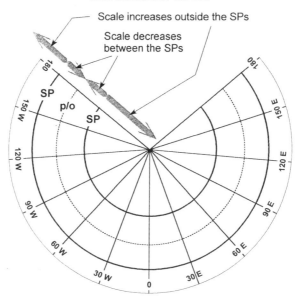

Fig. 11–3b   The cone opened out flat to show the appearance of Lambert's graticule.

The geometry of the basis of this projection is such that the latitudes of the two SPs are not quite equally spaced either side of the p/o. This is only critical for the cartographer who has to work the mathematics out, for the practical user the p/o can be considered as lying half way between the SPs. In examination questions if the value of the p/o or 'n' is given then use these values as required, otherwise use the sine of the latitude half way between the SPs.

11.6 On Lambert's projection:

Chart conv is:

Constant over the whole chart.

Correct at the p/o.

> Earth conv between the Equator and the p/o.

< Earth conv between the p/o and the Pole.

Scale is:

Correct along both SPs.

Contracted between the SPs to become least at the p/o.

Expanded outside the two SPs.

THE ⅔ : ⅙ RULE

11.7 Provided that the chosen SPs are not too far apart (up to a maximum of just over 12° of lat) the scale within the SPs and for a distance either side of the SPs (equal to a quarter of the distance between the SPs) can be considered as constant *for all practical purposes*. This means that practical constant scale charts can be produced to cover any lat spread of up to 20° by selection of the appropriate p/o and SPs. This spread is shown in Fig. 11–4 and is sometimes referred to as the ⅔ : ⅙ **Rule.** On such a chart the maximum scale error is less than 1% at the p/o and the N and S limits.

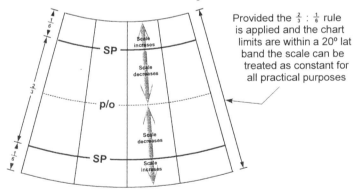

Fig. 11–4   The ⅔:⅙ rule for a Lambert's chart to be treated as constant scale for all practical purposes.

11.8 Some Lambert's charts cover a greater lat spread than 20° and these cannot be considered as having constant scale. Measurement of distance on such charts has to be made using a special variable scale plotted on the edge of the chart, or by use of the scale at the mid-latitude of the trk in the same way as on a Mercator chart.

APPEARANCE OF RLs AND GCs

11.9 If a straight line is drawn between two points on a Lambert chart (see Fig. 11–5) it can be seen to cross successive meridians at an angle which changes by the amount of chart conv between the meridians. A RL (which by definition has constant direction) between the same two points appears as a curve concave to the Pole of projection. It is worth noting that at the mid-point of the straight line and the RL they are running parallel to each other. This means that although curves are impractical to plot, the RL direction between two points can be ascertained by drawing a straight line trk between them and measuring the direction from the meridian at mid-point of the trk.

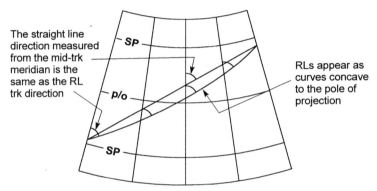

Fig. 11–5   Appearance of a RL and how to find the RL direction between points on a Lambert chart.

11.10 A straight line drawn E/W along the p/o will follow a GC since chart conv and earth conv are the same along the p/o. On the Polar side of the p/o where earth conv is greater than chart conv a straight line drawn E / W will lie closer to the p/o than the GC which appears as a curve concave to the p/o. Similarly on the Equatorial side of the p/o where earth conv is less than chart conv a straight line drawn E/W will lie closer to the p/o than the GC which appears as a curve concave to the p/o. Fig. 11–6 illustrates these cases.

11.11 For charts that fall within the ²/₃ : ¹/₆ rule the differences between chart conv and earth conv over the chart are small and straight lines can, *for all practical purposes*, be considered as GCs. Fig. 11–7 shows the true shape of a GC drawn obliquely across such a chart compared with the straight line drawn between the same start and finish points.

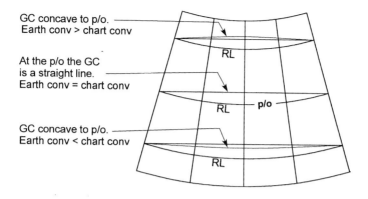

Fig. 11–6   The appearance of GCs running EW on a Lambert projection.

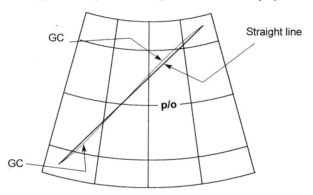

*Fig. 11–7   True appearance of a GC and an oblique straight line
joining two points either side of the plo.*

PLOTTING BRGs ON A LAMBERT CHART

11.12   Since straight lines on the Lambert's projection can be taken to represent GCs it follows that this makes Lambert's charts ideal for plotting radio brgs be they from a VHF Omni Range (VOR), Non Directional Beacon (NDB) or a ground based Direction Finding (DF) station. The form in which information is received from each of these ground-based sources can vary but in each case the (T) brg of the GC *from* the station must be calculated before plotting it as a straight line from the station's ground position on the chart. The various ways in which the above signals are converted for plotting purposes is dealt with in detail in Chapter 17. Ground DF brgs and VOR brgs emanate at their respective ground stations and once converted into a True bearing *from* the station are plotted as straight lines from N (T) at the ground station.

11.13 In the case of an aircraft taking a brg on an NDB the brg must first be converted to a brg from N (T) at the aircraft and the reciprocal (+ or − 180°) calculated. Chart conv between the DR position of the aircraft and the ground position of the NDB must be applied (in the correct sense) to this reciprocal brg before plotting from N (T) at the NDB ground position. Fig. 11–8 illustrates what happens if chart conv is not applied to the reciprocal.

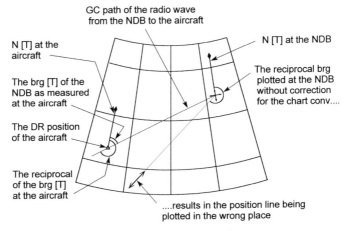

Fig. 11–8   The result of failing to apply chart conv.

11.14   In the case of plotting on a Lambert chart the calculation of the amount of chart conv to apply is found by the formula:

$$\text{chart conv} = \text{d'long} \times \text{'n'} \text{ (i.e. sine of the p/o)}$$

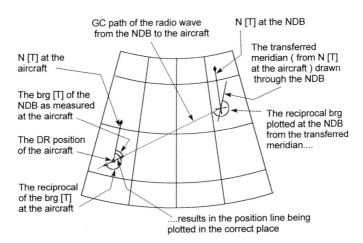

Fig. 11–9   Transferring a meridian to correct for chart conv.

This formula is more academic than practical but, since it may be needed to solve possible examination questions, candidates should commit it to memory. A more practical method can be used when plotting which does not involve calculating the value of the chart conv. Having worked out the reciprocal (T) brg at the aircraft, this is plotted from a line parallel to N (T) at the aircraft's DR position transferred to pass through the ground position of the NDB. This parallel datum is known as a **transferrred meridian** and the angle between it and the (T) meridian at the NDB is the chart conv between them. Fig. 11–9 illustrates this practical method of allowing for conv on a Lambert chart.

Example:
An aircraft takes a brg on an NDB which is positioned at 5236N 0029W. If the DR position of the aircraft is 5310N 0357W and the brg measured at the aircraft is 104 (T) what is the (T) brg to plot from N (T) at the NDB on a Lambert's chart whose p/o is 5600N ?
Answer:
d'long = 0357W – 0029W = 3° 28' = 3·467°
sine p/o (56°) = 0·829
Conv   = dlong × sine p/o
       = 3·467° × 0·829
       = 2·874143° say 3°
Brg of NDB from aircraft =   104 (T)
                 + or – 180°
Reciprocal bearing =   284 (T)
In this case Conv is +   3°
           Plot 287 (T) from NDB (see Fig. 11–10)

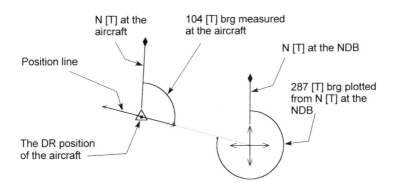

Fig. 11–10. Illustration of the mathematical worked example correcting for chart conv.

11.15   Whether conv has to be added or subtracted can be checked by means of a simple sketch. There are four possible cases:

N hemisphere, aircraft W of NDB (see Fig. 11–11a)
N hemisphere, aircraft E of NDB (see Fig. 11–11b)
S hemisphere, aircraft W of NDB (see Fig. 11–11c)
S hemisphere, aircraft E of NDB (see Fig. 11–11d)

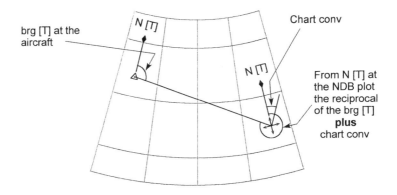

Fig. 11–11a   N Hemisphere, aircraft W of the NDB.

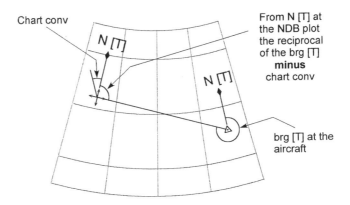

Fig. 11–11b   N Hemisphere, aircraft E of the NDB.

Figs. 11–11c and d also bring out the fact that **in the S hemisphere it is the S pole that is the pole of projection and N (T) is** *away* **from the pole.** Since candidates for the examinations may have to answer questions involving calculations similar to the example above Figs. 11–11a to d should be learned. Whether the cases are learned by rote or the diagrams studied for recall is a matter of personal preference.

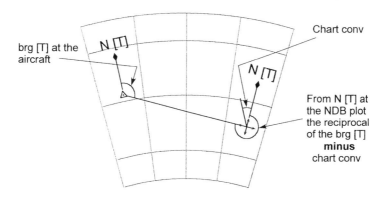

Fig. 11–11c   S hemisphere, aircraft W of the NDB.

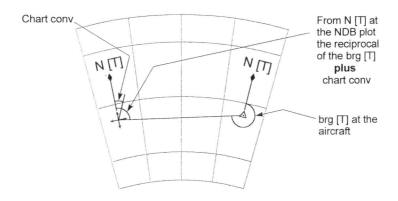

Fig. 11–11d   S hemisphere, aircraft E of the NDB.

11.16   Summary of the properties of the Lambert's projection:

Scale:

Correct (same as the RE scale) along the two SPs.

Contracts between the two SPs becoming least at the p/o.

Expands outside the two SPs.

On charts constructed to conform to the ⅔ : ⅙ Rule the scale can, *for all practical purposes*, be assumed as constant.

Conv:

Constant all over the chart.

Correct at the p/o.

Greater than earth conv between the p/o and the equator.

Less than earth conv between the p/o and the pole of projection.

Meridians:

Appear as straight lines radiating from the pole of projection.

Parallels of lat:

Appear as concentric arcs (360° × sine p/o) centred on the pole of projection.

RLs:

Curves concave to the pole of projection.

GCs:

Curves concave to the p/o, except for the meridians which are straight lines. Straight lines lying E/W along the p/o are GCs. On charts constructed to conform to the ⅔ : ⅙ Rule GCs can, *for all practical purposes*, be assumed to be straight lines.

Uses:

Plotting, topographical, radio navigation and meteorology charts for lats from 10° to 80°.

CHAPTER 12

POLAR STEREOGRAPHIC PROJECTION

12.1 This projection is formed by positioning a flat sheet of paper tangential over one pole on the RE and projecting the lat and long graticule onto the sheet from a light source positioned at the other pole. Figure 12–1a illustrates the lines of projection and Fig. 12–1b shows the appearance of the resulting chart. Note how the meridians radiate out from the pole as straight lines and the parallels are concentric circles all centred on the pole. All the meridians cross the parallels at 90° exactly as they do on the earth.

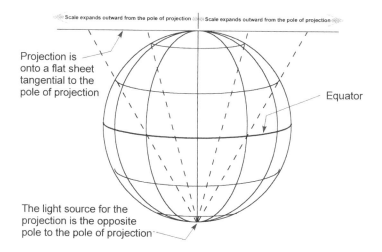

Fig. 12–1a   The Polar Stereographic method of projection.

12.2   The only point on the chart that has the same scale as the RE is at the pole of projection. The scale on the rest of the chart is expanding away from the pole. The rate of change of scale at any point is the same N/S as it is E/W so this projection is naturally orthomorphic and does not require any mathematical adjustment. The scale expands away from the

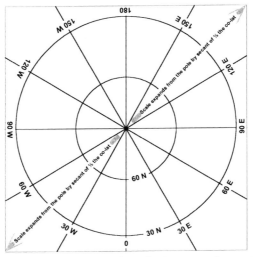

Fig 12–1b   The appearance of a Polar Stereographic projection.

pole as the **sec of ½ the co-lat** (see Fig. 12–2). The definition of the co-lat is:

90° – the lat of the parallel being projected

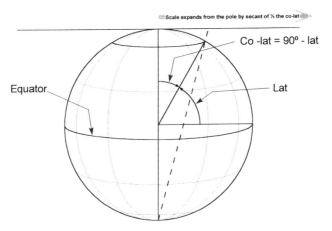

Fig. 12–2   Scale expanding by Secant of the ½ co-lat.

Example:
Scale at 80° lat = scale at the pole × sec ½ (90° – 80°)
                 = scale at the pole × sec ½ (10°)
                 = scale at the pole × sec 5°
                 = scale at the pole × 1·0038

Which indicates that at a distance of 600 nm (10° of lat) from the pole the scale expansion on this projection is only 0·38%. Checking other latitudes shows that at 70° lat scale expansion is 1·54%, at 60° lat it is 3·53% and although the equator can be projected the scale expansion is a massive 41·42%. *For all practical purposes* the scale can be regarded as constant within 600 nm of the pole of projection. Further than 600 nm from the pole scale can no longer be considered constant and the measurement of trk distances must be carried out using the latitude scale at the mid-lat point of the trk.

12.3 Conv is constant over the whole chart and is equal to conv at the pole, that is to say it is equal to d'long, the 'n' factor for the chart being 1 (the sine of 90°). With movement away from the pole to lower lats the earth conv decreases until it becomes zero at the equator. So chart conv is only correct at the pole and is greater that earth conv at all other lats.

Example:
At 80° lat earth conv $\quad$ = $\quad$ d'long × sine 80°
$\qquad\qquad\qquad\qquad\quad$ = $\quad$ d'long × 0·9848

This means that at 80° lat chart conv is approximately 1·5% in error. By 70° lat the error is around 6%, at 60° lat it is 13·4% and at the equator it is 100%. In the vicinity of the pole where the error is negligible, straight lines can, *for all practical purposes*, be considered as GCs. Since RLs are lines of constant (T) brg these will appear as curves concave to the pole of projection, the parallels of lat being one example, the one exception being the meridians which appear as straight lines and qualify as both RLs and GCs. It is worth noting that if an aircraft is flown along a meridian to the pole its (T) direction will change by 180° the instant it crosses the pole and starts to fly along the anti-meridian away from the pole.

12.4 Uses of this projection are limited to the polar regions. Even a relatively short flight in the vicinity of either of the poles can involve large changes in d'long, conv and (T) direction so the use of a suitably aligned grid overlay is not uncommon (see Chapter 2, paragraphs 2.11 and 2.12).

12.5 Summary of the properties of the Polar Stereographic projection:
Scale:
Only correct (same as the RE scale) at the pole of projection.
Expands away from the pole of projection as the sec of ½ the co-lat.
Conv:
Only correct at the pole of projection (equal to d'long).
Has a constant value over the whole chart.
Since earth conv decreases away from the poles to become zero at the equator the chart conv is greater than earth conv at all lats except the poles.

Meridians:
Appear as straight lines radiating from the pole of projection.
Parallels of lat:
Appear as concentric circles centred on the pole of projection.
RLs:
Appear as curves concave to the pole of projection, the one exception being the meridians which are straight lines and are both RLs and GCs.
GCs:
Appear as curves concave to the pole of projection, the one exception being the meridians which are straight lines and are both GCs and RLs. Within 600 nm of the pole of projection GCs can, *for all practical purposes*, be assumed to be straight lines.
Uses:
Plotting, topographical, radio aids and meteorology charts for use in the polar regions.

All the colour extracts from the 1:250 00 and 1:500 000 series of charts are produced here by the kind permission of the Aeronautical Charts section of the UK CAA.

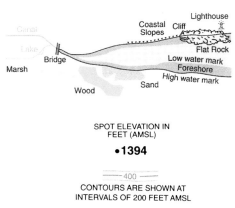

ELEVATION TINT LEGEND
HIGHEST GROUND
ELEVATION KNOWN IS
5414N 00224W

	2415ft	
FEET		*METRES*
Over		Over
2000		610
1400		427
1000		305
800		244
600		183
400		122
200		61
0		0

SPOT ELEVATION IN
FEET (AMSL)

•1394

———400———

CONTOURS ARE SHOWN AT
INTERVALS OF 200 FEET AMSL

Fig. 13-1a   Portrayal of natural features and relief on the 1:250 000 series of UK topographical charts

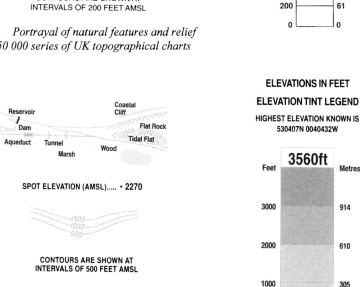

ELEVATIONS IN FEET

ELEVATION TINT LEGEND

HIGHEST ELEVATION KNOWN IS
530407N 0040432W

Feet	3560ft	Metres
3000		914
2000		610
1000		305
500		152
sea level		

SPOT ELEVATION (AMSL)..... • 2270

———1500———
———1000———
———500———

CONTOURS ARE SHOWN AT
INTERVALS OF 500 FEET AMSL

CAUTION

CONTOURS AND ELEVATION TINTS
BELOW 500 FEET AMSL ARE NOT
SHOWN ON THIS CHART.

Fig. 13-1b   Portrayal of natural features and relief on the 1:500 000 series of UK topographical charts

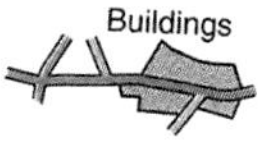

Buildings

Fig. 13-2a   Portrayal of towns and built up areas on the 1:250 000 series of UK topographical charts

BUILT-UP AREAS

City or large Town .... ⬠ over 2 Sq km

Town .... ☐ 1 to 2 Sq km

Small Town, Village or Hamlet .... ○ under 1 Sq km

Large Industrial Area ....

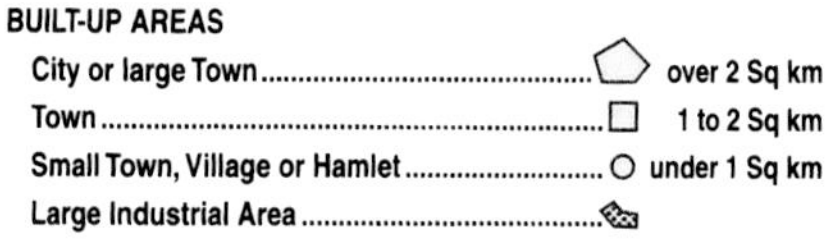

Fig. 13-2b   Portrayal of towns and built up areas on the 1:500 000 series of UK topographical charts

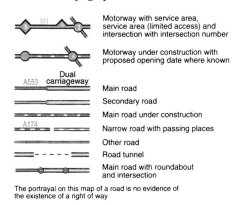

Motorway with service area, service area (limited access) and intersection with intersection number

Motorway under construction with proposed opening date where known

Main road

Secondary road

Main road under construction

Narrow road with passing places

Other road

Road tunnel

Main road with roundabout and intersection

The portrayal on this map of a road is no evidence of the existence of a right of way

Fig. 13-3a   Portrayal of roads on the 1:250 000 series of UK topographical charts

ROADS

Motorway, with Service Area ....

Dual Carriageway, with Service Area ....

Multi-level Intersection ....

Primary ....

Secondary and selected Minor ....

Under Construction ....

Bridge or Viaduct, Tunnel ....

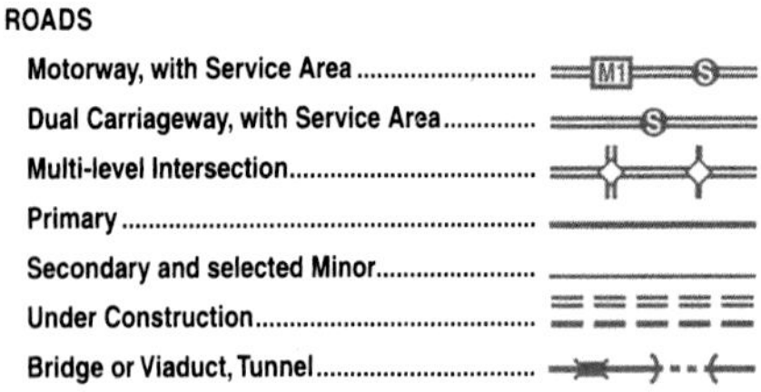

Fig. 13-3b   Portrayal of roads on the 1:500 000 series of UK topographical charts

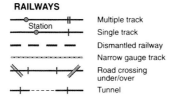

RAILWAYS

Station	Multiple track
	Single track
	Dismantled railway
	Narrow gauge track
	Road crossing under/over
	Tunnel

Fig. 13-4a   Portrayal of railways on the 1:250 000 series of UK topographical charts

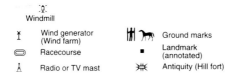

RAILWAYS

Multiple Track	
Single Track	
Narrow gauge Track	
Former railway, track removed (selected)	
Bridge or Viaduct, Tunnel	

Fig. 13-4b   Portrayal of railways on the 1:500 000 series of UK topographical charts

	Windmill		
	Wind generator (Wind farm)		Ground marks
	Racecourse	▪	Landmark (annotated)
	Radio or TV mast		Antiquity (Hill fort)

Fig. 13-5a   Portrayal of other, man made, features on the 1:250 000 series of UK topographical charts

GENERAL FEATURES

Reservoir under construction	
Power Station	PS ▪
Mine (selected)	✗
Racecourse or Racetrack	⬭
Landmark, annotated	▪
Hill Figure	
Monument (selected)	Δ

Fig. 13-5b   Portrayal of other, man made, features on the 1:500 000 series of UK topographical charts

AERODROMES - Field limits with hard runway pattern....... Civil
.......Government

- Showing disused runways as solid patterns

CUSTOMS AERODROMES are distinguished by a pecked line around the name of the aerodrome .... [MANCHESTER]

AERODROME LIGHT BEACON .... ☆ FIG ¦¦·¦·¦·¦ ☆ FIR ¦·¦·¦·¦

HELIPORT .... Ⓗ Ⓗ

MINOR AERODROME with runway pattern unknown or not portrayable ....

MICROLIGHT FLYING SITES - Intense Activity also takes place at certain Licensed and Unlicensed Aerodromes. See UK AIP ENR 1.1 .... Ⓜ

DISUSED or ABANDONED Aerodrome - shown for navigational landmark purposes only. See AIC 56/02 (Pink 34) ....

GLIDER LAUNCHING SITES - See UK AIP ENR 1.1.
a. Primary activity at locations showing Maximum Altitude of winch launch. AMSL .... G /2.5

b. Additional activity at locations showing Maximum Altitude of winch launch. AMSL G/2.5

c. Additional activity without cables .... G

HANG/PARA GLIDING - Winch Launch Sites showing Maximum Altitude of winch launch. AMSL. See UK AIP ENR 1.1. .... /2.5

ELEVATIONS of Active Aeronautical Sites are shown adjacent to the symbol. Shown in feet above Mean Sea Level (AMSL) 250 250

WINCH LAUNCHED ACTIVITIES. Maximum Altitude of cables is represented in thousands and hundreds of feet above mean sea level, calculated using a minimum cable height of 2000ft AGL plus site elevation. At some sites the cable may extend above 2000ft AGL. Due to the ground-based cable, aircraft should avoid over flying these sites below the indicated altitude.

Symbols depicting Non Winch Launch Hang/Para Gliding sites have been removed as they were not an accurate representation of the activity on any given day. Airspace users should be aware that single or groups of soaring or motorised Hang/Para Gliders can be found flying anywhere in the open FIR up to 15,000ft.

FREE-FALL PARACHUTING DROP ZONE - See UK AIP ENR 1.1.
Parachutists may be expected within the airspace contained in a circle radius 1·5NM or 2NM of the DZ up to FL150. Night parachuting may take place at any of the sites shown on this chart.

*AERODROMES WITH INSTRUMENT APPROACH PROCEDURES (IAPs) OUTSIDE CONTROLLED AIRSPACE.

Aerodrome having one or more IAPs outside Controlled Airspace .... ⟨⟨⟨

The symbol is aligned to the MAIN Instrument Runway (civil). Pilots who intend to fly to or route adjacent to aerodromes with IAPs are strongly recommended when flying within 10NM of the aerodrome to contact the aerodrome ATSU. Detailed IAP information is shown in the UK AIP.

ANNOTATION OF VERTICAL LIMITS FOR CONTROLLED AIRSPACE WHICH HAVE AN UPPER LIMIT OF FL245 ARE SHOWN WITH A PLUS (+) AFTER THEIR BASE LEVEL/ALTITUDE, eg 3000'·FL245 IS SHOWN AS 3000'+.
WHERE THE UPPER LIMIT IS BELOW FL245 BOTH BASE AND UPPER LIMITS ARE SHOWN.
AIRSPACE VERTICAL LIMITS ARE DEFINED BY ALTITUDE/FLIGHT LEVEL UNLESS OTHERWISE NOTED.
TINT BANDING DENOTES THE EXTREMITY OF CONTROLLED AIRSPACE. LINES WITHOUT TINT BANDING DENOTE LEVEL CHANGES WITHIN AREA.

FOR CHART CLARITY ONLY CENTRE LINE .... OF ADR's ARE SHOWN

ALL AIRSPACE NOT COVERED BY CLASSES A-F ....

NB. CONTROLLED AIRSPACE IS NOT DEPICTED ABOVE FLIGHT LEVEL 245 IN THE UK. ALL CLASS Ⓑ AIRSPACE IS ABOVE FL245. NO AIRSPACE IS DESIGNATED CLASS Ⓒ IN THE UK.

L10 Ⓐ FL45+

CTA Ⓓ 2500'·3500'

TMA Ⓔ 2000'·6000'

N5710 Ⓔ

FL55-FL235

Ⓐ
Ⓓ
Ⓔ
Ⓕ
Ⓖ

Low Level Corridor or Special Route................... 750'·2500'   or

Special Access Lane Entry/Exit
(⟋ indicates centre of lane.)

Visual Reference Point (VRP). Notified in UK AIP .... (Location identified by ⊕).

E/E. SHEPSHED

VRP TROWELL

MILITARY AERODROME TRAFFIC ZONES (MATZs) have the following vertical limits: SFC to 3000ft AAL within the circle and 1000ft AAL to 3000ft AAL within the stub.
Zone configuration may vary, often two or more MATZs are amalgamated to produce a Combined Zone (CMATZ). Controlling Aerodromes show the MATZ penetration frequency to be used. See UK AIP ENR 2.2.

MATZ LARS 126·5

STANDARD MATZ WITH TWO STUBS AND LARS

LOWER AIRSPACE RADAR SERVICE (LARS).
The abbreviation LARS has been added to the MATZ frequency to identify those participating MATZ ATS Units. Other participating LARS Units are identified by a LARS frequency box. The Service, Radar Advisory (RAS) or Radar Information (RIS), is available to all aircraft in unregulated airspace up to and including FL95 within approximately 30NM of each participating ATS Unit. See UK AIP ENR 1.6.

AREAS OF INTENSE AIR ACTIVITY (AIAA) ....
Areas are shown with name, vertical limits and where applicable contact frequency. Pilots of aircraft who transit these areas are strongly advised to make use of the Radar Service.

PORTREE ASR

BELFAST ASR

ALTIMETER SETTING REGION BOUNDARY (ASR) ....
NOTE: The airspace within (and below) all Control Zones, Terminal Control Areas and Control Areas (with the exception of the Worthing and Daventry CTAs) during their notified hours of operation, does not form part of the forecast QNH Altimeter Setting Region System. Pilots flying below the Transition Altitude, should use a QNH of an aerodrome situated within the lateral boundaries of that airspace. Alternatively, when flying within an aerodrome circuit, aerodrome QFE may be used. See UK AIP ENR 1.7.

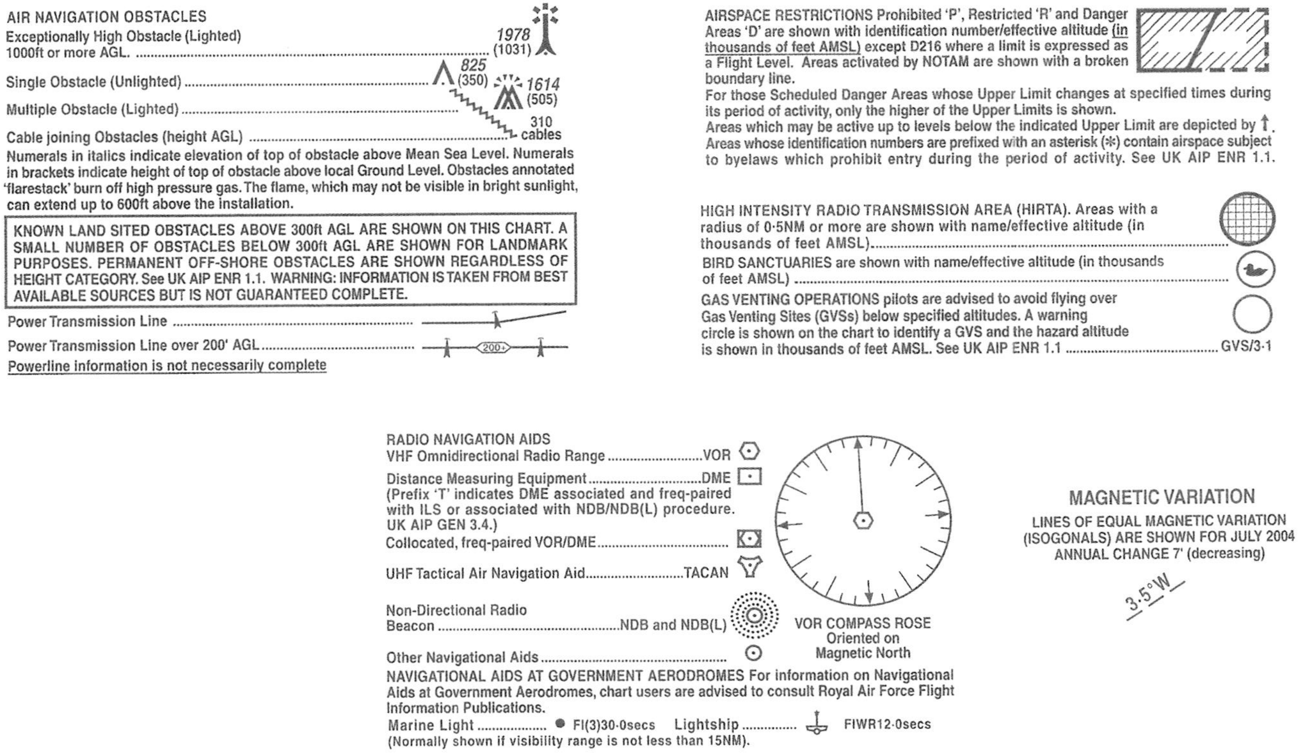

AIR NAVIGATION OBSTACLES

Exceptionally High Obstacle (Lighted) 1000ft or more AGL. 1978 (1031)

Single Obstacle (Unlighted) 825 (350)

Multiple Obstacle (Lighted) 1614 (505)

Cable Joining Obstacles (height AGL) .... 310 cables

Numerals in italics indicate elevation of top of obstacle above Mean Sea Level. Numerals in brackets indicate height of top of obstacle above local Ground Level. Obstacles annotated 'flarestack' burn off high pressure gas. The flame, which may not be visible in bright sunlight, can extend up to 600ft above the installation.

KNOWN LAND SITED OBSTACLES ABOVE 300ft AGL ARE SHOWN ON THIS CHART. A SMALL NUMBER OF OBSTACLES BELOW 300ft AGL ARE SHOWN FOR LANDMARK PURPOSES. PERMANENT OFF-SHORE OBSTACLES ARE SHOWN REGARDLESS OF HEIGHT CATEGORY. See UK AIP ENR 1.1. WARNING: INFORMATION IS TAKEN FROM BEST AVAILABLE SOURCES BUT IS NOT GUARANTEED COMPLETE.

Power Transmission Line ....

Power Transmission Line over 200' AGL ....

Powerline information is not necessarily complete

RADIO NAVIGATION AIDS

VHF Omnidirectional Radio Range .... VOR

Distance Measuring Equipment .... DME
(Prefix 'T' indicates DME associated and freq-paired with ILS or associated with NDB/NDB(L) procedure. UK AIP GEN 3.4.)

Collocated, freq-paired VOR/DME.

UHF Tactical Air Navigation Aid .... TACAN

Non-Directional Radio Beacon .... NDB and NDB(L)

Other Navigational Aids ....

NAVIGATIONAL AIDS AT GOVERNMENT AERODROMES For information on Navigational Aids at Government Aerodromes, chart users are advised to consult Royal Air Force Flight Information Publications.

Marine Light .... Fl(3)30·0secs Lightship .... FlWR12·0secs
(Normally shown if visibility range is not less than 15NM).

AIRSPACE RESTRICTIONS

Prohibited 'P', Restricted 'R' and Danger Areas 'D' are shown with identification number/effective altitude (in thousands of feet AMSL) except D216 where a limit is expressed as a Flight Level. Areas activated by NOTAM are shown with a broken boundary line.

For those Scheduled Danger Areas whose Upper Limit changes at specified times during its period of activity, only the higher of the Upper Limits is shown.

Areas which may be active up to levels below the indicated Upper Limit are depicted by ↑.

Areas whose identification numbers are prefixed with an asterisk (✳) contain airspace subject to byelaws which prohibit entry during the period of activity. See UK AIP ENR 1.1.

HIGH INTENSITY RADIO TRANSMISSION AREA (HIRTA). Areas with a radius of 0·5NM or more are shown with name/effective altitude (in thousands of feet AMSL).

BIRD SANCTUARIES are shown with name/effective altitude (in thousands of feet AMSL).

GAS VENTING OPERATIONS pilots are advised to avoid flying over Gas Venting Sites (GVSs) below specified altitudes. A warning circle is shown on the chart to identify a GVS and the hazard altitude is shown in thousands of feet AMSL. See UK AIP ENR 1.1 .... GVS/3·1

MAGNETIC VARIATION

LINES OF EQUAL MAGNETIC VARIATION (ISOGONALS) ARE SHOWN FOR JULY 2004
ANNUAL CHANGE 7' (decreasing)

3·5°W

VOR COMPASS ROSE
Oriented on
Magnetic North

Fig. 13-6a   Portrayal of aeronautical information on the 1:250 000 series of UK topographical charts

AERODROME - Civil .... ⊕

AERODROME - Civil, limited or no facilities. .... ◯

HELIPORT - Civil. .... Ⓗ

AERODROME - Government, available for Civil use. See UK AIP AD 1-1-1. ...... ◎

AERODROME - Government. .... ◉

HELIPORT - Government .... ⊕

MICROLIGHT FLYING SITES - Intense Activity also takes place at certain
Licensed and Unlicensed Aerodromes. See UK AIP ENR 1-1-5. .... Ⓜ

DISUSED or ABANDONED Aerodrome. Shown for navigational
landmark purposes only. See AIC 56/02 (Pink 34). .... ⊗

ELEVATIONS of Active Aeronautical Sites are shown adjacent to the symbol.
Shown in feet above Mean Sea Level. 250   250

CUSTOMS AERODROMES are distinguished by a pecked line around
the name of the aerodrome and elevation .... ⌐MANCHESTER¬
                                                                                                          ⌊1,257 ⌋

AERODROME LIGHT BEACON. .... ☆ FIG ⫶⌐⫶⁓⫶ ☆ FltR ⫶⁓⫶⁓⫶

FOR CURRENT STATUS, AVAILABILITY, RESTRICTIONS AND WARNINGS APPLICABLE TO
AERODROMES SHOWN ON THIS CHART CONSULT AIR INFORMATION PUBLICATIONS AND
AERODROME OPERATORS OR OWNERS. PORTRAYAL DOES NOT IMPLY ANY RIGHT TO USE
AN UNLICENSED AERODROME WITHOUT PERMISSION.

GLIDER LAUNCHING SITES. UK AIP ENR 1-1-5. .... Ⓖ

a. Primary activity at locations showing Maximum Altitude of winch launch. AMSL. ...... /2.5

b. Additional activity at locations showing Maximum Altitude of
winch launch. AMSL. .... Ⓖ /2.5

c. Additional activity without cables .... Ⓖ

HANG/PARA GLIDING - Winch Launch Sites showing Maximum Altitude of
winch launch. AMSL. See UK AIP ENR 1-1-5. .... ⧨

WINCH LAUNCHED ACTIVITIES. Maximum Altitude of cables is represented in thousands and
hundreds of feet above mean sea level calculated using a minimum cable height of 2000ft AGL
plus site elevation. At some sites the cable may extend above 2000ft AGL. Due to the
ground-based cable, aircraft should avoid over-flying these sites below the indicated altitude.

Symbols depicting Non Winch Launch Hang/Para Gliding sites have been removed as they were
not an accurate representation of the activity on any given day. Airspace users should be aware
that single or groups of soaring or motorised Hang/Para Gliders can be found flying anywhere
in the open FIR up to 15,000ft.

FREE-FALL PARACHUTING DROP ZONE. UK AIP ENR 1-1-5. .... ⊖
Parachutists may be expected within the airspace contained in a circle
radius 1.5NM or 2NM of the DZ up to FL150. Night parachuting may take place at
any of the sites shown on this chart

ANNOTATION OF VERTICAL LIMITS FOR CONTROLLED
AIRSPACE WHICH HAVE AN UPPER LIMIT OF FL245 ARE
SHOWN WITH A PLUS (+) AFTER THEIR BASE
LEVEL/ALTITUDE, eg 3000'-FL245 IS SHOWN AS 3000'+.
WHERE THE UPPER LIMIT IS BELOW FL245 BOTH BASE
AND UPPER LIMITS ARE SHOWN.
AIRSPACE VERTICAL LIMITS ARE DEFINED BY
ALTITUDE/FLIGHT LEVEL UNLESS OTHERWISE NOTED.
TINT BANDING DENOTES THE EXTREMITY OF
CONTROLLED AIRSPACE. LINES WITHOUT TINT
BANDING DENOTE LEVEL CHANGES WITHIN AREA.

FOR CHART CLARITY ONLY CENTRE LINE
OF ADR's ARE SHOWN ....

ALL AIRSPACE NOT COVERED BY CLASSES A-F. ....

Low Level Corridor or Special Route. ....

Radar Advisory Service Zone or Area. See UK AIP ENR 1-6.

Air Traffic Service Unit (ATSU) Area. See UK AIP ENR 1-15 ......
Reporting Point. ....
Shown only for ADRs and certain Recommended Routes.

Special Access Lane Entry/Exit. ....
(⌐ indicates centre of lane.)

Visual Reference Point (VRP). Notified in UK AIP ....
(Location identified by ⊕).

L10 Ⓐ FL45+

CTA Ⓒ 2500'-FL200

CTA Ⓓ 2500'-3500'

TMA Ⓔ 2000'-6000'

Ⓐ

Ⓒ

Ⓓ

Ⓔ

N571D Ⓕ
FL55-FL235   Ⓕ

Ⓖ

750'-2500'

△
E/E ↗
MERSEY LANE

VRP
SANDBACH

NB. CONTROLLED AIRSPACE IS NOT DEPICTED ABOVE FLIGHT LEVEL 245. IN THE UK ALL
CLASS Ⓑ AIRSPACE IS ABOVE FL245. NO AIRSPACE IS DESIGNATED CLASS Ⓒ IN THE UK.

ALTIMETER SETTING REGION BOUNDARY (ASR). ....
NOTE: The airspace within (and below) all Control Zones,
Terminal Control Areas and Control Areas (with the exception of the Worthing and Daventry
CTAs) during their notified hours of operation, does not form part of the forecast QNH Altimeter
Setting Region System . Pilots flying below the Transition Altitude, should use a QNH of an
aerodrome situated within the lateral boundaries of that airspace. Alternatively, when flying within
an aerodrome circuit, aerodrome QFE may be used. See UK AIP ENR 1-7.

PORTREE ASR

BELFAST ASR

MILITARY AERODROME TRAFFIC ZONES (MATZs)
have the following vertical limits: SFC to 3000ft AAL
within the circle and 1000ft AAL to 3000ft AAL within
the stub.
Zone configuration may vary, often two or more MATZs
are amalgamated to produce a Combined Zone (CMATZ).
Controlling Aerodromes show the MATZ penetration
frequency to be used. See UK AIP ENR 2-2.

4NM

5NM

MATZ
LARS
126·5

5NM

STANDARD MATZ WITH
TWO STUBS AND LARS

LOWER AIRSPACE RADAR SERVICE (LARS). The abbreviation LARS has been added to the
MATZ frequency to identify those participating MATZ ATS Units. Other participating Units are
identified by a LARS frequency annotation. The Service, Radar Advisory (RAS) or Radar
Information (RIS), is available to all aircraft in unregulated airspace up to and including FL95
within approximately 30NM of each participating ATS Unit. See UK AIP ENR 1-6-3.

Exceptionally High Obstacle (Lighted)
1000ft or more AGL 1978 (1031)

Single Obstacle (Unlighted) 825 (350)
Multiple Obstacle (Lighted) 1614 (505)
Cable Joining Obstacles .... cables

Numerals in italics indicate elevation of top of obstacle above Mean Sea Level. Numerals in brackets indicate height of top of obstacle above local Ground Level. Obstacles annotated 'flarestack' burn off high pressure gas. The flame, which may be visible in bright sunlight, can extend up to 600ft above the installation.

KNOWN LAND SITED OBSTACLES ABOVE 300ft AGL ARE SHOWN ON THIS CHART. A SMALL NUMBER OF OBSTACLES BELOW 300ft AGL ARE SHOWN FOR LANDMARK PURPOSES. PERMANENT OFF-SHORE OBSTACLES ARE SHOWN REGARDLESS OF HEIGHT CATEGORY. See UK AIP ENR 1-1.
WARNING: INFORMATION IS TAKEN FROM BEST AVAILABLE SOURCES BUT IS NOT GUARANTEED COMPLETE.

Marine Light .... ● Fl(3)30·0secs   Lightship... ⬨ FlWR12·0secs
(Normally shown if visibility range is not less than 15NM).

Controlled Airspace or ATZ with
surface level as lower limit...

RADIO NAVIGATION AIDS
VHF Omnidirectional Radio Range..................VOR
Distance Measuring Equipment.......................DME
(Prefix 'T' indicates DME associated and freq-paired with ILS or associated with NDB/NDB(L) procedure. UK AIP GEN 3-4-3.)
Collocated, freq-paired VOR/DME.
UHF Tactical Air Navigation Aid.....................TACAN
Non-Directional Radio Beacon...........NDB and NDB(L)
Other Navigational Aids...
For information on Navigational Aids at Government Aerodromes, chart users are advised to consult Royal Air Force Flight Information Publications.

VOR COMPASS ROSE
Oriented on
Magnetic North

Danger Areas 'D' are shown with identification number/ effective altitude (in thousands of feet AMSL) except D129 and D216 where upper limit is expressed as a flight level. Areas activated by Notam are shown with a broken boundary line.
For those Scheduled Danger Areas whose Upper Limit changes at specified times during its period of activity, only the higher of the Upper Limits is shown. Areas which may be active up to levels below the Indicated Upper Limit are depicted by ↑. Areas whose identification numbers are prefixed with an asterisk (✳) contain airspace subject to byelaws which prohibit entry during the period of activity. See UK AIP ENR 1-1-5.

MILITARY LOW FLYING SYSTEM this occurs in most parts of the UK at any height up to 2000ft above the surface. However, the greatest concentration is between surface and 1000ft and pilots should avoid this height band whenever possible. Detailed information can be found on CHART OF THE UK AREAS OF INTENSE AERIAL ACTIVITY (AIAA), AERIAL TACTICS AREAS (ATA) AND MILITARY LOW FLYING SYSTEM (UK AIP ENR 6-5-2-1).
◆◆◆◆◆◆◆◆◆

AIAA AND ATA AREAS....................
Areas are shown with name, vertical limits and where applicable contact frequency. Pilots of aircraft who transit these areas are strongly advised to make use of the Radar Service.

HIGH INTENSITY RADIO TRANSMISSION AREA (HIRTA). Areas with a radius of 0-5NM or more are shown with name/effective altitude (in thousands of feet AMSL).

BIRD SANCTUARIES are shown with name/effective altitude (in thousands of feet AMSL)...

GAS VENTING OPERATIONS pilots are advised to avoid flying over Gas Venting Sites (GVSs) below specified altitudes. A warning circle is shown on the chart to identify a GVS and the hazard altitude is shown in thousands of feet AMSL. See UK AIP ENR 1-1-5. ....GVS/3·1

MAXIMUM ELEVATION FIGURES (MEF)

32
Maximum Elevation Figures are shown in quadrangles bounded by graticule lines for every half degree of latitude and longitude. MEFs are represented in thousands and hundreds of feet above mean sea level. Each MEF is based on information available concerning the highest known feature in each quadrangle, including terrain and obstacles and allowing for unknown features.
NB THIS IS NOT A SAFETY ALTITUDE

MAGNETIC VARIATION

LINES OF EQUAL MAGNETIC VARIATION (ISOGONALS) ARE SHOWN FOR JULY 2004. ANNUAL CHANGE 7' (decreasing)

Fig. 13-6b   Portrayal of aeronautical information on the 1:500 000 series of UK topographical charts

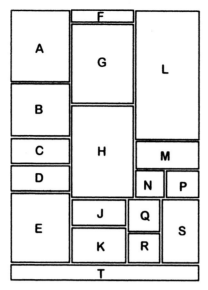

Fig. 13-7 A typical information panel from a 1:250 000 UK topographical map. The shape of box may vary to suit the particular map layout but the overall content will be the same. This box sits in the North Sea at the top right hand corner of the ENGLAND EAST sheet

(For legend decode see Para 13.9)

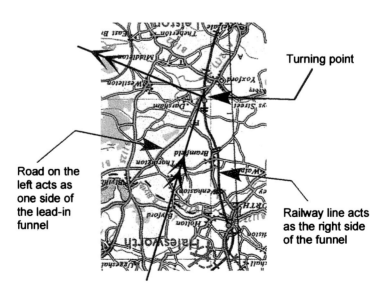

Turning point

Road on the left acts as one side of the lead-in funnel

Railway line acts as the right side of the funnel

Fig. 13–8   Example of funnel features.

CHAPTER 13

TOPOGRAPHICAL AND AERONAUTICAL MAPS AND CHARTS

13.1 The function of an aeronautical topographical map (or chart) is to provide a formalised pictorial representation of ground features that will help a pilot to plan and execute a flight that is to be carried out wholly, or partly, within visual contact of the ground. Map reading from the air is frequently referred to as an art and in a sense this is an appropriate statement since any topographical map is, in its own way, a work of art. In the case of topographical maps designed for aeronautical use, the starting point would be one of the projections discussed in the previous chapters. Which projection is used depends on what particular part of the earth's surface is to be portrayed. In general terms Mercator's projection is used in equatorial regions, Lambert's projection (with appropriate SPs) for mid-latitude regions and the Polar stereographic for polar regions. Transverse and Oblique Mercator's projections are used for some special cases (i.e. long narrow land masses or strip maps). Ground features are then applied, in their correct geographical position, on to the latitude and longitude graticule. Aeronautical information is then added as appropriate to complete the overall picture.

13.2 One of the first questions that arises in the production of a topographical map is 'how much and just what detail is to be shown?' To decide on the degree of detail to be shown, reference must be made back to 'scale' (see Chapter 8, paragraphs 8.5 to 8.8). The 'larger' the scale of a map the smaller the area it can portray within a given sheet size and the more detail can be fitted in. Conversely the 'smaller' the scale of a map the larger the area it can portray within a given sheet size but far less detail can be shown on it. The UK is currently covered on two different scales of topographical maps. The 1 : 500,000 series, printed on Lambert's projection, covers England, Scotland, Wales and Northern Ireland on three sheets and the 1 : 250,000 series, printed on a Transverse Mercator's projection (central meridian 2W) requiring 8 sheets to cover the same geographical region. It

147

follows that much more detail can be given on the 1 : 250,000 series than on the 1 : 500,000 series.

13.3 Details shown on the map must be things that a pilot can identify from his or her cruising level on a clear day. The 1 : 250,000 UK series is primarily intended for low level, relatively slow speed, cross-country navigation purposes. Like all maps designed for use in the air the 1 : 250,000 series also carries aeronautical information of a non-topographical nature (such as Controlled Airspace) restricted to those items applicable to *below 5000 ft above mean sea level (amsl)* and this series of maps should not be used above 5000 ft amsl without a 1 : 500,000 series map (all of which have full aeronautical information coverage up to 40,000 ft) as a back-up. From around 3000 ft amsl the field of view is quite good and it is possible to identify many features on the ground quite clearly. As a result it has been possible to utilise the excellent UK OS maps as the basis for the 1 : 250,000 series of aeronautical topographical maps. This gives more detail than is necessary for air work but is not a serious disadvantage.

13.4 In the case of the 1 : 500,000 series the intended use is for map reading at higher levels and higher speeds of flight. At high levels greater distances can be seen on a clear day but the amount of detail that can be identified on the ground will be reduced. High features such as hills become flattened to the pilot's view and most roads, other than motorways and trunk roads, become difficult to discern. Only large features like cities, coastlines and major rivers can be identified clearly and the reduced amount of detail shown on the 1 : 500,000 series reflects this changed situation. Map reading at high altitudes may be further complicated by the fact that the flight deck can restrict the view of a large area of the ground directly beneath the aircraft and for some miles around.

13.5 The information that is displayed on any aeronautical topographical map falls into one of three categories:

Natural features, i.e., coastlines, rivers, mountains etc.
Man-made features, i.e., towns, roads, railway lines, bridges etc.
Aeronautical information, i.e., boundaries and heights of areas of restricted airspace, geographic positions of ground based radio aid such as NDBs with their callsigns and frequencies, sites of special air activity such as gliding, etc.

How these features are portrayed follow fairly standard patterns. There are however some variations in presentation of man-made items on the different scale maps and these are discussed later in paragraph 13.7.

13.6 The main natural features are portrayed in fairly obvious colours, blue for water features and green for wooded areas. These rather idealistic colours are all very well but are not necessarily what the pilot will see. With changing seasons and weather the natural colours may change. The shapes of woods will remain pretty constant (even after felling) but flooding can alter the shape of water features for short periods of time and the colour may well be more like brown than blue at times. Relief, or height of the ground amsl, is shown by contour lines. These are lines joining places having a common height amsl and colours are used to shade the various contour layers to produce what is known as 'layer tinting'. The lowest layer is white and progressive layers are coloured with deepening amber tints, the darker the tint the higher the ground. By this method high ground is pictorially indicated and this is reinforced by individual high points being marked with a black dot and the height amsl printed in black beside it. In the UK heights are given in *feet* but maps produced in some countries use similar methods for indicating high ground but, and it is a big 'but', heights may be indicated in *metres*! Never take height readings on an unfamiliar map for granted – always check before using. For example, high ground shown as 700 m amsl is actully 2300 ft amsl. You have been warned! (Figs. 13–1a and 13–1b on the colour plates show the way natural features and relief are portrayed on these two UK topographical charts.)

13.7 Man-made features vary in their colouring depending on the materials used and the fashions at the time they were constructed. Furthermore colours can be changed, what is red today may be repainted yellow tomorrow. To cater for such variables, a set of conventions to cover all cases has been evolved for use on UK topographical charts:

Towns. These are portrayed in grey on the 1 : 250,000 series maps and in yellow on the 1 : 500,000 series maps. On the 1 : 250,000 series the shapes of quite modest built-up areas are given and in remote places individual buildings are shown. By contrast the 1 : 500,000 series only gives the shapes of the major cities, other towns merit small squares or dots depending on the size of the town and many small villages are not portrayed at all (see Figs 13–2 a and 31–2 b on the colour plates).

Roads. On the 1 : 250,000 series roads are outlined by parallel thin black lines and coloured according to designation. Motorways are in blue and trunk/main roads are in a brick red, secondary roads in a lighter shade of brick red and other tarred roads in white. For the aviator the lesser distinctions are of no real value. On the 1 : 500,000 series all roads are in red with no outlines. The line styles vary to signify Motorways, dual carriageways and lesser roads (see Figs. 13–3a and b on the colour plates).

Railway tracks. These are shown as solid black lines. Tracks have a small black slash across them at regular intervals, a single slash denoting a single track line and a double slash indicating two or more tracks. Where a track has been removed but the line of the original track bed is still visible from the air it is shown as a series of black dashes. Other symbols indicate features such as tunnels, bridges and level crossings (see Figs 13–4a and 13–4b on the colour plates).

Other man-made features may be visible from the air depending on the height of the aircraft above the ground. Some, such as giant figures or animals carved in chalk, can be seen from considerable altitudes and feature on both series of topographical maps; no matter what the natural colour of such ground marks they are portrayed, by shape, in solid black. Features such a lighthouses, windmills, radio masts, TV masts and racecourses which are far too diverse in shape and colour to be individually portrayed are given standardised symbols. Whilst all such features are marked in on the 1 : 250,000 series only the large features, like racecourses, are shown on the 1 : 500,000 series (see Figs 13–5a and 13–5b on the colour plates).

Aeronautical information is printed in blue (for Civil items) and purple (for Military items) on both the 1 : 250,000 and 1 : 500,000 series of maps. Apart from aerodromes, high obstructions (i.e. TV transmitter masts) and power transmission lines most of these items are not visible to the naked eye. Regulated airspace such as controlled, restricted and prohibited areas are designated by coded boundary lines along with information on the vertical extent of each designated area and the controlling authority. The geographical positions of ground based radio aids to navigation (such as NDBs) are given by means of standardised symbols along with their operating frequency and identifying callsign. Other symbols are used to signify sites of special aeronautical activities, such as gliding and parachuting (see Figs. 13–6a and 13–6b on the colour plates).

13.8 It is an examination requirement that candidates have a comprehensive knowledge of all of the above standard symbols. Although most have been given above, by far the best way to learn them is to study the information panels found on the edge of all topographical charts. One of each scale will be needed because as noted earlier in this chapter there are slight differences in the presentation of some features. It goes without saying that only current editions should be referred to as small changes do occur from time to time (usually with aeronautical information) and pilots are required to be up-to-date at all times.

13.9 At the time of writing, topographical maps have information displayed around the edges of the map and in a group, or groups, within the body of the map. The 1 : 250,000 series has the Sheet Number, Name and Edition printed in the top left and bottom right edge; along the bottom edge, repeated three times, are notes about the Military Low Flying System and these are repeated twice more along the top edge along with two warnings reminding users that the map aeronautical information only goes up to 5000 ft. In the centre of the top edge are the words TOPOGRAPHICAL CHART OF THE UNITED KINGDOM 1 : 250 000. Also round the edge are the values of the lats and longs where their lines reach the edge of the map. Fig. 13–7 shows the group layout of information on the 1 : 250,000 SHEET 6 ENGLAND EAST Edition 5. This particular map has an area of the North Sea in the NE corner which is convenient for grouping the information in one place; the disposition of information groups on other maps varies with the free space available on the map.

The layout in Fig. 13–7 decodes as follows:

A *Aerodrome* information giving type, name, elevation in ft, layout (where known), present usage and any special activities.
B *Controlled Airspace* information on Prohibited, Restricted and Danger areas.
C *Radio Navigation Aids.* Showing the symbols used to denote the different types of radio aids.
D *Obstructions.* All known land sited obstructions above 300 ft above the local ground level (AGL) are shown on the chart plus a small number of obstacles less than 300 ft AGL which are shown for landmark purposes. Permanent offshore obstructions are shown regardless of height. Different symbols are used to differentiate between those obstructions that are less than 1000 ft AGL and those that are more than 1000 ft AGL. The symbol is doubled to indicate a group of obstructions (such as a collection of tall factory chimneys) as opposed to a single obstruction (such as a TV transmission mast). The dot at the base of a symbol indicates the geographical position of the obstruction. Two numbers by each symbol give the height of the top of the obstruction amsl in **bold italics** and height above AGL in (smaller figures in brackets). A small ray symbol at the top of an obstruction symbol indicates that it carries obstruction lighting. Symbols for cables joining obstructions and power lines also appear in this block.
E *General information about the chart.* This block contains a repeat of the warning that the chart only shows aeronautical information up 5000 ft, copyright information, validity date of information on the chart and a contact address for the CAA.
F *Military Low Flying System.* A further reminder.
G *Controlled Airspace.* Symbols used to outline areas of regulated airspace, the different line types identifying the function of the enclosed area. The controlling authority and vertical extent of an area will also be given, either along a boundary line or within the area itself. Also in this block there is information about Military Aerodrome Traffic Zones (MATZ), Lower Airspace Radar Service (LARS), Areas of Intense Air Activity (AIAA) and Altimeter Setting Region Boundary (ASR).

H *General and specific warnings* applicable to the area covered by the chart. These cover a wide spectrum and are different for each chart. There is information on who to contact for specific information on various activities.

J *General Features.* Illustrating the conventional symbols used for roads, buildings, water features, woods and items such as racecourses and windmills.

K *Adjoining Sheets.* A diagram showing the Sheet number and Names of all the adjoining sheets and by how much they overlap each other.

L *UK Aerodrome Traffic Zones (ATZs).* A list of all ATZs within the chart area of coverage along with ATC frequencies.

M *Aerodromes with Instrument Approach Procedures (IAPs).* This shows the symbol used to denote IAPs **Outside Controlled Airspace.**

N *Magnetic Variation.* Showing how lines of equal magnetic variation (isogonals) are portrayed with their value, date of validity and annual rate of change. Note that isogonal values are given in half degrees. When flying in a zone between two isogonals use the mean varn, only changing the varn when crossing an isogonal into the next zone. Thus between the 3·5° W and 4·5° W isogonals use a variation of 4° W throughout.

P *Morse Code and ICAO Phonetic Alphabet.*

Q *Roads.* Showing how motorways and different classes of roads are portrayed. Unfortunately, the 1 : 250,000 topographical series has inherited the detailed road layout and classification from the OS maps on which it is based and this can prove an overkill for air work. However, at heights below 5000 ft (the limiting height for use of this series), motorways (shown in blue), main roads (shown in brick red), dual carriageways, and even major roundabouts can usually be clearly seen; it is the lesser roads that can become confusing.

R *Railways.* These are all shown in black with variations for multi-track, single track, dismantled and narrow gauge (which from the air look like single track), plus symbols for bridges, tunnels and stations.

S *Relief.* This shows the colour code for layer tinting, how spot elevations and contour lines are portrayed and a bold reminder that on this chart **ELEVATIONS ARE IN FEET (amsl).**

T *Scale.* **SCALE 1 : 250 000 TRANSVERSE MERCATOR PRO-JECTION** is printed above three linear scales, one in **Kilometres**, one in **Nautical Miles** and one in **Statute Miles** (see paragraph 8.5 and Fig. 8–1).

13.10 A look around the borders of a 1 : 500,000 series map will reveal a different layout but similar information. Some symbols have been deleted and others modified to suit the reduced details a pilot can expect to see when flying at greater altitudes. Likewise the Restricted Airspace details are now shown up to Flight Level 40 (FL 40 or 40,000 ft above the 1013 mb Standard Datum setting. See the Instrument and Meteorology syllabi for altimeter setting procedures). An item that appears only on the 1 : 500,000 series is:

Minimum Elevation Figures (MEF). The MEF is shown in each 30' × 30' box that contains any land mass. It gives the Thousands and Hundreds of ft of the highest terrain or known obstructions in the box. **It is not a safety height** (the reasoning behind, and calculation of, safety height is covered in depth in the altimetry sections of both the Instruments and Meteorology syllabi).

13.11   Pilots should be totally familiar with the symbols on the topographical maps that they use. As explained above, full details are available around the borders of topographical maps for reference at any time, but in a busy cockpit/flightdeck environment space to spread out a map, and time to do so, may be limited. Like so many aspects of navigation, time spent in study and preparation on the ground can save precious time in the air. Some people find trying to memorise columns of symbols extremely boring. Learning symbols can be made easier by making a game of it. Cut a hole of about 4 inches (10 cm) diameter in a piece of card, drop the card on the map and try to decode the items visible inside the hole. Look up any that do not come quickly to mind. Keep repeating the exercise on different parts of the map until decoding becomes second nature.

13.12   There are some basic rules about the best way to use topographical maps during pre-flight study and when map reading in the air:

Pre-flight:

Various ways of marking up a map for use with pilot navigation techniques were given in Chapter 7. In the preliminary stages of pre-flight planning study of the topographical details along a route will help in deciding which marking method is best suited to that particular route.

During the planning stages look for features that are unique along the route and are likely to be easily identified. In particular look out for combinations of different features that together form distinct pictures which are unlikely to be confused with anything else.

Look for what are termed 'funnel' features. These are ribbon features such as roads, rivers or railway lines that can act as a funnel into a turning point or destination. Such features may not be present at the end of every leg but when they are they can be as good as a signpost (see Fig. 13–8 on the colour plates).

It also pays to bear in mind the meteorological conditions that the flight is to be flown in. Under certain haze conditions visibility into sun may be poor and the only thing likely to be seen up sun will be reflections off water features. If such a situation is forecast concentrate most planning effort on features along the route that are down sun.

Try to get a clear picture how the beginning of each leg should look once the hdg has been set up. This is an insurance against a wrong compass hdg being set at the beginning of a leg. Suppose 352° (C) was set on in error for 325° (C), the expected view would be skewed off by almost 30°, an anomaly that should alert the prepared pilot to something being amiss.

In the air:

Map reading in the air is made easier if the map is orientated so that the trk on the map is pointing in the direction of the trk over the ground. This may require careful folding of the map prior to flight, especially if it is to be used in a cramped cockpit.

When map reading from a known position the technique is to read from map to ground. Look on the map to see what features should be coming into view ahead and to left and right, then look out in the relevant directions to verify those features on the ground. On the map mark places with the time as they are pinpointed, this will keep the progress of the flight up to date and help to make pilot navigation calculations easier.

When for any reason a pilot is uncertain of position the procedure for map reading is reversed (i.e. read from ground to map):

In a simple case of uncertainty, such as low cloud obscuring the ground for a period of time, once the ground becomes visible again it is a straightforward task to estimate the DR position on the map. Provided the planned elements of the flight plan have been adhered to since the last known position the map features in the vicinity of the DR position should match the features now visible on the ground.

Sometimes the situation can develop from being 'uncertain of position' to being 'lost'. If this occurs a definite plan of action known as **'lost procedure'** is needed. Certain questions should be asked and appropriate action taken if the answers call for it:

What is the Safety Height? Climb up if below it.

Does the route go near any Controlled Airspace? If so try and contact the Controlling Authority on RT for fixing assistance and guidance away from any Controlled area.

When and where was the last known position of the aircraft?

Have all the planned elements of the flight plan been adhered to since that time?

Are the compasses functioning correctly? Is the Directional Gyro Compass Indicator (DGI) correctly synchronised? Are there any magnetic items placed near the magnetic compass? If something is wrong correct the mistake and note the amount of hdg error that has to be allowed for in working out a DR positon.

Do not keep changing hdg in the hope of identifying some feature on the ground, such activity usually only serves to make matters worse by losing a record of the DR trks and GSs. By sticking to a steady hdg (even if it is found to be in error) it is possible to work out a DR position from which to start comparing the map features with the observed ground features.

13.13 It has been said that the secret of good navigation is not to get lost, something that cannot always be guaranteed. By careful pre-flight planning, route study, sticking to the flight plan, accurate flying, regular compass checks in flight and continual practise of pilot navigation techniques a pilot can greatly reduce the chances of getting lost on a map reading exercise. It is a true saying of most things in aviation, 'Time spent in preparation and continual practise makes for safe and enjoyable flying'. In the author's view if an hour spent in preparation on the ground can save a minute of hassle in the air then it is an hour well spent.

AERONAUTICAL CHARTS

13.14 A range of charts fall into this category, the sole purpose of which is to provide aeronautical information. These charts are for the most part white in colour with black printing, the only other colour used being pale blue to denote coastlines and sea areas; on a few charts (for instance Radar Vectoring Area charts) cities and towns are also portrayed by pale grey silhouettes. Types of chart include:

(a) *Low and High Altitude Area Charts*. Showing:
   (i)   *Aerodromes* with control areas, including MATZs where applicable.
   (ii) *Ground-based radio aids* to navigation with call-sign, channel number and/or frequency.
   (iii) *Reporting points* with name and lat and long.
   (iv) *Routes* with identity, levels, tracks and distances.
   (v)   *Holding* patterns with trks.
   (vi) *Danger*, prohibited and restricted areas with identification and levels of operation.
   (vii) *Offshore oil rig helicopter pads* and control zones.
   (vii) *Printed notices* covering Controlled Airspace communications and vertical limits, Airspace reservations, General notices and Airways frequency notices.

(b) *Aerodrome Charts.* These come in loose-leaf booklet form (A5), for ease of amendment. The number of pages for any aerodrome depends on the facilities provided at the aerodrome. Preceding the charts for an aerodrome are printed pages covering Aerodrome Operating Minima, Special Procedures (i.e. CAT II/III operations) and Noise Abatement procedures. Charts cover:

(i) *Aerodrome* layout with co-ordinates, elevation, runway(s) and frequencies for Ground, Tower, Radar and Air Traffic Information Services.

(ii) *Taxi* showing layout of taxiway with holding points plus the relative positions of the apron(s), ATC, terminal buildings and fire station.

(iii) *Ramp*: a large-scale layout of the apron area(s) showing the ramp (stand) positions plus a list of stand co-ordinates for programming INS.

(iv) *Departure and Arrival* giving trks and dists to and from en-route Airways reporting/joining points adjacent to the aerodrome.

(v) *Radar Vectoring Area* giving elevation limits and procedures to follow after a missed approach or a communications failure.

(vi) *NDB letdown* procedures to the various runways using the aids available at the aerodrome. Patterns are shown in plan view and in profile with trks, dists and altitudes (amsl and agl) for the touchdown point. Holding patterns are also given plus procedures for missed approach or communications failure.

SECTION 4
MISCELLANEOUS PROCEDURES

This section covers those aspects of navigation that have a direct bearing on flight safety, planning and airborne procedures.

The practicality of the flight safety aspects is fairly obvious and in the case of collision avoidance explains the rationale behind the Aviation Law rules for the rapid assessment of collision risk (i.e. an aircraft observed to be on a constant relative brg).

The chapter on Time and Time Conversions has considerable significance for commercial pilots whose work can take them to almost any quarter of the world and have them passing through time zones and crossing the International Date Line.

With the availability of so many automatic navigation devices on the flightdeck of commercial aircraft, the subject of plotting may seem obsolete. Nonetheless to get the maximum benefit from such aids requires a pilot to have a knowledge of the underlying principles behind them, hence the licence requirement for plotting.

In places there are references to earlier chapters and paragraphs. These are for the guidance of any reader who wishes to recap on a basic point before continuing with the main text.

CHAPTER 14

RELATIVE VELOCITY

14.1 Velocity is, as already defined, the movement of an object in terms of direction and speed in relation to a specified datum. Thus the TAS of an aircraft is its velocity in relation to the surrounding air whereas its GS is its velocity in relation to the earth's surface below it. The term **Relative Velocity** is used to define the direction and speed of one moving object in relation to another moving object. The relative velocity between two aircraft can be used to work out separation along airways, adjusting speed to achieve a specified overhead time at a reporting point or the assessment of possible collision risk. Furthermore the assessment of collision risk introduces the concept of a **Line of Constant Bearing (LCB)** which is also used in the calculation of the **Point of No Alternate (PNA)** (see later in Chapter 15).

CALCULATION OF THE RELATIVE VELOCITY BETWEEN TWO AIRCRAFT

14.2 The calculation of relative velocities is achieved by plotting vectors. The individual velocity vectors for the two aircraft are plotted from a common datum for a common period of time and the ends of the vectors are then joined up to give a vector of the relative velocity. The direction of the relative velocity will of course depend on which aircraft the relative movement is being observed from.

14.3 Fig. 14–1a shows the velocity vectors for two aircraft, 'A' on a trk of

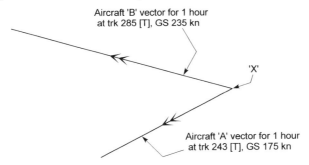

Aircraft 'B' vector for 1 hour
at trk 285 [T], GS 235 kn

'X'

Aircraft 'A' vector for 1 hour
at trk 243 [T], GS 175 kn

*Fig. 14–1a   One hour vectors for two aircraft departing from
a common datum point 'X'.*

159

243(T) at GS 175 kn and 'B' on a trk of 285(T) at GS 235 kn plotted from a common datum 'X' for one hour. Figure 14–1b shows the relative velocity vector drawn in, the arrows on this vector indicating the relative movement of aircraft 'B' as seen from aircraft 'A' (**333(T) at 156 kn**). In Fig. 14–1c the arrows are reversed indicating the relative movement of aircraft 'A' as seen from aircraft 'B' (**153(T) at 156 kn**).

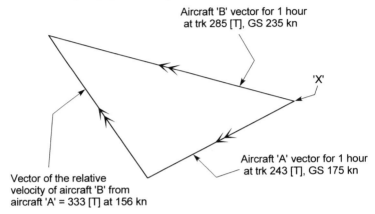

Fig. 14–1b   Vector of relative velocity of aircraft 'B' from aircraft 'A'.

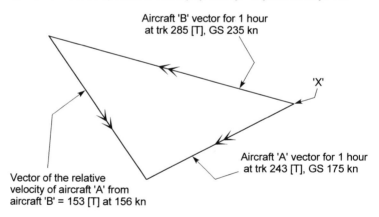

Fig. 14–1c   Vector of relative velocity of aircraft 'A' from aircraft 'B'

USES OF RELATIVE VELOCITY

14.4   Overtaking. The most basic case of the use of relative velocity is in the assessment of the position and time at which a fast moving aircraft will overtake a slower aircraft that is ahead of it on the same trk. The vector method for calculating the relative velocity mentioned in paragraph 14.2 works for *all* cases but is not necessary in this case where both aircraft are moving in the same direction and the only difference is their speeds. Fig. 14–2 shows two aircraft on a common trk, with aircraft 'D' (GS 275 kn) 48 nm ahead of aircraft 'E' (GS 335 kn) at 1100.

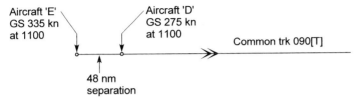

Fig. 14–2   Overtaking on a common trk.

The relative velocity of 'E' as seen from 'D' is in the direction of the trk at the difference in their GSs (**090(T) at 60 kn**).

With 'E' overtaking 'D' at 60 kn it will close up the 48 nm gap in 48 min.

By plotting either aircraft forward for 48 min at its GS the overtaking point can be found.

In this case it is some 220 nm ahead of 'D's position at 1100 hrs, or some 268 nm ahead of 'E's position at 1100, (see Fig. 14–3).

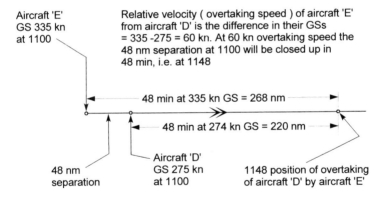

Fig. 14–3   Calculation of the point of overtaking.

14.5   Adjusting speed to achieve a revised ETA. For Air Traffic Control reasons a pilot may be requested to meet a revised (delayed) ETA by reducing the TAS of the aircraft to a specified value, this to be done at the latest time possible for achievement of the new ETA.

Example:
An aircraft is on a trk of 152 (T), TAS 390 kn and WV 230 / 55 with an ETA of 1024 at the next reporting point. At 0940 the pilot is instructed to reduce TAS to 350 kn so as to arrive over the reporting point at 1027. At

what time should the TAS be changed from 390 kn to 350 kn? (see Fig. 14–4.)

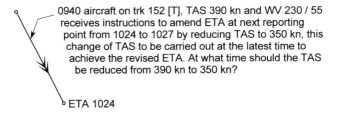

0940 aircraft on trk 152 [T], TAS 390 kn and WV 230 / 55 receives instructions to amend ETA at next reporting point from 1024 to 1027 by reducing TAS to 350 kn, this change of TAS to be carried out at the latest time to achieve the revised ETA. At what time should the TAS be reduced from 390 kn to 350 kn?

ETA 1024

Fig. 14–4   Reducing TAS to revise ETA, the scenario.

Solution:

The first step is to calculate the GSs the two TASs give (in some examination questions the GSs are quoted instead of TASs, thus making calculations easier for the candidate).

In this case a TAS of 390 kn will give a GS of 376 kn and a TAS of 350 kn a GS of 335 kn.

The original ETA was 1024 and the distance to run at 0940 is 44 min at GS 376 kn = 276 nm.

If, at 1940, the TAS was immediately reduced to 350 kn the amended ETA at the reporting point would be 1940 + (276 nm at GS 335 kn) = 1940 + 49·4 min = 1029·4 a loss of 5·4 minutes on the original ETA.

The revised ETA called for is 1027, a delay of only 3 minutes. Since 276 nm at the reduced TAS lost 5·4 minutes a simple ratio will solve for the distance required to lose 3 minutes:-

$$\frac{\text{Time lost (min)}}{\text{Distance (to reporting point)}} \quad \frac{5\cdot 4}{276} \quad = \quad \frac{3}{\text{'d'}}$$

Where 'd' is the distance, *measured back from the reporting point*, at which the reduced TAS must be started.

Rough check. Since 3 is just over ½ of 5·4 then 'd' must be just over ½ of 276, say about 150.

The circular slide rule readout gives **158 nm** as the distance to run at the reduced TAS.

At 0940 the distance to run was 276 nm so before reducing the TAS there is still (276 – 158) = 118 nm to fly at the original TAS which in this case was giving a GS of 376 kn. The time to reduce the TAS is:

0940 + (118 nm at 375 kn)
= 0940 + 18·8 min.
= **0958·8**.(see Fig. 14–5)

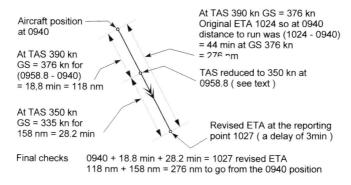

Fig. 14–5   Reducing TAS to revise ETA, the solution.

A final cross check can be made to confirm the answer. At 0958·8 there are 158 nm to go at the reduced GS of 335 kn = 28·2 min giving the revised ETA of 1027 as requested.

14.6   Calculation of collision risk. In Fig. 14–1 the establishment of the relative velocity between two aircraft that were diverging from a common starting point and time was demonstrated. Their individual positions after 60 min were joined by a line whose direction and length vectorially represented the relative velocity between the two aircraft for one hour. Had their positions after 30 min been plotted and then joined by a line, this line would be seen to be parallel to the line joining the 60 min positions. The same holds good for lines joining the 15 min positions, 45 min positions, in fact for any common time positions. Since the bearing is the same for all times it is known as a **Line of Constant Bearing(LCB)**. A pair of arrow-heads, pointing in towards each other, are used to denote that a line is a LCB (see Fig. 14–6).

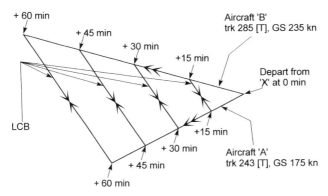

Fig. 14–6   Line of Constant Bearing (LCB).

163

14.7 By running the above diagram backwards using the same GSs the two aircraft would meet back at the starting point having maintained a steadily shortening LCB between them throughout the return journey (see Fig. 14–7). If they were at the same altitude a collision risk would exist at the point where the trks meet.

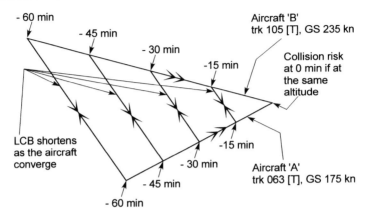

Fig. 14–7   Collision risk with aircraft converging whilst maintaining a LCB.

14.8 Consider the same two aircraft flying down the same trks at the same GSs as in Fig. 14–7 but with one of them starting some 30 nm further away from the point where the trks cross. Plotting common time positions and joining them with straight lines does not produce a LCB. (see Fig. 14–8) The two aircraft will not arrive at the crossing point of the trks at the same time and a collision risk does not exist.

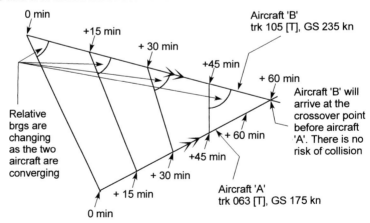

Fig. 14–8   Relative brgs that do not make a LCB signify no collision risk exists.

14.9 Only if a LCB exists between two converging aircraft flying at the same altitude is there a collision risk. If the bearing from one aircraft changes relative to another aircraft flying at the same altitude then a collision risk does not exist between them. These two statements give rise to some possible examination questions:

For two aircraft flying on converging trks at the same altitude calculate if a collision risk exists.

If a collision risk exists between two aircraft flying on converging trks at the same altitude calculate the position and time of the point of collision risk.

If a collision risk does not exist between two aircraft flying on converging trks at the same altitude calculate which aircraft will pass ahead of the other and by how many nm.

In examinations it is common practice to issue candidates with graph paper for solving any of the above type of questions. Trk, GS and the position of both aircraft *for a common time* are needed. These parameters may be given in the question or the candidate may have to work them out from other given information.

14.10 The decision whether a collision risk exists or not is straightforward. Plot both aircraft for a common time and draw the bearing between them, repeat the process for a later common time and check to see if the bearing is the same or changing. If they make a LCB a collision risk exists (see Fig. 14–7); if the bearing is changing a collision risk does not exist. (see Fig. 14–8.)

Example:

At 0843 aircraft 'X' (trk 112 (T), GS 160 kn) has aircraft 'Y' (trk 088 (T), GS 140 kn) flying at the same altitude on a brg of 170 (T) range 60 nm from 'X'.

Does a collision risk exist?

If a collision risk exists at what time will the collision risk occur?

If there is no collision risk which aircraft will cross in front of the other and by how many nm?

Answer:

Plot the 'X''s trk of 112(T) and mark it with the double arrow trk symbol pointing in the direction of 112(T).

Put a pinpoint symbol (a dot with a small circle around it) near the left hand end of this trk and label it with 'X' and the time 0843.

From this pinpoint plot a brg of 170 (T) and (using a suitable constant scale) measure 60 nm from 'X' down this brg.

Put another pinpoint symbol at this 60 nm point and label it with 'Y' and the time 0843.

From the pinpoint symbol for 'Y' plot 'Y''s trk of 088 (T) so that it crosses 'X''s trk. Mark with trk arrows.

What is now plotted is the situation at 0843, with both aircraft and their respective trks shown (see Fig. 14–9).

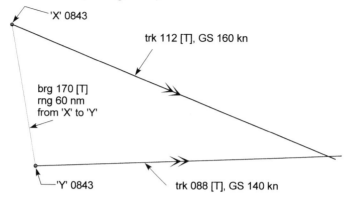

'X' 0843

trk 112 [T], GS 160 kn

brg 170 [T]
rng 60 nm
from 'X' to 'Y'

'Y' 0843

trk 088 [T], GS 140 kn

Fig. 14–9   The situation at 0843.

Plot each aircraft down its respective trk for an equal time interval. A time interval of 30 min is ideal as the movement will equal half the GS. Mark these new positions with the time to which they have been moved and join them with a line giving the brg between them. Fig. 14–10 shows the aircraft moved for 30 min down their trks, 'X' for 80 nm and 'Y' for 70 nm, both labelled with the time 0913.

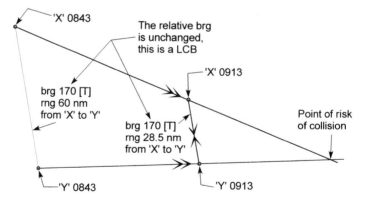

'X' 0843

The relative brg
is unchanged,
this is a LCB

'X' 0913

brg 170 [T]
rng 60 nm
from 'X' to 'Y'

brg 170 [T]
rng 28.5 nm
from 'X' to 'Y'

Point of risk
of collision

'Y' 0843

'Y' 0913

Fig. 14–10   Plotting forward to a common time and checking the new relative brg.

Measurement of the brg between 'X' and 'Y' at 0913 shows it to be the same as the brg between them at 0843. **It is a LCB and a collision risk exists.**
It is possible to measure from say 'X''s 0843 position to the point where the trks cross and using 'X''s GS calculate the time of collision. This method has the drawback that with trks that are converging at a shallow angle any

small error in plotting the trks will cause the position where the trks meet to be in error by several miles.

A far more accurate method is to use the relative closing speed. In the example the original distance apart at 0843 was 60 nm. A measurement of the LCB at 0913 shows the distance apart has shrunk to 28·5 nm. The LCB has a decreasing relative speed of:

$$(60 - 28\cdot5) \text{ nm in 30 min.}$$
$$= 31\cdot5 \text{ nm in 30 min.}$$
$$= 63 \text{ nm in 60 min.}$$
$$= \textbf{63 kn}$$

At 0843 the LCB was 60 nm long, it is closing up at a relative speed of 63 kn. So the 0 nm (collision point) will be reached in just under 60 min after 0843, the exact time **(t)** being found by the ratio:

$$\frac{60}{t} = \frac{63}{60}$$

The circular slide rule gives **t = 57 min**. Therefore the time of collision risk is 0843 + 57 min = **0940**.

Example:
At 1417 aircraft 'P' (trk 260 (T), GS 130 kn) has aircraft 'Q' (trk 286 (T), GS 150 kn) flying at the same altitude on a brg of 182 (T), range 70 nm. Does a collision risk exist?
If a collision risk exists, at what time will the collision risk occur?
If there is no collision risk, which aircraft will cross in front of the other and by how many nm?

Answer:
Plot the 'P''s trk of 260(T) and mark it with the double arrow trk symbol pointing in the direction of 260(T).
Put a pinpoint symbol near the right hand end of this trk and label it with 'P' and the time 1417.
From this pinpoint plot a brg of 182 (T) and (using a suitable constant scale) measure 70 nm from 'P' down this brg.
Put another pinpoint symbol at this 70 nm point and label it with 'Q' and the time 1417.
From the pinpoint symbol for 'Q' plot 'Q's trk of 286 (T) so that it crosses 'P''s trk. Mark with trk arrows.
What is now plotted is the situation at 1417, with both aircraft and their respective trks shown. (see Fig. 14–11)

Plot each aircraft down its respective trk for an equal time interval. Mark these new positions with the time to which they have been moved and join

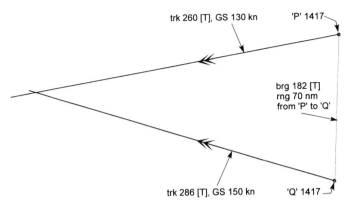

Fig. 14–11   The situation at 1417.

them with a line giving the brg between them. Figure 14–12 shows the aircraft moved for 30 min down their trks, 'P' for 65 nm and 'Q' for 75 nm, both labelled with the time 1447.

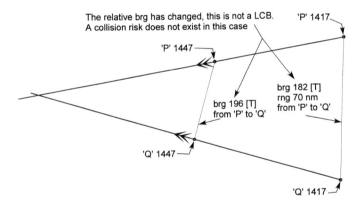

Fig. 14–12   Plotting forward to a common time and checking the new relative brg.

Measurement of the brg between 'P' and 'Q' at 1447 shows it not to be the same as the brg between them at 1417, **it is *not* a LCB therefore a collision risk does *not* exist** .

To calculate which aircraft will cross ahead of the other and by how many nm it is necessary to plot the LCB that these aircraft would have to be on for a collision risk to exist. To do this plot the aircraft from the point where the trks cross back up their trks for equal amounts of time. Joining these two points will plot the collision risk LCB. Figure 14–13 shows the positions plotted back for 30 min with the LCB plotted between them.

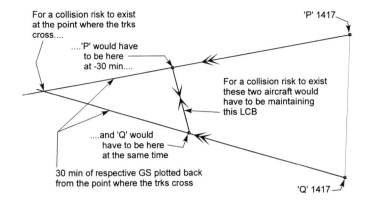

Fig. 14–13   Establishing the LCB that the aircraft would have to be on for a collision risk to exist.

Draw lines parallel to this LCB through the two 1417 aircraft positions. In this example the LCB through the 1417 position of aircraft 'Q' cuts the trk of aircraft 'P' between the 1417 position of 'P' and the crossover point of the trks. The LCB through the 1417 position of 'P' does not cut 'Q''s trk to the crossover point. The aircraft whose LCB cuts the trk of the other aircraft is the one that will reach the crossover point first. In the example aircraft, 'Q' will reach the crossover point ahead of aircraft 'P'.

Measuring the distance from 'P''s 1417 position to where the LCB through 'Q''s 1417 position cuts 'P''s trk will give the separation between the two aircraft at the crossover point, in this example it is 21 nm. (see Fig 14–14)

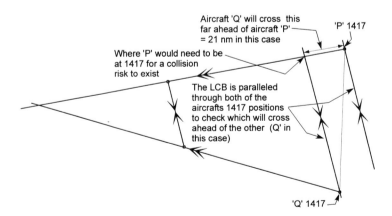

Fig. 14–14   Establishing which aircraft will pass in front of the other and by what distance.

169

CHAPTER 15

NAVIGATIONAL EMERGENCY DATA

15.1 Pilot training includes many hours of practice in handling emergencies in the air. Engine failure, asymmetric flight, forced landing, limited flight panel and many other such problems are grist to the mill for a good pilot. Preparation and practice are the pilot's insurance policy against the fortunately rare chance of being confronted with a real in-flight emergency. Some situations require navigational decisions to be taken. For instance a passenger is taken ill, is it quicker to continue to destination or return to the point of departure? This chapter deals with the various navigational emergencies and the pre-flight planning methods that provide the pilot with the answers before getting airborne.

CRITICAL POINT (CP)

15.2 The single leg case. The question posed above 'Is it quicker to go on or turn back?' gives rise to what is known as the **Critical Point (CP)** or 'equal time' point. Taking a single leg trk from 'A' to 'B' (see Fig 15–1) there must be a point along the leg where it is as quick to fly on to 'B' as it is to fly back to 'A'.

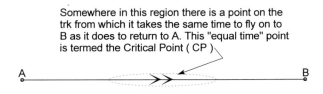

Somewhere in this region there is a point on the trk from which it takes the same time to fly on to B as it does to return to A. This "equal time" point is termed the Critical Point (CP)

A   B

Fig. 15–1   The Single leg Critical Point (CP)

If the **GS On (O)** to 'B' were the same as the return **GS Home (H)** back to 'A' then this equal time point, or CP would fall exactly half way between 'A' and 'B'. Such a situation will only occur in the rare condition of zero WV or with a WV exactly at right angles to the track. The normal effect of WV leads to different values for GS **O** and GS **H** resulting in the CP moving from the half way position on the leg, this movement always being into wind.

15.3 Fig. 15–2 shows the leg 'A' to 'B' of **total Distance (D)**. If from 'A' the **distance to the CP is called (d)** then the distance from the CP to 'B' must be **(D – d)**. The problem is to calculate **d** using the known total leg distance **D**, GS **O** and GS **H**.

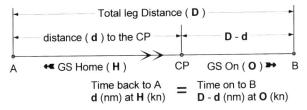

Fig. 15–2   *The basic elements of the single leg CP.*

Since the CP is an 'equal time' point the time to fly **(D – d)** (from the CP on to 'B') at GS **O** must be the same as the time to fly **d** (from the CP back to 'A') at GS **H**. The basic ratio formula:

$$\frac{\text{Distance}}{\text{Time}} = \frac{\text{GS}}{60} \quad \text{Transposes as Time} \quad = \frac{60 \times \text{Distance}}{\text{GS}}$$

Time from CP on to 'B' $\qquad = \dfrac{60 \times (\mathbf{D - d})}{\text{GS } \mathbf{O}}$

Time from CP back to 'A' $\qquad = \dfrac{60 \times \mathbf{d}}{\text{GS } \mathbf{H}}$

As these are equal times $\quad \dfrac{60 \times (\mathbf{D - d})}{\mathbf{O}} \quad = \quad \dfrac{60 \times \mathbf{d}}{\mathbf{H}}$

The 60s cancel, leaving $\qquad \dfrac{(\mathbf{D - d})}{\mathbf{O}} \quad = \quad \dfrac{\mathbf{d}}{\mathbf{H}}$

Cross multiplying gives $\qquad \mathbf{H\,(D - d)} \quad = \quad \mathbf{Od}$

$$\mathbf{HD - Hd} \quad = \quad \mathbf{Od}$$

$$\mathbf{HD} \quad = \quad \mathbf{Od + Hd}$$

$$\mathbf{HD} \quad = \quad \mathbf{d\,(O + H)}$$

$$\frac{\mathbf{HD}}{\mathbf{O + H}} \quad = \quad \mathbf{d}$$

This can best be set on the circular slide rule of the navigation computer in the form of the ratio:

$$\frac{\mathbf{H}}{\mathbf{O + H}} \quad = \quad \frac{\mathbf{d}}{\mathbf{D}}$$

Example:
An aircraft is to be flown from 'A' to 'B' Trk 105 (T), distance 372 nm, TAS 230 kn and WV 245 / 35. Calculate the distance and time from 'A' to the CP.

Answer:

Using the **L** slide of the navigation computer speed slide gives a GS **O** of 256 kn (hdg 111 (T)) for the trk 105 (T) and a GS **H** of 202 kn (hdg 279 (T)) for the reciprocal trk of 285 (T). **O** + **H** in this case is 256 + 202 = 458.

The ratio to set up on the circular slide rule is:

$$\frac{202}{458} = \frac{d}{372}$$

Rough check. 202 is just under half of 458 so **d** must be just under half of 372, say around 170 nm.

The circular slide rule readout for **d** is **164 nm** from 'A'.

Time from 'A' to the CP is 164 nm at the GS **O** of 256 kn. Rough check. Say 150 nm at 250 kn is ³/₅ of an hour or approximately 36 min.

The circular slide rule readout gives the time as **38·5 min.**

It is always possible to check the CP calculation by comparing the time to cover d at GS **H** with the time to cover **(D – d)** at GS **O**, if the CP has been correctly calculated they should be the same, give or take half a minute.

In the example above **d** of 164 nm at GS **H** of 202 kn.
Rough check. Say 150 nm at 200 kn is approximately 45 min.
The circular slide rule readout gives the time as **48·75 min.**
(D – d) = (372 – 164) = 208 nm at GS **O** of 256 kn.
Rough check. Say 200 nm at 250 kn is approximately 48 min.
The circular slide rule readout gives a time of **48·8 min** (see Fig. 15–3).

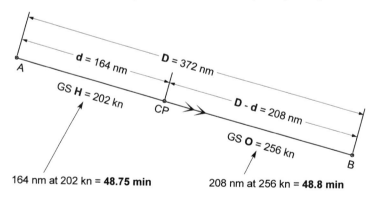

164 nm at 202 kn = **48.75 min**   208 nm at 256 kn = **48.8 min**

Fig. 15–3   Example of a single leg CP calculation.

15.4   The Multi-leg case. For reasons of safety and Air Traffic Control many flights have to be routed to their destination by circuitous means rather than in a direct line. A flight may consist of a series of legs of varying lengths and directions and solving the position of the CP requires the elimination of equal time from each end of the route to isolate that part to which the CP formula can be applied. Consider the three-legged route in Fig. 15–4 and the associated TAS and WV information.

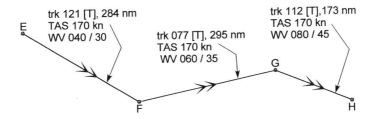

Fig. 15–4   Multi-leg CP calculation, basic scenario.

It pays to be methodical, so start by working out the flight plan along the entire route, 'E' to 'F', 'F' to 'G' and 'G' to 'H'. This will give GS **O** and time out on each leg (see Fig. 15–5).

Leg	TAS kn	WV	Trk (T)	Hdg (T)	GS kn	Dist nm	Time min
'E' to 'F'	170	040 / 30	121	111	162	284	105
'F' to 'G'	170	060 / 35	077	074	136	295	130
'G' to 'H'	170	080 / 45	112	104	130	173	80

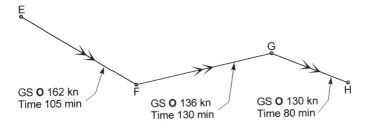

Fig. 15–5   Multi-leg CP calculation, GSs and times Out.

Now return to the first leg of the route and work out GS **H** 'F' to 'E' and the time it will take to fly from 'F' back to 'E', compare this time with the time to fly the last leg from 'G' to 'H' and note which is the longer time (see Fig. 15–6).

Leg	TAS kn	WV	Trk (T)	Hdg (T)	GS kn	Dist nm	Time min
'F' to 'E'	170	040 / 30	301	311	172	284	99

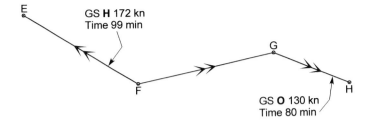

Fig. 15–6   Multi-leg CP calculation, comparison of time Home for the first leg with time On for last leg.

The leg back home from 'F' to 'E' is the longer by 99 min – 80 min = 19 min. So during the time to fly back 'home' from 'F' to 'E' all of the leg 'on' from 'G' to 'H' can be flown plus the last 19 min of the leg 'on' from 'F' to 'G'. This 19 min of leg 'F' to 'G' will be at 136 kn (the GS **O** for the leg 'F' to 'G'):

Rough check. Say 20 min at 120 kn GS gives approximate distance of 40 nm.
The circular slide rule readout gives the distance as 43 nm.
Plotting this distance back from 'G' towards 'F' will give a point (call it 'x') on the leg 'F' to 'G' from which it will take as long to fly on to 'H' via 'G' as it would to fly from 'F' back to 'E'. This leaves part of the 'F' to 'G' leg (from 'F' to 'x') somewhere along which the CP must lie. (See Fig. 15–7)

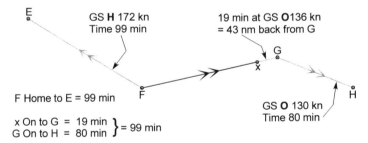

Fig. 15–7   Multi-leg CP calculation, elimination of equal time at each end of the route.

The part of the leg 'F' to 'x' can now be treated as a single leg (equal time having been eliminated from either side of these limits) for the calculation of the CP. GS **O** of 136 kn has already been found for the leg 'F' to 'G' (see Fig. 15–5) GS **H** for the leg 'G' back to 'F' is now calculated (see Fig. 15–8) and the distance from 'F' to 'x' obtained from total distance 'F' to 'G' minus the distance from 'G' to 'x' = 295 – 43 = 252 nm, this being the distance **D** for the CP calculation.

174

Leg	TAS kn	WV	Trk (T)	Hdg (T)	GS kn	Dist nm	Time min
'G' to 'F'	170	060 / 35	257	260	204	-	-

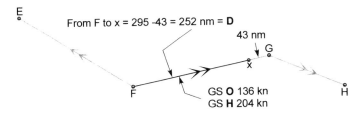

Fig 15–8   Multi-leg CP calculation the basic scenario of the leg from F to 'x'.

For 'F' to 'x':

D = 252 nm, **O** = 136 kn, **H** = 204 kn, **O** + **H** = 136 + 204 = 340

Setting up the ratio on the circular slide rule gives:

$$\frac{204}{340} = \frac{d}{252}$$

Rough check. 204 is approximately ⅔ of 340 so **d** must be in the region of ⅔ of 252, say around 160 nm.

The circular slide rule readout for **d** is **151 nm**.

The CP is therefore 151 nm from 'F' on the leg 'F' to 'G'. The total time from 'E' to the CP will be the time for the leg 'E' to 'F' plus the time to fly the 151 nm from 'F' to the CP at the GS **O** for the leg 'F' to 'G'.

This is 105 min + 66·5 min (151 nm at GS 136 kn) = **171·5 min**.

A final check on the accuracy of the calculations gives:

From CP on to 'G' = (295 – 151) = 144 nm at GS **O** of 136 kn	=	63·6 min.
From 'G' on to 'H' = 173 nm at GS **O** of 130 kn	=	80·0 min.
Total time on		= **143·6 min**

From CP back to 'F' = 151 nm at GS **H** of 204 kn	=	44·6 min.
From 'F' back to 'E' = 284 nm at GS **H** of 172 kn	=	99·0 min.
Total time back		= **143·6 min**

With the CP plotted on the chart the decision whether to carry on or turn back is simple. If past the CP carry on, if not turn back.

15.5   The reduced TAS case. For a given route and set of WVs a change in the value of the TAS of the aircraft will alter the position of the CP. One emergency likely to require a 'carry on or turn back' decision would be failure of one engine on a multi- engined aircraft. Since such a failure would also result in a decrease of the TAS a second CP, based on the 'engine-out' TAS, is needed to cater for this possible emergency. To demonstrate this consider the route in Fig. 15–4 but with a reduced 'engine-out' TAS of 150 kn. What is required first are the reduced TAS calculations of the various reduced GS **O** and GS **H** figures. In this case the reduced GS **O** for leg 'E' to 'F' and the reduced GS **H** for leg 'H' to 'G' need not be calculated to start with. These can be calculated later in the unlikely event of the reduced TAS CP not falling on the leg 'F' to 'G'. Figure 15–9 shows the reduced TAS calculations:

Leg	TAS kn	WV	Trk (T)	Hdg (T)	GS kn	Dist nm	Time min
OUT							
'F' to 'G'	150	060 / 35	077	073	116	-	-
'G' to 'H'	150	080 / 45	112	103	109	173	95·5
HOME							
'F' to 'E'	150	040 / 30	301	312	152	284	112
'G' to 'F'	150	060 / 35	257	261	183	-	

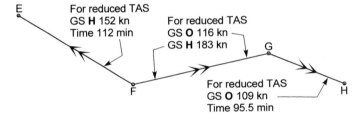

Fig. 15–9   Multi-leg CP calculation, revised GSs **O** and **H** for a reduced TAS.

The leg back home from 'F' to 'E' is (112 min – 95·5 min) = 16·5 min longer than the time to fly from 'G' to 'H' of 95·5 min. The equal time point 'x' is therefore 16·5 min at 116 kn (reduced GS **O** leg 'F' to 'G') = 32 nm back from 'G' towards 'F'. (See Fig. 15–10)

This leaves 295 nm – 32 nm = 263 nm, the distance **D** from 'F' to 'x' somewhere along which the CP must lie. Along this part of the route GS **O** = 116 kn and GS **H** = 183 kn giving **O** + **H** = 116 + 183 = 299. The ratio to set on the circular slide rule becomes:

$$\frac{183}{299} = \frac{d}{263}$$

Rough check. 262 is slightly less than 299 so **d** must be slightly less than

183. The computer readout gives **d = 161 nm**. Plotting this distance on from 'F' towards 'x' gives the position of the CP for the 'engine out' reduced TAS. (See Fig 15–11)

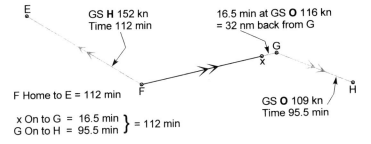

E
GS **H** 152 kn
Time 112 min

16.5 min at GS **O** 116 kn
= 32 nm back from G

G
x

F Home to E = 112 min   F

GS **O** 109 kn
Time 95.5 min

x On to G = 16.5 min
G On to H = 95.5 min } = 112 min

H

Fig. 15–10 Multi-leg CP calculation, elimination of equal time at each end of the route for the reduced TAS case.

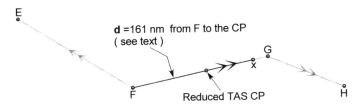

E

d =161 nm from F to the CP
(see text)

G
x

F   Reduced TAS CP   H

Fig. 15–11 Multi-leg CP calculation, position of the CP for the reduced TAS case.

A final check gives:

From CP on to 'G' = 295 nm – 161 nm = 134 nm at GS O of 116 kn =	69·4 min
From 'G' on to 'H' = 173 nm at GS O of 109 kn	= 95·5 min
Total time on	= **164·9 min**
From CP back to 'F' = 161 nm at GS H of 183 kn	= 52·8 min.
From 'F' back to 'E' = 284 nm at GS H of 152 kn	= 112·0 min.
Total time back	= **164·8 min.**

Since the 'reduced TAS CP' is only applicable after failure of an engine the time to reach the 'reduced TAS CP' has to be calculated at the 'all engines operating' GSs. In this case using the GSs O 'E' to 'F' and 'F' to 'G' at a TAS of 170kn (see Fig. 15–5). These give:

Time 'E' to 'F'	= 105 min.
Time 'F' to the 'engine out' CP at the GS O	
'F' to 'G' (all engines) = 161 nm at 136 kn	= 71 min.
Total time from 'E' to the 'engine out' CP	= **176 min.**

Which is 4·5 min beyond the 'all engines operating TAS CP' (See Fig. 15–12).

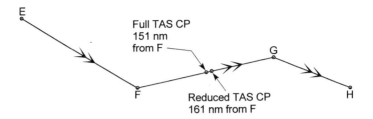

Fig. 15–12   Multi-leg CP calculation, comparison of the positions of the CP for the full and reduced TAS cases.

POINT OF NO RETURN (PNR)

15.6 The next navigational decision point is known as the **Point of No Return (PNR)**. As the name implies once the PNR has been passed it is impossible to return to the point of departure within the safe endurance of the aircraft and the pilot is committed to continuing on to the planned destination or a designated alternative airfield. From the fuel to be carried for the flight the safe **Endurance (E)** has first to be established. This is based on the available fuel and rate of fuel consumption for the planned cruising speed and altitude, (mandatory fuel carried for holding and diversion contingencies is never included when calculating the safe endurance E). As with the Speed/Distance/Time problems in Chapter 4 E is expressed in minutes for ease of use on the computer.

15.7 (PNR) Single leg case. Consider a single leg route from 'A' to 'B'. If the fuel available gives a safe endurance **E** which is insufficient to fly the round trip 'A' to 'B' and back again without landing then calculation of the PNR is essential. The formula for calculating the **Time out (To)** from 'A' to the PNR is evolved below for those who like to know how such things come about, being able to reproduce this proof is not part of the licence requirement so there is no need to commit it to memory.

Let GS out from 'A' to the PNR	=	O
Let GS home from the PNR back to 'A'	=	H
Let the distance from 'A' to the PNR	=	d
Let Time out from 'A' to the PNR	=	To (min)
Let Time home from the PNR back to 'A'	=	Th (min)
Let safe Endurance	=	E (min)

The ratio $\dfrac{d}{To} = \dfrac{O}{60}$ gives **d** $= \dfrac{To \times O}{60}$ 'X'

The ratio $\dfrac{d}{Th} = \dfrac{H}{60}$ gives **d** $= \dfrac{Th \times H}{60}$ 'Y'

'X' = 'Y' therefore $\dfrac{To \times O}{60} = \dfrac{Th \times H}{60}$

The 60s cancel out leaving $To \times O = Th \times H$ 'P'

The round trip from 'A' to the PNR and back to 'A' is:-

$$To + Th = E$$

Therefore $Th = E - To$ 'Q'

Substituting 'Q' for **Th** in 'P' gives:

$$
\begin{aligned}
To \times O &= (E - To)\,H \\
To \times O &= (E \times H) - (To \times H) \\
(To \times O) + (To \times H) &= E \times H \\
To\,(O + H) &= E \times H \\
To &= \frac{E \times H}{O + H}
\end{aligned}
$$

For solving on the circular slide rule this is rearranged as the ratio:

$$\frac{To}{E} = \frac{H}{O + H}$$

Candidates for Licence examinations should commit this ratio to memory and be able to apply it.

Example:
'A' to 'B' distance 624 nm. TAS 200 kn, Wind component + 20 kn out and – 20 kn home, safe endurance 5 hours and 20 minutes. Calculate the time and distance to PNR.

Answer:

E	=	5 hr 20 min	=	320 min.
GS **O**	=	TAS 200 kn + 20 kn	=	220 kn.
GS **H**	=	TAS 200 kn – 20 kn	=	180 kn.
O + **H**	=	220 + 180	=	400

The ratio to set on the circular slide rule is:

$$\frac{To}{320} = \frac{180}{400}$$

Rough check. 180 is just under half of 400 so **To** must be just under half of 320, say 140 to 150.

The circular slide rule readout makes **To = 144 min**.

Distance **d** to the PNR = 144 min at GS **O** of 220 kn.

Rough check. Approximately 2·5 hrs of GS **O**, say about 550nm.

The circular slide rule readout gives **d = 528 nm**.

A final check can now be carried out:

Th = **E** – **To** = 320 – 144 = 176 min at GS **H** of 180 kn confirms **d** as **528 nm**.

With a total distance from 'A' to 'B' of 624 nm once the aircraft has passed the PNR it cannot return to 'A' within the safe endurance and is committed to continue on to 'B'. (see Fig. 15–13)

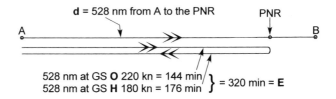

Fig. 15–13   Example of a single leg point of No Return (PNR).

15.8   (PNR) Multi-leg case. Where a multi-leg route is involved the sum of **To** and **Th** for each leg is worked out and these values are sequentially subtracted from the total safe endurance **E** until a leg is reached where **To** + **Th** for that leg is greater than the remaining endurance available at the beginning of the leg. The PNR must therefore lie on this leg and is calculated as for a normal PNR using the speeds and times for the leg and the value of the remaining endurance. Fig. 15–14 shows a route 'A' to 'E' via 'B', 'C' and 'D' with GS **O**, GS **H** and distance for each leg. The safe endurance **E** is 4 hours and 58 minutes = 298 min.

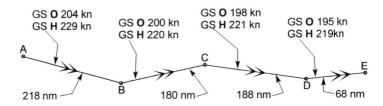

Fig. 15–14   Multi-leg PNR, a basic scenario.

For the leg   **O**   =   204 kn for distance 218 nm gives **To**   =   64 min
'A' / 'B'   **H**   =   229 kn for distance 218 nm gives **Th**   =   57 min
                              Total time 'A' to 'B' and back to 'A'   =   **121 min**
                E of 298 min – 121 min = **177 min endurance remaining**.

180

For the leg   **O**   =   200 kn for distance 180 nm gives **To**   =   54 min
'B' / 'C'   **H**   =   220 kn for distance 180 nm gives **Th**   =   <u>49 min</u>
                  Total time 'B' to 'C' and back to 'B'   =   **103 min**
Available endurance 177 min – 103 min = **74 min endurance remaining.**
For the leg   **O**   =   198 kn for distance 188 nm gives **To**   =   57 min
'C' / 'D'   **H**   =   221 kn for distance 188 nm gives **Th**   =   <u>51 min</u>
                  Total time 'C' to 'D' and back to 'C'   =   **108 min**
Available endurance remaining is 74 min, therefore the aircraft cannot fly to 'D' and return to 'C' within the safe endurance and the PNR must lie somewhere on the leg 'C' to 'D'.
Summarising for the leg 'C' to 'D':

$$
\begin{aligned}
\text{Safe endurance } \mathbf{E} \quad &= \quad 74 \text{ min.} \\
\mathbf{O} \quad &= \quad 198 \text{ kn.} \\
\mathbf{H} \quad &= \quad 221 \text{ kn.} \\
\text{Giving } \mathbf{O} + \mathbf{H} \quad &= \quad 419.
\end{aligned}
$$

The ratio to set on the circular slide rule is:

$$
\frac{\mathbf{To}}{74} \quad = \quad \frac{221}{419}
$$

Rough check. 221 is just over half of 419 so **To** (the time to the PNR) must be just over half of 74, say about 40 min.
The circular slide rule readout gives **To = 39 min**.
39 min at GS **O** of 198 kn gives the distance **d** from 'C' to the PNR = **129 nm.**
Cross checking, **Th** from PNR back to 'C' = 74 min – 39 min = 35 min at GS **H** of 221 kn = 129 nm.
Total time from 'A' to the PNR
= **To** 'A' to 'B' + **To** 'B' to 'C' + **To** 'C' to PNR.
= 64 min + 54 min + 39 min.
= **157 min.**

15.9 (PNR) Alternative solution. An alternative way of solving the PNR is first to calculate GS **O** and GS **H** and then work out the total time to fly out and home over a selected distance (it is common practice to use the distance that would be covered in 60 min at GS **O**, so dispensing with one calculation). With the total time taken to fly out and home over a known distance and a known value for **E**, the distance **d** to the PNR can be solved on the circular slide rule by setting the ratio:

$$
\frac{\mathbf{d}}{\mathbf{E}} \quad = \quad \frac{\text{Selected distance}}{\text{time out and home over selected distance}}
$$

A rework of the last part of the previous question from 'C' to the PNR with E=74 min, O=198 kn, H=221 kn. Selecting 198 nm for the calculation distance gives:

198 nm out at **O** of 198 kn	=	60·0 min.
198 nm home at **H** of 221 kn	=	53·8 min.
Total time out and home over 198 nm	=	**113·8 min.**

The ratio to set on the circular slide rule is:

$$\frac{d}{74} = \frac{198}{133·8}$$

Rough check. 198 is just over 1·5 × 113·8 so **d** must be just over 1·5 × 74 or around 120.
The circular slide rule readout gives **d = 129 nm.**

15.10   (PNR) Varying fuel flow case. A variation on the ratio method in paragraph 15.9 can be used to solve the PNR using the amount of usable fuel (excluding contingency fuel) and the fuel flow for the cruising speed and altitude. Fuel carried and fuel flow may be expressed by volume or by weight. Either can be used in this ratio method provided common units are used within each calculation. The method is to calculate the total fuel used out and back over an arbitrary distance (as before one hour's worth of distance out at GS **O** is a common figure to use since it will use one hour's worth of fuel flow, again reducing the number of steps to be calculated), with a known amount of usable fuel the ratio to be set on the circular slide rule is:

$$\frac{d}{\text{Usable fuel}} = \frac{\text{Selected distance}}{\text{Fuel used out and home over selected distance}}$$

This may seem like an unnecessary extension of the GS method of finding the PNR but in fact it is a far more accurate method when varying fuel flows are involved. On large aircraft, with fuel flows in thousands of kg/hr, as fuel is burnt off and the all-up-weight decreases, so will the fuel flow decrease. By the end of several hours flying the rate of fuel consumption will be considerably lower than at the start of the flight.

15.11   For a single track out and home route with decreasing fuel flow and insufficient fuel for a complete round trip the calculation of the PNR is a straightforward application of the formula in paragraph 15.10. Fig. 15–15 shows just such a case along with the relevant GSs, Fuel Available and Fuel Flows.

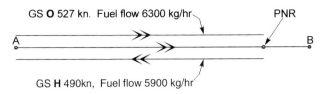

GS **O** 527 kn. Fuel flow 6300 kg/hr

PNR

A   B

GS **H** 490kn, Fuel flow 5900 kg/hr

Fuel available (excluding contingency fuel) = 27 000 kg

Fig. 15–15 Single leg PNR with decreasing fuel flow, a basic scenario.

The calculation of Total fuel used out / home over this distance is:
GS **O** = 527 kn so using 527 nm as the selected distance.

Fuel used out	=	527 nm at GS **O** 527 kn.
	=	60 min at 6300 kg / hr.
	=	**6300 kg.**

Fuel used home	=	527 nm at GS **H** 490 kn.
	=	64.5 min at 5900 kg / hr.
	=	**6350 kg.**

Total Fuel Used out and home over the selected distance
      =   6300 + 6350 kg.
      =   **12 650 kg.**

The ratio to set on the circular slide rule is:

$$\frac{d}{27\ 000} \qquad = \qquad \frac{527}{12\ 650}$$

Rough check. 27,000 is just over 2 × 12,650 so **d** must be just over 2 × 527, say in the region of 1100 nm.
The circular slide rule readout gives **d = 1127 nm.**

15.12 For a multi-leg out and home route the procedure is as follows:

Calculate the fuel required to fly the first leg out and home and subtract this amount from the total fuel available.

Repeat for the second leg subtracting the fuel required to fly out and home from the fuel remaining after the first leg calculation.

Proceed in this fashion in sequence down the route until a leg is reached where the total fuel out and home for the leg is greater than the remaining fuel available at the start of the leg.

The PNR must lie on this leg and is calculated in the same way as for a single leg route.

Fig. 15–16 shows such a multi-leg route. At this stage the GS, fuel flow and distance for each leg is given as these are the only required elements needed to illustrate the multi-leg PNR procedure. In an examination the candidate may have to work out the GSs **O** and **H** from given TAS, WV and trk before proceeding with the PNR calculation.

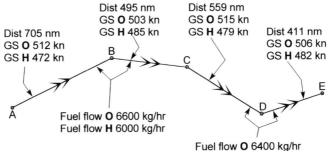

Dist 495 nm
GS **O** 503 kn
GS **H** 485 kn

Dist 559 nm
GS **O** 515 kn
GS **H** 479 kn

Dist 705 nm
GS **O** 512 kn
GS **H** 472 kn

Dist 411 nm
GS **O** 506 kn
GS **H** 482 kn

Fuel flow **O** 6600 kg/hr
Fuel flow **H** 6000 kg/hr

Fuel flow **O** 6400 kg/hr
Fuel flow **H** 6200 kg/hr

Fuel available (excluding contingency fuel) = 49 000 kg

Fig. 15–16   Multi-leg PNR with decreasing fuel flow, a basic scenario.

From/To	Distance (nm)	GS (kn)	Time (min)	Fuel flow (kg / hr)	Fuel used (kg)
Leg 1					
'A' to 'B'	705	512 (**O**)	82·5	6600 (**O**)	9 080
'B' to 'A'	705	472 (**H**)	90	6000 (**H**)	9 000

Total fuel used 'A' to 'B' and back to 'A'   **18 080 kg.**

Leg 2   Fuel available 49 000 kg – 18 080 kg = **30 920 kg.**

'B' to 'C'	495	503 (**O**)	59	6600 (**O**)	6 490
'C' to 'B'	495	485 (**H**)	61·2	6000 (**H**)	6 120

Total fuel used 'B' to 'C' and back to 'B'   **12 610 kg.**

Leg 3   Fuel available 30 920 kg – 12 610 kg = **18 310 kg.**

'C' to 'D'	559	515 (**O**)	65	6400 (**O**)	6 940
'D' to 'C'	559	479 (**H**)	70	6200 (**H**)	7 240

Total fuel used 'C' to 'D' and back to 'C'   **14 180 kg.**

Leg 4   Fuel available 18 310 kg – 14 180 kg = **4130 kg.**

'D' to 'E'	411	506 (**O**)	48·6	6400 (**O**)	**5200 kg.**

This is more than the 4130 kg of available fuel so the PNR must lie along the leg 'D' to 'E'. Proceed as for a single leg route:

GS **O** on leg 'D' to 'E' = 506 kn so use 506 nm as the selected distance.

Fuel used out	=	506 nm at GS **O** 506 kn.
	=	60 min at 6400 kg / hr.
	=	**6400 kg.**
Fuel used home	=	506 nm at GS **H** 482 kn.
	=	63 min at 6200 kg / hr.
	=	**6500 kg.**

Total fuel used out and home over the selected distance.
$$= \quad 6400 + 6500 \text{ kg.}$$
$$= \quad \textbf{12,900 kg.}$$
The ratio to set on the circular slide rule is:

$$\frac{d}{4130} = \frac{506}{12\,900}$$

Rough check. 4130 is approximately ⅓ of 12 900, so **d** must be about ⅓ of 506, say in the region of 150 to 170.
The circular slide rule readout gives **d = 162 nm** from 'D' on the leg 'D' to 'E' as the position of PNR.

The answer can be verified by working out the fuel used from the start of the leg to the PNR and back to the start of the leg. The total should check out against the fuel available at the start of the leg.

In the above example fuel available at 'D'   =   4130 kg.
                                   GS O   =   506 kn.
                                   GS H   =   482 kn.
Distance from 'D' to the PNR calculated as   =   162 nm.
Fuel used out   =   162 nm at 506 kn.
                  =   19·2 min (at 6400 kg / hr)
                  =   **2050 kg.**
Fuel used home   =   162 nm at 482 kn.
                   =   20·15 min (at 6200 kg / hr)
                   =   **2080 kg.**
Total fuel used out and home from 'D' to the PNR and back
                   =   2050 + 2080 kg.
                   =   **4130 kg.**
This checks out with the fuel available at the start of the leg.
The total time to reach the PNR from the moment of leaving 'A' is the sum of all the outbound times. In this case:
Time 'A' to 'B'   =   82·5 min.
Time 'B' to 'C'   =   59·0 min.
Time 'C' to 'D'   =   65·0 min.
Time 'D' to PNR   =   19·2 min.
Time 'A' to PNR   =   **225·7 min.**

POINT OF NO ALTERNATE (PNA)

15.13   The Point of No Alternate (PNA) only applies where the available alternate airfield lies some way off from the planned route and is too distant from the destination airfield to be reached from overhead the destination airfield within the safe limits of the contingency fuel carried. In such a case there will be a point along the route beyond which the alternate airfield cannot be reached within the safe fuel limits and the aircraft is committed to landing at the planned destination airfield. This point is called the PNA and any decision to divert to the alternate airfield must be taken before this point is passed. In practical terms this means the conditions for the destination airfield should be checked by RT just before the PNR is reached, in case a diversion is advisable.

15.14   The PNA is found by means of a constant scale geometrical solution carried out on the plotting chart. A Line of Constant Bearing (LCB) (see Chapter 14) is used in the solution of this problem along with the concept of a 'phantom' aircraft. The DR position of the aircraft is established for a point along the route some way before the PNA is likely to occur. A point before the aircraft is abeam the diversion airfield will usually suffice. From this DR position a trk is drawn in to the diversion airfield. This trk is not actually going to be flown but will be used to establish a LCB between the trk 'on' to destination and an imaginary (or 'phantom') aircraft assumed to be flying directly from the DR position so as to arrive at the diversion airfield at the end of the safe endurance. Fig. 15–17 shows a route with the trk to destination airfield 'B' marked in:

Diversion airfield 'C' is shown some way North and West of 'B'.

A DR position prior to coming abeam 'C' has been plotted on the chart and its time noted beside it.

A trk from this DR position to 'C' is plotted for the 'phantom' aircraft to fly along.

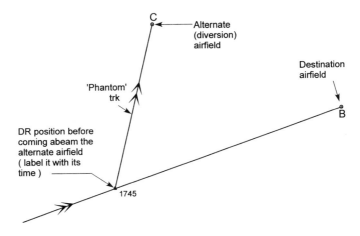

Fig. 15–17   Point of No Alternate (PNA) a basic scenario.

A LCB can now be established through:

The real aircraft's position on track to destination. and
The position of a 'phantom' aircraft flying from the DR position directly to the diversion airfield at a speed that will have it arriving at the end of the safe endurance.

To do this the GS of the 'phantom' aircraft must be calculated first. The distance of the direct trk from the DR position to the diversion airfield is measured using the appropriate scale for the plotting chart and the time (in minutes) from the DR position to the end of safe endurance ascertained. These two facts are then used to calculate the GS the 'phantom' aircraft must fly at to arrive at the diversion airfield just within safe endurance. Suppose the trk distance is found to be 297 nm and the time to run to the end of safe endurance is 115 minutes, the GS of the 'phantom' aircraft will have to be:

$$\frac{297 \text{ nm} \times 60}{115 \text{ min}} \quad \text{or, as a ratio on the navigation computer} \quad \frac{297}{115} = \frac{GS}{60}$$

Rough check. 60 is just over ½ of 115 so GS must be just over ½ of 297, say about 150 kn.
Computer readout gives 155 kn as the GS of the 'phantom' aircraft.

15.15   In paragraph 15.14 it was stated that this problem is solved geometrically using a constant scale. Although it is now common practice to use Lambert's projection for most plotting purposes, there are occasions when a variable scale chart such as Mercator's may have to be used and in such cases the construction that is explained below *must* be made using the (constant) longitude scale of the chart or even a Metric or Imperial rule. During construction an arc equal to the TAS has to be drawn so select a constant scale that will enable this to be done fairly large to reduce errors. Fig. 15–18 shows the construction which is built up as follows:

To scale plot in a vector for one hour of WV blowing OUT from the DR position. From the end of this wind vector strike a circle of radius equal to one hour of TAS. Where this cuts the actual trk to destination gives the aircraft's position (P) in one hour's time *according to the constant scale*. (This will not necessarily be the actual geographical DR position for one hours time except in the case of a constant scale chart where the latitude scale is being used for the PNA construction).
To the scale being used the length of the vector from the DR position to (P) gives GS to destination and the direction from the end of the wind vector to (P) gives the required hdg.
To the same scale a distance equal to one hour's movement at the GS of the 'phantom' aircraft is marked along the trk from the DR position towards the diversion airfield. This establishes the position of the 'phantom' aircraft (Q) for the same time that the actual aircraft will be at (P).
The LCB is then drawn by plotting a straight line through (P) and (Q) and extending it to cut the TAS circle at (R).
A line from the DR position to (R) gives the trk direction into the diversion airfield from the PNA and its vector length (to the constant scale) will give the GS.
The geographical position of the PNA is found by plotting a line parallel to this trk direction through the diversion airfield so as to intersect the actual trk into the destination airfield. The point of intersection is the PNA.

At the same time a line drawn from the end of the wind vector to (R) will give the hdg from the PNA to the diversion airfield.

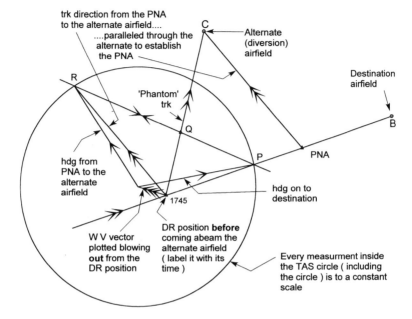

Fig. 15–18   Construction for solving the PNA.

Having found the PNA, plus hdg and GS to the diversion airfield, normal navigation techniques must be resumed and all distances must once more be measured by the appropriate scale for the chart in use.

CHAPTER 16

TIME AND TIME CONVERSIONS

INTRODUCTION

16.1 Earlier chapters in this book have shown time to be an intrinsic part of most navigational problems. So how has the measurement of time evolved? Early man would have appreciated the sequences of dark and light (one day), the complete cycle of the phases of the moon (a lunar month) and the passage of the seasons (one year). Observation showed that there were 28 days in a lunar month and there appeared to be 13 lunar months in a year. A slight error in the last observation came to light when users of this early form of calendar found that the seasons (a basis for planting and harvesting crops) were slipping in relation to their lunar based calendar by about one and a quarter days per year. The year was not 364 days long but more like 365¼ days in length.

16.2 The Julian Calendar. It was Julius Caesar (100 – 44 BC) who had the calendar modified to give the world the Julian Calendar of 365 days length for the year, the odd ¼ day being allowed for by adding one day every fourth year (a leap year). The passage of centuries once more showed the seasons slipping in relation to this calendar. The year based on the seasons was some 11¼ mins shorter than the 365¼ days assumed in the Julian Calendar so each leap year overcorrected by 45 mins. In four centuries this gave an over correction of three days and three hrs.

16.3 The Gregorian Calendar. In 1582 Pope Gregory XIII (1502–1585) had the Gregorian Calendar introduced which rectified the accrued error of the Julian Calendar and further reduced the error by making the century years leap years only if divisible by 400 (thus 1700 AD, 1800 AD and 1900 AD were not leap years but 2000 AD was). This reduced the accrued error in each 400 years from three days and three hrs to just three hrs, or put another way, it will take 3200 years for the Gregorian Calendar to slip one day. Most of continental Europe quickly went over to the Gregorian Calendar but the UK did not change from the Julian Calendar until 1752 by which time the UK was out of step with the rest of Europe by eleven days. When

189

the change was made there were riots in parts of the UK by people who thought that 11 days of their lives were being stolen!

16.4 Although the above paragraphs give the background to the Calendar in use today they do not explain the origins of how the length of the day is determined. For that it is necessary to mention a group of scientists who were living around the time of Pope Gregory XIII. The first of these was the Italian astronomer Galileo Galilei (1564–1642). Among his many achievements was the making of a telescope with which he observed the movements of the planets and confirmed the theory of Nicholas Copernicus (1473–1543) that the earth rotated on its axis and that earth and the other planets were in orbit about the sun. The Roman Church at the time regarded this as heretical. Galileo was made to recant his findings and as a result science in Italy was virtually brought to a standstill for decades.

16.5 In Denmark Tycho Brahe (1546–1601), another astronomer, spent years measuring and recording the movements of the planets. After the death of Tycho Brahe his brilliant one time assistant, Johann Kepler (1571 –1630) spent many more years analysing the mass of figures he left behind.

KEPLER'S LAWS OF PLANETARY MOTION

16.6 The result of Kepler's endeavours with Brahe's records are known today as Kepler's Laws of Planetary Motion which state:

The planets describe elliptic orbits, of which the sun is one focus.

An imaginary line joining a planet to the sun sweeps out equal areas in equal time.

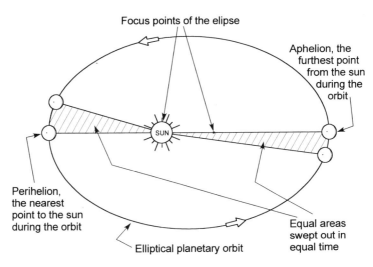

Fig. 16–1   Planetary orbit of the Earth around the Sun.

190

The square of the period of revolution of a planet is proportional to the cube of its average distance from the sun.

The first two of these laws are pertinent to the calculation of time (see Fig. 16–1). The third law is of interest to astronomers but plays no part in the subject matter of this Chapter.

16.7 From Fig. 16–1 it can be seen that in its elliptical orbit around the sun, for an imaginary line between the earth and the sun to sweep out equal areas in equal time, the speed of movement around the sun must vary. It is fastest at the point when it is closest to the sun (known as Perihelion) and slowest when it is at the point furthest from the sun (known as Aphelion). As well as moving at a varying speed on an elliptical path around the sun, the earth is also rotating at a constant speed about its own N/S axis, the N/S spin axis being inclined at 23° 30' from the vertical to the plane of the elliptical path around the sun (see Fig.16–2). At Perihelion the N pole is at maximum tilt away from the sun (the Winter Solstice) and at Aphelion the N pole is at maximum tilt towards the sun (the Summer Solstice).

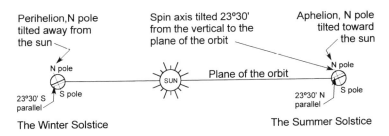

Fig. 16–2   The tilt of the Earth's spin axis to the Plane of Orbit.

THE SEASONS AND APPARENT MOVEMENT OF THE SUN

16.8 From Fig. 16–2 it can be seen that at Perihelion the sun will be vertically (90° to the earth's normal) overhead the parallel of 23°30'S and at Aphelion it will be vertically overhead the parallel of 23°30'N. It follows that at two points on its elliptical path the sun will be vertically over the equator. If all the vertically overhead points throughout the year are plotted on the surface of the earth a GC will be made giving the annual path of the sun over the earth known as the Ecliptic. (See Fig. 16–3) This path reaches its highest lats at the solstices and crosses the equator going Northwards at the Vernal Equinox (20 March, N hemisphere Spring) at a point known as the first point of Aries. Six months later it crosses the equator going Southwards at the Autumnal Equinox (22 or 23 September, N hemisphere Autumn) at a point known as the first point of Libra.

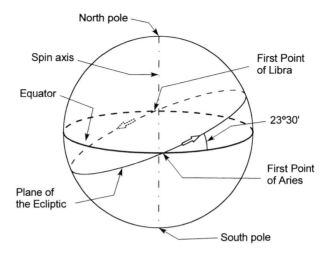

Fig. 16–3   The Plane of the Ecliptic.

If the daily path of the overhead position of the sun is plotted out it will appear to move along successive parallels of lat, changing lat by about 15' per day. The direction of rotation of the earth results in the sun appearing to move from E to W over the earth's surface. The tilt of the earth means that the length of the period of daylight will be least when the tilt is away from the sun and greatest when tilt is towards the sun, giving rise to the seasons (see Fig. 16–4).

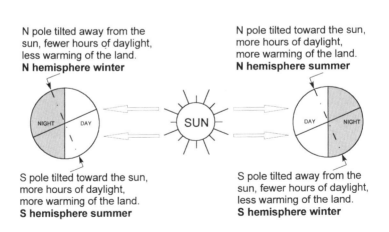

Fig. 16–4   How the tilt of the earth's spin axis varies the hours of day and night giving rise to the seasons.

DERIVATION OF TIME

16.9 The length of a day is measured by observing the interval between successive transits of a meridian by a chosen celestial body. The body chosen could be the sun, the moon, a star or even an imaginary celestial body. As already explained above, due to the rotation of the earth the sun appears to move from E to W over the earth's surface. This apparent E to W movement is also true of other celestial bodies but depending on their distance from the earth and their own movement in space the rates at which they appear to move will be different. It follows that the time interval between successive transits of an observer's meridian will be different for different celestial bodies. Most celestial bodies can be ruled out because the time taken for them to make two successive transits of a meridian does not contain a full natural cycle of daylight and darkness.

16.10   The Siderial Day. The celestial body chosen to measure the **Siderial Day** is *a fixed point in space*, such as a star at an infinite distance from the earth. Since the rotation of the earth is being measured against a fixed datum it follows that the resultant unit of time will be a true measure of the rotation of the earth through 360°. (see Fig. 16–5)

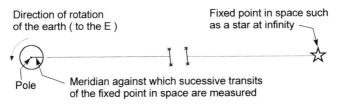

Fig. 16–5   Measurement of the Siderial Day.

The Siderial Day is important in astronomy but has the major drawback that it gets out of step with the natural daily sequence of light and dark which is based on the position of the sun. From Fig. 16–1 it can be seen that at any two points on opposite sides of the earth's elliptical path around the sun for the same time of the Siderial Day one will be in daylight and the other in darkness. This will always be the case, no matter in which direction the chosen fixed point in space lies.

16.11   The Apparent Solar Day is measured between two successive transits of the *sun* across a meridian on the earth. Because the earth is moving around the sun (anti-clockwise viewed from above the N pole) it will have to rotate more than 360° between successive transits. This means the Apparent Solar Day is longer than the Siderial Day (see Fig. 16–6).

193

Unfortunately because the speed of the earth varies on its elliptical path around the sun (see para. 16.7) the length of the Apparent Solar Day will also vary, being longest when its orbital speed is greatest (at Perihelion) and shortest when its orbital speed is least (at Aphelion).

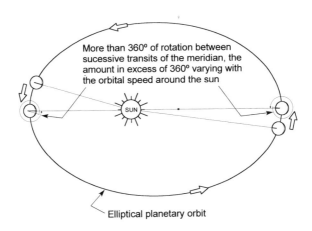

More than 360° of rotation between sucessive transits of the meridian, the amount in excess of 360° varying with the orbital speed around the sun

SUN

Elliptical planetary orbit

Fig. 16–6   The apparent Solar day.

16.12   Mean Solar Time and Civil Time. Since the Apparent Solar Day does not have a constant length it is not directly used in measuring time. An *imaginary* body called the **Astronomical Mean Sun** is assumed to orbit the earth at a constant speed, averaging out the variations in the Apparent Solar Day and giving a **Mean Solar Day** of constant length. The length of the Mean Solar Day is divided up into 24 equal hrs each containing 60 mins, each of 60 secs. Mean Solar Time is the basis of **Civil Time.** and the 24 hrs of a Mean Solar Day constitutes a **Civil Day.** The Siderial Day (see para. 16.10) has a constant length of 23 hrs and 56 mins of Civil Time.

16.13   The Siderial Year. The measurement of the time for the earth to make one elliptical orbit around the sun gives the length of a year. The **Siderial Year** is the measure of time between two successive conjunctions of the earth, sun and a *fixed point in space.* (see Fig.16–7) This is the true measure of one orbit of the earth around the sun and is approximately 365 days and 6 hours of Civil Time. The problem with the length of the Siderial Year is that the seasons gradually move in relation to any calendar based upon it (see paras. 16.4 and 16.7).

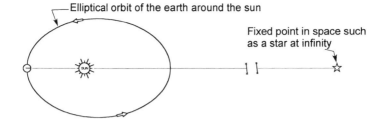

Measurement of sucessive conjunctions of earth, sun and a fixed
point in space gives the true time for the earth to orbit the sun

Fig. 16–7   Measurement of the Siderial Year.

16.14   The Tropical Year. Ideally what is required is a full cycle of the
seasons within a year and to have the seasons occurring at about the same
date(s) in each year. To obtain this it is necessary to base the length of the
year on the interval between successive passages of the sun through the first
point of Aries at the Vernal Equinox. This is some 365 days 5 hours and 48
¾ minutes of Civil Time and is known as the **Tropical Year**. It is the basis
of the Gregorian Calendar (see para. 16.3).

16.15   Local Mean Time (LMT). Relative to the Astronomical Mean Sun
the earth rotates 360° in 24 hrs of Civil Time, or in other words 15° per hr
or 1° per 4 mins. Time based on the position of the Astronomical Mean
Sun is known as **Local Mean Time (LMT)**. For an observer on the earth as

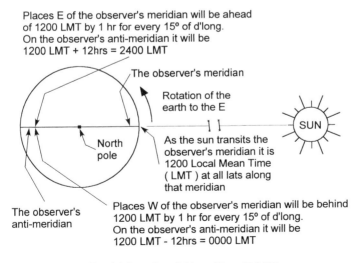

Fig. 16–8a   Local Mean Time (LMT).

the sun transits his or her meridian it will be midday according to the Astronomical Mean Sun, the time being 1200 hr LMT. No matter what the lat all points on the observer's meridian will have the same LMT. It follows that at the same moment on the observer's anti-meridian, the time will be different by 180° / 15° per hr = 12 hrs. With the earth rotating to the E all places to the E of the observer will have passed their midday point and have times later in the day than1200 hr LMT, the anti-meridian time being 1200 hr LMT + 12 hr = 2400 hr LMT. To the W of the observer all places will have times earlier in the day than 1200 hr LMT, the anti-meridian time being 1200 hr LMT – 12 hr = 0000 hr LMT. This identifies the observer's anti-meridian as the point from which LMT is measured clockwise round to the meridian of the Mean Sun. (see Fig.16–8a)

Fig. 16–8b shows two observers 'A' and 'B', on different meridians, with the measurement of their LMTs from their individual anti-meridians clockwise round to the meridian of the Mean Sun. In the example shown the LMT of 'A' is 1000 hr and the LMT of 'B' is 1500 hr. There is a difference of 5 hrs which means the d'long between 'A' and 'B' must be 5 hr × 15° per hr = 75° d'long.

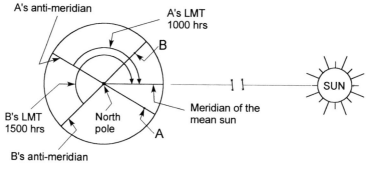

Fig. 16–8b   Relationship of LMT and D'long.

16.16   Greenwich Mean Time (GMT)/Co-ordinated Universal Time (UTC). If LMT were used as the basis for distributing international travel information there would be chaos. Departure and arrival points around the world with their different longs each operating on the LMT applicable to the meridian on which they were situated would result in almost incomprehensible time tables. The solution to this problem is the selection of one meridian as the Prime Meridian and to use the LMT of that meridian for all international communications involving time. The meridian chosen as the Prime Meridian is the one passing through Greenwich (see Chapter 1 para. 1.8) whose LMT is known as **Greenwich Mean Time (GMT)** or **Co-ordinated Universal Time (UTC)**. Conversion of LMT to UTC (GMT) and vice versa is by 'arc to time'. The d'long between the meridian through a place and the meridian through Greenwich is first converted to the time difference ('arc to time') between their LMTs (see para. 16.15) and this time is then applied, *in the correct sense*, to make the required conversion.

For places E of Greenwich:-

LMT *minus* 'arc to time' difference	=	UTC (GMT)
UTC (GMT) *plus* 'arc to time' difference	=	LMT

For places W of Greenwich:-

LMT *plus* 'arc to time' difference	=	UTC (GMT)
UTC (GMT) *minus* 'arc to time' difference	=	LMT

In other words *add* time if *moving Eastwards* and *subtract* time if *moving Westwards*.

16.17   Conversion of 'Arc to Time' is simplified by the use of a table to be found in the **Air Almanac**, a manual that candidates for the written examinations should study. A new edition is published every six months with updated tables of astronomical tables for navigational purposes. Examination Boards provided Candidates with an extract of an out-of-date Air Almanac for use during the examinations. Candidates without access to an Air Almanac for study, should be able to purchase a copy of the current examination extract from their relevant authority (in the UK the CAA or HMSO) rather than purchase a complete Air Almanac. The **Conversion of Arc to Time** table layout has seven columns. The first six columns on the left give conversions of whole degrees of long, (from 0° to 359°), into hrs and mins of time. The seventh column on the right gives conversion of minutes of long, from 0' to 59', into mins and secs of time. The table can be used either to convert d'long into time difference or to convert time difference into d'long.

Example:
Convert a d'long of 137°43' to time difference.
Answer:

137°	=	9 hrs 8 min	........3rd column
43'	=	2 min 52 sec	.........7th column
137°43'	=	**9 hrs 10 min 52 sec**	

Example:
Convert a time difference of 14 hrs 37 min 28 sec to d'long.
Answer:

14 hrs 36 min	=	219° d'long	..........4th column
1 min 28 sec	=	22' d'long	..........7th column
14 hrs 37 min 28 sec	=	**219°22' d'long**	

STANDARD TIME AND THE INTERNATIONAL DATE LINE

16.18   Use of LMT, as well as posing a world wide communication problem, can also complicate administration within a countries boundaries. For example two centuries ago in the UK, LMT was used throughout the country. In those days the UK was mainly an agricultural society, daily life was governed by the hours of daylight and local church clocks were set by the sun. The lack of high speed transport between places meant that the fact that LMT in London was some 20 min ahead of LMT in Bristol which was itself some 12 min ahead of LMT in Plymouth was not important. The industrial revolution brought about by the coming of the railways changed this tranquil way of life for ever. By the mid-19th century journeys that previously had taken days could be completed in hours. The preparation of railway timetables led to a need for a common **Standard Time** to be adopted for use throughout the country. The railways led the way by adopting the LMT of Greenwich (GMT) and issued its customers with an 'arc to time' table to enable them to work out the LMT of arrival and departure at stations anywhere in the country. With the speeding up of transport, countries throughout the world were all faced with similar problems and the Washington conference of 1884 (which selected the Prime meridian) also agreed on an international system of standard times. The UK adopted GMT as its Standard Time. Other countries adopted their own standard times, usually based on the LMT of a meridian close to the country's capital city which differed from GMT (UTC) by a whole number of hours or, in some cases a whole number of hours plus 30 minutes. Countries to the E of Greenwich keep standard times ahead of UTC (GMT), countries along the Greenwich meridian keep UTC (GMT) as standard time and countries W of Greenwich keep standard times behind UTC (GMT). There are some exceptions to these generalisations. For example:

If the capital city is on the extreme E or W of a country's land mass, the standard time chosen for the country may be that of a more centrally placed meridian well away from the capital city.

Some countries, such as the United States of America, Australia and Indonesia have extensive E to W territorial coverage with a d'long well in excess of 15°. In such cases more than one Time Zone, each with its own standard time, may be employed within the country's boundaries.

The land mass of Spain is almost entirely W of the Greenwich meridian but the standard time is 1 hr ahead of UTC (GMT) thus keeping Spanish clocks on the same time as their French neighbours.

Many countries, including the UK, put their clocks ahead by one hr during the summer months as a means of daylight saving.

In paragraph 16.15 it was shown that the 180° meridian could have two times 24 hrs apart, dependent on whether it was approached from the E or the W. Crossing the 180° meridian in an Easterly direction takes one into the Western hemisphere and changes the time by minus 24 hrs (or in other words changes the date by minus one day). It follows that crossing the 180° meridian in a Westerly direction will take one into the Eastern hemisphere and add one day to the date. This gives rise to the 180° meridian being termed the **International Date Line**. As mentioned in Chapter 1 para. 1.8, one of the factors in the selection of the Greenwich Meridian as the Prime Meridian was because it's anti-meridian passed through so few land masses it could be used as the International Date Line with the minimum of modification. The few territories and island groups that do straddle the 180° meridian have the International Date Line modified by taking it away from the 180° meridian and round the affected territories so as to keep all their administrative areas on a common date. The territories that fall within the areas of the modified International Date Line can be identified by the fact that their standard time difference from UTC (GMT) is more that 12 hrs (see LIST 1 mentioned below).

There are three lists of **Standard Times** in the Air Almanac. These lists fill four pages and give the Standard Time differences from UTC (GMT) for all the world. The three lists are made up as follows.

LIST I   Places Fast on UTC (GMT) – Mainly places E of Greenwich
    Add to UTC (GMT) to give Standard Time
    Subtract from Standard Time to give UTC (GMT)
LIST II   Places Keeping UTC (GMT)
LIST III   Places Slow on UTC (GMT) – Places W of Greenwich
    Subtract from UTC (GMT) to give Standard Time
    Add to Standard Time to give UTC (GMT)

Because of political changes territories sometimes split up or amalgamate and names get changed. The Air Almanac incorporates such changes in the Standard Times tables as each edition comes out.

CONVERSION BETWEEN LMT, UTC (GMT) AND STANDARD TIMES

16.19 Paragraphs 16.16 and 16.17 showed how conversion between LMT and UTC (GMT) is achieved by use of the Conversion of Arc to Time tables and para.16.18 showed how conversion between UTC (GMT) and Standard Time is achieved by use of the Standard Time tables. The common factor in both cases being UTC (GMT), it follows that to convert LMT to Standard Time, or vice versa, UTC (GMT) must be solved as an intermediate step.

    LMT<Arc to Time>UTC (GMT)<Standard Time Diff>**Standard Time**

It is advisable with time problems, particularly those involving flight times or the crossing of the 180° meridian, to convert into UTC (GMT) at the earliest possible stage and carry out all the intermediary workings in this form, only converting back to the required LMT or Standard Time as the final step in the calculations. Working in UTC (GMT) enables 'like' to be compared with 'like' and, as will be demonstrated by worked example, date changes on crossing the 180° meridian come out correctly without having to agonise about whether to add or subtract a day!

Example:
An aircraft is scheduled to depart from Tokyo (Japan) (35°30' N 134° 45' E) for a flight to Hawaii (USA) (21°20' N 158°10' W) at 0815 Standard Time on 21 November . The estimated flight time is 5 hrs and 35 mins. What is the LMT and local date of the ETA at Hawaii?
Answer:

Depart Tokyo......................	0815 ST Japan	Nov 21
Standard Time diff (Japan)...	- 0900 (to find UTC (GMT))	
Depart Tokyo......................	2315 UTC (GMT)	Nov 20
Flight time.......................	+ 0535	
ETA Hawaii.......................	0450 UTC (GMT)	Nov 21
Arc to time (158°10' W)......	- 1033 (to the nearest min)	
ETA Hawaii.......................	**1817 LMT**	**Nov 20**

Candidates should be aware that the rules for adding or subtracting are given at the top of each of the *Standard Time* lists and at the *bottom* of the *Conversion of Arc to Time* table. If in doubt check before proceeding. The above example highlights the chances of confusion if the calculations are not carried out in a methodical manner. Note that the time datum (LMT, UTC or ST) and the date is entered on completion of each step in the calculation, thus keeping track of the thought process.

SUNRISE AND SUNSET

16.20   Fig. 16–4 showed the tilt of the earth's spin axis to the vertical of it's elliptical path around the sun and how this varied the length of the

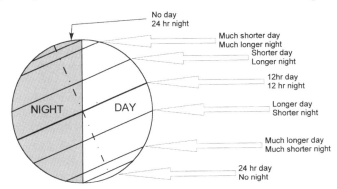

Fig. 16–9a   The Earth at Perihelion with the N Pole tilted away from the sun. The N hemisphere has fewer hours of daylight than night.

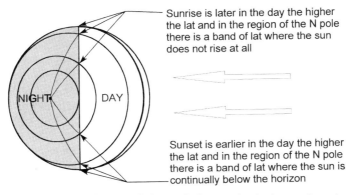

Fig. 16–9b   The Earth at Perihelion with the N Pole tilted away from the Sun.
Variations in sunrise and sunset times with lat.

hours of daylight. Figs. 16–9a and b illustrate in side and plan views
the earth at Perihelion with the N pole tilted away from the sun.

Note how the periods of day and night vary along different parallels of
lat, the further N of the equator a parallel is the fewer hours of daylight it
receives and in the region of the N pole there is a band of lat that does not
get any sunlight at all. In the S hemisphere with movement towards the S
pole the parallels are progressively receiving more hours of daylight and
there is a region around the S pole that is in continual daylight. Figs. 16–10a
and b illustrate how this situation is reversed when the earth is at Aphelion
with the N pole tilted towards the sun.

Along any chosen parallel of lat, as the earth moves on its elliptical path
around the sun, the length of daylight in a 24 hr period will vary between

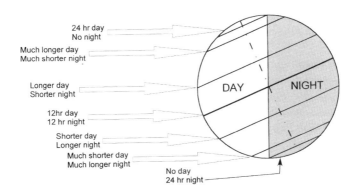

Fig. 16–10a   The Earth at Aphelion with the N pole tilted towards the sun. The N
hemisphere has more hours of daylight than night.

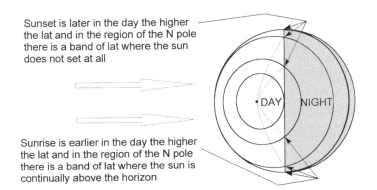

Sunset is later in the day the higher the lat and in the region of the N pole there is a band of lat where the sun does not set at all

Sunrise is earlier in the day the higher the lat and in the region of the N pole there is a band of lat where the sun is continually above the horizon

Fig. 16–10b   The Earth at Aphelion with the N Pole tilted towards the sun. Variations in sunrise and sunset times with lat.

the Perihelion and Aphelion extremes illustrated above. The length of daylight any parallel receives in a 24 hr period is a function of Hemisphere, Lat and Time of the Year (Calendar Date). The greatest changes throughout the year occur in the polar regions which vary from 24 hrs of continual daylight to 24 hrs of continual night. On the other hand in the region of the equator the number of hrs of daylight in any 24 hr period only vary from around 11 to 13 hrs throughout the year.

16.21   Sunrise and **Sunset** are taken from the moment the centre of the sun is observed to be on the horizontal to an observer at sea level. Because the earth's atmosphere refracts light the sun is actually visible when it is approximately 1° below the true horizontal. The times of SUNRISE and SUNSET listed in the *Air Almanac* are the times the sun's centre is observed as rising or setting on the visible horizon and not on the true horizontal.

16.22   Paragraph 16.8 and Fig. 16–4 showed how, during the course of one day, the path of the sun appeared to move over the earth from E to W tracking overhead one parallel of lat. It will of course appear to be tracking E to W along all other parallels (except those in continual polar night) but not directly overhead. Along any parallel of lat the length of the hrs of daylight will be the same for all meridians along that parallel. Therefore for any particular day and parallel of lat the observed LMT of Sunrise and Sunset must be the same for all meridians along that parallel. Paragraph 16.20 explained how the length of daylight varied with hemisphere, Lat and Calendar Date and it is these variables that are incorporated into the SUNRISE and SUNSET tables of the *Air Almanac*.

16.23   SUNRISE tables occupy the top half of the left-hand page and SUNSET tables the bottom half of the same page. Along the top of each table are Month blocks with Dates (for every third day) at the head of vertical columns. Down the left-hand side are listed lats starting with N 72° at the top and going down to 0° about two thirds of the way down, then moving into the S hemisphere going down to S 60°. Inspection reveals that starting from 0° the lat spacing is every 10° as far as N 30° and S 30°, from 30° lat to 50° lat the spacing is every 5° and from 50° lat the spacing is every 2°. The reason for this difference in line spacing is that at the lower lats where conv is small and changes slowly with change of lat the Sunrise and Sunset times also change slowly with change of lat. At higher lats conv changes faster with change of lat (with the sine of the lat) causing the Sunrise and Sunset times also to change more rapidly with change of lat. The reason for the gaps in the columns and lines is really one of sensible economy. To produce a table listing the LMT of Sunrise and Sunset for every day and every degree of lat would require twelve times the area of the present tables. The layout of the tables does however mean that the user has to interpolate the times for dates and/or lats not specifically listed.

Example:
What is the LMT of Sunrise on the 63°30' N parallel on 27 July?
Answer:
The SUNRISE tables list N 62° and N 64° for July 25 and July 28. What is required in this case is ¾ of the way between N 62° and N 64°, and ⅔ of the way between July 25 and July 28. Prepare a box four by three, extract the figures from the tables and enter them into the appropriate boxes (see Fig. 16–11a). The Sunrise times used in the Fig. are from an old Air Almanac and are probably not the same as the current edition, they are however typical for the lat and date. This use of out-of-date tables also applies to other worked examples in paragraphs 16.27 and 16.31 of this chapter.

	July 25 h m	July 26	July 27	July 28 h m
N 64	02 44			02 54
N 63 30				
N 62	03 06			03 14

Box prepared for interpolation with figure from the Air Almanac Sunrise tables inserted (bold). The unlisted dates and required lat are also inserted (light). The target box is shaded here for demonstration purposes only

Fig. 16–11a   Interpolation of the LMT of Sunrise from the
Air Almanac tables. Step 1.

On 25 July there is 0306 LMT – 0244 LMT = 22 mins difference between N 62° and N 64°. Interpolating for N 63°30' either add ¼ of 22 mins to 0244 LMT or subtract ¾ of 22 mins from 0306 LMT, in either case the answer is 0249·5 LMT. Doing the same for 28 July (time difference 20 mins) gives the time at N 63°30' as 0259 LMT. Enter these two times into their appropriate boxes. (see Fig. 16–11b)

	July 25 h m	July 26	July 27	July 28 h m
N 64	02 44			02 54
N 63 30	02 49.5 ☞	☞	☞ **02 56**	☜02 59
N 62	03 06			03 14

Interpolation for lat N 63 30 on July 25 and July 28

Fig. 16–11b   Interpolation of the LMT of sunrise from the Air Almanac tables. Step 2.

At N 63°30' the time difference between 25 July and 28 July is 0259 LMT – 0249·5 = 9·5 mins. The time of Sunrise at N 63°30' on 27 July is either 0249·5 LMT + ⅔ of 9·5 mins or 0259 LMT – ⅓ of 9·5 mins, in either case the answer, to the nearest min, is **0256 LMT**.

The solution could just as easily have been found by interpolating the Sunrise times on 27 July for N 62° and N 64° and then interpolating these time for N 63°30'. As Fig.16–11c shows the end result is the same as above.

	July 25 h m	July 26	July 27 h m	July 28 h m
N 64	02 44	☞ ☞	☞ 02 50.66	☜**02 54**
N 63 30			**02 56**	
N 62	03 06	☞ ☞	☞ 03 11.33	☜ 03 14

Interpolation for July 27 at N 64 and N 62 as the first step

Fig. 16–11c   Interpolation of the LMT of Sunrise from the Air Almanac Tables. Alternative route to the solution.

Some hints of a practical nature are worth mentioning:

When extracting figures from the Air Almanac, make sure that the correct table is entered (**SUNRISE** or **SUNSET** as appropriate) for the desired **Month** and **Date(s)** and the correct **Hemisphere** and **Lat(s)**

To reduce the risk of reading figures from the wrong line it is advisable to lay a rule, or the edge of a sheet of paper, under the line from which the figures are to be extracted.

Having extracted figures which have to be interpolated, note the earliest and latest times. *Any answer obtained that falls outside these limits must be wrong* and the interpolation should be reworked taking care to add and/or subtract in the correct sense.

These may seem obvious precautions to most people but the author has seen so many extraordinary answers produced by students who have not followed these basic checks that he feels they are well worth including them in this book.

16.24 Before leaving the SUNRISE and SUNSET tables, a look at the July tables reveal a series of empty rectangular boxes in quite a few of the high lat columns. Turning to the December tables reveal solid black rectangles boxes in the same general area of the tables. The empty boxes indicate that the sun does not set on that date at that particular lat (i.e. it is above the horizon for the full 24 hrs), the solid black boxes indicate that the sun does rise on that date at that particular lat (i.e. 24 hrs of darkness). These are the zones that have periods of continual daylight or darkness around the Perihelion and Aphelion points of the earth's orbit around the sun. (See para.16.20.)

MORNING CIVIL TWILIGHT AND EVENING CIVIL TWILIGHT

16.25 Just before Sunrise and just after Sunset there is a period of time when although the sun is not visible its light is refracted by the earth's atmosphere giving a degree of light known as **Twilight**. There are three zones of twilight depending on the depression of the centre of the sun below the visible horizon (the one used in assessing the time of Sunrise and Sunset):

Up to 6° of depression.....Civil Twilight. Out of doors operations are possible without artificial lighting and only the brightest stars are visible in the sky.

From 6° to 12° of depression.....Nautical Twilight. Out of doors operations are only possible with the aid of artificial lighting, bright stars are visible in the sky and at sea the horizon can be distinguished.

From 12° to 18° of depression.....Astronomical Twilight. The horizon is not visible at sea, most stars are visible in the sky but there is not quite total darkness which is deemed to occur when the depression is greater than 18°.

Nautical Twilight and Astronomical Twilight are of importance to seamen and astronomers but do not form part of a pilot's curriculum. However Civil Twilight is of significance to pilots, since during this period many daylight activities may be carried out in a normal and safe way without recourse to artificial lighting.

16.26　　The period of Civil Twilight before Sunrise is known as **Morning Civil Twilight** and after Sunset as **Evening Civil Twilight**. The *Air Almanac* lists the LMTs of the *beginning* of **Morning Civil Twilight** and the *end* of **Evening Civil Twilight** in exactly the same format as the SUNRISE and SUNSET tables. The Twilight tables are printed on the right-hand pages facing the SUNRISE and SUNSET tables, each pair of facing pages covering the same block of Calendar Dates. The method of interpolating the TWILIGHT tables to find the times for dates and lats not specifically listed is exactly the same as that demonstrated for interpolating the SUNRISE and SUNSET tables. (See para. 16.23)

16.27　　Comparison of the time of the beginning of Morning Civil Twilight and the time of Sunrise for a given Lat and Calendar Date will give the length of the period of Morning Civil Twilight for that Lat and Calendar Date. Similarly for a given Lat and Calendar Date the length of the period of Evening Civil Twilight can be found by comparing the Sunset time and the end of Evening Civil Twilight time. Because the times listed in the tables are the LMT of phenomena occurrence for all points along a given parallel of Lat on a given Calendar Date, this is one of the rare cases where it is possible to carry out comparisons of LMTs without converting into UTC (GMT) first. Some Morning Civil Twilight periods worked out from the tables for 28 June to 15 August are given below:

Sunrise at 10° N	05 43 LMT	July 1
Beginning of Morning Civil Twilight at 10° N	05 20 LMT	July 1
Length of Morning Civil Twilight at 10° N	23 mins.	July 1
Sunrise at 10° N	05 49 LMT	July 31
Beginning of Morning Civil Twilight at 10° N	05 27 LMT	July 31
Length of Morning Civil Twilight at 10° N	22 mins.	July 31
Sunrise at 60° N	02 42 LMT	July 1
Beginning of Morning Civil Twilight at 60° N	01 02 LMT	July 1
Length of Morning Civil Twilight at 60° N	1 hr 40 mins.	July 1

Sunrise at 60° N	03 37 LMT	July 31
Beginning of Morning Civil Twilight at 60° N	02 35 LMT	July 31
Length of Morning Civil Twilight at 60° N	1 hr 02 mins.	July 31

This demonstrates that along a parallel of lat close to the equator there is only a small change in the length of the period of twilight over a 30 day interval, the actual periods being fairly short. However at a higher parallel of lat the change in the length of the period of twilight over the same 30 day interval is quite large, the actual periods being much larger than at the lower parallel of lat. Repeating this exercise for 31 December the length of the period of Morning Civil Twilight at 10° N is found to be 22 mins and at 60° N it is 57 mins. So not only is the length of the twilight period longer at higher lats than at lats near the equator it also varies more between Summer and Winter. A similar pattern of length of twilight periods is to found for Evening Civil Twilight. Fig. 16–12a and b are reproductions of Fig. 16–9a and b with the Twilight Zone shaded in (not to scale) showing how at the higher lats, due to conv, a larger arc of long is in twilight than in the equatorial regions. With the earth rotating at a constant speed the length of the period of twilight will vary with the arc of long that is in twilight, being shortest in the equatorial region and getting longer as lat is increased toward the poles (but excluding the polar regions when they are in either 24 hrs of continual daylight or darkness).

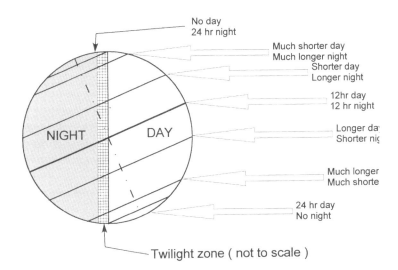

Fig. 16–12 a   The Earth at Perihelion with the N Pole tilted away from the sun, showing the twilight zone.

16.28 The June to August pages introduce another symbol in the TWILIGHT tables. This is an un-enclosed 'hatched' rectangle //// which signifies that at that Lat and Calendar Date the depression of the centre of the sun does not exceed 6° below the visible horizon between Sunset on one day and Sunrise on the following day. There is no night as such and twilight exists from Sunset on one day until Sunrise on the following day.

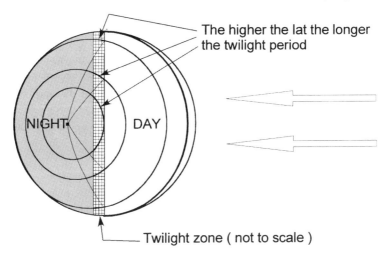

The higher the lat the longer the twilight period

Twilight zone (not to scale)

Fig. 16–12b   Plan view of the Twilight Zone showing how the twilight period increases at higher lats.

TYPES OF TIME PROBLEMS

16.29 In the Licence Examinations a variety of questions involving the use of some, or all, of the above tables are possible. The questions set are usually fairly straightforward, but they do require the candidate to be careful in reading the questions and methodical in working out the answers. Always enter the Calendar Date and the Time Datum beside all times when working out any time problem and remember that the SUNRISE, SUNSET and CIVIL TWILIGHT tables are all in LMT.

16.30 Below is a list of possible variations of questions involving the SUNRISE, SUNSET and CIVIL TWILIGHT tables only:

Question   Calculation of the length of the period of Morning Civil Twilight for a particular. Lat and Calendar Date.

Method   Extract the appropriate times of the beginning of Morning Civil Twilight and Sunrise from the tables (interpolating if necessary) and subtract the Morning Civil Twilight time from the Sunrise time.

Question Calculation of the length of the period of Evening Civil Twilight for a particular Lat and Calendar Date.

Method Extract the appropriate times of the end of Evening Civil Twilight and Sunset from the tables (interpolating if necessary) and subtract the Sunset time from the end of Evening Civil Twilight time.

Question Calculation of the period of time from Sunset on one day to Sunrise on the next day.

Method Extract the time of Sunset for the first day and the time of Sunrise for the *next* day from the tables (interpolating if necessary, with this type of question attention to the Calendar Dates is essential) and subtract the Sunset time (and Calendar Date) from the Sunrise time (and Calendar Date). Note: This is also the method for calculation of the length of the period of twilight where the //// symbol appears in the TWILIGHT tables.

Question Calculation of the period of daylight from Sunrise to Sunset for a particular Lat and Calendar Date.

Method Extract the appropriate Sunset and Sunrise times from the tables (interpolating if necessary) and subtract the Sunrise time from the Sunset time.

Question Calculation of the period of time from the beginning of Morning Civil Twilight to the end of Evening Civil Twilight for a particular Lat and Calendar Date.

Method Extract the appropriate end of Evening Civil Twilight and beginning of Morning Civil Twilight times from the tables (interpolating if necessary) and subtract the beginning of Morning Civil Twilight time from the end of Evening Civil Twilight time.

16.31 Paragraph 16.19 had an example of a question requiring conversions between LMT, UTC (GMT) and Standard Time and including a flight time. There are many variations that can be played with this type of question and the SUNRISE, SUNSET and TWILIGHT tables can be worked into them as part of the LMT element. It would take many pages to examine every possible variation but the worked example below should give candidates an insight into the way to approach such questions.

Example:
An aircraft is scheduled to depart from San Francisco (California, USA) (37°58' N 102°15' W) on an 11 hrs 35 mins flight to Amsterdam / Schiphol (Holland, the Netherlands) (52°19' N 004°46' E). The ETA is to be 30 mins

after Sunrise at Amsterdam / Schiphol on 12 November. Calculate the Local Standard Time and Calendar Date of departure from San Francisco.

Answer:

Stage 1	S/R 52°19' N	07 15 LMT	Nov 12
	Arc to time (4°46' E)	- 00 19 mins	
Stage 2	S/R 52°19' N	06 56 UTC (GMT) Nov 12	
	To arrive 30 mins after S/R	+00 30 mins	
Stage 3	ETA Amsterdam / Schiphol	07 26 UTC (GMT) Nov 12	
	Flight time	– 11 35	
Stage 4	Depart San Francisco	19 51 UTC (GMT) Nov 11	
	Std Time diff (Cal, USA)	– 05 00	
Stage 5	Depart San Francisco	**14 51 LST Cal**	**Nov 11**

Note the logical sequence for solving this particular problem:

Stage 1   Extract the LMT of Sunrise for 52°19'N on 12 November from the SUNRISE tables, interpolating between N 52° and N 54° (¹⁄₆ up OR ⁵⁄₆ down) and 10 and 13 November (²⁄₃ right OR ¹⁄₃ left).

Stage 2   Using the Long of Amsterdam / Schiphol and the CONVERSION OF ARC TO TIME tables convert the Sunrise time from LMT into UTC (GMT)

Stage 3   Add the 30 mins to the Sunrise time to find the ETA at Amsterdam / Schiphol in UTC (GMT).

Stage 4   Subtract the flight time from the ETA to give the time (and Calendar Date) of departure from San Francisco in UTC (GMT).

Stage 5   Using the STANDARD TIMES tables LIST III apply the conversion for California, USA to convert the departure time from San Francisco from UTC (GMT) into Local Standard Time.

In multi-choice question papers it is common practice to ask about more than one aspect of any calculation involving several steps. For example in the above problem the sort of multi-choice questions asked could be something like:

Q   The ETA at Amsterdam / Schiphol is:

a   0626 UTC Nov 12

b   0804 UTC Nov 12

c   0726 UTC Nov 12

d   0704 UTC Nov 12

Q Departure time from San Francisco is:-
a   1451 LST Nov 11
b   1801 LST Nov 12
a   0051 LST Nov 12
b   1351 LST Nov 11

A study of the incorrect answers on offer shows that they have all been obtained by wrong application of a + or a – at some point. Since this is the most common error in this type of calculation it means that a candidate who has made such an error may well find one of the choices matches up with the wrong answer he or she has obtained. Ironically the only time a candidate gets a definite indication that their working is wrong is when their answer is nowhere near any of the multi-choice answers on offer! Where interpolations are involved candidates who find that their answer differs by a min or two from one of the choices, should not waste time reworking, but select that choice as the answer.

CHAPTER 17

PLOTTING

17.1 With the array of navigation aids to be found on the flight deck of today's commercial aircraft, the need for actually navigating by plotting on a chart is minimal, even if space were available to do so. With the miniaturisation of electronics even quite small executive aircraft can carry an impressive navigation fit. Licence candidates may well feel like asking the questions, 'Why are plotting skills taught? Why should I be examined on something I may never use in practice?' In response to that the following may be said:

> The main purpose of requiring pilots to learn the basic skills of plotting is so that they are more aware of the best ways to use the many navigational aids available to them. It also gives them techniques for cross checking the airborne performance of automated equipment such as EFIS and FMS (see Chapters 23 and 24).
> Plotting practise also helps to develop a sense of where one is during a flight. The memory becomes trained as a matter of course to think about time, speed and distance covered. In the (rare) event of a major failure of an aircraft's automated navigation systems the trained mind should be able to take over the navigation task with the minimum of fuss and no panic!

Although the examination calls for plotting a flight on a chart, only a limited number of plotting techniques are required of the candidate. This chapter concentrates on the examination requirements to the exclusion of all other navigation techniques, of which there are many more than those covered below.

17.2 Chapters in Sections 1 and 2 introduced the basic navigation elements and techniques plus the concepts of deduced reckoning (DR) and fuel flow problems. Before launching into plotting on a chart some of these ideas need to be expanded and new items such as Climb and Descent introduced. Items from Chapters 14 and 15 such as revision of TAS to achieve a specific ETA, or calculation of a PNA could also be incorporated into an examination plot. Such additions to a plot would in fact stand on their own as separate questions and should not affect the way the rest of the examination plot is tackled by candidates.

THE BASIC ELEMENTS OF PLOTTING

DEAD RECKONING (DR)

17.3 The term DR can be used to encompass:

DR hdg, the calculated hdg to steer to make good a desired trk for a particular TAS and W/V, (see paragraph 5.14).

DR GS, the expected GS from a particular hdg / TAS and WV combination (see Chapter 5, para 5.12 and 5.14).

DR trk, the expected trk from a particular hdg/TAS and WV combination (see Chapter 5, para 5.12).

DR position, the estimated position of an aircraft at a specified time. This may be for the current time or some minutes ahead of the current time. By projecting from the last known actual position (a fix) along the DR trk at the DR GS for the appropriate time a DR position can be established for a specified time. This is known as **DRing ahead by trk and GS.** The symbol used to signify a DR position is a dot surrounded by a small triangle with the time beside it (see Fig. 17–1).

△ 0816

Fig. 17–1. The DR position symbol (with its applicable time noted beside it).

The method of DRing ahead by trk and GS only holds good if there has been no change of hdg or TAS since the fix. A change in either or both of these elements could alter the DR trk and/or the DR GS. The technique for DRing ahead where the hdg or TAS has changed at some time since the last fix is outside the licence requirements and therefore should not appear on an examination plot. However candidates should be aware of this limitation whenever DRing ahead during an actual flight.

Before moving on from DR it is important to emphasise that all DR elements are estimated (or expected) values and *not* actual values. A couple of tips about DR GS are worth a mention here, they may or may not prove of value in the examinations but certainly can save time and effort when airborne.

If when DRing ahead at DR trk and DR GS the movement is made for 6 minutes ($\frac{1}{10}$ of an hour) the distance to move along the DR trk will be $\frac{1}{10}$ of the DR GS. This is easily found by moving the decimal point one digit to the left (6 min at DR GS 325 kn = 32·5 nm along DR trk). Working in 6 minute steps can save a lot of time and effort!

For very rapid estimation of DR position (needed for some airborne procedures) it is a good idea to be aware of the average distance covered per minute in the aircraft being flown. For example in a light aircraft flying at 123 kn TAS the approximate distance covered per minute (ignoring the WV) is 2 nm. If the last actual fix was 17 minutes ago the current DR position must be somewhere in the vicinity of 2 × 17 = 34 nm down the DR trk from the fix. This rule of thumb way of DRing ahead is not as accurate as using the DR GS but is good enough for some situations as will be shown later in this Chapter.

THE PLOTTING OF POSITION LINES FROM GROUND STATIONS

17.4 A Position Line (P/L) is a line somewhere along which an aircraft was known to be at a certain time. The establishment of the actual position of the aircraft requires at least one other P/L crossing it at the same moment in time and at an angle close to 90°. In visual map reading conditions a P/L could be part of a straight stretch of railway line, major road, or even a coastline. Plotting is more commonly associated with P/Ls obtained from ground located radio stations. The types of ground stations, the informa- tion they supply and the procedures for plotting from each are given in paras. 17.5 to 17.8 below. When a P/L is plotted on a chart it is signified with a single arrow-head (pointing outwards) at each end of the line and the time the P/L was obtained written by it. (see Fig. 17–2) A P/L can be any length but when plotted on a chart it should be drawn so as to extend some way either side of the aircraft's DR position since the actual position should not be too far from this position.

Fig. 17–2   The Position Line (P/L) symbol (with its applicable time noted beside it).

17.5 Direction Finding (DF) Stations – usually based in Air Traffic Control (ATC) on airfields. These stations take bearings on **Radio Transmissions (RT)** from an aircraft whose pilot is requesting a bearing from the station. Depending on the type of bearing requested it is passed back to the pilot of the aircraft as:

QTE* The (T) bearing of the aircraft from N (T) *at the station.*
QDR* The (M) bearing of the aircraft from N (M) *at the station.*
QDM* The (M) heading to steer to reach the station in zero wind conditions. This
   is the reciprocal of QDR and is based on N (M) *at the station* and *not* on N (M)
   at the aircraft which could be different if the aircraft were some distance from
   the ground station.

QUJ* The (T) heading to steer to reach the station in zero wind conditions. This is the reciprocal of QTE and is based on N (T) *at the station* and *not* on N (T) at the aircraft which could be different (due to conv) if the aircraft were some distance from the ground station. In practice QUJ is rarely used to pass bearings but it is a useful tool in plotting calculations.

On charts the lat and long graticule is based on (T) directions and, apart from Grid navigation, plotting is normally conducted in terms of (T) directions. Of the above four types of bearing only two (QTE and QUJ) are based on N (T), and of these two only QTE is *from* the station. For normal plotting purposes QDM, QDR and QUJ have first to be converted into QTEs before they can be plotted from N (T) at the known position of the ground station. The rules for conversion are:

QUJ + or – 180° = QTE.
QDR + E (or – W) Var *at the station* = QTE.
QDM + or – 180° (= QDR) + E (or – W) Var *at the station* = QTE.
Alternatively
QDM + E (or – W) Var *at the Station* (= QUJ) + or – 180° = QTE.

Since these are radio bearings they will have travelled by the shortest route (i.e. along a GC) between the aircraft and the station. On charts where a straight line can, for all practical purposes, be assumed to be a GC (i.e. Lambert's and Polar Stereographic) the QTE can be plotted as a straight line directly from N (T) at the station. To plot the QTE from the station on a Mercator's chart the GC must first be converted to its RL equivalent before plotting it as a straight line from N (T) at the station. (See Chapter 9 starting at para. 9.16)

17.6 Very High Frequency Omnidirectional Radio Range (VOR) – automatic continual transmission stations of which there are two types, high-powered versions, most of which are located within the Airways System, and low-powered versions which are located as approach aids at some airports. A VOR transmits two signals, the phase difference between them being decoded by a receiver in the aircraft to give either a QDR or QDM based on N (M) *at the station*. The different ways of displaying VOR

---

* These three-letter codes, prefixed with the letter Q, are a relic from the days when air/ground communications were conducted solely in Morse Code by means of a Morse key. To reduce the amount of signals traffic a code known as the 'Q Code' was evolved. A booklet was published containing a different three-letter group for each of a series of standard messages, use of the appropriated group usually only requiring the addition of a few figures to send a message. The increased use of RT eventually did away with the Morse key but the continuing need to restrict the amount of signals traffic meant that some of the more frequently used elements of the Q Code have been retained. These days the most commonly used Q Codes deal with brgs (as above) and Altimeter settings and readings. (See the Instruments and Meteorology syllabi.)

information is part of the Radio syllabus. In plotting the main concern is with use of the end product, a QDR or QDM. The rules for converting QDRs and QDMs into QTEs and for plotting from N (T) at the station on different charts are exactly the same as described in paragraph 17.5 for the DF bearings.

17.7 Non-Directional Beacon (NDB) – radio beacons that transmit a signal radiating in all directions rather like the waves spreading out when a stone is dropped into still water. They are usually located at airfields or points on airway systems and operate on frequencies specifically for use by aircraft. Some transmitters used for public broadcasting may also be used by aircraft provided the frequencies are compatible with the aircraft's direction finding equipment. Apart from transmitting a continual signal the NDB has no further part to play in establishing a position line through the aircraft. Equipment on the aircraft takes a bearing on the incoming signal from the NDB. Depending on the display fit, this is shown as a **Relative Bearing (Rel brg)** measured clockwise round from the fore and aft axis through the nose of the aircraft on a **Relative Bearing Indicator (RBI)** (see Fig. 17–3a), or as a **Magnetic Bearing ((M) brg)** measured clockwise round from N (M) *at the aircraft* on a **Radio Magnetic Indicator (RMI).** (see Fig. 17–3b)

The pointer is indicating the bearing of the NDB it is tuned to clockwise round from the nose of the aircraft

Zero on the indicator dial is aligned with the fore and aft axis of the aircraft with zero indicating the direction of the nose of the aircraft

Fig. 17–3a   A Relative Bearing Indicator (RBI).

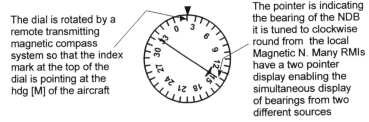

The dial is rotated by a remote transmitting magnetic compass system so that the index mark at the top of the dial is pointing at the hdg [M] of the aircraft

The pointer is indicating the bearing of the NDB it is tuned to clockwise round from the local Magnetic N. Many RMIs have a two pointer display enabling the simultaneous display of bearings from two different sources

Fig. 17–3b   A Radio Magnetic Indicator (RMI).

In the case of a Rel brg (see Fig. 17–3a) the information available to the pilot would be:

The Rel brg as displayed on the RBI.
The aircraft's (T) hdg (this may have to be resolved from (C) or (M) hdg as described in Chapter 2, paras 2.2 to 2.6).

The position of the NDB on the chart. This may be printed on the chart or the candidate may have to plot it on the chart from given lat and long co-ordinates. In the latter case care must be taken to plot it in the correct place, if the NDB is marked in the wrong place on the chart it follows that bearings plotted from it will be incorrectly positioned.

The aircraft's DR position (found by DR trk and DR GS since the last fix). The DR position is an essential part of the process as conv between the aircraft and the NDB is going to be needed and without an idea of the approximate long of the aircraft at the time of taking the brg the wrong value could be applied leading to an error in the plotted brg.

Fig. 17–4 shows a Lambert chart with the aircraft and ground position of the NDB marked on. A straight line is drawn from the NDB through the aircraft representing the GC path the radio wave has followed from the beacon to the aircraft. Marked in at the aircraft is the hdg of the aircraft from N (T) at the aircraft and the Rel brg from the nose fore and aft axis clockwise round to the GC. At the NDB's known ground position is indicated the, as yet uncalculated, bearing to be plotted from N (T) at the NDB.

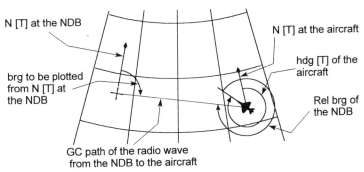

Fig. 17–4   Relative brg of an NDB measured from the nose of an aircraft, situation displayed on a Lambert chart.

The sequence for solving the brg to be plotted from the NDB is as follows:

To the Rel brg from the nose of the aircraft add the (T) hdg of the aircraft. This will give the (T) brg (from N (T) at the aircraft) of the GC *from* the aircraft *to* the NDB. If the answer comes out at more than 360° just subtract 360° from it to give the correct answer.

Any conv between the NDB and the aircraft's DR position must now be corrected. For plotting on Lambert or Polar Stereographic charts the most practical method is to transfer a line parallel to the N (T) meridian at the aircraft's DR position through the position of the NDB to give a Transferred Meridian. (See Chapter 11 para. 11.14 and Figs 11–9 and 11–10) The angle between this Transferred Meridian and N (T) at the NDB being the chart conv between the aircraft's DR position and the NDB.

To the (T) brg of the GC from the aircraft to the NDB add or subtract 180°. This gives the reciprocal brg from N (T) *at the aircraft*. Plot this brg from the Transferred Meridian at the NDB. Fig. 17–5 shows how the situation in Fig. 17–4 is resolved by this method.

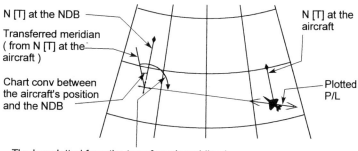

The brg plotted from the transferred meridian is:-
Rel brg of NDB + hdg [T] of the aircraft (- 360° in this case) + or - 180°

Fig. 17–5   Relative brg of an NDB measured from the nose of an aircraft, the plotting solution on a Lambert chart.

For plotting on a Mercator chart the (T) GC brg *from the aircraft* to the NDB *must* be converted to the equivalent (T) RL brg *from the aircraft* to the NDB *before working* out the reciprocal (T) RL brg to be plotted from N (T) at the NDB. Fig. 17–6 shows how the same situation as in Fig. 17–5 would appear on a Mercator chart.

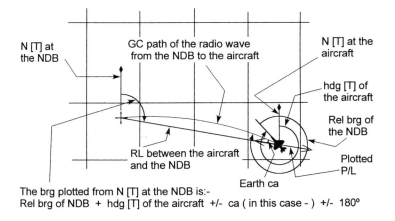

The brg plotted from N [T] at the NDB is:-
Rel brg of NDB + hdg [T] of the aircraft +/- ca (in this case -) +/- 180°

Fig. 17–6   Relative brg of an NDB measured from the nose of an aircraft, plotting solution on a Mercator chart, N hemisphere.

Remember the basic rules for converting GCs to RLs on a Mercator chart:

The ca is *always* applied at the point of measurement. (i.e. At the station for Ground D/F and VOR bearings and at the aircraft for ADF bearings on an NDB.)
The ca is *always* applied from the GC towards the equator and *never* towards the pole.

17.8 Distance Measuring Equipment (DME) – transponder beacons located within the airways system and at airfields. These beacons reply to interrogation signals from the aircraft, the response being displayed on the aircraft's receiver equipment as a range in nm from the ground station. Since the information is a range, the P/L through the aircraft will be an arc of a circle whose centre is the ground position of the DME and whose radius is the range being displayed. In practice DMEs are often co-located with VORs so that interrogation of both at the same time will result in a simultaneous fix being obtained (the curved range P/L from the DME crossing the straight line brg from the VOR at 90°, giving the ideal fix from two P/Ls). Fig. 17–7 shows such a simultaneous co-located VOR / DME fix.

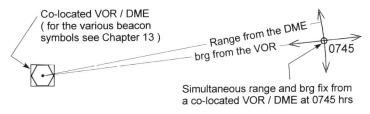

Fig. 17–7   Simultaneous fix from a co-located VOR/DME.

It is worth pointing out situations where the combination of a range P/L from a DME with a P/L from a non co-located source may need a further

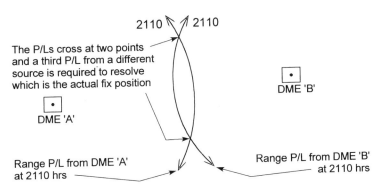

*Fig. 17–8   The need for a third P/L to resolve a fix position,
simultaneous ranges from two DME.*

P/L (obtained from a third source) to clarify the position of the aircraft. Figs. 17–8 and 17–9 show just such situations. In both cases there are two points where the P/Ls cross and further information is required to ascertain which position is the true one.

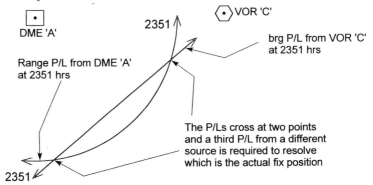

DME 'A'

2351

VOR 'C'

brg P/L from VOR 'C' at 2351 hrs

Range P/L from DME 'A' at 2351 hrs

The P/Ls cross at two points and a third P/L from a different source is required to resolve which is the actual fix position

2351

Fig. 17–9   The need for a third P/L to resolve a fix position, simultaneous range from a DME and brg from a non co-located VOR.

CLIMBING AND DESCENDING

17.9 Sometimes a plotting question has a climb and/or a descent in it. Working out a climb or descent is not very different from calculating hdg, GS, time and ETA for a level cruise. Consider the simple trk from 'A' to 'B' shown in Fig. 17–10a. It is required to plan a climb from 2000 ft overhead 'A' up to a cruising level of 26,000 ft and then a descent at the end of the cruise to arrive overhead 'B' at 10,000 ft. Certain items of information are required to enable the calculations to be carried out. These items may appear in questions in several different ways as will be explained later. The first thing to appreciate is that both the climb and the descent are treated as separate legs, even though they have the same trk direction as the cruise. Furthermore the distance from 'A' to the **Top of Climb (TOC)** and from 'B' back to the **Top of Descent (TOD)** have to be worked out and subtracted from the total distance from 'A' to 'B' to find the distance to be flown at the cruising level from TOC to TOD. Fig. 17–10b gives the side view of the situation and has the required elements for each calculation marked in.

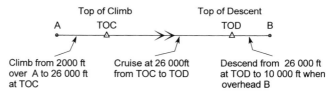

Top of Climb   Top of Descent

A   TOC   TOD   B

Climb from 2000 ft over A to 26 000 ft at TOC

Cruise at 26 000ft from TOC to TOD

Descend from 26 000 ft at TOD to 10 000 ft when overhead B

Fig. 17–10a   Plan view of a route with a climb and a descent.

220

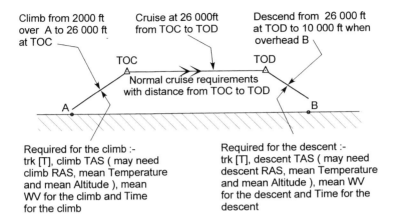

Required for the climb :-
trk [T], climb TAS (may need climb RAS, mean Temperature and mean Altitude), mean WV for the climb and Time for the climb

Required for the descent :-
trk [T], descent TAS (may need descent RAS, mean Temperature and mean Altitude), mean WV for the descent and Time for the descent

Fig. 17–10b   Side view of the same route with its climb, cruise and descent.

17.10   For the climb the required elements are:

Trk (T) which is the same as for the cruise and is measured directly from the chart.
Climbing RAS (for a climb at high levels this could be climbing Mach No). This is usually given in the question.
Mean temperature for the climb to enable **climbing TAS** to be calculated from the climbing RAS. This may be given in the question or have to be calculated as the mean temperature from temperatures given for the top and bottom of the climb (simply add the temperatures algebraically and divide by two).

For example in the case of Fig. 17–10b suppose the temperature at 2000 ft over 'A' was $+ 6°$ C and at the cruising level of 26,000 ft it was $- 40°$ C then the mean temperature for the climb would be:

$$(+ 6 – 40) / 2° \text{ C} = - 34 / 2° \text{ C} = - 17°C.$$

Sometimes the examination question gives the climbing TAS to use, in which case the above two items are not applicable.

Mean WV for the climb. Like the mean temperature the mean WV may be given in the question or have to be calculated from the mean of the WVs at the top and bottom of the climb. Adding the values together and dividing by two works for the Wind Speed but in certain cases can give the reciprocal of the Wind Direction.
For example there is no problem if the WV at the bottom of the climb were 240/30 and the WV at the top were 280/60, added together would give 520/90 which divided by two gives a **mean WV of 260/45**.
However when the Wind Directions at top and bottom of a climb lie either side of 000°, this method gives a reciprocal mean Wind Direction. For example, if the bottom and top WVs were 340/20 and 040/60 the added figures are 380/80

which when halved give 190/40! The mean speed is correct but the mean direction is patently the reciprocal of the correct answer. In cases where the bottom and top WVs lie either side of 000°, add or subtract 180° to the Wind Direction found by this method (i.e. 190° + or − 180° gives 010° as the mean Wind Direction).

Mean altitude of climb, needed to calculate the mean TAS from the mean RAS and mean temperature. Add together the altitudes at the bottom and top of the climb and divide by two. In the case of the climb in Fig. 17–10b this would be:

$$2000 \text{ ft} + 26,000 \text{ ft} / 2$$
$$= 28,000 \text{ ft} / 2$$
$$= \textbf{14,000 ft.}$$

Climbing time is needed so that, combined with the mean **climbing GS** calculated from the above elements, the **ground distance** from the start of the climb to TOC can be found and plotted on the chart. The time spent on the climb may be given in the question or it may need calculating from a given rate of climb over the altitude change involved. For example in Fig. 17–10b the starting altitude at 'A' is 2000 ft and at TOC it is 26,000ft, if the given rate of climb were 3000 ft per min the climbing time would be:

$$26,000 - 2000 \text{ ft} / 3000 \text{ ft per min}$$
$$= 24,000 \text{ ft altitude change} / 3000 \text{ ft per min}$$
$$= \textbf{8 min.}$$

17.11 **For the descent** the elements are similar to those for the climb. Just substitute the word 'descent' for the word 'climb' and 'TOD' for 'TOC', the distance from TOD to bottom of descent being plotted *from the bottom of descent back along the trk* to find the position of TOD on the chart. A possible variation that can be asked is, starting from a specific TOD, to calculate the rate of descent necessary to arrive overhead a point at a given altitude. The solution is to measure the distance from the position of the specified TOD to the overhead point of the bottom of the descent and use the calculated descent GS to find the descent time. The descent time (in min) divided into the change of altitude (in ft) involved on the descent will give the required rate of descent (in ft per min).

17.12 The calculations involved in preparing a Flight Plan for the route shown in Fig. 17–10b are given below. To demonstrate the process from start to finish different WVs, temperatures and rate of climb to those in the paragraph 17.10 examples will be used. The associated log-keeping procedures will be ignored at this stage, log-keeping is dealt with later in this Chapter.

Example:

An aircraft is to be flown from 'A' to 'B', a distance of 253 nm, trk 090 (T). The aircraft is to climb from 2000 ft overhead 'A' to a cruising altitude of

26,000 ft. Mean RAS for the climb 195 kn, mean rate of climb 2000 ft per min. Cruise RAS 265 kn. The aircraft is to descend from cruising altitude to arrive overhead 'B' at 10,000 ft. Mean RAS for the descent 180 kn, mean rate of descent 1600 ft per min. Forecast WVs and temperatures are:-

At 'A' 2000 ft	WV 150 / 30	temp + 12° C
26,000 ft level	WV 200 / 60	temp – 42° C
At 'B' 10,000 ft	WV 170 / 40	temp – 8° C

Calculate the hdgs and times for the climb, the cruise and the descent.

Answer:
For the climb:
Mean altitude
= (2000 + 26,000) ft / 2 = 28,000 ft / 2 = **14,000 ft**
Mean temp.
= (+ 12 – 42)° C / 2 = – 30° C / 2 = **– 15° C**
Mean WV
= (150 / 30 + 200 / 60) / 2 = (350 / 90) / 2 = **175 / 45**
Climbing time
= (26,000 – 2000) ft / 2000 ft per min
= 24,000 ft / 2000 ft per min
= **12 min.**

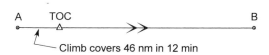

Fig. 17–11   The climb, plotting TOC.

Mean climbing RAS 195 kn, mean altitude 14,000 ft, mean temp –15° C gives a mean climbing **TAS of 238 kn** (see Chapter 4, para. 4.6).
Trk 090 (T), mean climbing TAS 238 kn, mean climbing WV 175 / 45 gives a climbing **hdg of 101 (T)** at a mean climbing **GS of 230 kn** (See Chapter 5, para. 5.14).
Mean climbing GS 230 kn for a climbing time of 12 min gives a distance of **46 nm** along trk from 'A' to the TOC. (see Fig. 17–11)
For the descent:
Mean altitude
= (26,000 + 10,000) ft / 2 = 36,000 ft / 2 = **18,000 ft**
Mean temp
= (- 42 – 8)° C / 2 = – 50° C / 2 = – **25° C**

Mean WV
= (200 / 60 + 170 / 40) / 2 = (370 / 100) / 2 = **185 / 50**
Descent time
= (26,000 – 10,000) ft / 1600 ft per min
= 16,000 ft / 1600 ft per min
= **10 min**.
Mean descending RAS 180 kn, mean altitude 18 000 ft, mean temp –25° C
gives a mean descending **TAS of 234 kn**.
Trk 090 (T), mean descending TAS 234 kn and mean descending WV
185/50 gives descending **hdg of 102 (T)** at a mean descending **GS of 233 kn**.
Mean descending GS 233 kn for a descending time of 10 min gives a distance of **39 nm** *back* along trk from 'B' *to* the TOD. (See Fig. 17–12).

Fig. 17–12   The descent, plotting TOD.

For the cruise:
Cruise RAS 265 kn, altitude 26,000 ft, temp – 42 C gives a cruise **TAS of 386 kn**. (See Chapter 4, para. 4.7 for TAS > 300 kn.)
Cruise distance from TOC to TOD = Total distance from 'A' to 'B' less the combined climb and descent distances

= 253 – (46 + 39) nm
= 253 – 85 nm
= **168 nm**.

Trk 090 (T), cruise TAS 386 kn, WV at 26,000 ft 200 / 60 gives a cruise **hdg of 099 (T)** at a **GS of 403 kn**.
Cruise distance 168 nm at GS 403 kn gives a **cruise time of 25 min** from levelling off at TOC to starting descent at TOD. (see Fig. 17–13)

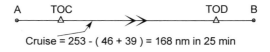

Fig. 17–13   The Cruise, Distance and Time.

Summary of flight plan:
Climb on hdg 101 (T) for **12 min** from 2000 ft overhead 'A' to TOC (49 nm from 'A').
Cruise on hdg 099 (T) for **25 min** from TOC to TOD (a distance of 168 nm).
Descent on hdg 102 (T) for **10 min** from TOD to 10,000 ft overhead 'B' (a distance of 39 nm).
Total time for flight = 12 + 25 + 10 min = **47 min.** (see Fig. 17–14.)

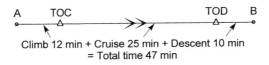

Fig. 17–14   Total time for the climb, cruise and descent.

THE PLOTTING SEQUENCE

17.13   The basic plotting sequence is an ongoing process which is repeated throughout the flight from start to finish. Expressed in the simplest terms the process consists of the following stages:
Gathering information to up-date the position of the aircraft.
From the latest position reassess TMG, GS and WV.
Assess and implement any alterations needed to hdg and/or ETA as a result of changes detected.

THE PLOTTING CHART

17.14   The plotting process is carried out on a chart which must have as a minimum a lat and long graticule and isogonals. Natural features such as coastlines may be shown along with the location, identification of type and call sign of ground located radio aids. Over the years the charts used for training and examination purposes have varied very little and charts based on the Lambert's projection have been used for a couple of decades and look set to stay that way in the foreseeable future. Currently the chart being used is the Jeppesen Europe LO 1 / 2. This is a Lambert's projection with airways routes and radio aids overlaid; it has the advantage that trks and dists between turning points and reporting points are printed on the chart **BUT A WORD OF WARNING**: there are two possible traps for the unwary when it comes to plotting. Being an airways chart the **trks are in degrees [M]** and will need to be converted to [T] for use with the forecast W/V (never mix [M] and [T] in the same calculation). Some airways legs have their total **dist broken down into sectors** between en route reporting points and care must be taken not to miss a sector out when looking for the total dist.

THE NAVIGATION LOG FORM

17.15   Good log-keeping is the secret of good plotting, a well kept log makes it easy to access the latest state of affairs and a well laid out log form can act as an *aide mémoire*; gaps in the columns indicating that a process has not yet been carried out. Log forms can vary in layout but all should have columns for recording items like time, trk, hdg, dev, varn, Alt/FL, temp, RAS / Mach No, TAS, GS, dist, time, ETA, incoming information, etc. While content is essential the actual layout is a matter of personal taste. For example, candidates may find the log form used below (which just happens to be the author's preferred layout) differs in detail from log forms from other sources. For the UK examinations candidates may use whatever type of log form they please. The author strongly advises candidates to choose a log form layout that suits them personally and get plenty of practise in using it. Do not forget to take blank copies with you for use in the examinations. Most log forms have a Time column on the left hand side and an ETA column on the right-hand side. Between these two lie other columns arranged in functional groups. The author's preferred log form layout has the left-hand side dealing with the direction elements first, thus:

Time	Trk	WV/	Hdg	Var	Hdg	Dev	Hdg
	(T)	/drift	(T)		(M)		(C)

In the centre of the log is a wide space (about $\frac{1}{3}$ of the total width of the sheet) for **Observations**. The space allows room for calculations of bearings to plot and other items like climbs and /or descents. Between the **Observations** space and the ETA column are the speed, distance and time (to go) elements, thus:

Mach/	Pressure/	TAS	GS	Dist	Time	ETA
No /RAS	Alt /COAT					

Had a log form been used for the calculations of the climb example given in paragraph 17.12 the final result would look something like Fig. 17–15a.

The stages used in completing each line of the log are shown in Fig. 17–15b. Numbers give the sequence of working and arrows indicate the transfer of information from the **Observations** space into specific columns.

PLOTTING THE POSITION OF AN AIRCRAFT

17.16   The established position at which an aircraft is *known* to have been at a particular time (as opposed to a DR position which is an *estimated* position) is known as a **fix**. In plotting, a fix can be established by several

Time	Trk [T]	W V/drift	Hdg [T]	Var	Hdg [M]	Dev	Hdg [C]	Observations	Mach No/RAS	Pressure Alt/COAT	TAS	GS	Dist	Time	ETA
	090	175/45	101					'A' CLIMBING 2000 ↗ 26000FT 'TOC' MEAN ALT = (2000 + 26000) / 2= 28000 / 2 = 14000 FT.	195	14000 / -15	238	230	46	12	
								ALT CHANGE = 26000 - 2000 = 24000 FT AT 2000 FT / MIN = 12 MIN MEAN TEMP = (+12 -42) / 2 = -30 / 2 = -15C.							
								MEAN W V = (150/30 + 200/60) / 2 = 350/90 / 2 = 175/45							

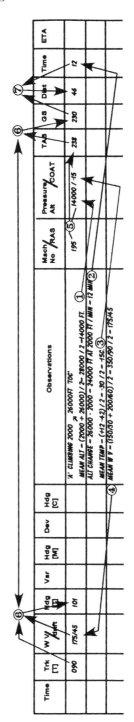

Fig. 17–15a The log sheet, the climb entries

Fig. 17–15b The log sheet, the climb entries showing the sequence of the calculations

different methods. These are described in paragraphs 17.17 to 17.20 along with the symbols used to identify them, by type, on the chart. Fixes should always have the applicable time marked beside them on the chart.

TYPES OF FIX

17.17   Visual observation whilst map reading (visual fixes are known as **pinpoints** and are marked on the chart with a dot surrounded by a small circle). It is easier to obtain visual pinpoints at lower altitudes than at high level. Pinpointing requires good visibility and a clear field of view to the ground directly beneath the aircraft, cloud and the restricted downward view from the flight deck of most modern airliners make obtaining visual pinpoints from high altitude almost impossible. Nonetheless pinpoints are sometimes given in training and examination plotting questions, often as a starting point. Candidates should mark the position accurately with the pinpoint symbol and the time of the fix beside it. (see Fig.17–16)

$$1728 \; \odot$$

Fig. 17–16   The Pinpoint symbol (with its applicable time noted beside it).

17.18   A radar fix , as a range and bearing 'to' or 'from' a ground feature displayed on the radar screen. To plot the radar fix the ground feature has to be located on the chart and the bearing plotted 'from' it crossed by the range P/L. Radar fixes are denoted by a cross surrounded by a small circle with the time of the fix beside it. In plotting questions radar fixes are given with Time, Range and Bearing 'to' or 'from' an identified (by lat and long) ground feature . If the bearing given is 'from' the ground feature this is the bearing to plot. If the bearing given is 'to' the ground feature the bearing to plot is the reciprocal of the given bearing (i.e. 'to' brg + or – 180° = 'from' brg). (See Fig. 17–17). Radar signals follow GC paths and the rules for plotting GC brgs must be applied for the type of chart in use. This is especially true at high lats and for long radar ranges.

Fig. 17–17   The Radar Fix symbol (with its applicable time noted beside it).

17.19   A simultaneous fix from two P/Ls crossing at (or very close to) 90°. One example of this type of fix was given in paragraph 17.8 and Fig. 17–7 where a brg and range were obtained at the same time from a co-located VOR / DME. A simultaneous fix can also be obtained from sources that are not co-located provided the P/Ls cross at or near to 90° at the time they are obtained. The selection of the best stations to inter-rogate in order to obtain a simultaneous fix requires knowledge of the current DR position of the aircraft in relation to the ground stations in the area. The rough rule-of-thumb for finding the DR position (see para. 17.3) is accurate enough for this purpose. Simultaneous fixes are marked on the chart by plotting the two P/Ls and drawing a small circle round the fix position where the lines cross. The time is recorded against *each* posi-tion line *and* the fix. (see Fig. 17–18) Even though in this case it may seem like overkill, writing the relevant time beside *every* item on the plot is a very good habit to get into. Without time tags to identify their place in the sequence of events, fixes, DR positions and P/Ls become almost mean-ingless and the task of trying to make plotting sense of them almost impossible. The same applies to marking trks and WV vectors with their appropriate arrows.

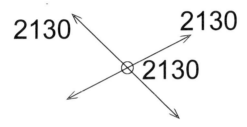

Fig. 17–18   A simultaneous fix with brg P/Ls from two widely separated ground station.

17.20   A running fix made up of P/Ls obtained at different times; the earlier P/Ls being transferred forward (using DR trk and GS) to the time of the later P/L to give a fix for the time of the later P/L. The principle behind this transferring concept is as if the earlier P/Ls are being carried forward on the aircraft's back, along trk at GS for a given time interval. The ideal running fix is made up of three P/Ls which cut each other at approximately 60°. The origin of this type of fix is a nautical one. The rec-iprocals of three well spaced out brgs taken as a ship sails past a prominent feature (such as a lighthouse, island or headland) being plotted on a chart as P/Ls radiating from the feature's position. The earlier P/Ls are then moved forward (at the ship's equivalent of DR trk and GS) to the time of the last P/L. The result (in a perfect world) being three P/Ls all passing through the same point to fix the ship's position at the time of the last P/L. (see Fig. 17–19) *Note that the transferred P/Ls are annotated with double arrow-heads and are given the time they have been transferred to.*

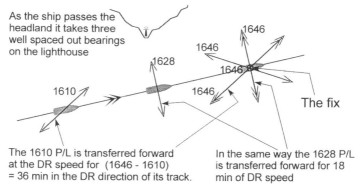

Fig. 17–19   A running fix, the nautical origin.

Two factors can upset the conditions for an ideal running fix:

The accuracy of the brgs taken.

The actual direction and speed of movement of the ship being slightly different from the estimated values used in transferring the P/Ls.

As a result of such error inputs the three P/Ls may produce a small triangle known as a 'cocked hat'. In such cases the centre of the triangle is taken as the fix position thus averaging out the errors. (see Fig. 17–20)

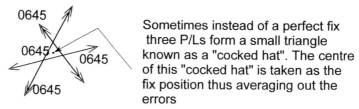

Fig. 17–20   The 'Cocked Hat' fix.

The principle of the running fix can be applied in aviation plotting with the P/Ls being obtained when in transit past a ground station such as a VOR or an NDB. Furthermore, provided the bearings are at, or around, 60° to each other a running fix can be made up from P/Ls obtained from a mixture of sources. (see Fig. 17–21) 'Cocked Hat' fixes also occur in aviation plotting for similar reasons to those mentioned for the shipping fix.

In the example in Fig. 17–21 note how the final fix does not lie on the DR trk. Since the fix is an *actual* position and the DR trk only an *estimated* trk this often happens during a plot and is no cause for alarm. When transferring, as long as a P/L is moved in the *direction* of the DR trk at the DR GS, it will finish up in the right place to give a reasonable fix

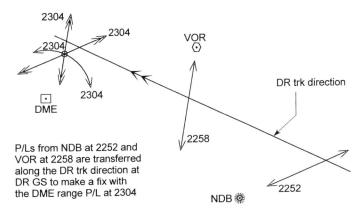

Fig. 17–21   An airborne running fix from mixed sources.

(when combined with other P/Ls) even if the DR trk is displaced well to one side of the actual TMG. A case in point is the transferring of a DME range P/L which is a curve, being the arc of a circle centred on the ground position of the DME station. The only way such a range P/L can be transferred forward is by moving the whole circle in the direction of the DR trk at DR GS for the appropriate time. A construction line is drawn *from* the DME station *in the **direction** of the DR trk* and the station transferred forward *at the DR GS* to the time of the last P/L, the range circle being redrawn from the transferred station to give the transferred range P/L. (See Fig. 17–22)

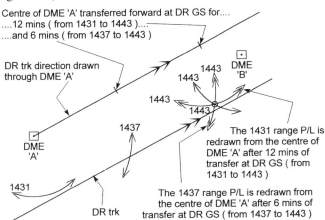

Fig. 17–22   An airborne running fix from DME stations.

EXAMINATION PLOT

17.21   An examination plot can never be the same as a plot carried out in the air. In the air it is the task of the plotter to get the information needed and also to select which aids to interrogate at any time. In examinations all the plotting information is presented in one go. The candidate has to take this tabulated mass of information and break it into a series of manageable packets. Reading through an examination plotting paper reveals key items of information:

The start point of the plot. Is it an actual position or is it a DR position?
Cruising levels and speeds. Do they change at any point?
Forecast WVs and temperatures.
Is a Climb and / or a Descent to be worked out at any point?
Fixes which have to be plotted. What types are they?
WVs which have to be calculated.
DR positions to be plotted (for alteration of hdg or the assessment of conv).
Alterations of hdg and revision of ETA to be calculated.
Possible pilot navigation requirements.

17.22   The way to approach a plotting examination is to treat it as a series of separate problems that are linked to each other in a string, the most up-to-date information being carried forward from one step to the next in the sequence. This may be modified where examiners find it necessary to ensure that all candidates use the same inputs for a particular plotting process. In such cases instructions will be given in the question paper as to what specific values are to be used in place of information resolved in the previous step. The key to successful plotting is to be methodical. Work towards understanding the processes and *concentrate on accuracy in the first instance.* Speed will come with practise and experience. Newcomers to plotting who try for speed before acquiring accuracy invariably have troubles with the subject. A well proven sequence to follow is:

Record on the log sheet all the given starting information and plot on the chart the applicable starting point (fix or DR position) with its time beside it.
Having got the start plotted, read ahead only as far as the next major item on the plot.
Compute and plot all the elements to solve this first stage.
Where possible update information (such as WV, TMG, GS, ETA etc.) resulting from completion of the first stage.
Read ahead to the next major item and repeat the process using the most up-to-date information.
Repeat to the end of the plot, remembering to maintain the log and annotate all items on the chart with their correct symbols and times.

17.23   The plot which now follows sets out to use as many aspects of plotting as possible in one exercise. To achieve the maximum number of variables in this plot it has been necessary to select aids which best illustrate plotting methods rather than the more practical options that would be used on a real flight. Also included is some pilot navigation of the type commonly used on airways flying. (see Chapter 7, para. 7.23 and Figs 7–27a, b and c) Questions involving pilot navigation do not as a rule require anything to be plotted on the chart, the log entries usually suffice. Candidates should be on the lookout for any pilot navigation question(s) within the examination plot, if they are not recognised for the simple thing that they are, a lot of time can be wasted on unnecessary plotting.

DEMONSTRATION PLOT

17.24 Candidates will need the following plotting instruments:

Navigation Computer. This must be of the circular slide rule type and not a programmed electronic type (not allowed in examinations).
Straight-edge.
Protractor (square plotter type).
Dividers.
Compasses (continually changing round combined dividers / compasses can waste time in an examination, it is advisable to have one of each).
Pencils (HB for the log and 2H or 3H for the chart work). It is a good idea to have a supply of sharpened pencils to hand *before* the examination starts, sharpening pencils after the examination starts wastes precious time.
Pencil sharpener. Just in case.
Eraser.

The demonstration plot that follows is carried out on a Lambert's projection chart with no airways overlay. The chart is reproduced within this publication with the kind permission of the Aeronautical Charts section of the United Kingdom Civil Aviation Authority. The fact that it is not the current Jeppersen chart is not important, what is important is to learn the procedures used and the method of log keeping. Start slowly and aim for accuracy, speed will come once accuracy is acquired.

THE INFORMATION

An aircraft is en route tracking from 'F' (6400N 2200W) to 'M' (5800N 0625W), hdg 122 (T), FL235, temp -35C, RAS 260 kn, DR GS 403 kn.

1310   DR Position 6328N 2015W
1313   VOR 'G' (6400N 1702W) QDM 078
1322   DME 'G' range 73 nm
1331   VOR 'E' (6530N 1400W) QDR 212
        What is the fix position at 1331?

1352 NDB 'H' brs 298 RBI (hdg 122 (T))
1358 Ground D/F station 'L' (5900N 0300W) passes QTE 293
1404 VOR 'M' (5800N 0625W) 153 'TO'
What is the fix position at 1404?
What is the mean WV since 1331?
1410 DR position alter hdg for 'M'
What is the hdg (M) to steer?
What is the ETA at 'M'?
1417 Doppler drift and GS, 4S, 425 kn.
1425 Pinpoint overhead 'M'. Alter hdg for 'I' (6030N 0100W), FL230, use
WV 020 / 60, temp -30°C, RAS 263 kn.
What is the hdg (M) to steer?
What is the ETA at 'I'?
1451 NDB 'M' brs 183 RBI
NDB 'I' brs 005 RBI
Alter hdg direct for 'I'
What is the new hdg (T)?
1455 DME 'I' range 60 nm.
What is the revised GS and ETA at 'I'?
1506 Overhead 'I' alter hdg for 'J' (6230N 0600E), FL230, use WV 030 /
50, temp -30°C, RAS 263 kn
What is the hdg (M) to steer?
What is the ETA at 'J'?
1515 Message received. 'The aircraft is to descend to arrive at 5000 ft
overhead 'J', the descent is to be at 1000 ft per minute and the start
of the descent is to be delayed to the latest time that will achieve this
objective. WV at 5000 ft at 'J' is 350 / 30 temp + 10° C. Mean TAS
for the descent 240 kn.'
What is the position of the Top of Descent (TOD)?
What is the ETA at TOD?
What is the hdg (M) for the descent?
What is the revised ETA for overhead 'J' at 5000 ft?

PROCEDURE FOR THIS PLOT

17.25 From the information at the start and at 1310:

In the first line of the log enter 1310 in the **Time** column and in the **Observations**
space enter the DR position information. The appropriate given information is
entered in the **RAS, Press Alt/temp** and **GS** columns. The TAS is now calculated
on the navigation computer and entered in the **TAS** column. In this case a
compressibility correction is necessary as the initial TAS > 300 kn. (see Chapter
4, para. 4.7)

The trk from 'F' to 'M' is drawn on the chart and annotated with two arrows in the direction of movement.

The DR position for 1310 is plotted on the chart and indicated with a triangle symbol. The time 1310 is marked on the chart beside the DR position. To plot a given position accurately on a chart with curved parallels and straight meridians use a straight edge to draw in the meridian through the position first, the required latitude can then be measured along this meridian with the aid of dividers and the latitude scale.

17.26   Reading ahead. At 1313, 1322 and 1331 information about three P/Ls is given followed by a request for the position at 1331. This must be calculated and plotted before proceeding beyond 1331:

ENTER 1313 in the **Time** column of the second line on the log form and in the **Observations** space enter the source of the information and what it is.

Carry out the calculations to enable the P/L to be plotted (in this case QDM converted to QTE, see para. 17.5).

Plot the P/L, mark the ends with single arrow-heads to signify it is a P/L and write the time (**1313**) beside it.

This P/L has to be transferred forward in the *direction* of the DR trk (i.e. in the *direction* of the plotted trk from 'F' to 'M') at the DR GS from 1313 to 1331, a period of 18 min. The **GS**, **Dist** and **Time Min** columns are used in calculating and recording the distance the P/L is to be transferred. The process of transferring this P/L is dealt with at the fix time of 1331.

If more than one line is needed to complete the calculations in the **Observations** space mark the **Time** column with a tick to show the information applies to the time above the tick.

ENTER 1322 in the **Time** column of the next line of the log form and in the **Observations** space enter the information details.

Since this is a range from a DME station no calculations are needed prior to plotting the range P/L.

Plot the range P/L (in the region of the DR trk) as the arc of a circle of radius the range from the DME. Mark with P/L arrows and the time (**1322**).

This P/L has to be transferred forward in the *direction* of the DR trk (i.e. in the *direction* of the plotted trk from 'F' to 'M') at the DR GS from 1322 to 1331, a period of 9 min. The **GS**, **Dist** and **Time Min** columns are used in calculating and recording the distance the P/L is to be transferred. The process of transferring this range P/L is dealt with at the fix time of 1331.

ENTER 1331 in the **Time** column of the next line of the log form and in the **Observations** space enter the information details.

Carry out the calculations to enable the P/L to be plotted, in this case QDR converted to QTE (see para. 17.5).

Plot the P/L, mark the ends with single arrow-heads to signify it is a P/L and write the time (**1331**) beside it.

TRANSFER THE 1313 P/L TO 1331. From where the 1313 P/L crosses the DR trk measure the calculated transfer distance forward along the DR trk and put a mark. The transferred P/L must pass through this point and be parallel to the 1313 P/L. With the point of a (sharp) pencil on the transfer mark bring the square plotting protractor up against it and rotate the protractor until the squared grid lines lie parallel over the top of the 1313 P/L. The edge of the protractor is now parallel to the 1313 P/L and passing through the transfer mark ready for the transferred P/L to be drawn along it. Draw the line and mark its ends with double arrows to indicate it is a transferred P/L and give it the time it has been transferred to (**1331** in this case).

TRANSFER THE 1322 RANGE P/L TO 1331. Unlike the 1313 straight P/L the 1322 P/L is part of a circle and to transfer it requires the centre of the circle (the DME station) to be moved in the *direction* of the DR trk at the DR GS and the arc of the circle redrawn from the transferred centre. The square plotting protractor is used to draw a line parallel to the DR trk from the centre of the DME station and the calculated transfer distance is marked off down this line from the DME station. From this mark the original range arc is redrawn to give the transferred range position line (mark its ends with double arrows and give it the transferred time of **1331**).

THE FIX AT 1331. In the ideal case the original 1331 P/L and the two transferred P/Ls should all cross at a common point giving a perfect fix. Errors in plotting sometimes result in a 'cocked hat' (see para. 17.20) in which case the centre of the triangle should be taken to be the fix position.

ENTER THE 1331 FIX position in the log and underline <u>**1331**</u> in the **Time** column to indicate a fix at that time.

Fig. 17–23 shows the logsheet entries (reduced in size to fit the page) and a corner of the chart with the plot so far.

17.27 Reading ahead the next items are P/Ls at 1352, 1358 and 1404 and a fix to be found at 1404. *Note that there was nothing about finding a WV or TMG at 1331. This is because there is no definite position information available prior to 1331, only an estimated DR position at 1310. A TMG, GS or WV can only be found between established fixes, **NEVER** between (an estimated) DR position and (an actual) fix.*

ENTER 1352 in the **Time** column of the next line of the log form and in the **Observations** space enter the information details.

Carry out the calculations to enable the P/L to be plotted. The procedure for converting and plotting an RBI brg of an NDB transmission is to be found at para. 17.7. In this case the DR position at 1352 is in the region of the 12W meridian and the square plotting protractor is used to draw a line parallel to the 12W meridian through the position of NDB 'H' to give the transferred meridian from which the P/L is to be plotted.

Plot the P/L from the transferred meridian and label with the P/L arrows and the time (**1352**).

Time	Trk [T]	W V/drift	Hdg [T]	Var	Hdg [M]	Dev	Hdg [C]	Observations	Mac/No /RAS	Pressure Alt /COAT	TAS	GS	Dist	Time	ETA
1310			122					△ 6328N 2015W	260	23 500 / -35	385	403			
1313								VOR 'G' QDM 078 + 180 = QDR 258							
								- 19W VAR = QTE 239 PLOT							
1322								DME 'G' RNG 73 NM PLOT				✓	121	18	
1331								VOR 'E' QDR 212 -18W VAR = QTE 194 PLOT				✓	60,5	9	
								✕ 6212N 1540W							
✓															

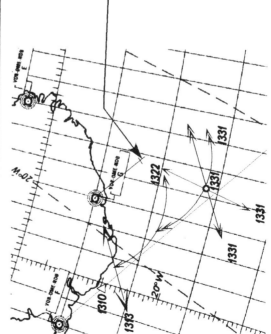

Construction for transfer of the 1322 DME range P/L from 'G' by DR trk (direction) and GS

Fig. 17–23   Demonstration plot, the fix at 1331

237

This P/L has to be transferred from 1352 to 1404, a time interval of 12 min. Calculate and log the details as before.

ENTER 1358 in the **Time** column of the next line of the log form and in the **Observations** space enter the information details.
Since this is a QTE it can be plotted from N (T) at 'L' with no further calculations required. Mark with the P/L arrows and the time (**1358**).
This P/L has to be transferred from 1358 to 1404, a time interval of 6 min. Calculate and log the details as before.

ENTER 1404 in the **Time** column of the next line of the log form and in the **Observations** space enter the information details.
Carry out the calculations to enable the P/L to be plotted. Whenever a VOR brg is given as 'TO' it is a QDM and if given as 'FROM' it is a QDR (in both cases based on N (M) at the station). This is a similar calculation to the one at 1313, (note that the varn at 'M' is 11W, three-quarters of the way between the 8W and the 12W isogonals on the chart).
Plot the P/L and mark with the P/L arrows and the time (**1404**).

TRANSFER THE 1352 and 1358 P/Ls TO 1404 . The method is the same as used to transfer the 1313 P/L to 1331. Be sure to move the 1352 P/L for 12 min of DR GS and the 1358 P/L for only 6 min of DR GS.

ENTER THE 1404 FIX POSITION in the log and underline <u>1404</u> in the **Time** column.

17.28 At 1404 as well as the fix position the question also wanted the WV since 1331. The 1331 fix and the 1404 fix are both *actual* positions. Since a steady hdg and TAS has been maintained between these two fixes it is a reasonable assumption that a steady TMG and GS have also been maintained between them and these can be extracted from the plot.

DRAW A STRAIGHT LINE joining the 1331 fix to the 1404 fix and extend this line some distance beyond the 1404 fix (the reason for this will be seen later). This is the TMG from 1331 to 1404, mark it with the trk double arrow pointing *from* the 1331 fix *to* the 1404 fix.

MEASURE THE TMG direction from the meridian half way between the two fixes and enter this information in the **Observations** space of the log.

MEASURE THE DISTANCE between the two fixes and enter this information in the **Observations** space of the log along with the time interval between the two fixes.

COMPUTE THE GS from this distance and time interval using the navigation computer (see Chapter 4, para. 4.14) and enter this under the **GS** column.

Fig. 14–24 shows the logsheet entries from 1358 to 1404 (reduced in size to fit the page) and the relevant part of the chart.

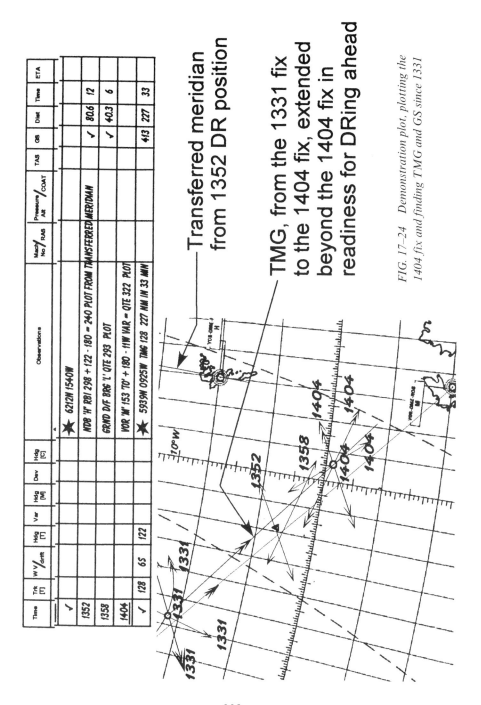

Time	Trk [T]	W V /drift	Hdg [T]	Var	Hdg [M]	Dev	Hdg [C]		Observations		Mach/ No / RAS	Pressure Alt / COAT	TAS	GS	Dist	Time	ETA
	✓								6212N 1540W	★							
1352									NDB 'H' RBI 298 + 122 - 180 - 240 PLOT FROM TRANSFERRED MERIDIAN					✓	80.6	12	
1358									GRMD D/F BRG 'L' QTE 293 PLOT					✓	40.3	6	
1404									VOR 'W' 153 70' + 180 - 11W VAR – QTE 322 PLOT								
	✓	65	122						5939N 0925W TMG 128 227 NM IN 33 MIN	★				413	227	33	

Transferred meridian from 1352 DR position

TMG, from the 1331 fix to the 1404 fix, extended beyond the 1404 fix in readiness for DRing ahead

FIG. 17–24 Demonstration plot, plotting the 1404 fix and finding TMG and GS since 1331

All the elements are now available to enable the WV to be found on the navigation computer by the trk and GS method. (see Chapter 5, para. 5.11)

COMPUTE THE WV from hdg, TAS, TMG and GS. Enter this WV in both the **Observations** space and the **WV/drift** column.

17.29 The next item on the question paper is at 1410 asking for an alteration of hdg and revised ETA for 'M'. This involves establishing the DR position at 1410, plotting and measuring the required trk and distance from there to 'M' and finally the computation of hdg, GS, time and ETA.

PLOT THE DR POSITION FOR 1410. As the same hdg and TAS is being flown between 1404 and 1410 as was being flown between 1331 and 1404 it can reasonably be assumed that the TMG and GS will be the same in both cases. On this assumption extension of the TMG (from 1331 to 1404) beyond 1404 to 1410 at the GS found will give the DR position for 1410. Mark the position on the chart with the triangular DR symbol and the time (**1410**).

ENTER 1410 in the **Time** column of the next line of the log form and put a DR triangle symbol in the **Observations** space and the words **ALTER HDG FOR 'M'**.

DRAW A LINE FROM THE DR POSITION TO 'M' and mark it with the double arrow trk symbol pointing towards 'M'. This is the DR trk to reach 'M'.

MEASURE this DR trk direction and distance and enter their values in the **Trk (T)** and **Dist** columns on the 1410 line of the log. Read the mean varn for this trk from the chart and enter it into the **Var** column. Ticks may also be put in the **WV/drift** and **TAS** columns of the 1410 line to indicate no change to their values since the last entry.

COMPUTE HDG (T) AND GS using the navigation computer (see Chapter 5, para. 5.14) and enter the results in the **Hdg (T)** and **GS** columns on the 1410 line of the log. Apply the varn to the hdg (T) to give the hdg (M) and enter this value into the **Hdg (M)** column on the same line.

COMPUTE THE TIME TO GO from the distance to go and the GS (see Chapter 4, para. 4.14) and enter the value in the **Time Min** column on the 1410 line of the log. Add this time to 1410 to give the ETA at 'M', enter it in the **ETA** column.

Fig. 17–25 shows the logsheet entries for 1410 (reduced in size to fit the page) and the relevant part of the chart.

17.30 The Doppler drift and GS at 1417 is used to confirm the calculation of trk (hdg (T) + S Doppler drift) and GS from the 1410 DR position to 'M'. At 1425 the question indicates that the aircraft is fixed as being overhead 'M', with instructions to alter hdg for 'I'. There are changes to the FL, WV, temperature and RAS. In effect all the previous calculations can be ignored from this point on, and a completely new start made.

Time	Trk [T]	W V/drift	Hdg [T]	Var	Hdg [M]	Dev	Hdg [C]	Observations	Mach No/RAS	Pressure Alt/COAT	TAS	GS	Dist	Time	ETA
✓		000/ 52						WV 000 / 52							
1410	146	✓	142	12W	154			△ ALTER HDG FOR 'M'			✓	426	105	15	1425
1417								DOPPLER DRIFT 4S, GS 425 KN CHECKS OUT							

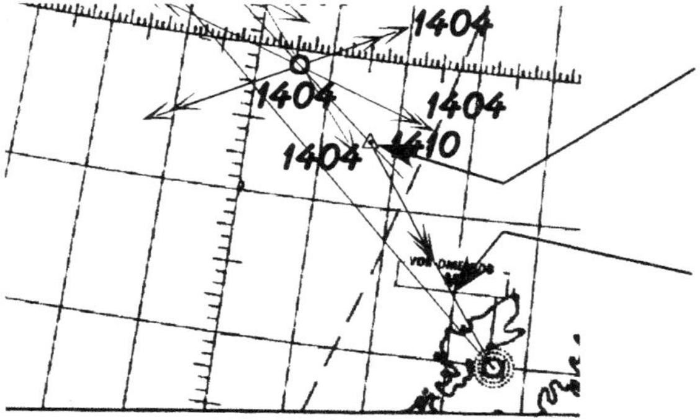
1404
1404
1404
1404
1410
1410 DR position found by plotting down the extended TMG for 6 min of the mean GS between the 1331 and 1404 fixes.
New DR trk and distance from the 1410 DR position to 'M'.

Fig. 17–25 DRing ahead and altering hdg for 'M'

ENTER 1425 in the **Time** column of the next line on the log sheet and in the **Observations** space put a pinpoint symbol (a dot with a small circle round it) and the words **'M' ALTER HDG FOR 'I'**. In their appropriate columns enter the new WV, RAS, FL (Pressure Altitude) and temperature. Compute the new TAS (see Chapter 4, para. 4.7, RAS to TAS where TAS > 300 kn) and enter it in the **TAS** column.

DRAW IN THE TRK FROM 'M' TO 'I' on the chart and mark it with the double arrow trk symbol pointing towards 'I'. Read the mean varn for this trk from the chart and enter it into the **Var** column on the 1425 line of the log.

MEASURE the trk direction and distance from 'M' to 'I' and enter their values in the **Trk (T)** and **Dist** columns on the 1425 line of the log.

COMPUTE HDG (T) AND GS using the navigation computer (see Chapter 5, para. 5.14) and enter the results in the **Hdg (T)** and **GS** columns on the 1425 line of the log. Apply the varn to the hdg (T) to give the hdg (M) and enter this value into the **Hdg (M)** column on the same line.

COMPUTE THE TIME TO GO from the distance to go and the GS (see Chapter 4, para. 4.14) and enter the value in the **Time** column on the 1410 line of the log. Add this time to 1425 to give the ETA at 'I', enter it in the **ETA** column.

17.31   At 1451 the RBI shows a back brg of 183° relative on the NDB at 'M' and a forward brg of 005° relative on the NDB at 'I' with instructions to alter hdg directly towards 'I'. This is pure pilot navigation and requires nothing to be plotted on the chart. The reciprocal of the back bearing will give the relative TMG from 'M' and the forward brg the relative required trk to 'I'. The angular difference from the relative TMG to the relative required trk gives the required change of hdg (in degrees) and the direction (Port or Starboard) of that change.

ENTER 1451 in the **Time** column of the next line on the log sheet and in the **Observations** space write **NDB 'M' 183 RBI + 044 -180 = 047 TMG**. On the next line of the **Observations** space write **NDB 'I' 005 RBI + 044 = 049 REQ TRK**. TMG to req trk = 2 S On the next line of the Observations space write **Alter hdg 2S for 'I'**. Enter **046** into the **Hdg (T)** column.

17.32   At 1455 a DME range gives distance to go to 'I' and a GS check and revision of ETA at 'I' is asked for. Subtract distance to go from total length of leg to give distance gone. Subtract start time of leg from 1455 to give time gone. From distance gone and time gone the GS can be computed. From GS and distance to go the time to go can be computed and added to 1455 to give the revised ETA.

ENTER 1455 in the **Time** column of the next line of the log sheet and in the **Observations** space write **DME 'I' rng 60 nm**. On the next line in the Observations space write **224 – 60 = 164 nm gone in 30 min = 328 kn GS**. Enter **328** in the **GS** column and **60** in the **Dist** column.

Time	Trk [T]	W/V /drift	Hdg [T]	Var	Hdg [M]	Dev	Hdg [C]	Observations	Mach No/RAS	Pressure Alt /COAT	TAS	GS	Dist	Time	ETA
1425	048	020/60	044	11W	055			⊙ 'M' ALTER HDG FOR 'I'	263	23 000 /-30	371	320	224	42	1507
1451	✓							NDB 'M' 183 RBI +044 -180 = 047 TMG							
	✓		046					NDB 'I' 005 RBI +044 = 049 REQ TRK							
	✓							ALTER HDG 2S FOR 'I' PILOT NAVIGATION							
1455	✓							DME 'I' RNG 60 NM							
	✓							224 - 60 = 164 NM GONE IN 30 MIN = 328 KM GS			328		60	11	1506

Apart from plotting the trk from 'M' to 'I' there is no need for further plotting on this leg as all the working is by pilot navigation. Even the DME rng from 'I' at 1455 need not be plotted even though it is shown here.

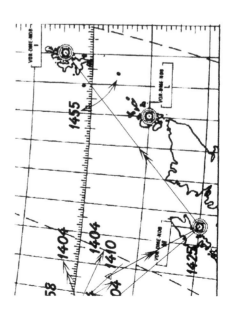

Figure 17–26 Pilot Navigation Leg.

243

COMPUTE THE TIME TO GO from the distance to go and the GS and enter the time in the **Time** column. Add the time to 1455 to give the ETA which is entered in the **ETA** column.

Fig. 17–26 shows the logsheet entries from 1425 to 1455 (reduced in size to fit the page) and the relevant part of the chart.

17.33   At 1506 the aircraft is overhead 'I' and altering hdg for 'J'. RAS, FL and temperature are unchanged (therefore TAS is also unchanged). There is a new WV given and the trk will have to be plotted and its direction and distance measured. Entries in the log follow the same pattern as at the start of the previous leg as do the calculations of hdg, GS and ETA. Figure 17.27 shows the logsheet entries for 1506 (reduced in size to fit the page) and the relevant part of the chart.

17.34   The instructions at 1515 mean that a descent has to be calculated to arrive at 5000 ft over 'J', delaying the start of the descent till the last possible moment. At this point candidates may wish to refer back to paragraphs 17.9 to 17.12 (which covered both climbs and descents) to refresh their memories before proceeding. A run through information shows that there is available:

Altitude at the cruising level (i.e. TOD).
Altitude at bottom of the descent.
The rate of descent in ft / min.
WV and temperature at the cruising level (i.e. TOD).
WV and temperature at the bottom of the descent.
Mean RAS for the descent.
The trk (T) for the descent (the same as the cruise trk (T)).

From this information the following can be calculated and computed:

Mean altitude for the descent (by averaging the altitudes at the top and bottom of the descent).
Total change of altitude in the descent (by subtracting the bottom of descent altitude from the TOD altitude).
Time taken on the descent (total change of altitude / rate of descent).
Mean WV and temperature for the descent (by averaging the WV and temperatures at the top and bottom of the descent).
Mean TAS for the descent (from mean altitude, temperature and RAS).
Mean hdg (T) and mean GS for the descent (from trk (T), mean WV and mean TAS).
Mean hdg (M) for the descent (applying local varn to hdg (T)).
Distance covered on the descent (from mean GS and time taken on the descent).
TOD (by plotting distance covered on the descent from 'J' back along the trk towards 'I').
ETA at TOD (by subtracting distance on the descent from the total leg distance 'I'

Time	Trk [T]	W V/drift	Hdg [T]	Var	Hdg [M]	Dev	Hdg [C]	Observations	Mach No/RAS	Pressure Alt/COAT	TAS	GS	Dist	Time	ETA
1506	058	030/50	054					O/H "I" ALTER HDG FOR "J"	263	23 00 / -30	371	326	234	43	1549

This is a straightforward plotting of the required trk, measuring the direction and distance and then computer work to solve hdg, GS, time and ETA

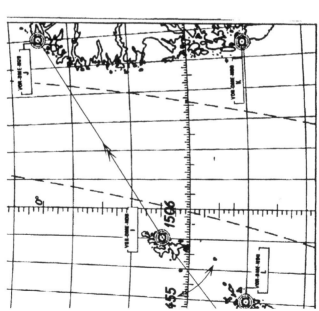

Fig. 17–27 Computing the leg 'I' to 'J'.

to 'J' to give distance from 'I' to TOD and then compute the time from 'I' to TOD at the cruising GS).

Revised ETA at 5000 ft overhead 'J' (by adding the descent time to the ETA at TOD).

Fig. 17–28 shows the logsheet entries for this (reduced in size to fit the page) and the relevant part of the chart. Note how a line was left below the 1506 line (for the calculation of the ETA at the TOD) before the descent calculations were carried out. The whole process is in fact much simpler than the rather long explanation makes it look. The secret is to be methodical and keep an organised log, plus plenty of practice. And practice is something every good pilot knows about.

17.35 Figs. 17–29 and 17–30 on pages 260 and 261 show the complete logsheet and chart for the exercise just described. Both are shown smaller than actual size to allow them to fit the page without folding.

17.36 Finally there are two types of peripheral questions that get introduced into plotting examination questions from time to time. These involve asking for:

The information to be expected from a specified ground-based radio aid when at a given position.

The maximum reception range of information from a ground-based radio aid.

In themselves these are not true plotting items but are used by the examiners to check out a candidate's, knowledge of the practical use of radio aids:

An example of the first case above would have been to ask for the QDR from the VOR at 'K' (5902N 0530E) when the aircraft reached the calculated TOD on the demonstration plot. To do this plot the TOD and draw a line from 'K' through the TOD. Measure the angle of this line from N (T) at 'K' to give the QTE and apply the varn at the VOR to convert the QTE to the QDR. On the plot the QTE is 342, varn at 'K' 4W gives **QDR 346.**

An example of the second case above would have been to ask for the long of the earliest time that a brg could be expected to be to be received from the VOR at 'M' while on the leg cruising from 'F' to 'M'. To do this the formula for calculating the maximum range of a line-of-sight radio transmission has to be remembered from the Radio Aids syllabus.

Maximum Range (nm) = $1·25 (\sqrt{h1} + \sqrt{h2})$.
Where:
h1 = height of ground transmitter (ft amsl).
h2 = altitude of the aircraft (ft amsl).

Time	Trk [T]	W V/drift	Hdg [T]	Var	Hdg [M]	Dev	Hdg [C]	Observations	Mach No/RAS	Pressure Alt/COAT	TAS	GS	Dist	Time	ETA
1506	058	030/50	054					O/H 'I' ALTER HDG FOR 'J'	263	23 00 / -30	371	326	234	43	1549
✓								'I' TO TOD 234 - 82 = 152 NM				✓	152	28	1534
1534		101 /40	052					△ TOD 23 000 ↘ 5000 FT	240	14 000 / -10	300	273	82	18	1552

Calculation of TOD position and ETA at TOD. Descent hdg, GS, distance and time plus revised ETA at 5000 ft overhead 'J'.

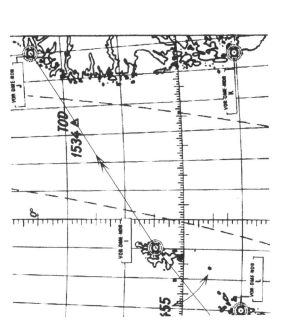

Fig. 17–28 Descent Calculations.

247

In the plot assuming the VOR is at sea level this gives:

Maximum Range (nm) $= 1\cdot25\,(\sqrt{0} + \sqrt{23\,500})$
$= 1\cdot25 \times 153\cdot3$
$= \mathbf{191\cdot6\ nm.}$

When plotted from 'M' back down the trk towards 'F' the maximum range of 191·6 nm cuts the trk at the **11W** meridian.

INTENTIONALLY BLANK

Time	Trk [T]	WV/drift	Hdg [T]	Var	Hdg [M]	Dev	Hdg [C]	Observations	Mach No/RAS	Pressure Alt/COAT	TAS	GS	Dist	Time	ETA
1310			122					△ 632BN 2015W	260	23 500 / -35	385	403			
1313								VOR 'G' QDM 078 + 180 = QDR 258				✓	121	18	
✓								-19W VAR = QTE 239 PLOT				✓	60,5	9	
1322								DME 'G' RNG 73 NM PLOT							
1331								VOR 'E' QDR 212 -18W VAR = QTE 194 PLOT							
✓								✳ 6312N 1540W							
1352								NDB 'H' RBI 298 + 122 - 180 = 240 PLOT FROM TRANSFERRED MERIDIAN					80.6	12	
1358								GRND D/F BRG 'L' QTE 293 PLOT					40.3	6	
1404	128	65	122					VOR 'W' 153 TO' + 180 -11W VAR = QTE 322 PLOT	263	23 000 / -30					
✓								✳ 5939N 0925W TMG 128 227 NM IN 33 MIN				413	227	33	1425
✓		000/52						WV 000/52							
1410	146	✓	142	12W	154			△ ALTER HDG FOR 'W'			✓	426	105	15	
1417								DOPPLER DRIFT 4S, GS 425 KN CHECKS OUT							
1425	048	020 060	044	11W	055			'W' ALTER HDG FOR 'Y'	263	23 000 / -30	371	320	224	42	1507
1451								NDB 'W' 183 RBI +044 -180 = 047 TMG							
✓							046	NDB 'Y' BRG 005 RBI +044 = 049 REQ TRK							
✓								ALTER HDG 25 FOR 'Y' PILOT NAVIGATION							
1455								DME 'Y' RNG 60 NM							
✓								224 - 60 = 164 NM GONE IN 30 MIN = 328 KN GS				328	60	11	1506
1506	058	030 50	054					O/H 'Y' ALTER HDG FOR 'J'	263	23 00 / -30	371	326	234	43	1549
✓								'J' TO TOD 234 - 82 = 152 NM				✓	152	28	1534
1534		101/40	052					△ TOD 23 000 × 5000 FT	240	14 000 / -10	300	273	82	18	1552

Fig. 17.29   Demonstration plot, the log

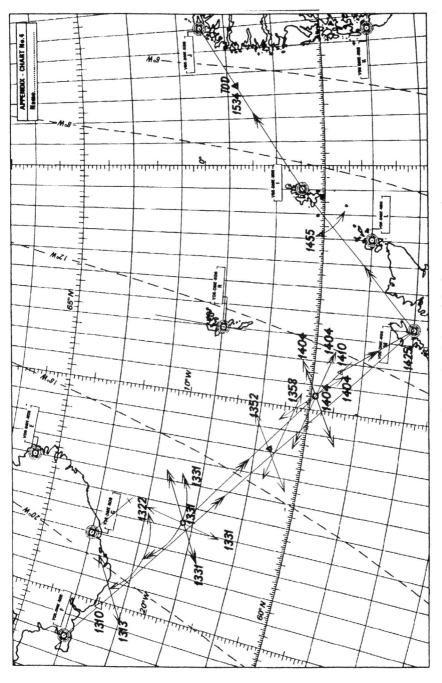

Fig. 17–30 The completed chart of the demonstration plot.

MAGNETISM
AND COMPASSES

The Earth possesses a weak magnetic field that has for many centuries been used by man as an aid to navigation, by using crude compasses to find direction. Unfortunately the Earth's magnetic field does not possess symmetry and is continually changing at a very slow but uneven rate, factors that were not critical when travel was slow and most journeys were of a local nature. As the speed of travel and distances covered have increased, more refined compass systems have been designed and for over a century the Earth's magnetic field has been continually monitored so that variation information on maps and charts can be kept up to date.

Modern theories of magnetism get into quantum physics, an area that is fine for scientists but not needed for practical piloting. Pilots need to have a working knowledge of the properties of magnetism and the magnetic compass systems used in aircraft, and it is these requirements that are to be found in this section.

CHAPTER 18

MAGNETISM AND EARTH MAGNETISM

18.1   Man has known of the existence of magnetic materials for thousands of years. Lumps of material (known as lodestone) that occurred in nature were observed to attract small iron objects, and, if suspended on a string or if placed on wood and floated on water, would swing round to take up a rough North/South alignment, producing a primitive form of compass.

18.2   Magnets come in many shapes and forms but they all exhibit a basic set of properties. For this part of the navigation syllabus it is necessary to study these properties but only to consider straight bar magnets. Like the circular slide rule (see Chapter 3, paragraph 3.6), where no knowledge of logarithms was needed, in the syllabus there is no need to delve into the theory of magnetism as long as the basic facts are known along with an understanding of how magnet materials react to each other.

18.3   Placing a piece of white card on a bar magnet and shaking iron filings onto the card will result in the filings making a pattern when the card is gently tapped or vibrated (see Fig. 18–1). The pattern taken up by the iron filings gives a visual picture of the lines of force generated by the magnetic field of the bar magnet. These lines of force can be seen to be

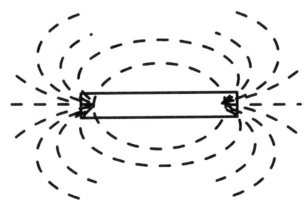

Fig. 18–1   Magnetic field of a bar magnet.

255

converging at two points located just inside the ends of the bar magnet; these two points are known as the POLES of the magnet. Magnetic poles cannot exist in isolation; they always come in pairs. If a bar magnet is cut in two, each piece will become a smaller (and weaker) bar magnet in its own right, each piece having two poles which are weaker than the original.

18.4 Certain conventions are ascribed to the poles and lines of magnetic force. To distinguish between the two poles one is labelled RED and the other BLUE. If a bar magnet suspended on a thread or mounted on a pivot is allowed to swing freely it will eventually settle down in a roughly North/South direction with the *same* pole always pointing in a Northerly direction. It is this North-seeking pole that is termed the RED pole, the other, South-seeking, pole being termed as the BLUE pole. The behaviour of magnets is such that it is apparent the lines of force have movement. This movement, by convention, is assumed to flow through the magnet from the blue pole to the red pole and through the space surrounding the magnet back into the blue pole (see Fig. 18–2).

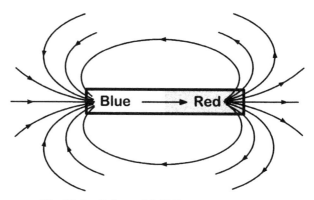

Fig. 18–2   Poles and field flow conventions.

Following these conventions, if two magnets are brought together so that their red poles are facing each other, the out-flowing lines of force will be in conflict and repulsion will be felt. Similarly, if two blue poles are brought towards each other the conflicting in-flowing lines of force will repel each other. However, if the red pole of one magnet is brought towards the blue pole of the other magnet, the flow of the lines of force will coincide and the two magnets will be drawn to each other. This gives rise to the rule that:

Like poles repel each other and **unlike poles attract** each other.

The strength of the repulsion and attraction force is strongest when the distance between the poles is small, the strength decreasing as the distance between the poles is increased. The rate of change of these forces is inversely proportional to the square of the distance between the poles of the two magnets.

18.5   The sensitivity, or magnetic moment, of a magnet depends on two factors, how physically far apart the red and blue poles of the magnet are and how magnetically strong are its poles. A given value of sensitivity can be obtained with either a long bar magnet with weak poles or a short bar magnet with strong poles. In magnetic compasses the magnets must be able rapidly to detect and align with the earth's weak magnetic field. This requires the magnets in the compass to have high sensitivity but low inertia, usually achieved by employing pairs of short magnets with high polar strength.

18.6   Very few materials possess magnetic properties. In fact, magnetism in any significant detectable strength is confined to ferrous materials, i.e. iron, steel and various alloys of steel. It is the magnetic properties of these ferrous materials that need to be understood.

18.7   Most ferrous materials have the potential to become magnetised. Some, classified as **HARD IRON**, require a great deal of work input to magnetise them, but once magnetised, will retain their magnetism for very long periods of time, measured in terms of years. Such magnetism is said to be *permanent* magnetism and occurs in steel alloys. Equally, 'hard' iron, once magnetised, requires an equal amount of work to demagnetise it. Other groups of ferrous material only exhibit magnetic properties when under the influence of an existing magnetic field, reverting to a non-magnetic state when removed from the influence of the magnetic field. Such ferrous material is classified as **SOFT IRON** and its magnetism as *induced* or *transient* magnetism; pure iron falls into this category. Obviously there are ferrous materials that lie between these two extremes and exhibit a mixture of these characteristics. Magnetism in these materials tends to decay with the passing of time, the rate of decay varying dependent on where it lies within the spectrum.

18.8   One explanation for these differences is that each molecule in the material is in its own right a tiny magnet. When the molecules are distributed in a random fashion throughout the material their individual magnetic fields cancel each other out (see Fig. 18–3a) and the material does not display an overall magnetic field. However, if the molecules are aligned

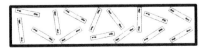

Fig. 18–3a   Random molecules, non-magnetised iron.   *Fig. 18–3b   Molecules aligned in sequence, magnetised iron.*

with their red poles all pointing in the same direction the individual fields become unified to create a large magnetic field (see Fig. 18–3b).

18.9   In the case of 'hard' iron one can imagine each molecule as only able to turn on a stiff and rusty pivot, so that getting the molecules to move from a random state to an aligned state (or vice versa) will require considerable effort. On the other hand imagine the 'soft' iron molecules as being mounted on frictionless pivots and each being held in a random fashion by its own very light coil spring. Placing a piece of 'soft' iron in the influence of a magnetic field will result in the molecules freely swinging round on their pivots to align with the influencing field; thus the whole becomes a magnet in its own right. Remove the influence and the coil springs will return each molecule to its random state and the 'soft' iron loses its overall magnetism.

18.10   Methods of magnetising 'hard' iron:
(a) Placing a 'hard' iron bar in the influence of an existing magnetic field and, without changing its alignment, subjecting it to vibration or hammering over a long period of time (see Fig.18–4). Each shock shakes the molecules, allowing them to turn slowly to align with the influencing field. The more the molecules turn, the stronger the magnetic field in the 'hard' iron bar will become. If the process is continued until all the molecules are aligned, the strength of the magnetic field in the 'hard' iron bar will be at its maximum and further vibration or hammering will have no effect; the material is then said to be *magnetically saturated*. Aircraft components made from 'hard' iron can have small amounts of permanent magnetism induced in them by the earth's magnetic field if subjected to vibration or hammering during manufacture.

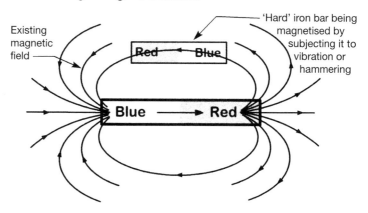

Fig. 18–4   Magnetising a 'hard' iron bar in an existing magnetic field.

(b) Placing a 'hard' iron bar on a flat non-magnetic surface and stroking it with one end of a strong magnet over and over again in the same direction (see Fig. 18–5). Each stroke will attract the opposite polarity of each molecule, pulling it slowly round into alignment with its fellow molecules to create a magnetic field in the iron bar – a truly slow and tedious method of magnetising a bar of 'hard' iron.

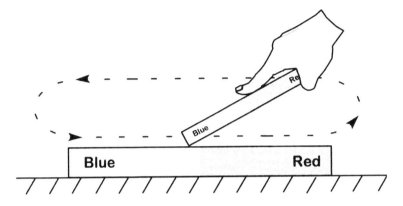

Fig. 18–5   Magnetising a 'hard' iron bar by stroking with a powerful magnet.

18.11 Methods of inducing magnetism in 'soft' iron:

(a) Placing the 'soft' iron bar in the influence of an existing magnetic field as in Fig. 18–4. In this case no vibration or hammering is needed. The 'soft' iron will automatically become magnetised, the polarity of the induced magnetism following the red, blue, red, blue sequence. If the 'soft' iron bar is now turned through 180° the original induced polarities will not go with the bar, the end that originally was red will now become blue and vice versa thus maintaining the red, blue, red, blue sequence. It is the existing magnetic field that dictates the polarity of the magnetism induced in the 'soft' iron.

(b) Winding a coil of wire around a rod of 'soft' iron and passing a direct electrical current through the wire (see Fig. 18–6). This method generates a magnetic field within the coil which can be controlled by the number of turns used on the coil and the direction and value of the voltage. Switching the direction of flow of current through the coil changes the direction of magnetic flow through the 'soft' iron rod, at the same time reversing the red and blue poles. By selecting a suitable voltage for the size of the rod and the number of turns on the coil it is possible to control the strength of the induced magnetism up to the magnetic saturation value. These last two properties are used in the detector units of remote-reading compasses (see Chapter 21).

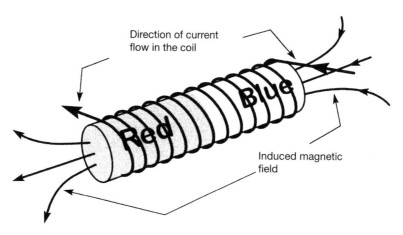

Fig. 18–6 Inducing transient magnetism in a 'soft' iron rod by means of passing a current through a coil.

18.12 Methods of de-magnetising 'hard' iron:

(a) Placing the 'hard' iron magnet in a strong magnetic field so that it lies at 90° to the field and subjecting it to shock by hammering for a long period of time.

(b) By heating the 'hard' iron magnet to around 900°C. Heating to this intensity causes the molecules to vibrate and lose their uniformity and on cooling they assume a random, non-magnetic, state.

Both of the above methods are destructive and totally unsuitable for de-magnetising precisely manufactured aircraft components or structures.

(c) Using a coil similar to that used to induce magnetism in 'soft' iron, only employing a varying alternating current to generate rapidly changing polarities which destabilise the alignment of the molecules in the 'hard' iron destroying the permanent magnetism. This process is known as degaussing and is non-destructive.

18.13 Methods of de-magnetising 'soft' iron:

(a) In the case of induced magnetism caused by an existing magnetic field, as in Paragraph 18.11(a), moving the 'soft' iron out of the influence of the said magnetic field will result in it losing its induced magnetism.

(b)   In the case of induced magnetism due to electrical current in a coil, as in para 18.11(b), switching the electrical current off will result in the 'soft' iron losing its induced magnetism.

18.14   The earth has a magnetic field which behaves as if a large but weak bar magnet were in its interior, and since it is the red pole of a freely suspended magnet that points towards N(M) it follows that by the accepted convention the N(M) pole must be a blue pole (see Fig. 18–7). Unfortunately, as well as being weak for its size, the axis of this hypothetical bar magnet does not coincide with the earth's spin axis nor does its centre coincide with the earth's centre. This means that as well as the N(M) and S(M) poles not coinciding with the N(T) and S(T) poles, they are not geographically opposite each other. The situation is further complicated by the fact that the magnetic field is not stationary within the earth and the positions of the magnetic poles are slowly moving around the true poles at a rate of somewhere in the region of once every 960 years. The N(M) pole is to be found in Canada in the region of 70°N 95°W and the S(M) pole in Antarctica in the region of 72°S 155°E.

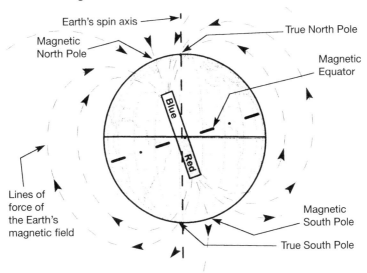

Fig. 18–7   The earth's magnetic field.

18.15   Not only are the lines of force of the earth's magnetic field out of alignment with the true North/South direction on the earth, and slowly changing as the magnetic poles move, they are also distorted in places due to ferrous deposits in the earth's crust. A freely suspended magnet of the type used in a compass will align itself with the direction of the earth's magnetic field at the point of measurement, which in most cases will not coincide with the direction of N(T). The angular difference between the direction of the local magnetic meridian (the one the needle lines up with) and the direction of the local true meridian is called **Magnetic Variation** or plain **Variation** (varn). Depending on location, the value of varn can range from 0° to 180°, the latter occurring at places along a line joining the N(T) and N(M) poles and again on a line joining S(T) and S(M) poles. Varn at a position is designated East or West depending on whether the magnetic meridian at the position lies East or West of the true meridian. How varn is shown on charts and the rules for applying varn to a magnetic direction to calculate the true direction are to be found in Chapter 2.

18.16 Referring back to Fig. 18–7 it can be seen that at the N(M) pole the lines of force of the earth's magnetic field are going into the earth at 90° to the local horizontal. Similarly, at the S(M) pole the force lines are coming out at 90° to the local horizontal. At both these places a freely suspended magnet would point straight up and down. Half way between the two magnetic poles it can be seen that the magnetic force lines are parallel to the local earth horizontal in a band all around the earth. This band is known as the **magnetic equator** and anywhere along it a freely suspended magnet would come to rest parallel to the earth horizontal. Moving from the magnetic equator towards either magnetic pole the lines of force can be seen to be entering the earth at an ever-increasing angle. In the North magnetic hemisphere the red pole of a freely suspended magnet will progressively **dip** down in line with the earth's field. The same will occur in the South magnetic hemisphere except it will be the blue pole of the magnet that will progressively dip down. Fig. 18–8 illustrates how the dip of the force field varies from the S(M) pole to the N(M) pole relative to the local horizontal. If **T** (the total force field) at each of these points is broken into its **H** (horizontal) and **Z** (vertical) components (see Fig. 18–9), it can be seen that the H component which defines the magnetic meridian, and to which

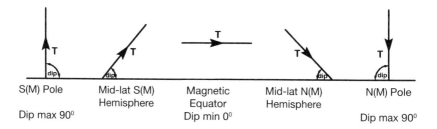

S(M) Pole	Mid-lat S(M) Hemisphere	Magnetic Equator	Mid-lat N(M) Hemisphere	N(M) Pole
Dip max 90⁰		Dip min 0⁰		Dip max 90⁰

Fig. 18–8   How the dip angle of T (the Total force of the earth's magnetic field) changes from the S(M) Pole to the N(M) Pole.

a magnetic compass tries to align, is strongest along the magnetic equator and has a zero value at both magnetic poles. In the region of both magnetic poles the H component is too small to permit the use of a magnetic compass to define direction in the horizontal plane, especially as the Z component, which is trying to pull the compass needle out of the horizontal, is strongest in these regions.

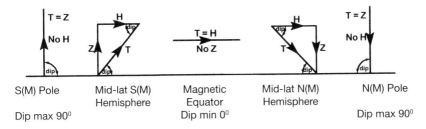

| S(M) Pole | Mid-lat S(M) Hemisphere | Magnetic Equator | Mid-lat N(M) Hemisphere | N(M) Pole |

Dip max 90⁰ ... Dip min 0⁰ ... Dip max 90⁰

Fig. 18-9   How the breakdown of T into H (the horizontal component) and Z (the vertical component) changes from the S(M) Pole to the N(M) Pole.

From the above: Z/T = Sine dip   H/T = Cosine dip   Z/H = Tangent dip

At a given magnet lat, knowing any two from T, H, Z or dip the other unknowns can be calculated. For most practical purposes T can be considered as a constant, and once known at one magnetic lat can be used to calculate H, Z or dip at any other magnetic lat where only one of these elements is known.

Example:
At a place in the magnetic N hemisphere H has a value of 0·6 and Z a value of 0·25, what is the dip angle and what is the value of T? What is the value of H at a place where dip is 49°?

Answer:
Z/H = tan dip   0·25/0·6 = tan dip   = 0·4167   **dip = 22° 37′**
H/T = cos dip   H/cos 22° 37′ = T   = 0·6/0·9233   **= T = 0·6498**
H/T = cos dip   T × cos 49° = H   = 0·6498 × 0·6561 **= H = 0·4580**

18.17   Unlike the lat and long grid used to define position, the magnetic elements do not have uniformity. Varn can be anything from 0° to 180° and lie to the East or the West of the true meridian. Furthermore, due to the slow movement of the magnetic poles, the value of varn at any give point on the earth can change with the passage of time. This rate of change in varn (known as *secular* change) also differs from place to place. Since varn is essential in converting M direction to T direction the values and rates of secular change are monitored and regularly updated on the appropriate aeronautical charts. Lines drawn on a chart joining places where varn has the same value are called *isogonals*; these lines will also be annotated with the value of the varn and the year to which it is applicable. On an out-of-date chart the varn information can be brought up to date by either changing the values on the printed isogonals or moving their positions on the chart. The amount of annual change can be found in the information boxes located around the edge of the chart. On some charts small numbered arrows printed at intervals along the isogonals indicate the direction and amount (in n.m.) of the annual movement of the isogonals. The golden rule is always to use a current chart wherever possible. *Use of an out-of-date chart should only ever be a last-resort option.* A word of caution: in some parts of the world the isogonals happen to run roughly North/South, when these appear on a chart care must be taken not to confuse them with the local true meridian. There are two isogonals along which the value of varn is zero, these are called *agonic lines*. One agonic line runs roughly North/South through the American continents, the other takes a more convolute path through Europe, the Near East and Yemen, turning Northward passing through Pakistan, Russia, round Siberia and Japan and South again near Singapore, finally tracking through Western Australia.

18.18 Two other magnetic lines that only appear on special magnet charts are *isoclinals*, lines joining places having the same magnetic dip (the zero isoclinal which defines the magnetic equator is also known as the *aclinic* line), and *isodynes*, lines joining places having the same horizontal directive force. Due to slight variations in the total force field the isoclinals and the isodynes do not have the symmetry that might be mathematically expected.

18.19 As well as the changes in varn due to the slow movement of the magnetic poles, other regular changes take place on a daily and annual basis and also on an approximate 11-year cycle thought to be related to sunspot activity. These regular changes to varn are fortunately of insufficient magnitude to affect normal navigation. Far more significant to navigation are the unpredictable magnetic storms caused by emissions from unusually large sunspots that occur at irregular intervals. These magnetic storms, often lasting for up to three days, are usually accompanied by an aurora borealis display as the solar winds funnel into the magnet poles. These storms can cause temporary changes to the value of varn lasting up to an hour with errors exceeding 5° in the Polar Regions. The horizontal component of the earth's magnetic field may also be weakened and propagation of some radio frequencies affected.

CHAPTER 19

DIRECT READING MAGNETIC COMPASSES

19.1 A direct reading magnetic compass (alternatively known as a standby compass) is a compass where the all-in-one sensing and display unit has to be located within the pilot's field of view for it to be readable. In effect this means it must be mounted somewhere on the flight deck, usually on the instrument panel.

19.2 There are two main groups of direct reading magnetic compasses, the older horizontal card type (see Fig. 19–1a), usually to be found in vintage and veteran aircraft, and the newer more compact vertical card type (see Fig. 19–1b).

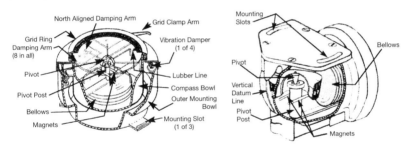

Fig. 19–1a Section through a typical horizontal type direct reading compass.

Fig. 19–1b Section through a typical vertical type direct reading compass.

19.3 As well as readability, any direct reading compass has three basic requirements: *Horizontality*, *Sensitivity* and *Aperiodicity*.

(a) *Horizontality*. To sense H (the horizontal component of the earth's field – see paragraph 18.16) and to make it easy to read, the magnet(s) in a direct reading magnetic compass needs to be as near horizontal as possible.

(b) *Sensitivity*. The magnet(s) employed must be sensitive enough to detect and respond to the weak pull of the earth's magnetic field, and friction in the pivot must be kept as low as possible.

(c) *Aperiodicity*. The system needs to be 'dead beat', that is to say it

265

should be quick to settle back to a steady M(N) indication whenever manoeuvring the aircraft or turbulence has displaced the indication. Any tendencies to oscillation must be damped out.

19.4 A single freely suspended bar magnet will have Z (the vertical component of the earth's field – see paragraph 18.16) pulling one end down (red pole in the N(M) hemisphere, blue pole in the S(M) hemisphere) until it aligns with T (the total component of the earth's field – see paragraph 18.16). In other words it will assume the local angle of dip making it difficult to read, particularly in high magnetic lats. Furthermore, a single bar magnet is unlikely to possess the degree of sensitivity required in an aircraft compass. In direct reading magnetic compasses a compromise solution is employed whereby pairs of short, powerful, magnets are pendulously mounted below a low-friction pivot point (see Fig. 19–2).

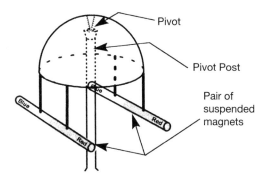

Fig. 19–2   Pendulous suspension of a pair of magnets.

The turning couple set up by the weight of the magnet system trying to get directly below the pivot point of the pendulum opposes the turning couple generated by Z acting on the magnets. This greatly reduces the effect of the local dip, and the magnet system settles down closer to the horizontal

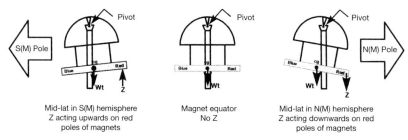

Fig. 19–3   Side view, looking West, showing how pendulous suspension reduces the effect of Z.

making it easier to detect H and also easier to read (see Fig. 19–3). How far from the horizontal it settles is a variable depending on the local value of Z, the weight of the magnets and the length of the arm of the pendulum. At the magnetic equator, where the value of Z is zero, the magnets are truly horizontal with their CG directly below the pivot, but as Z increases in value towards the poles the amount of tilt out of the horizontal increases. Apart from the magnetic equator case the system *always* achieves equilibrium with *the CG of the magnets lying on the equatorial side of the pivot*, that is to say N of the pivot in the S(M) hemisphere and S of the pivot in the N(M) hemisphere.

19.5 The whole compass system is built into a sealed bowl filled with clear liquid, the liquid acting as a damping agent and at the same time reducing the effective weight of the system on the pivot as well as lubricating it. Various liquids are used but all need certain characteristics such as a low viscosity, transparency, a low freezing point, a high boiling point, a low coefficient of expansion and non-corrosiveness. Most compasses are filled with some form of industrial alcohol. An expansion chamber in the bowl compensates for any changes in liquid volume due to temperature variations, preventing the formation of bubbles that can cause swirl and destroy the damping properties of the liquid. In the horizontal type of direct reading compass a set of thin lightweight arms radiates out from the pivot acting as dampers. One arm is aligned with the magnets and is in effect a N(M) seeking arm. This arm is painted white so that it is clearly visible against the rest of the bowl's interior which is painted black. In the vertical card type it is the card, stamped out of a thin sheet of light alloy, which acts as the damper as well as forming a dome for the pivot. Again the interior is painted black; the compass headings, painted in white on the card, are viewed through a window which has a white vertical datum line painted on it.

19.6   **Compass checks.** These fall into three main categories:
  (a)   Damping and pivot friction tests which are carried out prior to installing a compass in an aircraft, before a compass swing (see Chapter 20) or any time the accuracy of the compass is suspect.
  (b)   Pre-flight checks.
  (c)   In-flight checks.

Damping checks are designed to find out how quickly a compass needle returns to alignment after being deflected. A small handheld magnet is used to deflect the compass needle by 90° and then held there for 20 seconds to allow any liquid swirl to settle down. On removal of the handheld magnet from near the compass a stopwatch is used to time how long it takes for the needle to return to within 5° of the original heading. Depending on the compass model and the magnetic lat, tables are available giving the acceptable lower and upper time limits. Typical horizontal direct reading compass limits are between 4 to 7 seconds and vertical direct reading compass limits are 2 to 3 seconds. Times lower that the given limits indicate underdamping, and greater times indicate over-damping, both of which are undesirable and render the compass unserviceable.

A pivot friction test uses a handheld magnet to deflect the compass needle by 10°, holding it for 10 seconds and then removing the handheld magnet and noting the heading on which, without the assistance of vibration or tapping, the compass needle settles down. The exercise is repeated, deflecting the needle 10° the other way, and the two final readings compared; they should be within 2° for a horizontal direct reading compass and within 2½° for the vertical reading type. This test is normally repeated on four headings 90° apart. Readings that are higher than the laid down limits are an indication of too much pivot friction and render the compass unserviceable.

Pre-flight checks to be carried out on a direct reading compass include:
(a) No obvious damage such as dents.
(b) Compass securely fixed to its mounting, with no rotational freedom.
(c) No discoloration of the liquid or signs of sediment.
(d) No sign of bubbles in the liquid.
(e) Any lighting system checked to ensure it is working and provides sufficient illumination.
(f) In the case of a horizontal reading type, check the grid ring has full and free movement, the grid clamp functions properly, there is no metal to metal contact within the anti-vibration mountings and the bowl is free to rock smoothly fore and aft, and sideways.
(g) Prior to take-off, check the heading against the runway direction on line up.

In-flight carry out regular comparison checks against other compass systems and any other heading-providing equipment on the flight deck.

19.7   Under smooth flight conditions a direct reading magnetic compass quickly settles down to give a steady heading indication. However, problems can arise when the compass is subjected to acceleration. Any acceleration will felt by, and act directly on, the pivot of the compass system. Because the magnets are pendulously suspended they are not acted on directly by the acceleration and lag behind the pivot due to inertia. Effectively this is the same as applying a force through the CG of the magnets in the opposite direction to the acceleration. The displacement of the CG of the magnets to the equatorial side of the pivot (see Fig.19–3) means that any acceleration, other than in a magnetic North/South direction, will set up a turning moment which causes the magnets to swing around the pivot. During the period of any acceleration, false heading indications occur due to this inertia-induced turning of the magnets.

Accelerations occur:
(a)   when speed is being changed in straight line flight, or
(b)   during a turn from one heading to another.

19.8   Straight-line acceleration errors. Fig. 19–4a, b, c and d show (in plan view) four situations of straight-line accelerations taking place at a mid-lat in the N(M) hemisphere. Fig. 19–4a shows an aircraft accelerating in a straight-line toward W(M) and Fig. 19–4b shows an aircraft accelerating in a straight-line toward E(M). In both cases the effect of lag on the CG causes the magnets to turn and *falsely* indicate as if a turn were starting *towards N(M)*, or in other words, *towards the nearer magnetic pole*. *Decelerations* cause the magnets to turn in the opposite way to those caused by accelerations and result in false indications of a turn *away from the nearer magnetic pole*.

Fig. 19–4c shows an aircraft accelerating in a straight line toward N(M) and Fig. 19–4d shows an aircraft accelerating toward S(M), in both cases no turn is imparted on the magnets. Since the pivot and CG are in line with the acceleration the only effect is on the angle the magnets take up relative to the horizontal, *increasing* the value when accelerating *towards the nearer*

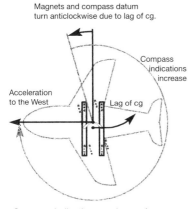

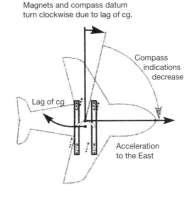

Fig. 19–4(a) Acceleration to W(M),
   mid-lat magnetic N hemisphere

Fig. 19–4(b) Acceleration to E(M),
   mid-lat magnetic N hemisphere

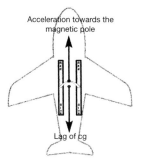

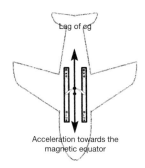

Fig. 19–(c) Acceleration to N(M),   Fig. 19–(d) Acceleration to S(M),
mid-lat magnetic N hemisphere   mid-lat magnetic N hemisphere

magnetic pole and *decreasing* the angle when accelerating *away from the nearer magnetic pole*. In the S(M) hemisphere the acceleration errors are a mirror image of those in the N(M) hemisphere. That is to say N(M) or S(M) accelerations cause no errors, and W(M) and E(M) accelerations cause errors of an apparent turn towards the S, or *nearer, magnetic pole*.

19.9   In both hemispheres an acceleration in a straight-line toward W(M) or E(M) always results in the ***compass falsely indicating a change of heading as if a turn were taking place towards the nearer magnetic pole***. For a given amount of straight-line acceleration or deceleration it can be seen that maximum errors occur on headings of W(M) and E(M), while zero errors occur on headings of N(M) and S(M). Straight-line accelerations or decelerations on intermediate magnetic headings will produce errors of magnitude between these two extremes. Straight-line accelerations or decelerations are usually of short duration; consequently their effects tend to be short lived. Several factors affect the magnitude of any acceleration error:

(a)   *Magnetic lat.* The higher the lat the greater the value of Z and the greater the displacement of the CG from under the pivot. The further the CG is displaced from under the pivot, the greater the turning moment imparted by a given acceleration becomes.

(b)   *Aircraft heading.* The closer the heading is to W(M) or E(M) the greater the magnitude of the error, the closer the heading is to N(M) or S(M) the nearer to zero magnitude the error becomes.

(c)   *Magnetic moment of the magnets.* Since this has to be a design compromise between polar strength of the magnets (to give sensitivity) and weight (to help the pendulosity reduce the effect of dip), compasses vary in design and consequently how they react to acceleration. The stronger the magnets the more the resistance to being deflected from H but greater the attraction of Z. The greater the weight the smaller the displacement of the CG but the greater the effect of lag due to inertia.

(d) *The rate of the acceleration.* Rapid accelerations (or decelerations) cause larger errors than gentle accelerations (or decelerations).

With such a mix of variables it is impossible to quote exact values for acceleration errors.

19.10 Turning errors. Fig. 19–5 shows, in plan view, Port (heading decreasing) and Starboard (heading increasing) turns being carried out at a mid-lat position in the N(M) hemisphere. During any turn there is always acceleration acting toward the centre of the turn at right angles to the heading of the aircraft. This means that when passing through N(M) and S(M) headings the compass system is subjected to either an E(M) or W(M) acceleration, and when passing through E(M) and W(M) headings the acceleration is acting toward either N(M) or S(M). Paragraph 19.8 illustrated that the maximum errors due to acceleration occurred when the accelerations were in an E(M) or W(M) direction. Therefore, during a turn, maximum errors occur when heading through N(M) or S(M), and reduce to zero as the heading passes through E(M) or W(M).

19.11 From Fig. 19–5 it can be seen that when the aircraft is on a heading *toward the **nearer** magnetic pole* the acceleration into the centre of the turn cause the needles to rotate in the same direction as the aircraft is turning. When on headings *toward the magnetic equator* the effect is reversed and the needles rotate in the opposite direction to that in which the aircraft is turning. This is true for both Port and Starboard turns. The effect of turning error when headings are *toward the **nearer** magnet pole* is for the compass to under-indicate the amount of heading change that has taken place. If requiring to stop the turn on a particular heading, the roll-out should commence before the compass indicates the required heading. The opposite is the case when turning *toward the magnetic equator*, the compass over-indicates the amount of heading change and roll-out on to any required heading should be delayed until the compass heading has gone beyond the desired heading. In the S(M) hemisphere the same rules apply, since the CG of the magnet system is also displaced to the equatorial side of the pivot, creating a mirror image of the effects seen in the N(M) hemisphere. To summarise:

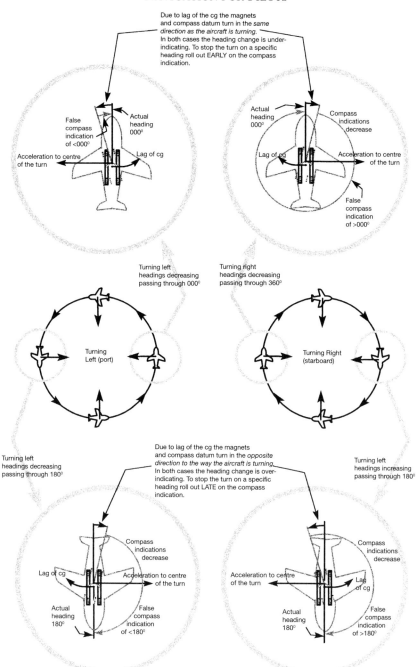

Fig. 19–5 Turning errors in the magnetic N hemisphere

Turns toward the *nearer* magnetic pole. Needles turn same way as the aircraft is turning, amount of heading change is under-indicated, roll out early onto a desired heading.

Turns toward the magnetic equator. Needles turn the opposite way to the way the aircraft is turning, amount of heading change is over-indicated, roll out late onto a desired heading.

CHAPTER 20

COMPASS CALIBRATION (COMPASS SWINGING)

20.1   In Chapter 19 it was explained that a direct reading magnetic compass has to be installed in a position where it is visible to the pilot at all times. This means installing it, accurately aligned with the aircraft's fore-and-aft axis, somewhere on the flight deck, usually on the instrument panel. The flight deck is not the best place for accurate functioning of the compass since the surrounding structure may well contain ferrous material with magnetic properties sufficiently strong to cause the compass needle to deviate from its alignment with N(M). It is almost impossible to build an aircraft that does not contain ferrous material somewhere in its structure and a percentage of this ferrous material is liable to contain magnetic properties, either permanent, transient or induced, or, more likely, a mixture of all three properties. Even aircraft of identical design are unlikely to have the same magnetic signature. Bearing in mind that the magnetic force of the earth is very weak, it does not require a large magnetic effect from the airframe to deflect the compass needle from the local magnetic meridian. It is the possible misalignment of the compass bowl and the presence of aircraft magnetism in the vicinity of the compass that give rise to the bulk of compass **deviation (dev)**. The compass calibration and correction procedures explained in this Chapter should, in theory, eliminate all the devs found to be affecting the compass in an aircraft. In practice there may be residual dev left after the correction process has been completed and this residual dev needs to be recorded on a card kept near the compass where it can be referred to by the pilot. The compass calibration and correction consists of three stages:

(a)   To determine the deviations present on a series of designated headings.

(b)   To correct for these deviations as far as is practical.

(c)   To determine and record any residual deviation.

20.2   Misalignment of the compass bowl causes a dev that is the same on all (C) headings equal to the amount of misalignment. Figure 20–1

274

Coeff A

The compass bowl has two, or more, curved mounting slots through which bolts are used to secure it in place in the aircraft. These slots allow for small radial movements to obtain correct alignment with the fore and aft axis of the aircraft during the installation. However if the compass bowl is misaligned during the installation the same dev error, equal to the misalignment, occurs on *all* *compass* headings.
If this dev is plotted out on a graph it generates a straight line.

The magnitude of this error is the same on all headings and is known as coeff A.

With the compass bowl misaligned to the left of the fore and aft axis of the aircraft the straight line plots out to the right of the zero axis on the graph, giving a + value to coeff A as shown in the diagram. For a misalignment to the right the line plots out to the left of the zero axis on the graph and gives a - value to coeff A.

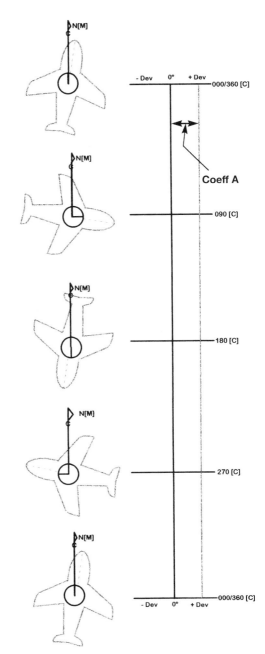

Fig. 20–1   Coefficient A.

275

Coeff B

If the Blue pole of the aircrafts magnetism is in the nose of the aircraft (and, by inference, the Red pole is in the tail) as the aircraft alters its heading the position of the Blue pole relative to the compass changes.

The minimum effect is when the Blue pole is in line with the compass and the local magnetic meridian. This occurs on headings of 000/360 [C] and 180 [C].

The maximum effect is when the Blue pole is at right angles to the *compass needle* (not the magnetic meridian). This occurs on headings of 090 [C] and 270 [C].

When all the devs due to a Blue pole in the nose are plotted out on a graph a positive sine curve is generated. The maximum dev on 090 [C] is known as coeff B and in the case of a Blue pole in the nose has a + value. For an aicraft with a Blue pole in the tail the devs generate a negative sine curve and coeff B has a - value.

The value of dev on any heading is equal to :-
coeff B x sin hdg [C]

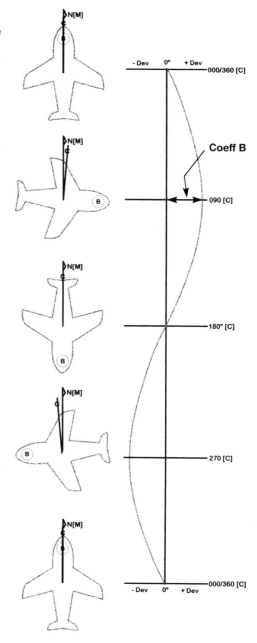

Fig. 20–2   Coefficient B.

Coeff C

If the Blue pole of the aircrafts magnetism is in the right wing of the aircraft (and, by inference, the Red pole is in the left wing) as the aircraft alters its heading the position of the Blue pole relative to the compass changes.

The minimum effect is when the Blue pole is in line with the compass and the local magnetic meridian. This occurs on the headings of 090 [C] and 270 [C].

The maximum effect is when the Blue pole is at right angles to the *compass needle* (not the magnetic meridian). This occurs on the headings of 000/360 [C] and 180 [C].

When all the devs due to a Blue pole in the right wing are plotted out on a graph a positive cosine curve is generated. The maximum dev on 000/360 [C] is known as coeff C and in the case of a Blue pole in the right wing has a + value. For an aircraft with a Blue pole in the left wing the devs generate a negative cosine curve and coeff C has a - Value.

The value of dev on any heading is equal to :-
    coeff C x cos hdg [C]

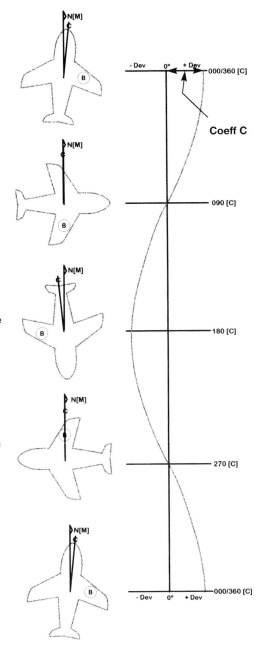

Fig. 20–3   Coefficient C.

shows an aircraft with the compass bowl installed with its datum offset to the left of the fore-and-aft axis of the aircraft. On every heading the compass indication measured against the misaligned bowl is less than the magnetic heading (measured from N(M) to the fore-and-aft axis of the aircraft) by the amount of misalignment. This constant dev due to misalignment of the compass is known as COEFFICIENT A (Coeff A) and gives the number of degrees the bowl needs to be turned and whether the readings need to be increased or decreased to get it correctly aligned with the fore-and-aft axis of the aircraft.

20.3   Aircraft magnetism is made up of a collection of magnetic influences within the aircraft's structure, but it can be treated as if it were three single bar magnets acting through the centre of the compass, one fore-and-aft, one laterally and one vertically. A magnet acting vertically through the compass does not cause dev in level flight and, for all practical purposes, can be ignored. The strength and disposition of all the magnetic fields in an aircraft dictate the size and position of the poles of the two representative horizontal magnets. The fore-and-aft representative magnet can have its Blue pole in the nose or tail and the lateral representative magnet can have its Blue pole to the right or left of the compass, and each causes a different dev depending on the heading (C) of the aircraft. These separate devs are analysed in detail in Figs 20–2 and 20–3.

20.4   On any heading (C) the total dev is the summation of the individual devs caused by coeffs A, B and C on that heading (C), and is written as:

$$\text{dev on any hdg(C)} = A + B \sin \text{hdg(C)} + C \cos \text{hdg(C)}$$

The purpose and objective of compass calibration and correction (known as *compass swinging* from the days when sailing ships were swung around their mooring buoys to facilitate compass corrections) is to calculate the coeffs A, B and C from total devs observed on selected headings and then to correct them.

20.5   Measuring the dev. On any heading the dev affecting a compass is found by comparing the compass reading in the aircraft against the reading of an external high quality landing compass located some distance from the aircraft and thus not affected by the aircraft's magnetism. The correct heading M is found by lining up the landing compass with the aircraft fore and aft axis. In the case of large aircraft this may involve the use of temporary datum rods, screwed into special locations on the underside of the aircraft, as an aid to alignment. To ensure that the compass readings are as accurate as possible, the site used for compass swinging needs to be free of any miscellaneous magnetic influences such as underground cables or, in the case of grass airfields, pierced steel planking. Any site proposed for compass swinging should be checked for local magnetic anomalies by use of two landing compasses taking reciprocal bearing of each other on a series of headings across the site; if the site is magnetically 'clean' the bearings should consistently differ by 180°. Large airports usually have a magnetically free area specifically prepared for compass calibration purposes. As well as being free of anomalous magnetism the site needs to be large enough for the aircraft to be manoeuvred round for readings to be taken on a series of headings. Other considerations to be taken into account are the strength of the surface being able to support the weight of the aircraft and the location of the site, which should be well away from operational movements on the airfield.

20.6   Calculation of the coefficients. Paragraph 20.4 stated that:

dev on any hdg(C)   = A + B sin hdg(C) + C cos hdg(C)

Applying this formula on the four Cardinal headings gives:

dev on 000/360 (C)   = A + B sin 000° + C cos 000°
                                    = A + B (0) + C (+1)
                                    = A + C

dev on 090 (C)   = A + B sin 090° + C cos 090°
                              = A + B (+1) + C (0)
                              = A + B

dev on 180 (C)   = A + B sin 180° + C cos 180°
                              = A + B (0) + C (–1)
                              = A – C

dev on 270 (C)   = A + B sin 270° + C cos 270°
                              = A + B (–1) + C (0)
                              = A – B

This enables the calculation of the coeffs to be resolved from the total devs obtained on the Cardinal [C] points during a compass swing, as follows:

dev on N(C) + dev on E(C) + dev on S(C) + dev on W(C)
                                              4

$$= \frac{(A + C) + (A + B) + (A - C) + (A - B)}{4} = \frac{+ 4A}{4} = \text{coeff A}$$

$$\cdots\cdots\cdots$$

$$\frac{\text{dev on E(C)} - \text{dev on W(C)}}{2}$$

$$= \frac{(A + B) - (A - B)}{2} = \frac{A + B - A + B}{2} = \frac{+ 2B}{2} = \text{coeff B}$$

$$\cdots\cdots\cdots$$

$$\frac{\text{dev on N(C)} - \text{dev on S(C)}}{2}$$

$$= \frac{(A + C) - (A - C)}{2} = \frac{A + C - A + C}{2} = \frac{+ 2C}{2} = \text{coeff C}$$

This can be expressed in a simpler form as:

$$\frac{\text{devs N} + \text{E} + \text{S} + \text{W}}{4} = \text{coeff A}$$

$$\frac{\text{devs E} - \text{W}}{2} = \text{coeff B}$$

$$\frac{\text{devs N} - \text{S}}{2} = \text{coeff C}$$

Example Question:
Calculate the coeffs A, B and C from the following (C) and (M) readings found on the cardinal headings during a compass swing.

358 (C)	351(M)
090 (C)	091(M)
179 (C)	182(M)
270 (C)	265(M)

Answer:

358 (C)	351 (M)	dev on North	$= -7°$
090 (C)	091 (M)	dev on East	$= +1°$
179 (C)	182 (M)	dev on South	$= +3°$
270 (C)	265 (M)	dev on West	$= -5°$

$$\textbf{coeff A} = \frac{\text{devs N} + \text{E} + \text{S} + \text{W}}{4} = \frac{-7 + 1 + 3 - 5}{4} = \frac{-8}{4} = \textbf{--2°}$$

coeff B $= \dfrac{\text{devs E} - \text{W}}{2} = \dfrac{+1 - (-5)}{2} = \dfrac{+1 + 5}{2} = \dfrac{+6}{2} = \textbf{+3°}$

coeff C $= \dfrac{\text{devs N} - \text{S}}{2} = \dfrac{-7 - (+3)}{2} = \dfrac{-7 - 3}{2} = \dfrac{-10}{2} = \textbf{-5°}$

20.7   Correcting the coeffs A, B and C.

Coefficient A. Whenever a compass swing produces a coeff A with a value other than 0° it is indicating that the compass bowl is not lined up with the fore and aft axis of the aircraft. To correct for this error the current heading is noted, the bolts holding the compass bowl are slackened, the bowl gently rotated until the indicated heading has been changed by the amount of coeff A and the bolts are retightened. This correction is normally only required on the first compass swing after a compass has been installed and should not be required on subsequent compass swings unless it has been disturbed. In the example above, coeff A came out to be –2° indicating that the compass bowl needs turning on its mountings by 2° to reduce the (C) reading by 2°. Since coeff A is a constant, this correction can be carried out on any heading, for instance on 270 (C) the bowl needs turning until the compass indicates 270 + A = 270 + (–2) = 268 (C).

Coefficient B. By definition (see Fig. 20–2) this is the dev on 090 (C) caused by the fore-and-aft effect of aircraft magnetism. When the Blue pole is in the nose of the aircraft coeff B has a + value and when the Blue pole is in the tail of the aircraft coeff B has a – value. Since coeff B varies with the sin heading (C) the correction for coeff B can only be carried out on headings where the value of sine is 1, i.e. 090 (C) (sin 090° = +1) or 270 (C) (sin 270° = –1). If carrying out the correction on 090 (C) the correction to be applied is B with its sign (+ or –) unchanged; if making the correction on 270 (C) the sign of B must be changed before applying it to the heading. Coeff B is corrected by generating an equal but opposite magnetic field along the fore-and-aft axis of the aircraft by means of a pair of magnets mounted in a corrector box situated directly above or below the compass. These are mounted one above the other on a pair of geared bevel wheels which rotate in opposite directions when a key turns a small driving bevel wheel that links them (see Fig. 20–4 for a schematic diagram).

The arrangement of the corrector magnets that compensate for coeff B is such that when in the neutral position they lie exactly athwartships with Blue over Red and Red over Blue. Whenever the small bevel wheel is turned, the two large bevel wheels rotate in opposite directions and start to move one pair of similar poles toward the nose and the other pair of poles

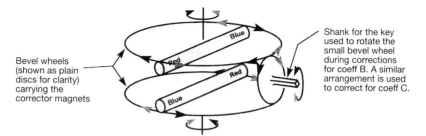

Bevel wheels
(shown as plain
discs for clarity)
carrying the
corrector magnets

Shank for the key
used to rotate the
small bevel wheel
during corrections
for coeff B. A similar
arrangement is used
to correct for coeff C.

Fig. 20–4 Schematic diagram of compass corrector box mechanism.

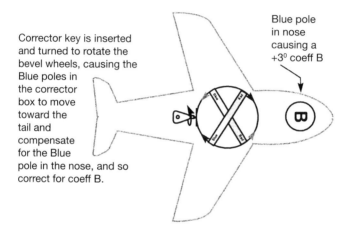

Corrector key is inserted
and turned to rotate the
bevel wheels, causing the
Blue poles in
the corrector
box to move
toward the
tail and
compensate
for the Blue
pole in the nose, and so
correct for coeff B.

Blue pole
in nose
causing a
+3⁰ coeff B

Fig. 20–5 Correcting for a + coefficient B on 090 (C).

toward the tail. The further the wheels turn, the closer together each pair of like poles become and the stronger their total effect. In the worked example in paragraph 20.6 coeff B came out at +3°. Correcting for coeff B of +3° on 090 (C), the corrector key is inserted to engage the shank of the small bevel wheel and turned slowly until the compass heading changes to 090 + (+3) = 093 (C). Correcting for coeff B of +3° on 270 (C), the final reading required is 270° – (+3) = 267°(C). Just the one correction is needed on **either** 090°(C) **or** 270°(C) but **not both**.

Coefficient C. By definition (see Fig. 20–3) this is the dev on 000/360 (C) caused by the athwartships effect of aircraft magnetism. When the Blue pole is to the right of the compass coeff C has a + value and when the Blue pole is to the left of the compass coeff C has a – value. Since coeff C varies with cos heading (C), the correction for coeff C can only be carried out on headings where the value of cos is 1, i.e. 000 (C)/360 (C) (cos 000° = +1) or 180 (C) (cos 180° = -1). If carrying out the correction on 000/360 (C), the correction to be applied is C with its sign (+ or –) unchanged; if making the correction on 180 (C) the sign of C must be changed before applying it to the heading. The method of correction is the same as that used to correct for coeff B except that it uses a second pair of magnets mount at 90° to, and piggy-backing, the ones used to correct for coeff B. The coeff C corrector box has its own keyway for turning its magnets. In the worked example in paragraph 20.6 coeff C came out at –5°. Correcting for coeff C of –5° on 000 (C), the corrector key is inserted to engage the shank of the small bevel wheel and turned slowly until the compass heading changes to 000° + (–5) = 355 (C). Correcting for coeff C of –5° on 180 (C), the final reading required is 180° – (–5) = 185 (C). Just the one correction is needed on **either** 000/360 (C) **or** 180 (C), but **not both**.

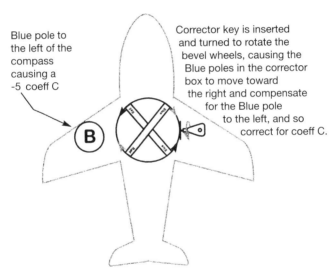

Fig. 20–6 Correcting for a – coefficient C on 000/360 (C).

20.8   Residual dev. When a coeff A has been corrected by realigning the compass it is usual practice to check the devs on the Cardinal points again and recalculate the coeffs. This should confirm whether the original coeff A has been successfully reduced to zero and show up any minor changes in coeffs B and C due to the moving of the compass. After coeffs B and C have been corrected a further swing, called a 'check swing', is carried out to determine if there is any residual dev to record. A 'check swing' is usually carried out on eight headings 45° apart. Maximum allowable values for residual deviation on any heading are:

(a)   (+ or –) 3° on direct reading compasses (see Chapter 19).

(b)   (+ or –) 1° on remote reading compasses (see Chapter 21).

20.9 The occasions when there is a requirement to carry out a compass swing are:

(a)   When a compass is first installed, or a replacement compass is fitted.

(b)   When structural replacements are made to the aircraft of components that may have a magnetic effect on the compass.

(c)   Before putting the aircraft back into service after long-term storage.

(d)   At specified intervals laid down in the servicing schedule.

(e)   When an aircraft is given a new *permanent* operating area involving a large change of magnetic latitude.

(f)   If the aircraft has been struck by lightning.

(g)   If the compass has been subjected to shock (such as a heavy landing).

(h)   If carrying an unusual ferromagnetic cargo.

(i)   Any time the accuracy of the compass is suspect.

20.10   HEADING OF MAXIMUM DEVIATION

A purely academic question that is sometimes set in examinations is to ask the candidate to calculate the value and hdg of maximum dev (before correction) due to a set of given coeffs A, B and C. As an example, consider the coeffs found in paragraph 20.6; what is the value of the maximum dev due to a combination of coeffs A = –2°, B = +3° and C = –5° and on what hdg (C) would it occur?

Coeff A, being a constant, is going to bias the final answer toward its sign, in this case – (or dev W), so the overall maximum dev must have a – sign.

Start by sketching the aircraft on N(C).

Draw in (to scale) vectors for the given coeffs B and C. In this case a vector of 3 in the nose (coeff B +3 a Blue pole in the nose) and a vector of 5 to the left (coeff C –5 a Blue pole to the left).

Using guidelines, draw in the Blue pole vector that coeffs B and C represent.

Measuring the length of this vector gives the maximum deviation that coeffs B and C together can cause.

Measure, by protractor, the angle clockwise from the vector round to the next cardinal point; in this case N.

Rotating the aircraft clockwise through this angle and then in further steps of 090°, 180° and 270° will place the vector in line with N(C) (no dev) or at 90° E or W of N(C) (maximum dev).

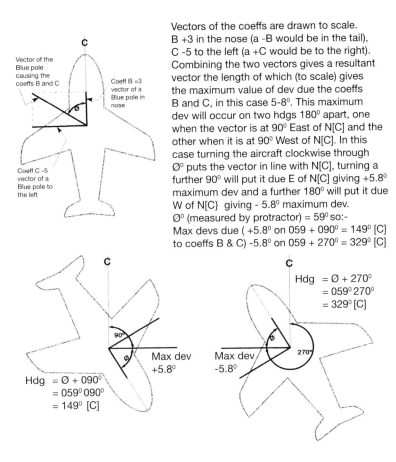

Vectors of the coeffs are drawn to scale. B +3 in the nose (a -B would be in the tail), C -5 to the left (a +C would be to the right). Combining the two vectors gives a resultant vector the length of which (to scale) gives the maximum value of dev due the coeffs B and C, in this case 5-8⁰. This maximum dev will occur on two hdgs 180⁰ apart, one when the vector is at 90⁰ East of N[C] and the other when it is at 90⁰ West of N[C]. In this case turning the aircraft clockwise through Ø⁰ puts the vector in line with N[C], turning a further 90⁰ will put it due E of N[C] giving +5.8⁰ maximum dev and a further 180⁰ will put it due W of N[C} giving - 5.8⁰ maximum dev. Ø⁰ (measured by protractor) = 59⁰ so:-
Max devs due (+5.8⁰ on 059 + 090⁰ = 149⁰ [C] to coeffs B & C) -5.8⁰ on 059 + 270⁰ = 329⁰ [C]

Vector of the Blue pole causing the coeffs B and C

Coeff B =3 vector of a Blue pole in nose

Coeff C -5 vector of a Blue pole to the left

Hdg = Ø + 090⁰
= 059⁰ 090⁰
= 149⁰ [C]

Max dev +5.8⁰

Max dev -5.8⁰

Hdg = Ø + 270⁰
= 059⁰ 270⁰
= 329⁰ [C]

Fig. 20-7 Maximum dev due to coefficients B of +3⁰ and C of -5⁰

Adding the value of coeff A to the max dev of its sign gives the overall maximum dev.

Fig. 20–7 illustrates the process for the coeff B of +3° and coeff C of –5°, which gives maximum devs of +5·8° on a hdg of 149 (C) and –5·8° on a hdg of 329 (C). If the coeff A of –2° is now applied, with its sign unchanged, to both maximum devs the final maximum dev due to all three coeffs comes out as **–7·8°**. At the same time the hdg must be mathematically misaligned by applying coeff A with its sign changed to all hdgs. The hdg on which the maximum dev occurs is 329 – (–2°) = 329 + 2° = **331 (C)**.

An alternative way to solve for Ø and the maximum dev vector is to do a rough sketch and used trigonometry.
In the example above:

tan Ø = C / B = 5 / 3 = **1·6666** which gives Ø = **59°02'**

C / Vector length = sin 59°02' so Vector length = C ÷ sin 59°02' = 5 / 0·8575 = **5·84**

CHAPTER 21

REMOTE READING COMPASSES

21.1 In Chapter 19 certain drawbacks of Direct Reading Compasses were discussed, these included:

(a) The need for them to be installed on the flight deck where they are visible to the pilot, meaning they are in a position where the deviation effects of aircraft magnetism and electrical circuits are likely to be high.

(b) They only display hdg (C), which needs correcting for dev and varn to obtain hdg (T).

(c) They are subjected to acceleration and turning errors.

Two more drawbacks can be added to this list:

(a) The priority of other instruments on the flight deck sometimes means the Direct Reading Compass gets mounted in a position that is not directly in front of the pilot's line of sight, leading to parallax reading errors.

(b) Being an enclosed instrument, it has no means of automatically transmitting hdg information to any other position or piece of navigational equipment.

21.2 These drawbacks are addressed in Remote Reading Compass systems by employing an electrical **Directional Gyro Indicator (DGI)** for ease of reading and stability in turns (see DGI in the Instrument syllabus), which is continually monitored and corrected for drift by a remote N(M) sensing detector unit. The detector unit is mounted in a wing tip or the fin, well away from the worst effects of aircraft magnetism. Unlike the free magnets in a direct reading compass, the detector unit has no moving parts, it is mounted aligned parallel with the aircraft's fore-and-aft axis on a universal joint which allows for movement in pitch and roll but is fixed in azimuth. The base of the detector unit is weighted so that in normal flight conditions the unit lies horizontal to the earth's surface. The electrical DGI is wired to transmit its hdg information to other pieces of equipment and, in some models, can have dev and varn offsets put in by the pilot so that the compass indicates hdg (T).

21.3   The heart of the system is the detector unit that contains flux valves set at different angles to each other. In paragraph 18.11(b) the induction of a magnetic field into soft iron by means of a coil and an electrical current was discussed. It is a carefully controlled adaptation of this process that is employed in the flux valves. Fig. 21–1 illustrates a single flux valve that consists of two soft iron strips joined by a short soft iron rod, the strips are prevented from touching each other by a thin layer of insulating material. A coil around the rod has a carefully controlled alternating current passing through it. The combination of the amount of soft iron, the number of turns on the coil and the current used is designed to make the soft iron strips just reach magnetic saturation at each peak of the a.c. cycle. Being an alternating current, the induced magnetism dies away to zero 90° after the cycle peaks, and 90° after that it peaks again with its polarity changed. At any instance the induced magnetism in the two strips have equal strength but opposite polarity which cancel each other out so that there is *no overall change of magnetic field* to induce a current into the pick-off coil wound around the two soft iron strips. Placing the flux valve horizontally in the earth's magnetic field results in both strips detecting the same constant component of H. The strength and polarity of this component of H depends on the angle that the flux valve lies relative to the local magnetic meridian. The addition of the earth-induced magnetism means that magnetic saturation in one polarity will take place before the a.c. cycle

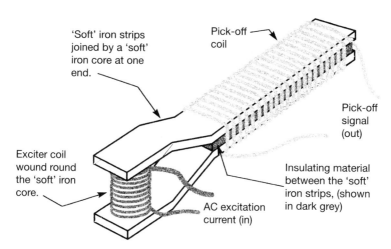

Fig. 21–1 A single flux valve, showing the exciter and pick-off coils.

peaks and will not start to die away until a similar interval after the a.c. peak. During this extended period of magnetic saturation in one strip the changing opposite polarity in the other strip is not affected and the two fields no long cancel each other out. An overall change of magnetic field occurs during the extended saturation period and this induces a 'blip' of alternating current in the pick-off coil. The amplitude and phasing of the 'blip' varies with the polarity and strength of the earth-induced magnetism. As the a.c.-induced magnetism in the strips are 180° out of phase with each other, two 'blips' are induced in each a.c. cycle. A typical exciter coil current uses 400 cycles per sec with a pick-off coil rate of 800 a.c. 'blips' per sec.

21.4   An example of a typical detector unit is the three radial arm layout used in the Sperry CL series of compasses. This has a single central exciter coil that simultaneously induces alternating magnetic fields in three flux valves set at 120° to each other, and soft iron 'collector horns' at their outer end to assist in sensing the earth's magnetic field. On installation, one flux valve is usually aligned parallel to the fore-and-aft axis of the aircraft.

Fig. 21–2 shows, in plan view, the layout of a Sperry detector unit with each flux valve lying at a different angle to H. Polarity and strength of earth-induced magnetism is different in each flux valve, which in turn results in a different current issuing from each flux valve pick-off coil. The pick-off currents are fed to three vertical coils set at 120° to each other behind the dial of the electrical DGI unit, where they reproduce the direc-

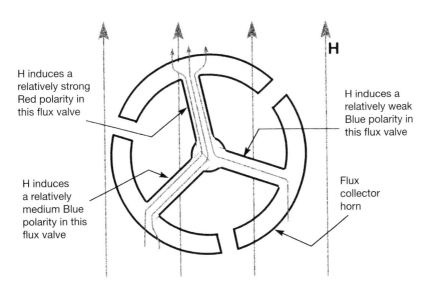

Fig. 21–2   Sperry detector unit with three flux valves at 120° to ach other radiating from a central exciter coil.

289

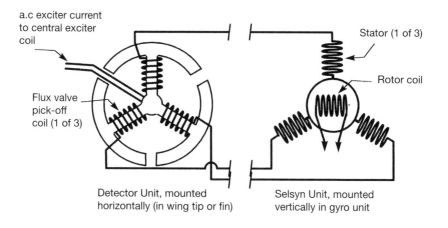

Fig. 21–3   Transmission system, detector to flight deck.

tion of the earth's field in a pulsing vertical form. Positioned in this pulsing field is a rotor coil mounted on the shaft to the display card of the DGI. This coil is mounted on the shaft so that it is at 90° to the pulsing field when the gyro is correctly aligned with N(M), in which position the pulsing field does not induce any current into the rotor coil (see Fig. 21–3).

If for any reason the DGI become desynchronised, the rotor coil is taken out of the 90° position to the pulsing field and a current is induced in it. Current from the rotor coil passes to an amplifier, then via an annunciator coil and transductors to a precession coil which causes the DGI to precess back to the synchronised position at *a rate of between 2° to 5° per minute.* This arrangement is known as a Self-Synchronous (or Selsyn) unit. Depending on which way the correcting current is flowing, the annunciator coil causes an arm marked with a dot and a cross flag to move to left or right behind a small window on the face of the DGI indicator dial. Display of a steady dot or a steady cross indicates the DGI is not synchronised, a slowly alternating dot/cross, dot/cross display indicates that the DGI is hunting around the synchronised heading. The DGI has a manual resetting control for initial synchronisation during pre-flight checks or if at any time the DGI becomes desynchronised in flight. The manual reset control has a dot and a cross on it to indicate the correct way to turn the control when resetting. If a steady dot is showing in the annunciator window, turn the control toward the dot on the control until the annunciator flag flicks from dot to cross as the synchronised point is reached; if a steady cross is showing turn toward the cross on the reset control. *Always* check the DGI reading against the direct reading magnetic compass after manual resetting because if the manual resetting control is accidentally turned the wrong way the annunciator flag will flick over as the rotor coil reaches its other 90° position with the DGI 180° out of correct synchronisation.

21.5 *Pre-flight checks.* Remote reading compasses use precise electric voltages and, depending on manufacturer and model, there is an indicator, usually in the form of a light, that shows only when the correct voltages are supplied to the compass when it is switched 'ON'. This indicator should be checked both pre-flight and regularly during flight. If the indicator fails to show that the correct voltage is being supplied, the compass should not be used other than as an electrical DGI, a DG switch on the unit being used to cut out the monitoring from the detector unit. Check that the compass is synchronised with the detector unit by noting that the annunciator flag is hunting dot/cross/dot/cross. Check that the compass has not been set up 180° out; this is an essential check if manual synchronisation has to be carried out.

21.6 *Acceleration and turning errors.* Unlike direct reading magnetic compasses there is no pendulous magnetic system with a displaced CG to cause problems during accelerations. In straight and level accelerations the detector unit being locked in azimuth does not falsely indicate a turn taking place. The bottom-weighted detector unit may tilt out of the earth's horizontal sufficiently to cause small false signals to be passed to the stator coils. However, the amount of error passed to the DGI is limited by the self-synchronous rate of 2° to 5° per minute and self-corrects at the same rate once the acceleration ceases. The same arguments apply in a turn where the DGI compass card and rotor coil move around the gyro maintaining them in synchronisation with the aircraft's hdg. Again small errors can accrue due to the detector unit tilting out of the earth's horizontal, but these will only become significant in a sustained turn. The self-synchronous unit will quickly correct any small errors that accrue during a heading change that does not involve a sustained turn. Errors accrued in a sustained turn will take longer to self-synchronise and are best corrected by manual resetting as soon as the turn is stopped.

21.7 *Compass calibration and correction.* Placing the detector unit in a wing tip or the fin where the effects of aircraft magnetism are weak does not remove the need to carry out calibration and correction checks. Misalignment of the detector unit can occur during installation (giving rise to coeff A) and what little aircraft magnetism is present still needs to be compensated for (coeffs B and C). The compass swing and calibration of coeffs A, B and C are exactly the same as described in Chapter 20, the only difference is in the way these are corrected:

Coefficient A is corrected by first checking to ensure the compass is switched 'ON', the voltage indicator shows voltages are correct and that the compass is synchronised with the annunciator hunting. Then mathematically apply the value of coeff A to the present hdg and then use the course setting knob to *select and hold* the resultant required hdg. This will cause a desynchronised indication in the annunciator window. The bolts holding the detector unit in place are then slackened and the unit slowly rotated until the annunciator window returns to a dot/cross display. At this point coeff A has been corrected and the bolts are then re-tightened and the course setting knob is released. On models of remote reading compasses that have variation setting controls, if coeff A is 2° or less it can be removed at the variation setting and the lubber line of the variation control moved to realign with 0° variation.

Coefficient B is corrected on *either* 090 (C) *or* 270 (C). Proceed as for correcting coeff A, applying coeff B as applicable, i.e. 090°(C) + (coeff B) or 270°(C) – (coeff B), up to the point where the required hdg is being held with the course setting knob. A coeff B corrector control, found either in a separate corrector box or built into the amplifier, is then used to control the d.c. voltage supplied to a coil wound round a soft iron rod mounted fore and aft above the detector unit. The voltage is adjusted until the annunciator flag returns to a dot/cross display indicating that coeff B has been compensated for and synchronisation has been achieved with the desired hdg. The course setting knob is then released.

Coefficient C is corrected in a similar way as for correcting coeff B except that coeff C is corrected on *either* 000/360 (C) *or* 180 (C), applying coeff C as applicable, i.e. 000/360°(C) + (coeff C) or 180°(C) – (coeff C). A coeff C corrector control, to be found beside the coeff B corrector control, is used to adjust the d.c. voltage to a coil wound round an athwartships soft iron rod mounted above the detector unit.

After the corrections for coeffs A, B and C are completed a check swing is carried out to ascertain if there is any residual dev. The maximum residual dev allowed for a remote reading compass is (+ or –) 1°.

Section 6

Advanced Flight Deck Systems

Advances in microprocessors and computer technology in the latter part of the 20th century have given rise to many changes on the flight deck. Compared to the original layout of Concorde's flight deck, which was pretty much ancient technology by the time it first flew, today's 'glass' cockpit is far less cluttered and pilot friendly. In fact, technology has picked off specialist trades from the flight deck crew one by one, first the Signaller, then the Navigator, followed by the Flight Engineer. Only two pilots are needed to operate the majority of modern airliners and computers take much of the strain. This does not relieve the pilot of responsibility for the flight and all pilots need to know what the various computers can do and how to operate and monitor them. This section contains chapters on Inertial Navigation, Flight Management and Electronic Flight Instrument Systems.

CHAPTER 22

INERTIAL NAVIGATION SYSTEMS

22.1 Inertial navigation systems are self-contained within the aircraft and require no outside assistance from air, ground or satellite radio transmissions. The principle of any inertial navigation system is to measure all the accelerations that have taken place from the moment the aircraft starts to taxi, convert them into current speed(s) and total direction and distance moved from the start point, and display this as a lat and long. The system is also able to display many other navigation functions, which are explained later in this chapter. The basic requirements for such a system are:

(a)   Accurate input of the start position.
(b)   Accurate measurement of acceleration in the earth's horizontal plane.
(c)   A means of converting accelerations into speeds and distance moved from the start point.

22.2 *Accurate input of the start position.* Normally this is to 0·1 minute of lat and/or long. On airports with parking ramps the INS nose-wheel position for each ramp is listed in the airport documents and the individual ramp position is often displayed on a board visible to the pilot from the flight deck of a parked aircraft. At many international airports, flight plans, including the INS information, are electronically downloaded directly from Operations Planning. Whatever the method of inputting the information it is the pilot's responsibility to ensure the start position is correctly programmed into the INS along with all other navigation information.

22.3 *Accurate measurement of acceleration in the earth's horizontal plane.* This is a complex problem due to a combination of several factors. In flight an aircraft moves in both pitch and roll and the flight takes place above a sphere which is rotating and moving through space. Two methods of isolating the horizontal accelerations are currently available, the 'stable platform' and 'strap-down' methods.

22.4 The *'stable platform'* method uses two accelerometers mounted at 90° to each other on a gymbal-mounted platform corrected for movement in pitch, roll and azimuth by three rate-type gyros and three motors. The normal alignment of the two accelerometers is N/S and E/W although polar flights often use orientations based on along and across the mean GC trk. The INS computer is programmed to correct for earth rotation and movement in space plus transport errors due to change in lat and long.

22.5   The *'strap-down'* method (known as an **Inertial Reference System** or **IRS**) employs three accelerometers and three rate gyros. Each of the three axes of the aircraft has one accelerometer and one rate gyro aligned, or 'strapped', to it so that all accelerations along, and all rotations around, each axis are being continually sensed. The IRS computer is programmed to interpret these signals into N/S and E/W accelerations as well as correcting for earth rotation, movement through space and transport errors.

22.6   *The principles of accelerometers.* Accelerometers come in various forms; those that are used in INS employ a 'force-feed-back' system whereby the acceleration is measured by the force needed to cancel out the acceleration. The simplest form of the 'force-feed-back' accelerometer is based on a pendulum that is only free to swing along the axis of measurement. Pendulums obey Newton's laws of motion.

Newton's first law states that a body will remain in a state of rest or uniform motion in a straight line unless compelled to change its state by a force acting on it. This means that if no force is acting along the swing axis of the pendulum it will hang with its CG vertically below its pivot.

Newton's second law states that the rate of change of momentum of a body is proportional to the applied force causing the change of momentum and

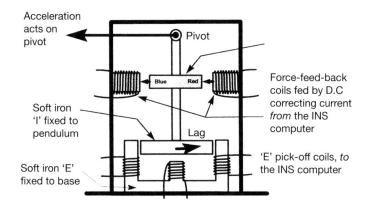

Fig. 22–1   Principle of a pendulum accelerometer.

takes place in the direction of the applied force. This law means that when a force (acceleration) acts at an angle to the accelerometer axis of measurement only, a vector of the acceleration is sensed by that accelerometer. This is the reason that two accelerometers are needed, set at 90° to each other, the combined readings from each being reassembled in the computer to resolve the direction and strength of the acceleration acting on them.

Newton's third law states that to every action there is an equal and opposite reaction. This means that when acceleration acts on the pivot of a pendulum, the base of the pendulum lags and swings in the opposite direction to the acceleration at a rate equal to the acceleration.

22.7   Fig. 22–1 illustrates the principle of a simple pendulum 'force-feed-back' accelerometer. The pivot allows the pendulum to swing only along the axis in which acceleration is to be measured. At the bottom of the pendulum the weight is formed by the horizontally mounted soft iron 'I' bar of an 'E/I' bar pick-off sensor. The soft iron 'E' part of the sensor lies on its back with its outer legs either side of the 'I' bar. When the pendulum is truly vertical (no acceleration acting on the pivot) the air gaps between the ends of the 'I' bar and the outer legs of the 'E' are identical. When an acceleration acts on the pivot the pendulum reacts by swinging in the opposite direction, closing up one air gap and opening the other. When the air gaps are identical the AC exciter current induces an alternating magnetic field in the 'E/I' bar system which at any moment has identical strength but opposite polarity in the outer legs of the 'E'. This results in the AC currents induced in the pick-off coils around the outer legs of the 'E' being of equal strength but 180° out of phase. When these pick-off currents are fed to the computer they cancel out giving a zero acceleration signal. When acceleration is sensed, the swing of the pendulum upsets the air gaps and the strength of the polarities induced in the outer legs of the 'E' is changed, one being stronger, the other weaker. The strength of the 180° out of phase AC currents induced in the two pick-off coils are no longer identical and when fed to the computer do not totally cancel out, leaving an error signal. From the phase of the error signal the computer is programmed to determine which way the pendulum has swung. The computer converts the error signal into a DC current, the direction of which is directly related to the direction of the acceleration; this current is used to force the pendulum to oppose the swing (see below), increasing in strength until a balance point is reached. The direction and strength of the DC current needed to achieve balance are directly related to the direction and strength of the acceleration being sensed. Located mid-way down the pendulum arm is the force-feed-back device which consists of a small permanent magnet mounted on the pendulum and a pair of soft iron rods with coils wound round them mounted to the case, one either side of the permanent magnet. The wiring around the soft iron rod is arranged so that when a correcting DC current is fed to the coils, magnetism is induced into the soft iron rods with like polarities facing inwards toward the permanent magnet. This repels one end of the permanent magnet and attracts the other, forcing the pendulum to one side. The direction and strength of the DC current controls the polarity and strength of the induced magnetism and hence the direction and force of swing of the pendulum. 'E/I' bar controlled force-feed-back systems are extremely sensitive, having instantaneous reaction to any change in acceleration. There are several variations in the design of accelerometers used in INS but all employ some form of force-feed-back system.

STABLE PLATFORM INS

22.8   *A stable platform INS* carries its accelerometers on a gimbal-mounted platform, the gimbals having movement about the aircraft's roll and pitch axes and the platform has movement in azimuth about the earth's vertical. All movements of the gimbals and the platform are driven by motors controlled by signals from three force-feed-back rate gyros mounted on the platform; these gyros are known as **Rate Integrating Gyros (RIG)**. A normal rate gyro has a spring or torsion bar that causes the gyro to precess with any turn being sensed in the plane in which it has no freedom. A rate integrated gyro has no spring or torsion bar. When such a rate gyro senses a movement in the plane in which it has no freedom, precession of the gyro tilts the 'I' bar of an 'E/I' pick-off generating an error signal that is used, via motors, to move the whole assembly back to the start position cancelling the tilt caused by the precession. Fig. 22–2 shows a rate integrated gyro with no freedom about the vertical axis. Yaw of the

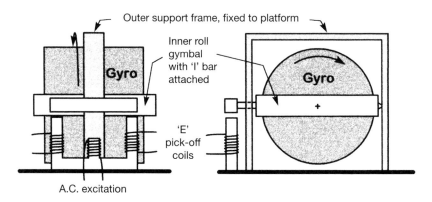

Fig. 22–2   Principle of a force-feed-back rate gyro.

platform causes the gyro to precess and roll the gimbal and 'I' bar, so upsetting the air gaps of the 'E/I' pick-off, the error signal being used to move the platform the opposite way to the original yaw.

The three rate integrated gyros on the stable platform are mounted so that:

One has no freedom about an E/W axis and reacts to any tilt toward N or S.

The second has no freedom about a N/S axis and so reacts to any tilt toward E or W.

And the third has no freedom about a vertical axis and so reacts to any movement in azimuth.

Signals from the gyros are sent to the INS computer which resolves them into appropriate voltages to be sent to the motors to counter the sensed movement of the platform. Fig. 22–3 illustrates the layout of the components of a stable platform.

22.9   The process of converting accelerations into navigational information is carried out in the INS computer. An integration process is used

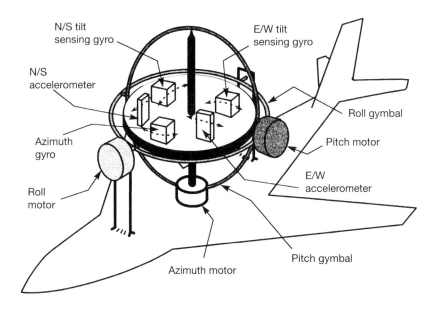

Fig. 22–3   Stable platform, layout of gimbals, motors and sensors.

to convert acceleration into speed and speed into distance travelled. 'Integration' is the assembling of the whole by the summation of all the parts over a given period of time:

Acceleration when integrated with respect to time gives speed.
Speed integrated with respect to time gives distance travelled.

In INS these integration processes commence the moment the aircraft starts to move from its parked position (in the case of airliners this includes the 'push-back' from the terminal). Starting from a known position and zero speed the current N/S and E/W speeds and distances travelled are resolved within the INS computer. The computer is also programmed to convert the current N/S and E/W speeds into current trk and GS and the N/S and E/W distances into the current brg and dist from the start position. Since the aircraft is flying above a sphere, the computations use

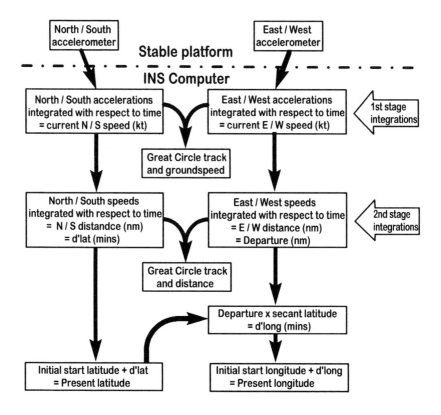

Fig. 22–4   The integration and position update process.

spherical trigonometry and the resultant trks and brgs are GC trks and brgs.

N/S dist (nm) = d'lat (see Chapter 1, paragraph 1.11), the computer applies this to the start lat to give the ***current lat read-out***.

E/W (nm) = dept (nm); in Chapter 3 paragraph 3.11 it was shown that Dept = d'long x cos lat, therefore d'log = Dept x sec lat. Tapping the current lat output to get sec lat enables the d'long to be computed which, when applied to the start long, gives the ***current long read-out***.
   The whole process is shown in the flow chart at Fig. 22–4.

22.10   Given in the instrument syllabus is an explanation of DGI errors due to the earth's rotation and transporting a gyro over the earth's surface. All that is needed here is to re-state these errors and their correction rates:

Error in	Correction for Earth's rotation	Correction for transport	
Tilt N/S	None	$\dfrac{\text{GS N/S}}{60}$	°/ hr
Tilt E/W	15 cos lat °/ hr	$\dfrac{\text{GS E/W}}{60}$	°/ hr
Azimuth	15 sin lat °/ hr	$\dfrac{\text{GS E/W}}{60}$	tan lat °/ hr

These same errors affect the gyros on the INS platform and the computer is programmed to feed in corrections based on knowledge of the current position and the N/S and E/W GSs. These errors are fundamental in the process of levelling and aligning the platform prior to initial taxiing of the aircraft and will be met again in paragraph 22.13. Further corrections are programmed into the computer to correct for the corriolis effects due to curved path of the aircraft over the earth's surface and the curved path of the earth through space.

22.11   ***Schuler Loop.*** An INS stable platform, being maintained in the earth's horizontal, is found to behave like a pendulum whose length is the same as the radius of the earth with its pivot at the centre of the earth. Such a pendulum is not affected by accelerations of the aircraft but if anything does disturbs the platform it will oscillate at a period of 84.4 min, a period consummate with a pendulum of length equal to the radius of the earth. Any disturbance results in the platform oscillating about a mean position with a see-sawing motion going through one full cycle every 84.4 min. During a full oscillation errors in GS occur, sometimes reading high at other times low, the extent of the error depending on the size of the disturbance. Over the full cycle period of 84.4 min the GS errors even out, the mean GS being the correct GS. This oscillation is known as the Schuler Loop. During workshop servicing, the platform can be deliberately disturbed and the period of the displacement cycle checked, any deviation from 84.4 min being used to tune the system.

22.12 *INS errors* are classified as either '*Bounded*' or '*Unbounded*' errors. As the names imply, Bounded errors do not increase with the passage of time whereas Unbounded errors do. False signals from the accelerometers will result in a constant Bounded GS error which, with the passage of time, results in increasing Unbounded distance and position errors. Referring back to Fig. 22–4 it can be seen that any errors at the 1st integration (speed) will be Bounded errors whereas errors at the 2nd integration (dist) will be Unbounded. There are several causes of INS errors:

(a) *Initial levelling of the platform.* If the platform is not correctly levelled, the accelerometers will continually be sensing a small component of gravity which will result in a constant Bounded GS error at the 1st stage of integration and an increasing Unbounded dist gone error at the 2nd stage of integration.

(b) *Initial alignment of the platform.* If the platform is not correctly aligned there will be a constant Bounded trk error equal to the amount of misalignment; with the passage of time this will give rise to an increasing Unbounded cross trk error.

(c) *Real wander of the rate integrated gyros.* The gyros employed are extremely accurate and ground tuning virtually eliminates real wander. A constant real wander on the levelling gyros of 0.1°/hr would cause a Bounded GS error of 6 kt, the same real wander rate on the azimuth gyro would cause a Bounded cross trk error of 0·05°. With such bounded errors at a GS of 600 kt, the Unbounded cross trk error after 1 hr would be about 0·5 nm and the Unbounded along trk error would be 6 nm, from which it can be seen that real wander on the levelling gyros is a major cause of errors in the INS. Fortunately, the real wander rates on INS gyros are closer to 0·01°/hr; rates as high as 0·1°/hr being rare. In flight, factors such as heavy turbulence can cause small amounts of unpredictable random wander.

(d) *Accelerometer and Computer errors.* Small errors in computation may occur due to minor imperfections in these components. In general errors, due to these sources are far smaller than those caused by gyro wander.

(e) **Inherent errors.** For absolute accuracy the true shape of the earth (an oblate spheroid) and the height of the aircraft above the earth's surface should be taken into account. Most INS ignore these factors as the errors are small and only become appreciable after covering great distances. Overall accuracy of an INS comes down to the degree of accuracy demanded by the operator and how much technology the operator is prepared to pay for it.

OPERATING PROCEDURES

22.13   *The initial levelling and alignment* of the platform can only be carried out on the ground with the aircraft stationary. The whole process takes about 15 min from switching on to being ready for use in the NAV mode. The aircraft's nose wheel position, accurate to the nearest tenth of a minute of lat and long, must be entered into the computer very early in the process. During the initial levelling and alignment the Inertial referencing function of the computer is caged and the accelerometers are used to level the platform. With the aircraft stationary the accelerometers should be sensing zero acceleration, but this will only happen if the platform is truly level. If the platform is not level one, or both, of the accelerometers will sense an element of gravity generating signals to the computer that are used to level the platform. Once the platform is level the initial alignment takes place using a process known as 'gyro compassing'. With the platform truly aligned with N(T), the N/S tilt sensing gyro will sense zero tilting and the E/W tilt sensing gyro will sense a tilt rate of 15 cos lat °/hr (see the table in paragraph 22.10). If the platform is not truly aligned, the N/S tilt sensing gyro will detect some of the E/W tilt and the resulting error signal is used to power the azimuth motor, turning the platform until zero tilt is sensed by the N/S tilt sensing gyro. Once levelling and alignment is completed and the INS switched to the NAV mode, the Inertial reference is un-caged, the platform is kept level and aligned by the three rate integrated gyros and the two accelerometers assume their function of measuring acceleration in the earth's horizontal plane.

THE FLIGHT DECK CONTROLS FOR INS, usually consist of a Mode Selector and a **Control Display Unit (CDU)**.

22.14   *The Mode Selector* (see Fig. 22–5) has a five-position Selector Control and two warning lights. Apart from one emergency function, the Mode Selector is only used during initial levelling and alignment and once

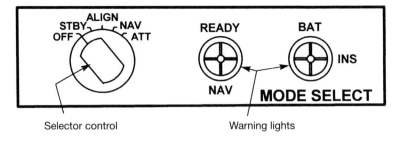

Selector control   Warning lights

Fig. 22–5   A typical INS Mode Selector.

switched to NAV should be left in that mode throughout the flight. It is common practice for the Mode Selector to be mounted well away from the CDU to prevent accidental switching from the NAV mode during flight. The five positions of the Selector Control are:

OFF   Power is switched off.

ST BY   Power is switched on. The navigation unit starts a fast warm up, the CDU is turned on, the digital computer is turned on and the Inertial reference is caged. The initial levelling procedure commences. The aircraft's ground position should be programmed into the CDU with the mode selector in this position.

ALIGN   Initial alignment takes place, taking approximately 15 min, during this period Waypoints can be inserted into the CDU and checked for accuracy. Once the alignment is successfully completed the green READY NAV illuminates.

NAV   Normal navigation operations can be carried out once levelling and alignment are completed. The aircraft must not be moved until NAV has been selected and verified by the Green READY NAV light illuminating. If NAV is selected straight from OFF the INS will automatically sequence through the ST BY and ALIGN procedures provided the aircraft is parked and the initial position programmed in the CDU. If for any reason the selector control is switched from NAV, the platform *must* be re-aligned; this can *only* be done on the ground with the aircraft parked. *Switching from NAV during flight loses all navigation functions for the rest of that flight.* To lessen the chances of inadvertent switching from NAV, the selector control has a safety lock built in whereby the control can only be turned after pulling the control out to release the lock.

ATT This is an emergency back-up for the vertical reference systems to the attitude indicator, automatic flight control system and radar stabilisation. In the event of failure of the normal vertical reference systems the INS platform can supply the attitude information, but selecting ATT means switching from NAV and the loss of all INS navigation functions for the rest of that flight.

The two warning lights are:

READY NAV A green light that illuminates when alignment has been achieved.

BAT INS A red light that illuminates if the INS has automatically shut down due to low battery power when operating on stand-by battery power. A stand-by battery is carried to cover for any interruptions to the normal supply of electrical power to the INS. The only other time this battery is used is for a few sec during alignment to check that sufficient power is available to start with.

22.15 *The Control and Display Unit (CDU)* (see Fig. 22–6) has left and right display panels, a keypad for insertion of navigation information, a Waypoint selector, a Waypoint FROM/TO display, a data selector control, an AUTO/MAN selector control and three warning lights.

The Data Selector Control is used to select requested navigation information for display in the left and right display panels as in the table below:

Data Selector	Left Display Panel	Right Display Panel
TK/GS	*Current GC trk (T)* to nearest 0.1°	*Current GS* to nearest kt
HDG/DA	*Current hdg (T)* to nearest 0.1°	*Drift Angle* Left or Right of hdg to nearest degree
XTK/TKE	*Cross trk dist,* Left or Right of desired trk, to nearest 0·1 nm	*Trk Angle Error,* Left or Right of desired trk, to nearest degree
POS	*Present Position,* to nearest 0·1 min of lat	*Present Position,* to nearest 0·1 min of long

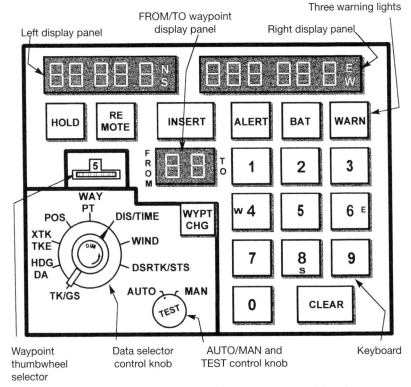

Fig. 22–6   A typical INS Contrl and Display Unit (CDU).

WAY PT   ***Waypoint Position***, to   ***Waypoint Position***, to
nearest 0·1 min of lat   nearest 0·1 min of long
(the Waypoint displayed is the one selected by the
Waypoint Thumbwheel)

DIS/TIME   *GC dist*, to nearest nm   *Time*, to nearest 0·1 min at
current GS
Depending on the setting of other controls the
DIST/TIME readout can be:
(a)   From present position to the next Waypoint.
(b)   From present position to a selected Waypoint.
(c)   From any selected Waypoint to another selected
Waypoint.

WIND	*Wind Direction (T),*	*Wind Speed*
	to nearest degree	to nearest kt

(the WIND function only works if the INS has a TAS input. With no TAS input the display screens remain blank when WIND is selected)

DSRTK/STS	*Desired Initial GC trk*	*System Status*	
	between the two Waypoints in the FROM/TO display, To nearest degree (T)	1st Fig	**1** if in NAV mode **0** if not in NAV mode
		2nd & 3rd Figs	Action Code or Malfunction Code
		4th Fig	Always blank
		5thFig	Current Performance Index
		6th Fig	Desired Performance Index (normally **5**)

The **AUTO/MAN (TEST)** control:

With **AUTO** selected the INS is linked to the aircraft's Automatic Flight Control System (AFCS) and the aircraft is automatically flown along the GC route sequentially through the Waypoints programmed into the INS computer.

With **MAN** selected the INS is not linked with the AFCS and the aircraft is being flown manually; by selecting XTK/TKE with the Data Selector, deviations from the desired GC trk can be monitored.

TEST is a push button control that has two functions:

On the ground, pushing the TEST button checks that the warning lights and all the electronics in the display panels are functioning.

When using the DSRTK/STS to check the status (see the WARN light below), pushing the TEST button switches between the Malfunction and Action Codes.

The three warning lights:

The **ALERT** warning light is an **amber** light. When the aircraft is being flown in the AUTO Mode this light illuminates for 2 min before reaching a Waypoint and goes out once the Waypoint is passed and the AFCS has altered hdg for the next Waypoint along the route. In the MAN Mode the light comes on 2 min before a Waypoint but starts to blink as the Waypoint is passed and does not go out until the Waypoint change is manually carried out.

The **BAT** warning light is an **amber** light. This light illuminates if the aircraft's electric power supply to the INS is interrupted and the INS is operating on stand-by battery power. Most INS have either 15 or 30 minutes of stand-by battery power after which time if the aircraft's electric supply is not restored to the INS it automatically shuts down and the **red BAT INS** light on the MODE SELECTOR comes on.

The **WARN** warning light is a **red** light. A self-checking system in the computer puts this light on whenever it detects an out-of-tolerance situation that requires prompt action. The Data Selector should immediately be set to DSRTK/STS and the Malfunction and Action Codes extracted (the 2nd and 3rd figures and the TEST button). Referring to the INS operational manual with the codes gives the appropriate action to be taken.

CHECKS

22.16 *Insertion of Initial lat.* Paragraphs 22.2 and 22.13 mentioned the need to insert the Initial Position into the CDU early in the levelling and aligning process and the fact that the position needed to be accurate to the nearest 0.1 min of lat and long. At the alignment stage the N/S tilt-sensing gyro 'Gyro Compasses' the platform until it senses zero tilt, at which point the E/W tilt-sensing gyro would be sensing a tilt rate of 15 cos (present) lat °/hr. The computer is programmed to compare the actual rate sensed with the rate it expects to sense based on the Initial Position lat entered into the CDU. If the Initial Position lat has been entered with a significant error the computer will be unable to balance the actual and expected tilt rates. The detection of this out-of-tolerance condition will result in the illumination of the WARN light on the CDU. Following the Malfunction and Action Codes process will pinpoint the error. Insertion of an accurate Initial Position lat is also very important bearing in mind that two of the corrections for the earth's rotation and one of the corrections for transport (see paragraph 22.10) require accurate input of the present lat throughout the flight.

22.17 *Insertion of Initial long.* An error in the insertion of the Initial long has no detrimental effect on the levelling and alignment of the platform, and there is no way by which the computer can automatically detect such an error. An incorrectly inserted Initial long should be detected when carrying out the Waypoint checks (see below), but if an error in the Initial long is discovered after the aircraft has started to move there are two possible options open (other than returning to the ramp and starting all over again):

(a)   Depending on the INS type it may be possible to apply a correction to the present long, equal to the d'long error.

(b)   If the present long cannot be corrected, all the Waypoints can be reprogrammed with the same d'long error as the present long.

22.18   *Insertion and checking of Waypoints*. Insertion of Waypoints is carried out in sequence, starting with the first one along the route. The Waypoint Thumbwheel Selector is used to give a number to each Waypoint as it is inserted with the Data Selector turned to the WAY PT position. To recall any Waypoint, set the Data Selector to WAY PT and dial the number of the required Waypoint with the Thumbwheel. This enables a full check of Waypoint lats and longs to be carried out against the flight plan, an essential precaution if an electronically downloaded route is being used. A second, and better, check is to use the DIS/TIME and DSRTK/STS positions on the Data Selector to check distance and initial GC trk between successive pairs of Waypoints along the route and cross-check them with the flight plan. If any Waypoint is incorrectly entered it will result in errors in dists and initial GS trks in the legs to and from it. Present position is given the Waypoint number of **0** by the computer, so the first leg is FROM **0 TO 1** in the Waypoint FROM/TO display panel. If the first leg dist and/or initial GS trk is found to be in error and the leg from **1** to **2** is not in error, then it is the Initial Position that must have been incorrectly entered and needs correcting.

22.19   *Radial Error Rate*. This is a check to monitor the performance of an INS installation over a period of time. At the end of each flight, before shutting down, the ramp position being occupied is entered into the CDU as if it were a new Waypoint. The Data Selector is turned to DIST/TIME to give the distance (in nm) between the indicated INS Present Position and the ramp position where it actually is. Dividing this by the total time in the NAV Mode (in hrs) gives the Radial Error Rate (in nm/hr) for that flight. Records of Radial Error Rates are used to monitor the performance of an INS and provide early warning of any sudden deterioration in overall performance.

STRAP DOWN IRS

22.20   *The Ring Laser Gyro (RLG)*. Strictly speaking a RLG is not a gyro since it does not have a rotating mass that possesses properties of rigidity

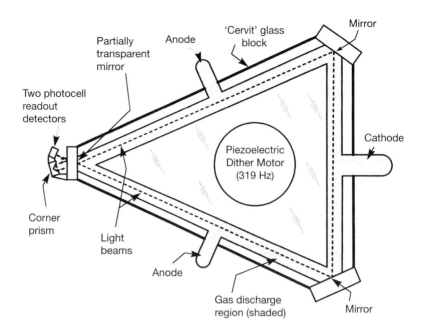

Fig. 22–7   Schematic layout of a typical Ring Laser Gyroscope (RLG).

and precession, what it does do is to emulate a rate gyro in that it measures rates of rotation about a fixed axis. A RLG employs a pair of laser beams moving in opposite directions around an enclosed path set at 90° to a fixed axis. Fig. 22–7 shows the layout of a typical RLG, made up of a solid triangular block of 'Cervit' (an extremely hard, temperature stable, glass) with a triangular path very accurately drilled through it linking mirrors set at each corner. All the air is evacuated from the drilled pathways and a small charge of helium-neon gas injected in its place. The pathways have a cathode and two anodes located as shown in Fig. 22–7. A high voltage is passed between the anodes and the cathode and the gas becomes ionised emitting an orange-pink light, which by design is made to turn into two beams having identical frequencies but travelling in opposite directions around the pathways. The mirrors serve two purposes: as well as reflecting the beams around the pathways they act as filters, absorbing all light frequencies other than the selected light frequency they are designed to reflect. The mirror at the end of the longer sides of the triangle is partially transparent and allows some of each beam of light through, one directly and the other via a corner prism, to the detector unit where their frequencies are optically compared. When no rotation is taking place about the axis

310

to which the RLG is fixed (or 'Strapped') the two light beams have exactly the same distance to travel to get round the triangle, taking exactly the same time and with no change to their frequencies. When identical frequencies are optically compared in the detector unit they match and do not produce a moving fringe (error) pattern. Rotation around the axis to which the RLG is 'strapped' takes the mirrors with it so that one light beam has mirrors moving toward it, effectively shortening its path round the triangle, whilst the other beam has the mirrors moving away from it, effectively lengthening its path round the triangle. The effect is that one light beam is compressed, shortening its wavelength whilst the other light beam is stretched, increasing its wavelength. When the two different wavelengths are optically compared they produce a moving fringe pattern which the computer is programmed to decode as to the direction and rate of rotation taking place about the axis to which the RLG is 'strapped'.

The relationship between input rate of rotation and the output frequency is linear, but at very low input rotation rates the output frequency can become non-linear and at certain threshold values it can suddenly drop to zero. This is known as a 'lock- in' and is caused by the beams becoming synchronised due to small amounts of energy from the beams back-scattering into each other. To overcome this problem a piezoelectric dither motor is fitted which vibrates the RLG about its input axis throughout the 'lock-in' region,

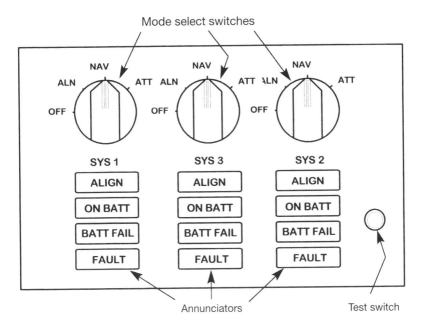

Fig. 22–8   Triple-channel Mode Selector Unit.

311

unlocking the beams and enabling the small movements of the fringe pattern to be read. The output of the RLG is corrected for the dither motion. This is an essential addition to the LRG since it is a necessary requirement that rates of rotation as low as 0·001°/hr be detectable for IN/IR systems to work effectively, and 'lock-in' could lead to undesirable errors.

22.21 *The Mode Selector Unit (MSU).* The MSU of a strap-down IRS has similar switching and functions to the stable platform INS; the only differences are that since strap-down IRS uses digital signal processing and RLG there is no need for a warm-up period requiring a STBY position on the selector, and the use of annunciators to replace warning lights. Fig. 22–8 shows a triple-channel MSU for use in aircraft with triple IRS, such a unit being connected to a CDU having a selection switch enabling individual IRS units to be interrogated. The functions of the annunciators are:

ALIGN   White light. Steady illumination when the system is in the align mode.
Flashes on and off if there is a failure in the alignment procedure.

ON BATT   Amber light. Illuminates to indicate that power to the system has automatically switched from the normal (115 V AC) to battery (28 V DC).

BATT FAIL   Amber light. Illuminates when battery power source falls below 18 V DC.

FAULT   Amber light. Illuminates when any system failures are detected.

22.22 *The Inertial System Display Unit (ISDU)* controls and functions of an IRS are similar to those of the CDU of an INS, though some variations in layout may be found between different manufacturers and models. The initial alignment still requires the aircraft to have its position accurately inserted and the aircraft to remain stationary during the process. The IRS computer program takes into account all the factors that the INS computer handled plus corrections for gravity and the fact that the laser beams are measuring movement relative to space and not the earth; from the inputs it can resolve the earth's horizontal, N(T) and long. The alignment phase is initiated by turning the mode selector switch to either the **ALIGN** or **NAV** position, the **NAV** position being the preferred option. During the align phase the **ALIGN** annunciator illuminates with a steady light but will start to flash on and off if the aircraft is moved before the system has reached the nav ready phase and the switch turned to the **NAV** position. If the **ALIGN** annunciator starts to flash, the mode selector must be turned to **OFF** for at least 3 secs before restarting the align process. The total time from starting the align process to reaching the nav ready state varies with the latitude of the start position, this can vary from 2·5 min at the equator up to 10 min at 70° N or S. Due to degrading of the systems navigation performance accuracy at lats higher than 70° N or S alignment may not be obtainable at these lats. At lats above 70° N or S, extending time in the Align mode to 15 min may improve the alignment, but longer than 15 min has little extra effect.

ALIGNMENT TESTS

22.23   *Reasonableness test.* Immediately the initial lat and long is entered into the ISDU the IRU checks it against the shut down lat and long. If the two positions do not agree within stored limits, the MSU ALIGN annunciator will start to flash. If the initial position's co-ordinates are rejected as having been incorrectly entered they should be replaced with the correct co-ordinates. If on the other hand a new IRU has been installed or the aircraft repositioned without use of the IRU, the re-entering of identical initial lat and long co-ordinates will override the test and the co-ordinates be accepted.

22.24   *System Performance Test.* When the alignment process is completed, the IRU automatically compares the initial position entered in the ISDU with its computed lat. If they are within given limits the test is passed and the system is ready for use in the **NAV** mode. If the limits are exceeded the test is failed and the **ALIGN** annunciator light flashes and the IRU will not enter the **NAV** mode until a new position is entered whose lat passes the system performance test. If two identical initial positions are entered consecutively and both fail the test, the **ALIGN** annunciator changes from flashing to steady and the **FAULT** annunciator illuminates; these will not shut off until a acceptable initial position has been entered into the ISDU.

CHAPTER 23

FLIGHT MANAGEMENT SYSTEMS

23.1 **A Flight Management System (FMS)** consists of two major units, a *Flight Management Computer (FMC)* and a *Control and Display Unit (CDU)*. The primary function of an FMS is the automatic amalgamation and analysis of ongoing navigation and performance data to obtain the most efficient operation of the aircraft in terms of adherence to the flight plan and fuel economy.

23.2 *The role of the FMC* is the collection of all the inputs, from various sources, relevant to the navigation and performance of the aircraft. Fig. 23–1 illustrates a typical information distribution via data busses; actual cases will vary according to the specific equipment installation in an aircraft.

23.3 *Components of a typical FMC*

(a) A 'bubble' memory holding the bulk of the navigation and performance data bank.

(b) A *Random Access Memory (RAM)* holding specific navigation and performance data for the active and secondary flight plan.

(c) A *Programmable Read Only Memory (PROM)* for the operation programme.

All the above will vary according to aircraft type and the aircraft operator's route structure. Route structure can be pre-recorded onto magnetic tape and downloaded into the 'bubble' memory via a portable database loader unit. Updates of navigation procedures, navigation aids and route structures are carried out, via the data loader, at laid down time intervals, usually every 28 days.

23.4 *Contents of a typical performance database*

(a) *Engine Pressure Ratios (EPR)* covering all aspects of flight for the aircraft type.

314

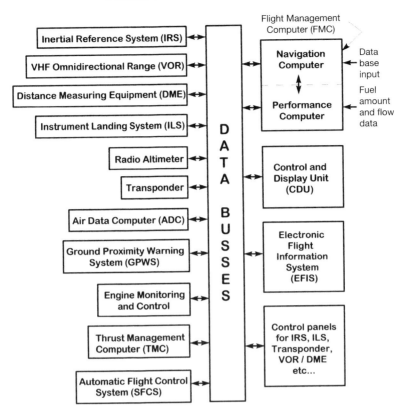

Fig. 23-1   Simplified diagram of a typical information distribution via data busses.

(b)   *Speeds* for Climb (**CLB**), Cruise (**CRZ**), Descent (**DES**) and Holding (**HOLD**) to give best fuel economy. Allied to the speeds are rate of climb in CLB, maximum endurance in HOLD and the time and distance in DES.

All the parameters are programmed to adjust for altitude and temperature changes.

23.5   *Order of priority the FMC uses to select aids for position fixing.*
FMC are programmed to select the best combination of aids available at the time for the computation of the most accurate position of the aircraft, altitude and ground speed. This involves automatic tuning of receivers to search for DMEs and VORs within range of the aircraft's present position and the selection of ILS for update of position during the approach phase

of a flight. Accuracy of DME is deemed to be better than VOR accuracy, so priority is given to scanning for DME, one VOR to three DMEs being a typical scan ratio. Three DMEs providing a simultaneous three-position line fix provide a more accurate position than a VOR/DME fix from a co-located source. The automatic selection sequence follows a decreasing scale depending on aid availability. The hierarchy sequence is:

(a) *1ˢᵗ option.* With IRS in Normal Mode plus VOR and DME all available, automatic selection of the RADIO/INERTIAL MODE takes place.

(b) *2ⁿᵈ option.* IRS in Normal Mode available but no DME or VOR available, automatic selection of the INERTIAL MODE ONLY takes place.

(c) *3ʳᵈ option.* With VOR and DME available but no IRS in Normal Mode available, automatic selection of the RADIO MODE ONLY takes place.

(d) *4ᵗʰ option.* With no IRS in Normal Mode, VOR or DME available, but with TAS (from the ADC), valid hdg (M) (from an AHRS), an IRS in Reversionary Mode with Set Heading bit and last known W/V all available, automatic selection of the DEAD RECKONING MODE takes place.

In the event that the FMC is unable to meet any of the above requirements, no Navigation Mode is selected and the Navigation function is lost.

23.6   ***The role of the CDU*** is to provide the means by which the pilot and the FMC communicate with each other. Fig. 23–2 illustrates the layout of a typical FMS CDU. Different manufacturers produce CDUs with variation to the illustrated layout but all FMS CDUs have alphanumeric keys, page change keys, scroll keys, a selection of function keys, line keys, annunciators and a ***Cathode Ray Tube (CRT)*** which may be either monochrome or colour. The model illustrated has a CRT with a display of 14 lines of text each of 24 characters; some models have as few as nine lines of text. Colour CRTs use the colours to highlight certain important items, the colours used being matched as near as possible with the colours used on the Electronic Flight Information System (EFIS). That is to say, Blue (cyan) for Vertical information, Green for both Lateral information and Index selections, Magenta (pink) for TO a Waypoint, Yellow for FROM a Waypoint, Orange for Flight Plan names and White for Titles and Prompts.

23.7   ***Information blocks on the CRT*** are accessed via the function keys. The table below outlines what information is to be found by using the different keys:

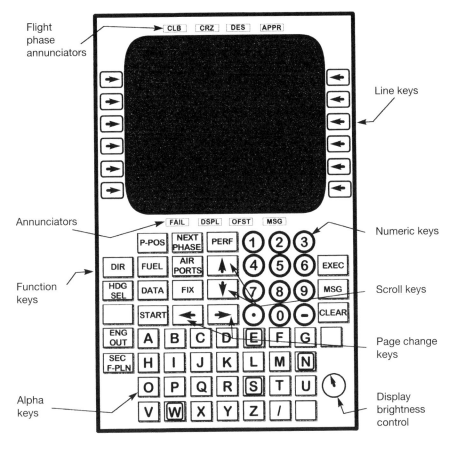

Fig. 23–2 A typical FMS Control and Display Unit (CDU).

Key	Selection of this function ...
P-POS	shows the active navigation page and displays aircraft's present position.
NEXT PHASE	changes the navigation leg display to the start of the next phase of the flight plan.
PERF	displays the performance pages.
DIR	allows entry of revisions to the flight plan directly from present position to any waypoint.

317

FUEL   displays the fuel pages.

AIR-PORTS   displays the navigation legs page which contains the next airport along the current flight plan route.

HDG SEL   displays the headings to be flown automatically via the FMS.

DATA   displays the data index pages. These pages cover data relative to vertical, lateral, sensors, performance, key waypoints, navigation, maintenance, aircraft configuration and history.

FIX   displays the aircraft's position for checking or updating.

START   displays the 'START DATA REQUIRED' pages enabling the flight crew to construct and initiate flight plans.

ENG OUT   displays the performance data pages that relate to engine out operations.

SEC F-PLAN   displays the secondary flight plan facility to enable re-clearance or return-leg planning.

EXEC   enables the promotion of a temporary plan to an active status. When the FMCS has sufficient data to create an active plan the bar illuminates and stays illuminated until the temporary plan has been activated or cancelled (cancellation is by pressing the P POS function key).

MSG   acknowledges any message displayed on the CDU and telling the computer the message will be either stored or erased.

CLEAR   deletes incorrect scratch pad entries.

23.8   *CRT Display* There are many pages of data that can accessed for displaying on the CRT (see paragraph 23.7 above), far more than can be detailed within the scope of this chapter. Fig. 23–3 is an example of one such page and illustrates how information is presented and advisory cues given to the pilot. Cues given include:

↓ (a) On the top line to indicate that active page requires information inserted.

 (b) On the bottom line to indicate the function key to press to scroll the page on.

↑ On the bottom line to indicate the function key to press to scroll the page back.

→ (a) On the top line to indicate that next page requires information inserted.

 (b) Opposite one of the line keys on the right-hand side to indicate that the pilot has an option to display more information or initiate a process.

← Opposite one of the line keys on the left-hand side to indicate that the pilot has an option to display more information or initiate a process.

? Indicates a request for the pilot to enter information.

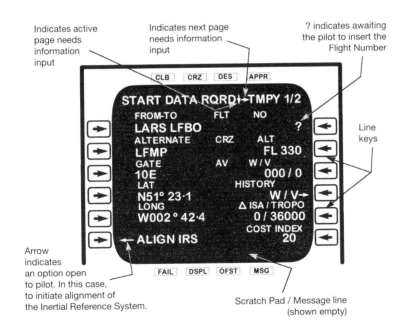

Fig. 23–3   An example of a CRT page display.

23.9   The first thing to notice is that there are two sizes of lettering. The page title at the top and the lines opposite the line keys are in larger print than the intermediate lines of text. The smaller print identifies the data printed immediately below it, this data being either a default value, a computer calculated value or a pilot entered value. The page shown is typical of that displayed when the **START** function key is pressed to initiate the construction of a flight plan.

The top line gives the page name (**START DATA RQRD**) then arrows ($\downarrow\rightarrow$) indicating that information is required on both the active and the following page. This is followed by (**TMPY**) indicating that the data being entered by the pilot is a temporary flight plan (i.e. not a standard company flight plan stored in the data bank). Finally (**1/2**) indicating that this is page 1 of 2 pages.

In line two (**FROM-TO**) and (**FLT NO**) identify what the data in the next line three is.

In line three the ICAO location indicators for the departure and arrival point are given having been entered by the pilot, there is as yet no flight number showing but a (**?**) at the end of the line indicates that the computer is waiting for the pilot to insert this information.

Lines four and five show that the alternate airfield and the cruise FL data have been entered by the pilot.

Lines six and seven show the gate, or stand, number has been entered along with the default W / V.

In lines eight to eleven on the left-hand side are the gate co-ordinates for the IRS start point; if these are stored in the FMC data 'bubble', download to the page should be automatic, otherwise the pilot has to enter them in. The arrow pointing to the line key gives the pilot the option to call up W / V data from the history bank. The (**ISA / TROPO**) data is at default.

Lines twelve and thirteen show the default (**COST INDEX**) and a arrow beside (**ALIGN IRS**) is giving the pilot the option to initiate alignment of the IRS.

Line fourteen is used for the scratch pad and messages. The alphanumerical keys are used to enter new information, or changes, into the scratch pad where it can be checked before it is entered into the page proper. If the entry is correct it is transferred to its location on the page by pressing the line key adjacent to its destination. If the entry is incorrect it can be deleted by pressing the **CLEAR** function key. In Fig. 24–3 the flight number is being requested by the use of a **?**. When the pilot first types in the flight number it appears in the scratch pad where it can be checked before transferring it to the page by pressing the line key next to the **?**. If a small correction is needed to any item already on a page the item must first be transferred to the scratch pad by pressing the line key next to the item. After correction the line key is again used to restore the item to the page. Corrections can only be carried out in the scratch pad. The line also is where alert messages from the computer to the pilot are displayed, such messages are drawn to the pilot's attention by the **MSG** annunciator illuminating. Any scroll cues appear at the right-hand end of the line.

23.10   Referring back to Fig. 24–2, the four flight phase annunciators in the row above the CRT light up white (advisory) in accordance with the current phase of a flight. For example, during the climb phase the **CLB** annunciator illuminates while the CRT displays the flight plan page with the climb data on it. The four annunciators below the CRT are alert and advisory signals, The **FAIL** (amber light) illuminates whenever the FMS performance is lower than that required for the current phase of a flight. The other three annunciators are white (advisory) lights. The **DSPL** annunciator lights up whenever the page displayed on the CRT is not relevant to the current phase of the flight. The **OFST** annunciator lights up whenever a lateral offset has been entered into the FMS. The **MSG** annunciator lights up to draw attention to a message display on the bottom line of the CRT.

23.11   Specific start-up and pre-flight checks will vary with the aircraft type, equipment fit and the manufacturer and model of the FMS. Basic checks should include ensuring that all items of equipment monitored by the FMS are on and functioning correctly, all switch lights and annunciator lights tested to make sure they will function correctly if needed, brightness control set to the desired level and the flight plan and fuel checks carried out.

CHAPTER 24

ELECTRONIC FLIGHT INSTRUMENT SYSTEMS

24.1   The development of smaller and more powerful data processors and their application to aircraft instrument displays has lead to today's 'glass cockpit' where CRTs have relegated many of the traditional pressure- and gyro-driven mechanical displays to secondary stand-by roles. The CRTs of an **Electronic Flight Instrument System (EFIS)** are able to display selected information pertaining to the current phase of a flight to the exclusion of unwanted information, thus making the pilot's task easier. An EFIS has a Control Panel and two CRT colour display units, one an *Attitude Display Indicator (ADI)* and the other a *Horizontal Situation Indicator (HSI)*. A processor known as a *Symbol Generator (SG)* is continually updated with (electronic) inputs from the Air Data Computer (ADC), the Autopilot flight director computer and the FMS plus heading and altitude information from the IRS. The SG is also connected to the EFIS control panel, the ADI and HSI; pilot selections on the EFIS control panel decide what is shown on the two CRTs.

24.2 The EFIS Control Panel is divided into two areas, the ADI controls and the HSI controls, the HSI controls having a further sub-area for the control of data when operating in the PLAN mode.

The *ADI controls* consist of a manual brightness control for the ADI CRT (**BRT**), a Decision Height selector (**DH**), DH display (**DH REF**) and DH reset button (**RST**).

The *HSI Mode selector* enables selection of the HSI display to match the operational mode of the flight. There are four main modes:

A **FULL VOR** or **FULL ILS** mode that has a full compass rose display similar to a non-electronic HSI display.

An **EXP**anded **VOR** or **EXP**anded **ILS** mode that is oriented with hdg (M) at 12 o'clock with the aircraft symbol near the bottom of the screen and an arc of 80° of the compass rose at the top of the screen.

A **MAP** mode similar to the **EXP** modes but oriented with trk (M) at 12 o'clock and route information within the selected range (such as Waypoints and TRK (M)) plotted in plan form.

322

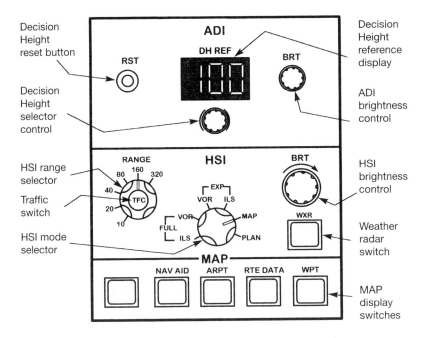

Fig. 24–1   Layout of a typical EFIS Control Panel.

A **PLAN** mode that is displayed oriented to N (M) showing the flight plan route in plan form.

The *HSI Range selector* gives the pilot the option of selecting the range (ahead of the aircraft) to be displayed on the HSI CRT when operating in either the **MAP** or **PLAN** modes. This control sometimes has a Traffic switch (**TFC**) for display of *Traffic Alert and Collision Avoidance System (TACS)* information on the HSI.

When in the **MAP** mode other information can be selected as required via push buttons that light up when selected; items such as navigation aids (**NAV AID**) and aerodromes within the selected area (**ARPT**), flight plan altitudes and ETAs at waypoints (**RTE DATA**), waypoints (**WPT**) and weather radar returns (**WXR**).

24.3   The ADI reduces the pilot's scanning workload by combining the functions of many of the traditional attitude instruments in one display (see Fig. 24–2). The central part of the display is an electronic artificial horizon with an aircraft symbol in front of a moving horizon with a blue sky above and a yellow/brown earth below. There are pitch attitude scales above and below the horizon and a roll scale around the top. When a Flight Director is engaged, white command bars are displayed. Depending on the model many other functions can be superimposed, some permanently, others selected as required. Listed below are some of items that can be displayed (see Fig. 24–2):

In the bottom right-hand corner of the display is the selected Decision Height (DH) and the current reading from the radio altimeter. Above 1000 ft this is in alphanumerical form (main picture), but below 1000 ft it changes to a dial form with a marker bug at the DH and a numerical readout and a decreasing arc for the altitude from the radio altimeter (see corner scrap).

In the bottom left corner the Mach No and GS are displayed when the speed is in excess of Mach 0.4 (not shown on the diagram because the speed is too low).

Down the left side is an airspeed scale with the command airspeed readout shown digitally (at the top) and as a bug (on the scale), the current airspeed is shown digitally inside a wide airspeed indicator symbol which moves up and down with speed changes.

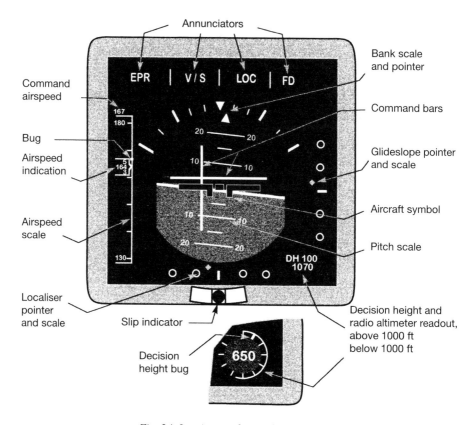

Fig. 24–2   A typical ADI display.

324

Along the bottom and right side are Localiser and Glideslope pointers and scales.

Annunciators along the top (reading from left to right) give information on the performance of Autothrottle, Automatic Flight Director System (pitch), Automatic Flight Director System (roll) and Autopilot plus Flight Director. Each annunciator performs a series of status reports; the display in Fig. 24–2 gives an example of one possibility in each position.

Most ADI displays have a standard (non-electronic) slip indicator below the CRT.

24.4   The HSI. As stated in paragraph 24.2, the HSI mode selector gives the pilot the choice of mode that can be displayed on the HSI.

The **FULL VOR** and **FULL ILS** modes are 360° compass rose displays with the aircraft in the centre of the screen, the ILS mode additionally having a glideslope deviation scale. These displays are the same as non-electronic HSI displays both in presentation and use.

The **EXP VOR** and **EXP ILS** modes display the same information as the full modes but in an expanded form, concentrating on the sector ahead of the aircraft. The aircraft symbol is located near the bottom of the screen with **hdg (M)** oriented to the 12 o'clock position, with an arc of the compass rose (40° either side of the aircraft's hdg) at the top of the screen. The hdg (M) is displayed above the arc of the compass rose in numerical form. Present trk (M) and the localiser course are shown as straight lines from the aircraft symbol to the compass arc. All four Full and Expanded displays have the WV vector arrow and speed at bottom left of the screen and the localiser deviation scale under the aircraft symbol. Both expanded modes can have the weather radar information displayed by switching the **WXR** switch located on the Control panel to ON. Weather returns are colour coded according to the intensity of the signal returns. Generally Red is used to denote the areas of strongest returns, Amber for medium returns and Green for the lowest returns. Magenta is used to indicate turbulence.

The layout of the **MAP** mode is similar in some respects to the expanded VOR and ILS modes in that the position of the aircraft symbol, the WV vector and 80° of compass arc are the same. However, in this mode it is the **trk (M)** that is oriented to 12 o'clock on the screen. The range ahead displayed on the screen depends on the range selected on the Control panel, the *half range* value being displayed at the mid-point of the trk (M) line.

Fig. 24–3 depicts a typical MAP display showing the aircraft to Starboard of the flight plan route and on trk (M) direct for waypoint XYZ bypassing waypoint UVW. With waypoint XYZ selected (using the FMS)

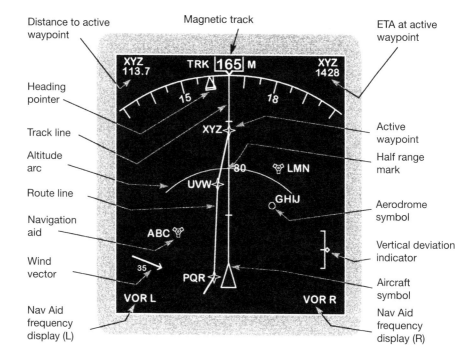

Distance to active waypoint

Magnetic track

ETA at active waypoint

Heading pointer

Track line

Altitude arc

Route line

Navigation aid

Wind vector

Nav Aid frequency display (L)

Active waypoint

Half range mark

Aerodrome symbol

Vertical deviation indicator

Aircraft symbol

Nav Aid frequency display (R)

Fig. 24–3   Typical HSI display in MAP mode.

as the active waypoint, the dist and ETA to XYZ are displayed at the top left and right of the screen. The relative positions of navigation aids that are within operational range are shown as a result of **NAV AID** being selected on the Control panel. The type of aid, its identification and frequency are automatically displayed at the bottom left and right of the screen. When an aid is tuned in its symbol is displayed in green (see colour coding below). With **ARPT** selected on the Control panel all aerodromes held in the database that fall within the selected map area are displayed by a circle and identity. When the Mode Control Panel (MCP) is used to initiate a programmed altitude change an Altitude arc is displayed, the point where it crosses the trk being the position at which the desired altitude will be reached. Displayed only during descent is a vertical deviation indicator showing any deviation from the programmed vertical profile, the scale limits being ±400 ft. Fig. 24–3 covers most of the symbols used in an HSI display; further clarification is obtained by use of a colour code (first mentioned in Chapter 23, paragraph 23.6). The colour code breaks down as follows:

Green	Indicates active (or engaged) flight mode displays.
White	Indicates present status information, scales and armed flight mode displays.
Magenta (pink)	Indicates command information, symbols, pointers and fly-to condition.
Cyan (blue)	Indicates background and non-active information.
Red	Indicates warning.
Amber	Indicates faults, cautionary information and flags (see paragraph 24.5).
Black	Indicates blank areas or off condition.

The layout of the **PLAN** mode display has the same details at the top of the screen as the MAP mode display. That is to say an 80° arc of the compass with the trk (M) in the 12 o'clock position, current hdg marker, dist to next waypoint and ETA (in Z time) to next waypoint. The rest of the screen has a diagram of the active FMS flight plan *oriented to North*; this is particularly useful for cross checking against the flight plan data. Use of the range selector on the control panel can expand parts of the route for more detail, especially useful for checking terminal area manoeuvring.

24.5 *EFIS failure flags.* As mentioned in the previous paragraph, these are Amber in colour, and typically appear on the screen as boxes superimposed over the failed item.

ADI display failure flags include:

SEL SPD (Command speed symbol and/or display failed), **SPD** (Speed data from ADC invalid, or display failed), **MACH** (Mach data from ADC invalid), **FD** (Flight director failed in pitch and roll), **ATT** (Attitude data from source invalid), **LOC** (LOC receiver or display failed), **G/S** (GS receiver or display failed), **DH** (DH data failed while at or above 1000 ft), **RA** (RA data failed while at or above 1000 ft).

HSI display failure flags include:

TRK (HDG) (Trk or hdg data unreliable), **MAP** (FMC-generated map display failed), **VTK** (FMC vertical trk data unreliable), **VOR 1** (or **2**) (VOR failed), **ADF 1** (or **2**) (ADF failed), **VOR (LOC)** (VOR or LOC signal unreliable in VOR or APP mode).

24.6   Specific start-up and pre-flight checks will vary with the aircraft type, the navigation fit and the manufacturer and model of the EFIS installed. Basic checks should include ensuring that all items of equipment that are linked to the EFIS are on and functioning properly, all switch lights and warning lights tested to make sure they will function, brightness controls and the range and mode selectors tested. With these basics out of the way the details of the route flight plan should be cross-checked against the loaded flight plan; this task is made easier with the HSI in the PLAN mode.

CHAPTER 25

GLOBAL POSITIONING SYSTEM

25.1   Global Positioning System (GPS) is a fully operational space-based global fixing and time determination system available for use by commercial airlines. It is not unique, a similar Russian military system called Glonass has been offered to commercial aviation and the European Space Agency is in the process of setting up a system to be known as Galileo and promises to offer a degree of accuracy far better than anything currently available. The ultimate aim of ICOA is to have a Global Navigation Satellite System (GNSS) that will meet a set of strict performance requirements; whether this will ultimately be met by just one system or a combination of systems is yet to be resolved. In the meantime, pilots need to make themselves familiar with the principles of how these systems operate, as satellite navigation in one form or another looks set to become a major feature on the flight deck. A brief look at GPS, currently the most common system around, is as good a starting point as any.

25.2   GPS is a USA military system, the potential accuracy of which varies with the receiver equipment. Equipment capable of interrogating the very highest degree of GPS accuracy is currently only available to the American Armed Forces and a few other carefully vetted organisations. Though delivering a lower degree of positioning accuracy, GPS receivers on the open market provide global fixing that more than matches the legal requirements of commercial aviation. GPS is made up of three segments, a Satellite Segment (in space), a Control Segment (on the ground) and a User Segment (either on the earth's surface or in an aircraft). Fig. 25–1 shows how these segments communicate with each other.

25.3   The Space Segment (see Fig. 25–2) consists of 24 satellites (21 operational and 3 on standby) orbiting the earth at approximately 11,000 nm (20,200 km) and taking approximately 12 hr to complete a full orbit. The satellites are equally distributed between six separate orbiting paths that are inclined at 55° to the equator and spaced out so that at any time at least five satellites can be viewed from any point on the earth.

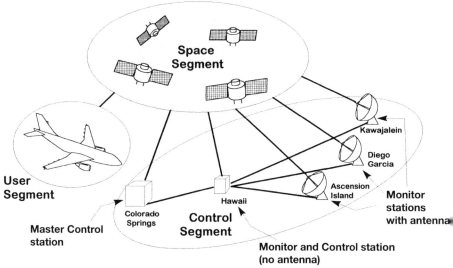

Fig. 25–1   The three major GPS segments.

25.4   *Pseudo-Random Code.* Each satellite has its own unique encoded signal known as a pseudo-random code, which it transmits along with its position and the precise time of transmission, repeating itself every millisecond. The user GPS receiver uses the message to identify and track individual satellites for ranging purposes. There are two types of pseudo-random code, one giving access to a Precise Positioning Service (PPS) only available to vetted users and the other a Standard Positioning Service (SPS) available for general public use. Since the middle of the year 2000 the SPS position accuracy has been improved and is now virtually the same as PPS accuracy. Three satellites are the minimum needed to obtain a two-dimensional fix provided the altitude of the user is known, for a full three-dimensional fix four satellites are needed.

25.5   *The Navigation Message.* This is information superimposed on the code for the PPS and SPS and is normally updated every four hrs. The navigation message contains information on GPS time of transmission, ephemeris (where each satellite is within the constellation), clock data and almanac (orbital data for the entire constellation) plus additional information on satellite health and coefficients for calculation of UTC.

25.5   **The Control Segment.** This consists of a Master Control Station located in Colorado Springs and four Monitoring stations located around

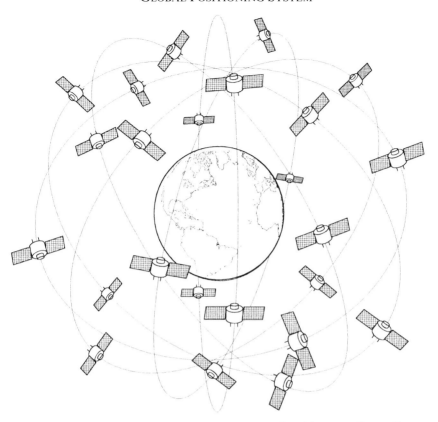

Fig. 25–2   The GPS constellation of 21 operational and three standby satellites.

the globe within about 15° of the Equator. The stations keep track of all satellites within their view and pass information on to the Control stations for control of the satellites' clock, orbital state and navigation messages. The satellites are frequently updated with new data for the navigation messages.

25.6   The User Segment. Almanac data is stored in the user's receiver and on start-up the receiver checks the almanac to see which satellites should currently be in sight from its present location; it then searches for the appropriate codes. Once a satellite is detected the user starts to receive and process the navigation information from that satellite. It then establishes ranges to all the satellites detected and, from knowing their positions, is able to compute the aircraft's position, speed and time. This process is known as *pseudoranging*. With the receiver's clock fully synchronised with the satellites (atomic) clocks, three or more satellites give fixes with the satellite ranges all passing precisely through the fix position. If the receiver's clock is out of synch the ranges obtained will form a 'Cocked Hat' fix (see Chapter 17, paragraph 17.20). The computer in the receiver recognises this error and goes through a trimming process to correct the error and at the same time correct its clock.

25.7   Receiver Displays. These vary from manufacturer to manufacturer and model to model. All have a CDU or a control panel with key pads for entering flight planning details and have displays of items such as position, trk, GS, ETA and, if a TAS input is connected, the WV. The display will also have the ability to display satellite status, which satellites are in view and being tracked and the integrity status and signal quality.

25.8   This introduction to GPS is brief in the extreme and is only intended to give the student pilot an idea of the very basic ideas behind global positioning by satellites. Students will find that if ever (which is very likely) they have to convert onto an aircraft type with global positioning equipment there will be vast amounts of technical literature on the subject waiting for them on the conversion course.

TABLE OF ABBREVIATIONS

<	less than	conv	convergency
>	more than	cos	cosine
AC	Alternating Current	CP	Critical Point
ADI	Attitude Display Indicator	CRT	Cathode Ray Tube
ADC	Air Data Computer	**D**	Total Distance of leg in calculation of the Critical Point
AFCS	Automatic Flight Control System	**d**	distance to the Critical Point from the start of the leg
ASI	Airspeed Indicator		
ATD	Actual Time of Departure	DC	Direct Current
brg	bearing	DH	Decision Height
(C)	Compass (direction)	d'lat	difference in latitude
°C	Degrees Celsius (centigrade temperature)	d'long	difference in longitude
CA	Closing Angle	Dept	Departure
ca	conversion angle	dev	deviation
CAS	Calibrated Airspeed	DF	Direction Finding (ground station)
CDU	Control and Display Unit	DGI	Directional Gyro Indicator
CG	Centre of Gravity	DME	Distance Measuring Equipment (ground-based radio aid)
ch'lat	change in latitude (another name for d'lat)		
ch'long	change in longitude (another name for d'long)	DR	Deduced (Dead) Reckoning
		E	East (direction)
		E	Endurance (can be expressed in time or fuel available)
COAT	Correct Outside Air Temperature		
coeff	coefficient	EAS	Equivalent Airspeed
Comp.Corr.	Compressibility Correction	EFIS	Electronic Flight Instrument System

ETA	Estimated Time of Arrival	INS	Inertial Navigation System
FD	Flight Director	ISA	International Standard Atmosphere
ft	feet		
FMC	Flight Management Computer		
		ISDU	Inertial System Display Unit
FMS	Flight Management System		
		kg	kilograms (weight)
(G)	Grid (direction)	kn	knots (nautical miles per hour – speed)
g / cub m	grams per cubic metre (atmospheric density)		
		kph	kilometres per hour (speed)
GC	Great Circle	lat	latitude
GMT	Greenwich Mean Time	lb	pounds (weight)
		LCB	Line of Constant Bearing
gnm	ground nautical miles		
GNSS	Global Navigation Satellite System	LMT	Local Mean Time
		long	longitude
GPS	Global Positioning System	lt	litres (volume)
		m	metres (distance)
griv	grivation	M No	Mach Number
GS	Ground Speed	(M)	Magnetic (direction)
H	Home (as in Groundspeed Home)	mb	millibars (atmospheric pressure)
H	Horizontal component of the Earth's magnetic field		
		MCP	Mode Control Panel
		min	minutes (time)
hdg	heading	MSU	Mode Selector Unit
HSI	Horizontal Situation Indicator	mph	statute miles per hour (speed)
hr	hours (time)	msl	mean sea level
IAS	Indicated Airspeed	N	North (direction)
IAT	Indicated Air Temperature	n	constant of the cone
		NDB	Non-Directional Beacon (ground-based radio aid)
ILS	Instrument Landing System		
Imp Gal	Imperial Gallons (volume)	nm	nautical miles (distance)

O	Out or On (as in Groundspeed Out)	**t**	time (in minutes)
P	Port (to the left)	**T**	Total force field of the earth's magnetism
P/L	Position Line		
p/o	parallel of origin	**TACS**	Traffic Alert and Collision Avoidance System
PNA	Point of No Alternate		
PNR	Point of No Return	**TAS**	True Airspeed
RA	Radio Altimeter	**TAT**	Total Air Temperature
RAS	Rectified Airspeed		
RBI	Relative Bearing Indicator	**TE**	Track Error
		Th	Time home
RE	Reduced Earth	**TMG**	Track Made Good
Rel	Relative (as in Relative bearing)	**To**	Time out
		TOC	Top Of Climb
RL	Rhumb Line	**trk**	track
RLG	Ring Laser Gyro	**US Gal**	United States Gallons (volume)
RMI	Radio Magnetic Indicator		
		UTC	Co-ordinated Universal Time (name now given to GMT)
RT	Radio Telegraphy		
RW	Runway		
S	South (direction) or Starboard (to the right)		
		varn	variation
		VOR	Very High Frequency Omni Range (ground-based radio aid)
SAT	Static Air Temperature		
sec	secant		
SG	Specific Gravity	**W**	West (direction)
SP	Standard Parallel	**WV**	Wind Velocity
st m	statute miles (distance)	**Z**	Vertical component of the Earth's magnetic field
(T)	True (direction)		

INDEX

aerodrome symbols, 151
aeronautical information, 150
Air Almanac, 197
air density, 35
airspeed indicator, 35
accelerometer, 296
aclinic line, 264
actual time of departure, 94
altering heading for destination, 86
altering heading to regain track, 86
altering heading to parallel track, 82
anti-meridian, 4
apheloin, 190
apparent movement of the sun, 191
apparent solar day, 193
arc to time conversion, 197

bar magnet, 255
bearing to an NDB, 216
blue pole, 256

calibrated airspeed, 35
cardinal points, 3
central meridian, 125
change in latitude, 8
change in longitude, 8
charts, 103
chart information layout, 151
civil time, 194
climbing, 220
closing angle, 83
closing angle lines, 96
'cocked hat' fix, 230
Coefficient A, 275
Coefficient B, 276
Coefficient C, 277
collision risk, 163

compasses, 265, 287
compass acceleration errors, 268, 291
compass aperiodicity, 265
compass calibration, 274, 291
compass checks, 268, 291
compass deviation, 18, 274
compass horizontality, 265
compass sensitivity, 265
compass turning errors, 271, 291
compass direction, 18
compressibility correction, 36
conformality, 105
constant of the cone, 133
contour lines, 149
convergency, 21
convergency on:
    Lambert's projection, 135
    Mercator's projection, 113
    polar stereographic projection, 145
conversion angle, 118
conversion factors for:
    distances, 27
    speeds, 34
    volumes, 71
    weights, 71
co-ordinated universal time, 196
correct outside air temperature, 35
critical point, 170
cross-wind component on a runway, 65

day, 189
dead reckoning, 213
departure, 30

derivation of time, 193
descending, 220
detector unit, 289
deviation, 18, 274
difference in latitude, 8
difference in longitude, 8
dip, 262
direction, 15
direction finding station, 214
direct reading compass, 267
distance, 26
distance marks on track, 92
DME, 219
doppler, 51
drift, 48
drift components on a track, 99

earth, 1
earth magnetism, 261
east, 4
economical cruising level, 78
Electronic Flight Instrument Systems, attitude displays, 323
control panel, 322
horizontal displays, 325
E/I bar pick-off, 297
emergency data, 170
estimated time of arrival, 80
estimation of closing angle, 86, 96
estimation of distance, 102
estimation of track angle, 88
estimation of track error, 81

equator, 4
feet, 32

Flight Level, 153
Flight Management
    Systems:
    computer, 314
    control and display
        unit, 316
flux valve, 288
fraction marks on track,
    92
fuel consumption, 76
fuel flow, 76
fuel volume, 71
fuel weight, 71
funnel features, 153

Global Positioning
    System:
    space segment, 329
    control segment, 330
    user segment, 331
graduated scale, 106
grams per cubic metre, 35
Great Circle, 4
Greenwich Mean Time,
    196
Greenwich meridian, 6
Gregorian calendar, 189
grid direction, 23
grivation, 24
ground-radio aid
    symbols, 152
ground speed, 41
ground speed home, 170
ground speed out (or on),
    170

hard iron, 257
heading, 17
heading / TAS vector, 47
head-wind components:
    on a runway, 65
    on a track, 99
hours, 194

Imperial gallons, 71
indicated airspeed, 34
indicated air
    temperature, 38
Inertial Navigation
    Systems:

integration flow chart,
    300
errors, 302
checks, 308
control and display
    unit, 305
mode selector, 303
radial error rate, 309
instrument error, 35
International Date Line,
    198
International Standard
    Atmosphere, 35
isoclinals, 264
isodynes, 264
isogonal, 16, 264
isogriv, 189

Julian calendar, 189

Kepler's laws of
    planetary motion,
    190
kilograms, 71
kilometres, 27
knots, 34
kilometres per hour, 34

Lambert's conic
    projection, 130
latitude, 5
layer tinting, 149
line of constant bearing,
    163
litres, 71
Local Mean Time, 195
longitude, 6
lost procedure, 154
lunar month, 189

Mach number, 38
magnetic direction, 16
magnetic equator, 262,
    264
magnetic variation, 16,
    262
magnetism, 255
man-made features, 150
map reading in the air,
    153
maximum deviation, 284
maximum drift angle, 99
maximum ground speed,
    49

mean altitude, 222
mean sea level (MSL), 35
mean solar time, 194
mean temperature, 221
mean wind velocity, 221
Mercator's projection,
    108
meridians, 4
metres, 32
millibars, 35
minimum elevation
    figures, 153
minimum ground speed,
    49
minutes (time), 194
minutes (angular
    measurement), 5

natural features, 148
nautical miles, 26
navigation computer:
    AIRSPEED window,
        35
    circular slide rule, 28
    Mach no. index, 63
    triangle of velocities,
        56
    wind components on a
        R/W, 65
navigation log form, 226
non-directional beacon,
    216
north, 3

oblique Mercator's
    projection, 128
obstruction symbols, 151
one-in-sixty rule, 80
Ordnance Survey maps,
    127
orthomorphism, 105, 108
overtaking, 160

paralleling track, 82
parallel of latitude, 5
parallel of origin, 133
Perihelion, 190
pilot navigation, 80
pinpoint fix, 228
pitot pressure, 35
plane of the ecliptic, 192
plotting, 212

plotting radio bearings
on:
a Lambert's chart, 137,
217
a Mercator chart, 117,
218
point of no alternate, 185
point of no return, 178
polar stereographic
projection, 143
poles, 3
position, 3
position error, 35
position line, 224
pounds, 71
pre-flight planning, 80,
153
pressure altitude, 35
prime meridian, 6

QDM, 214
QDR, 214
QTE, 214
QUJ, 215

radar fix, 228
radio magnetic indicator,
100, 216
railway tracks, 149
rate integrated gyro, 298
rectified airspeed, 34
red pole, 256
reduced earth (RE), 107
regulated airspace
symbols, 152
relative rearing indicator,
216
relative velocity, 159
relief features, 148

remote reading compass,
287
residual deviation, 283
rhumb line, 12
ring laser gyro, 309
roads, 149
running fix, 229
runway, 65

scale, 106
Schuler loop, 301
seasons, 191
sidereal day, 193
sidereal year, 194
simple conic projection,
130
small circles, 5
simultaneous fix, 228
soft iron, 257
south, 3
specific gravity, 72
speed, 34
stable platform, 298
standard closing angle,
84
standard parallel, 130
standard time, 198
starboard, 48
static air temperature, 38
static pressure, 35
statute mile, 26
strap-down IRS
alignment, 312
strap-down IRS tests, 313
sunrise and sunset, 200
surface wind velocity, 66
symbols used in plotting,
47, 213

tail-wind components, 99

temperature rise with
speed, 38
time, 41
time home, 178
time marks on track, 92
time out or on, 178
top of climb, 220
topographical maps and
charts, 147
total air temperature, 38
towns, 149
track, 47
track error, 81
track made good, 81
transferred meridian, 139
transferred position lines,
229
transverse Mercator's
projection, 125
triangle of velocities, 47
tropical year, 195
true Airspeed, 34
true direction, 16
twilight, 205
two-thirds, one-sixth
rule, 135

United States gallons, 71

variation, 16, 262
vector triangle problems,
50
velocity vectors and
symbols, 47
VOR, 225

water features, 148
weights, 71
west, 4
wind velocity, 47

	Trinidad	England
Total images	36,854	22,479
Average per person	732	450
Average per male	614	283
Average per female	849	613
Based on the maximum of 300 inspected:		
Woman on own	1,006	450
Man on own	696	359
Woman with children	159	100
Man with children	111	68
Couple, average per man	16	16
Couple, average per woman	9	7
Draws attention to what wearing	576	142
'Faux model'	198	3
Trying to look hot but not selfie	354	52
Shoes	20	1
Bling	172	3
Hat/cap	254	52
Nails	34	4
Swimsuit	116	83
Pregnancy	79	5
DJ equipment	49	0
'Gangsta'	253	0
Brands	147	6
Food alone	253	65
Food and people	126	79
Drinks alone	61	23
Drinks and people	352	568
Cars	93	70
Motorbike	11	21
Garden	0	48
At work	343	12
Religion associated	147	5
Holiday	243	1,199
Scenery	81	173

Figure 1 Analysis of most recent 150 images posted and the most recent 150 tagged images, from the profiles of 50 informants per field site

	Trinidad	England
Beach	355	116
Birthday	47	25
Christmas	74	47
Wedding	140	168
Sports	65	251
Tongue out	5	127
Wearing silly outfit/fancy dress	31	178
Dog	52	100
Cat	32	36
Babies/toddlers (on own)	315	612
Carnival	137	0

Figure 1 *(Contd.)*

	Trinidad		England	
	Total posts	Total people	Total posts	Total people
Total	3,093		1,841	
Two girls	123	12	122	15
Two girls kissing	0	0	8	5
Pouting	15	5	12	3
Event	70	19	1	1
Baby/toddler	78	19	36	11
Baby only	36	12	54	6
Image is not them, but is another person	111	28	91	21
Image is neither them or another person (i.e. not a human being)	497	36	205	21
Embellishment	185	25	10	3
Retro	33	12	2	2
Meme	97	17	18	7
Pulling a face	8	6	72	11
Hot	283	22	53	7
Carnival	19	8	0	0
Holiday/scenery	29	10	40	10
'Gangsta'	29	11	4	1

Figure 2 Analysis of profile pictures of 50 informants per field site (total posts and the total of people who posted them)

	Trinidad		England	
	Total posts	Total people	Total posts	Total people
Total	1,002		927	
'Faux lesbian' pose	0	0	24	4
Mirror	114	14	34	10
Hot	205	16	58	8
No make-up	0	0	3	3
Pulling a face	10	4	196	18
With others	116	20	474	32
On their own	557	28	138	29

Figure 3 Analysis of selfies that appeared in the most recent 150 images posted by 50 informants per field site

smartphone. Figure 4 is a survey of the last 20 postings on the walls of the same 100 individuals, giving us a sample of 2,000 postings.

Issues of anonymity and privacy

All our informants were told that we might use their posted material within educational materials and signed consent forms. Sometimes they requested to first see the particular images that we have reproduced here, which we then supplied. We do not, however, have consent for some people who appear in the background or alongside our informants, so we have tried to render them anonymous. This is especially true of The Glades, since consent there tended to be from individuals. In the more socialised world of El Mirador, Jo was often able to get consent from whole families or groups. Since we prefer natural images this has led to a bias of representation, with the balance in favour of individuals rather than groups; this is especially true of images from The Glades. People in The Glades also had a general concern with the public exposure of baby images, so we decided to anonymise these regardless of consent.

When it comes to memes and other public images, we have tried to investigate the legal basis for the reproduction of such images. This research resulted in a clear conclusion that no one actually knows at this point of time what is or is not legal. Our response has been to focus on what we would call 'real' ethics. The purpose of this book is clearly educational, and without these images that purpose could not have been achieved. As academics we believe strongly in the merits of education

	Trinidad		England	
	Total posts	Total people	Total posts	Total people
Eco/ climate	7	3	14	5
IT/ science	16	10	11	9
Banter	17	10	39	19
School/ work	5	3	11	6
Football	13	7	40	8
Purchases	13	7	4	4
Facts	9	4	15	10
Mood	39	18	33	11
Bored	4	3	0	0
Spectacle	13	8	3	1
Family	27	15	136	29
National	7	7	5	4
Gender banter	10	10	14	14
Selfies				
Home	19	7	0	0
School/ Work	13	9	0	0
Other	11	8	30	15
Total	43	24	30	15
Music				
Total links to videos	41	22	21	11
Foreign	36	17	9	7
Local	5	5	5	4
Memes				
Total	125	36	45	14
Cartoon	35	14	19	12
Moral	21	10	15	6
Political	0	4	9	7
Romance	7	5	0	0
Religion	11	6	0	0
Posts				
Video	92	28	55	19
Mapped status	7	1	22	12
Embellishment	6	3	0	0

Figure 4 Analysis of most recent 20 postings on the timelines of 50 informants per field site (total posts and the total of people who posted them)

	Trinidad		England	
	Total posts	Total people	Total posts	Total people
Photos				
Food only	8	4	9	9
Food and people	7	5	6	5
Drinks only	7	7	4	4
Drinks and people	11	7	62	19
Cars	4	3	7	6
Religion	21	17	5	2
Work	22	8	19	7
Holiday	23	8	45	13
Beach	15	6	2	2
Film/television/celebrity	11	5	7	6
Birthdays	18	10	29	15
Weddings	15	7	3	3
Festive greetings	13	9	2	2
Death	6	4	11	7
News	4	3	13	7
Sports	17	9	24	10
Babies	19	8	44	11
Gaming	39	19	4	4

Figure 4 *(Contd.)*

per se. Nor do we envisage that any harm will come to anyone through their inclusion in this book, which is the issue that we feel should be at the heart of 'real' ethics, as opposed to the labyrinthine world of copyright and intellectual property law.

If someone recognises themselves here and wishes they had not been included, or some company claims prior rights, we will remove their image in further editions of the book. In our field work people generally were very happy to contribute to what they felt was a worthwhile purpose; indeed, the main complaint was when they wanted to be named and we had to insist upon anonymity to protect others. With respect to self-reference we decided to use our first names, Jo and Danny, for casual reference and our surnames, Miller and Sinanan, when referring to ourselves as authors of publications.

Notes

Chapter 1

1 Miller, D. 2011. *Tales from Facebook*. Cambridge: Polity Press.
2 Miller, D. et al. 2016. *How the World Changed Social Media*. London: UCL Press. Chapter 11, 155–77.
3 Sinanan, J. 2017. *Social Media in Trinidad*. London: UCL Press.
4 For example Miller, D. 1994. *Modernity: An Ethnographic Approach*. Oxford: Berg. Miller, D. and Sinanan, J. 2014. *Webcam*. Cambridge: Polity Press.
5 For example Miller, D. 1994a. Miller, D. and Sinanan, J. 2014.
6 Miller, D. 2016. *Social Media in an English Village*. London: UCL Press.
7 Fox, K. 2004. *Watching the English*. London: Hodder & Stoughton.
8 Based on the records of the local medical practice.
9 Miller, D. 2016. Sinanan, J. 2017.
10 Miller, D. 2016. Chapter 3, 45–91.
11 Barthes, R. 1981. *Camera Lucida: Reflections on Photography*. New York: Hill and Wang. Benjamin, W. 1970. *Illuminations*. London: Jonathan Cape. Sontag, S. 1978. *On Photography*. London: Allen Lane.
12 Bateson, G. and Mead, M. 1962. *Balinese Character: A Photographic Analysis*. New York: New York Academy of Sciences.
13 For example Caiuby Novaes, S. 2010. 'Image and Social Sciences: The Trajectory of a Difficult Relationship.' *Visual Anthropology* 23: 278–98. Chaplin E. 1994. *Sociology and Visual Representations*. London: Routledge. Mitchell, M. J. T. 2005. *What Do Pictures Want?* Chicago, IL: University of Chicago Press.
14 For example Danforth, L. and Tsiaras, A. 1982. *The Death Rituals of Rural Greece*. Princeton, NJ: Princeton University Press. Daniels, I. 2010. *The Japanese House*. Oxford: Berg. Pinney, C. 1997. *Camera Indica*. London: Reaktion Press.
15 Bourdieu, P. 1990. *Photography: A Middle-brow Art*. Cambridge: Polity Press.
16 Edwards, E. 2012. *The Camera as Historian: Amateur Photographers and Historical Imagination 1885–1918*. Durham, NC: Duke University Press.
17 Sarvas, R. and Frohlich, D. 2011. *From Snapshots to Social Media – The Changing Picture of Domestic Photography*. London: Springer-Verlag. 133.
18 Keightley, E. and Pickering, M. 2014. 'Technologies of Memory: Practices of Remembering in Analogue and Digital Photography.' *New Media and Society* 16: 576.
19 See Van Dijck, J. 2007. *Mediated Memories in the Digital Age*. Stanford, CA: Stanford University Press.
20 See especially the contributions and bibliography within Gómez Cruz, E. and Lehmuskallio A., eds. 2016. *Digital Photography and Everyday Life: Empirical Studies on Material Visual Practices*. London: Routledge.
21 Rose, G. 2012. *Doing Family Photography*. Surrey: Ashgate. Poole, D. 1997. *Vision, Race, and Modernity*. Princeton, NJ: Princeton University Press.
22 Slater, D. 1995. 'Domestic Photography and Digital Culture' In Lister, M., ed. *The Photographic Image in Digital Culture*. London: Routledge. 129–46. The study of these domestic photographs has flourished since the publication of Chalfen, R. 1987. *Snapshot Versions of Life*. Bowling Green, OH: Bowling Green University Press.

23 Bourdieu, P. 1990.
24 General works on the relationship between anthropology and photography include Edwards, E. 1992. *Anthropology and Photography 1860–1929*. London: Royal Anthropological Institute. Edwards, E. and Hart, J. 2004. *Photographs, Objects, Histories*. London: Routledge. Edwards, E. 2012. 'Objects of Affect: Photography Beyond the Image.' *Annual Review of Anthropology* 41: 221–34. Pinney, C. 2011. *Photography and Anthropology*. London: Reaktion. An unusual example of an anthropological work that does focus on visual images in social media is Autenrieth, U. P. and Neumann-Braun, K., eds. 2011. *The Visual Worlds of Social Network Sites: Images and Image-based Communication on Facebook*. Baden-Baden: Nomos, Edition Reinhard Fischer.
25 There is a sustained literature on visual anthropology, to which one of the most consistent contributors has been Sarah Pink. However, the emphasis has been more methodological and conceptual compared to this book, where the aim is description and cross-cultural comparison. See Pink, S. 2006. *The Future of Visual Anthropology: Engaging the Senses*. London: Routledge. Pink, S. 2007. *Doing Visual Ethnography: Images, Media and Representation in Research*. London: Sage. Revised and expanded 2nd edition.
26 Goffman, E. 1979. *Gender Advertisements*. New York: Harper and Row.
27 Larsen, J. 2008. 'Practices and Flows of Digital Photography: An Ethnographic Framework'. *Mobilities* 3(1): 141–60.
28 Another useful journal article in that respect was Murray, S. 2008. 'Digital Images, Photosharing, and our Shifting Notions of Everyday Aesthetics'. *Journal of Visual Culture* 7(2): 147–63.
29 Shifman, L. 2013. *Memes in Digital Culture*. Cambridge: MIT Press. 37–54.
30 The site http://knowyourmeme.com/ is the best attempt we have come across to try and find the source of some of the most popular memes.
31 We recognise that this discussion is quite attenuated. A more detailed account that includes the various stages of development in social media photography may be found in Miller, D. 2015. *Photography In the Age of Snapchat*. London: Royal Anthropological Institute.

Chapter 2

1 During his ethnography Miller and his co-worker Ciara Green interviewed over 350 individuals, including 80 at the four local secondary schools. These were mostly 16–18-year-old pupils, but also included some teachers.
2 Nicolescu, R. 2016. *Social Media in Southeast Italy*. London: UCL Press.
3 Miller, D. 2016.
4 A tagged picture is one in which the picture is linked to your name by the person who posted it online. As a result people searching your name will see these pictures whoever originally posted them.
5 If we follow the usual 'technical' definition of a selfie – a photo taken by the subject of that photo on their camera phone – it is not always possible to be certain that an image is in fact a selfie. As a result we tend to include within this genre many close-ups that might in fact have been taken by someone else.
6 To be precise, among the Facebook postings of school-age children there were 288 images with others and 63 on their own.
7 For examples of Instagram pictures from The Glades see Miller, D. 2016 and Miller, D. 2015. These also discuss other genres of the selfie such as the 'uglie'; these are not discussed here since they relate more to Snapchat than to Facebook.

Chapter 3

1 Sinanan, J. 2017.
2 Miller, D. and Sinanan, J. 2014. 11–113. See also Carsten, J. 2003. *After Kinship*. Cambridge: Cambridge University Press.
3 Bolter, J. and Grusin, R. 2000. *Remediation: Understanding New Media*. Cambridge: MIT Press.

4   Both the culture of BFF and 'indirects' are equally common in The Glades. However, they have migrated from Facebook to Twitter and are therefore discussed in Chapters 3 and 5 of Miller, D. 2016.
5   Miller, D. 2014a. 224, 236.
6   See Miller, D. 1994a. 245–52. This defines bacchanal as the confusions and disorder which arise from gossip and scandal, and as a revelation of truth.

Chapter 4

1   Miller, D. 1997. 'How Infants Grow Mothers in North London.' *Theory, Culture and Society* 14: 67–88. Phoenix, A., Woolett, A. and Lloyd, E., eds. 1991. *Motherhood: Meanings, practices and ideologies*. Thousand Oaks, CA: Sage Publications.
2   See   http://www.dailymail.co.uk/femail/article-2595450/These-selfies-make-livid-Why-cancer-survivor-JENNI-MURRAY-angry-stars-helped-raise-millions-posting-photos-no-make-up.html
3   Lupton, D. 2013. *The Social Worlds of the Unborn*. London: Palgrave Macmillan. Murray, M. 2013. '"Staying with the Baby": Intensive Mothering and Social Mobility in Santiago de Chile.' In Faircloth, C., Layne, L. and Hoffman, D. eds, *Parenting in Global Perspective: Negotiating Ideologies of Kinship, Self and Politics*, 151–66. London: Routledge.
4   Miller, D., ed. 1995. *Unwrapping Christmas*. Oxford: Oxford University Press.
5   Chalfen, R. 1969. 'Photography's Role in Tourism: Some Unexplored Relationships.' *Annals of Tourism Research* 6(4) (1979): 435–47. Lo, I., McKercher, B., Lo, A., Cheung, C. and Law, R. 2011. 'Tourism and Online Photography.' *Tourism Management* 32(4): 725–73. Urry, J. 1990. *The Tourist Gaze*. London, Thousand Oaks, New Delhi: Sage.
6   Bourdieu, P. 1986. *Distinction: A Social Critique of the Judgement of Taste*. London: Routledge. Sahlins, M. 1976. *Culture and Practical Reason*. Chicago, IL: University of Chicago Press.
7   See Miller, D. et al. 2016. Chapter 9.
8   The way this is often expressed in anthropology is that in many societies women represent what is understood as natural and men what is cultural. See Ortner, S. 1972. 'Is Female to Male as Nature Is to Culture?' *Feminist Studies* 1: 5–31.
9   Ormston, R. and Curtice, J. 2015. *British Social Attitudes 32*, National Centre for Social Research   http://www.bsa.natcen.ac.uk/latest-report/british-social-attitudes-30/social-class/subjective-social-class.aspx

Chapter 5

1   A very clear example where the task of looking good online is evidently a socially constructed burden rather than mere vanity is found in Nicolescu, R. 2016.
2   Yelvington, K. 1995. *Producing Power: Ethnicity, Gender and Class in a Caribbean Workplace*. Philadelphia, PA: Temple University Press. 22.
3   Similar observations were made about the importance of showing oneself in a work environment in our field site in South India. See Venkatraman, S. 2017. *Social Media in South India*. London: UCL Press.
4   Yelvington examines social relations as linked to gender, class and ethnicity, whereas Prentice emphasises this as the site for a process of self-creation and the relationship to both people and work. Yelvington, K. 1995. 164. See also Prentice, R. 2008. 'Knowledge, Skill and the Inculcation of the Anthropologist: Reflections on Learning to Sew in the Field.' *Anthropology of Work Review*, 29 (3): 54–61.
5   Alim, H. S., Ibrahim, A. and Pennycook, A. 2008. *Global Linguistic Flows: Hip Hop Cultures, Youth Identities, and the Politics of Language*. London: Routledge.
6   This is also found among those in The Glades living in social housing.
7   Not being taken for granted is one of the main reasons why traditionally Trinidadian women avoided marriage even after they had children. See Miller, D. 1994a. Chapter 4.
8   Meighoo, K. 2003. *Politics in a 'Half Made Society': Trinidad and Tobago, 1925–2001*. Kingston: Ian Randle Publishers. Ryan, S. 1972. *Race and Nationalism in Trinidad and*

Tobago: A Study of Decolonization in a Multiracial Society. Toronto: University of Toronto Press. Singh, K. 1994. *Race and Class Struggles in a Colonial State: Trinidad 1917–1945.* Kingston: The University of the West Indies. Yelvington, K. 1995. *Op. cit.*

9 Singh, K. 1994. 12.

10 Naipaul, V. S. 1967 (2001). *The Mimic Men.* London: Vintage Books; 1961 (2003). *A House for Mr Biswas.* London: Pan Macmillan; 1959 (2000). *Miguel Street.* Oxford: Heinemann Educational Publishers.

11 Ironically the actress who played this role, Miley Cyrus, then adopted a highly sexualised dance form, 'twerking', that certainly looks indebted to Caribbean dance forms such as wining. Though in the interests of scholarship Nicki Minaj (who was born in Trinidad) has insisted that they are different and that she – Nicki Minaj – wines.

12 See Miller, D. 1994a. 233–45.

13 Barnes, R. and Eicher, J. B. 1992. *Dress and Gender: Making and Meaning in Cultural Contexts.* New York: Berg. Gilbertson, A. 'A Fine Balance: Negotiating Fashion and Respectable Femininity in Middle-class Hyderabad, India.' *Modern Asian Studies* 48(1): 120–58. Khan, A. 2004. *Callaloo Nation: Metaphors of Race and Religious Identity among South Asians in Trinidad.* Durham, NC and London: Duke University Press. Mahmood, S. 2005. *Politics of Piety: The Islamic Revival and the Feminist Subject.* Princeton, NJ: Princeton University Press.

14 O'Young, W. 2000. 'Diaspora and Transnationalism: The Case of the Chinese in Trinidad and Tobago.' MA diss., University of the West Indies, St Augustine.

15 Fan, C. 1999. 'Migration in a Socialist Transnational Economy: Heterogeneity, Socioeconomic and Spatial Characteristics of Migrants in China and Guangdong Province.' *International Migration Review* 33 (4): 954–87. Kuhn, P. 2008. *Chinese Among Others: Emigration in Modern Times.* Lanham: Rowman and Littlefield Publishers.

16 Wang, X. 2016. *Social Media in Industrial China.* London: UCL Press.

17 Liu, H. 2005. 'New Migrants and the Revival of Overseas Chinese Nationalism.' *Journal of Contemporary China* 14 (43): 291–316.

18 Madianou, M. and Miller, D. 2012.

19 Compare Bourdieu, P. 1986. Bennett, T. et al. 2009. *Culture, Class, Distinction.* London: Routledge.

Chapter 6

1 Macfarlane, A. 1987. *The Culture of Capitalism.* Oxford: Blackwell. Chapter 4. Thomas, K. 1983. *Man and the Natural World: Changing Attitudes in England 1500–1800.* London: Allen Lane.

2 Chevalier, S. 1998. 'From Woollen Carpet to Grass Carpet: Bridging House and Garden in an English Suburb.' In Miller, D., ed. 1998. *Material Cultures.* London: UCL Press.

3 Miller, D. 1998. *A Theory of Shopping.* Cambridge: Polity Press and especially Miller, D. 1997. *Op. cit.,* 67–88.

4 Fox, K. 2004.

5 Fox, K., 2004.

6 Miller, D., 2016.

Chapter 7

1 Miller, 1994a.

2 We would not wish to over-generalise here. There are actually very striking differences in the attitudes to public display between The Glades and our corresponding study based in Southeast Italy. Nicolescu, R. 2016.

3 Sennett, R. 1974, 1976. *The Fall of Public Man.* Cambridge: Cambridge University Press.

4 The details of this argument are found in Miller, D. 1994 (b). 'Style and Ontology.' In Friedman, J., ed. *Consumption and Identity.* Amsterdam: Harwood Academic Publishers.

5 Miller, D. 2011. 40–52. Miller, D. and Sinanan, J. 2014. 162–91.

6   Ho, C. 2000. 'Popular Culture and the Aestheticization of Politics: Hegemonic Struggle and Postcolonial Nationalism in Trinidad Carnival.' *Transforming Anthropology* 9(1): 3–18. Mahase, R. 2008. 'Plenty a Dem Run Away' – Resistance by Indian Indentured Labourers in Trinidad, 1870–1920.' *Labor History* 49(4): 465–80. Sankerelli, B. 1998. 'Indian Presence in Carnival.' *The Drama Review* 42(3): 203–12.

7   Miller, 1994a. 82–134.

8   A film we have made about such a company can be found within the Trinidad films at http://www.ucl.ac.uk/why-we-post

9   The place where the costumes are invented, created and sold, and where the band is organised.

10 Miller, D, 1994a. 245–53.

11 Anderson, B. 1983 and 1991. *Imagined Communities*. London and New York: Verso.

12 See Miller, D. 2011. 40–52.

Chapter 8

1   Sinanan, J. 2017.

2   We have tried to use spelling that to our ears best conveys the meaning as well as the sound to a non-Trinidadian reader of English, favouring intelligibility over phonetics.

3   In direct quotations 'D:' stands for Danny (who carried out these interviews) and 'I:' for the informant.

4   Haynes, N. 2016. *Social Media in Northern Chile*. London: UCL Press.

5   At which point Danny admits saying silently to himself: Hallelujah.

Chapter 9

1   Autenrieth, U. P. and Neumann-Braun, K. 2011. Empson, R. 2011. *Harnessing Fortune: Personhood, Memory and Place in Mongolia*. Oxford: Oxford University Press. McKay, S. 2006. *Satanic Mills or Silicon Islands? The Politics of High-Tech Production in the Philippines*. New York: Cornell University/ILR Press. Uimonen, P. 2013. 'Visual Identity in Facebook.' *Visual Studies* 22(2): 122–35.

2   Miller, D., 1994a. *Op. cit.*

3   The argument developed here corresponds to Chapter 6 in Miller, D., 1994a. 257–90.

4   Thomas, K. 1983. *Man and the Natural World: Changing Attitudes in England, 1500–1800*. Oxford: Oxford University Press.

5   Macfarlane, A. 1978. *The Origins of English Individualism*. Oxford: Basil Blackwell.

6   Miller, D. 2015.

7   Miller, D. 2016.

References

Alim, H. S., Ibrahim, A. and Pennycook, A. 2008. *Global Linguistic Flows: Hip Hop Cultures, Youth Identities, and the Politics of Language*. London: Routledge.

Anderson, B. 1983 and 1991. *Imagined Communities*. London and New York: Verso.

Autenrieth, U. P. and Neumann-Braun, K., eds. 2011. *The Visual Worlds of Social Network Sites: Images and Image-based Communication on Facebook*. Baden-Baden: Nomos, Edition Reinhard Fischer.

Barnes, R. and Eicher, J. B. 1992. *Dress and Gender: Making and Meaning in Cultural Contexts*. New York: Berg.

Barthes, R. 1981. *Camera Lucida: Reflections on Photography*. New York: Hill and Wang.

Bateson, G. and Mead, M. 1962. *Balinese Character: A Photographic Analysis*. New York Academy of Sciences, New York, N.Y.

Benjamin, W. 1970. *Illuminations*. London: Jonathan Cape.

Bennett, T., Savage, M., Silva, E., Warde, A., Gayo-Cal, M. and Wright, D. 2009. *Culture, Class, Distinction*. London: Routledge.

Bolter, J. and Grusin, R. 2000. *Remediation: Understanding New Media*. Cambridge: MIT Press.

Bourdieu, P. 1990. *Photography: A Middle-brow Art*. Cambridge: Polity Press.

Bourdieu, P. 1986. *Distinction: A Social Critique of the Judgement of Taste*. London: Routledge.

Caiuby Novaes, S. 2010. 'Image and Social Sciences: The Trajectory of a Difficult Relationship.' *Visual Anthropology* 23: 278–98.

Carsten, J. 2003. *After Kinship*. Cambridge: Cambridge University Press.

Chalfen, R. 1987. *Snapshot Versions of Life*. Bowling Green, OH: Bowling Green University Press.

Chalfen, R. 1969. 'Photography's Role in Tourism: Some Unexplored Relationships.' *Annals of Tourism Research* 6(4) (1979): 435–47.

Chaplin, E. 1994. *Sociology and Visual Representations*. London: Routledge.

Chevalier, S. 1998. 'From Woollen Carpet to Grass Carpet: Bridging House and Garden in an English Suburb.' In Miller, D., ed. *Material Cultures*. London: UCL Press.

Danforth, L. and Tsiaras, A. 1982. *The Death Rituals of Rural Greece*. Princeton, NJ: Princeton University Press.

Daniels, I. 2010. *The Japanese House*. Oxford: Berg.

Edwards, E. 1992. *Anthropology and Photography 1860–1929*. London: Royal Anthropological Institute.

Edwards, E. 2012. 'Objects of Affect: Photography Beyond the Image.' *Annual Review of Anthropology* 41: 221–34.

Edwards, E. and Hart, J. 2004. *Photographs, Objects, Histories*. London: Routledge.

Empson, R. 2011. *Harnessing Fortune: Personhood, Memory and Place in Mongolia*. Oxford: Oxford University Press.

Fan, C. 1999. 'Migration in a Socialist Transnational Economy: Heterogeneity, Socioeconomic and Spatial Characteristics of Migrants in China and Guangdong Province.' *International Migration Review* 33 (4): 954–87.

Fox, K. 2004. *Watching the English*. London: Hodder & Stoughton.

Gilbertson, A. 'A Fine Balance: Negotiating Fashion and Respectable Femininity in Middle-class Hyderabad, India.' *Modern Asian Studies* 48 (1): 120–58.

Goffman, E. 1979. *Gender Advertisements*. New York: Harper and Row.

Gómez Cruz, E. and Lehmuskallio A., eds. 2016. *Digital Photography and Everyday Life: Empirical Studies on Material Visual Practices*. London: Routledge.

Haynes, N. 2016. *Social Media in Northern Chile*. London: UCL Press.

Ho, C. 2000. 'Popular Culture and the Aestheticization of Politics: Hegemonic Struggle and Postcolonial Nationalism in Trinidad Carnival.' *Transforming Anthropology* 9(1): 3–18.

http://knowyourmeme.com/

http://selfiecity.net/

Keightley, E. and Pickering, M. 2014. 'Technologies of Memory: Practices of Remembering in Analogue and Digital Photography.' *New Media and Society* 16(4): 576–93.

Khan, A. 2004. *Callaloo Nation: Metaphors of Race and Religious Identity among South Asians in Trinidad*. Durham, NC and London: Duke University Press.

Kuhn, P. 2008. *Chinese Among Others: Emigration in modern times*. Lanham: Rowman and Littlefield Publishers.

Liu, H. 2005. 'New Migrants and the Revival of Overseas Chinese Nationalism'. *Journal of Contemporary China* 14(43): 291–316.

Lo, I., McKercher, B., Lo, A., Cheung, C. and Law, R. 2011. 'Tourism and Online Photography.' *Tourism Management* 32(4): 725–73.

Lupton, D. 2013. *The Social Worlds of the Unborn*. London: Palgrave Macmillan.

Macfarlane, A. 1987. *The Culture of Capitalism*. Oxford: Blackwell.

Macfarlane, A. 1978. *The Origins of English Individualism*. Oxford: Wiley.

Madianou, M. and Miller, D. 2012. *New Media and Migration*. London: Routledge.

Mahase, R. 2008. 'Plenty a Dem Run Away' – Resistance by Indian Indentured Labourers in Trinidad, 1870–1920.' *Labor History* 49 (4): 465–80.

Mahmood, S. 2005. *Politics of Piety: The Islamic Revival and the Feminist Subject*. Princeton, NJ: Princeton University Press.

McKay, S. 2006. *Satanic Mills or Silicon Islands? The Politics of High-Tech Production in the Philippines*. New York: Cornell University/ ILR Press.

Meighoo, K. 2003. *Politics in a 'Half Made Society': Trinidad and Tobago, 1925–2001*. Kingston: Ian Randle Publishers.

Miller, D. 2016. *Social Media in an English Village*. London: UCL Press.

Miller, D. 2015. *Photography in the Age of Snapchat*. Royal Anthropological Society.

Miller, D. 2011. *Tales from Facebook*. Cambridge: Polity Press.

Miller, D. 1998. *A Theory of Shopping*. Cambridge: Polity Press.

Miller, D. 1994a. *Modernity: An Ethnographic Approach*. Oxford: Berg.

Miller, D., ed. 1995. *Unwrapping Christmas*. Oxford: Oxford University Press.

Miller, D. 1997. 'How Infants Grow Mothers in North London.' *Theory, Culture and Society* 14: 67–88.

Miller, D. 1994b. 'Style and Ontology.' In Friedman, J., ed. *Consumption and Identity*. Amsterdam: Harwood Academic Publishers.

Miller, D. and Sinanan, J. 2014. *Webcam*. Cambridge: Polity Press.

Mitchell, M. J. T. 2005. *What Do Pictures Want?* Chicago, IL: University of Chicago Press.

Murray, M. 2013. '"Staying with the Baby": Intensive Mothering and Social Mobility in Santiago de Chile.' In C. Faircloth, L. Layne and D. Hoffman, eds. *Parenting in Global Perspective: Negotiating ideologies of kinship, self and politics*, 151–66. London: Routledge.

Murray, S. 2008. 'Digital Images, Photo-sharing, and our Shifting Notions of Everyday Aesthetics.' *Journal of Visual Culture* 7(2): 147–63.

Naipaul, V. S. 1967 (2001). *The Mimic Men*. London: Vintage Books.

Naipaul, V. S. 1961 (2003). *A House for Mr Biswas*. London: Pan Macmillan.

Naipaul, V. S. 1959 (2000). *Miguel Street*. Oxford: Heinemann Educational Publishers.

Nicolescu. R. 2016. *Social Media in Southeast Italy*. London: UCL Press.

Ormston, R. and Curtice, J. 2015. British Social Attitudes *32, National Centre for Social Research* http://www.bsa.natcen.ac.uk/latest-report/british-social-attitudes-30/social-class/subjective-social-class.aspx

O'Young, W. 2000. 'Diaspora and Transnationalism: The Case of the Chinese in Trinidad and Tobago.' MA diss., University of the West Indies, St Augustine.

Phoenix, A., Lloyd, E.and Woolett., A., eds. 1991. *Motherhood: Meanings, Practices and Ideologies*. Thousand Oaks, CA: Sage Publications.

Pink, S. 2007. *Doing Visual Ethnography: Images, Media and Representation in Research*. London, Thousand Oaks, New Delhi: Sage. Revised and expanded 2nd edition.

Pink, S. 2006. *The Future of Visual Anthropology: Engaging the Senses*. London: Routledge.

Pinney, C. 2011. *Photography and Anthropology*. London: Reaktion Books.

Pinney. C. 1997. *Camera Indica*. London: Reaktion Books.

Prentice, R. 2008. 'Knowledge, Skill and the Inculcation of the Anthropologist: Reflections on Learning to Sew in the Field.' *Anthropology of Work Review* 29(3): 54–61.

Rose, G. 2012. *Doing Family Photography*. Surrey: Ashgate.

Ryan, S. 1972. *Race and Nationalism in Trinidad and Tobago: A Study of Decolonization in a Multiracial Society*. Toronto: University of Toronto Press.

Sahlins, M. 1976. *Culture and Practical Reason*. Chicago, IL: University of Chicago Press.

Sankerelli, B. 1998. 'Indian Presence in Carnival.' *The Drama Review* 42(3): 203–12.

Sarvas, R. and Frohlich, D. 2011. *From Snapshots to Social Media – The Changing Picture of Domestic Photography*. London: Springer-Verlag.

Scher, P. 2003. *Carnival and the Formation of a Caribbean Transnation*. Gainesville, FL: University Press of Florida.

Sennett, R. 1974, 1976. *The Fall of Public Man*. Cambridge: Cambridge University Press.

Sinanan, J. 2017. *Social Media in Trinidad*. London: UCL Press.

Shifman, L. 2013. *Memes in Digital Culture*. Cambridge: MIT Press.

Singh, K. 1994. *Race and Class Struggles in a Colonial State: Trinidad 1917–1945*. Kingston: The University of the West Indies.

Slater, D. 1995. 'Domestic Photography and Digital Culture.' In Lister, M., ed. *The Photographic Image in Digital Culture*. London: Routledge. 129–46.

Sontag, S. 1978. *On Photography*. London: Allen Lane.

Thomas, K. 1983. *Man and the Natural World: Changing Attitudes in England, 1500–1800*. Oxford: Oxford University Press.

Uimonen, P. 2013. 'Visual Identity in Facebook.' *Visual Studies* 22(2): 122–35.

Urry, J. 1990. *The Tourist Gaze*. London, Thousand Oaks, CA and New Delhi: Sage.

Van Dijck, J. 2007. *Mediated Memories in the Digital Age*. Stanford, CA: Stanford University Press.

Venkatraman, S. 2017. *Social Media in South India*. London: UCL Press.

Wang, X. 2016. *Social Media in Industrial China*. London: UCL Press.

Yelvington, K. 1995. *Producing Power: Ethnicity, Gender and Class in a Caribbean Workplace*. Philadelphia, PA: Temple University Press.

Index

aberrant instances appearing to refute
    generalisations 140
adulthood, representation of 74, 82–8
alcohol, use of 15–17, 47, 78, 87, 114
Alsatian dogs 128
Amway distributers 174–6
Anderson, B. 176
anime 47
anthropology 10, 201–6
    comparative 201
    nature of 202–4
anthropomorphising 126

'babe' shots 82
baby photographs 31–5, 55, 62–6, 135–9
bacchanal 55, 166, 180–4
baking 83–4
Barthes, R. 7
Bateson, G. 7
Benjamin, W. 7
'best friends forever' (BFF) 43–4
bio-politics 155
birth process 62, 136, 195–6
birthday celebrations 40–1, 68–9
'bling' culture 23, 46, 137, 155, 164–5
blurring of images 6–7
'boldface' 153
boredom 47, 51, 99–100
boundaries, policing of 190, 193, 204
Bourdieu, P. 7–9
branded goods 112

cancer 58–9
card-giving 33
Carnival 53–6, 153–68, 171, 189–90,
    195, 202–3
    and the values of transience 155–67
cars, perceived importance of 115–16
casual dress 98–9
cats and dogs 125–31, 141–2
celebrity 23, 45
chemotherapy 58–9
Chevalier, Sophie 133
children, relationships to 88, 128, 203
Chinese migrants 121–2
Christianity 145, 171
Christmas 33, 69–70, 153–5, 167–9, 203
class distinctions 57, 89–90, 108–16
clothing *see* dress

collages 32–3
comments added to photographs 100
community values 180
compromising photographs 18
conspicuous consumption 102
conspicuous display, absence of 140
cooking at home 84
cosmopolitanism 109
cover photographs 98
cultural capital 123
cultural diversity 2–3, 8, 55, 206
cultural heritage and cultural
    orientation 118, 121–2
cultural values and norms 204
cupcakes 84, 178–9
'cute' images 32–3, 37

death 69–71
debunking 146
dieting 83
dogs 132, 193–4; *see also* cats and dogs
domesticity and domestication 132–3
dress 19, 23–4, 45–6, 49–52, 71, 79–80,
    91, 137–40, 157–9, 173, 190
    for work 96–8
    see also fancy dress
drinks shown in posts 115
dualism in Trinidadian values 203

'El Mirador' 4–6, 31, 95, 201
Englishness and English values 7, 151–2,
    202, 204
entrepreneurial activity 173–7
environmental concerns 178, 205
essentialism 202–3
ethical issues 6
ethnicity 96, 116–23
ethnography 2, 5, 7, 9, 61, 66, 153, 201
Evangelism 171
extended families 35, 66, 101, 118, 168, 202

Facebook 1–2, 5–6, 9–22, 27–9, 33, 47–8,
    57–8, 61–2, 69–71, 85, 90, 95, 98–100,
    123, 126, 129–43, 146, 154–8, 161–2,
    165–70, 173–84, 195, 198–200,
    206–7
    radical changes in 17–18, 22
Faith Community church 174, 176
family, concept of 55

family photographs 26, 35, 67, 71, 101–2
fancy dress 75–6, 139
fashion 23
fathers and fatherhood 34, 55, 136
'faux model' phenomenon 45, 137, 160
femininity 83, 90, 105
fetes 155–60
fights between schoolchildren 166–7
finger nails 164–5
fingers splayed out 15
'first time' photographs 66–7
Flickr 7
food, images of 47, 69–70, 80–1, 112, 114
football and football shirts 27, 75–8
footwear 45, 92, 98
formal appearance and formal
    occasions 13, 25, 101–2
Fox, Kate 2–3, 140, 152
freedom, sense of 202
'freeing up' 160–1, 190
friendship 22, 42–4, 50
Frohlich, D. 8, 10
'fuck', use of the word 144–5, 200
fun, enjoyment of 15–17, 20, 26, 50
funny cats 141–2

gaming 41–3, 47
'gangsta' image 102–4, 117, 123, 161
gardens
    pictures of 133
    visits to 72–3
gay culture and gay rights 28, 88–9
gender relations and gender
    roles 45, 56, 68, 95–6, 101–8,
        198, 205
generalisations 202–5
gesturing 12–16, 75
ghetto 109
'girls' night out' phenomenon 87
'The Glades' 2–6, 66, 95, 201
global influences and genres 109–10, 121
Goffman, E. 9
gold, display of 165, 187–8
'Goldilocks strategy' (Miller) 152
graduation photographs 25, 52–3
The Great British Bake Off 83–4
Green, Ciara 138

hairstyles 46–7, 98–9, 119–20, 164
Haynes, N. 195
hen parties 85, 87
high heels 45–6
hip-hop culture 102–3, 161
holiday photographs 19–20, 71–3, 80, 139
home improvements 133
homogenisation, cultural 206
homosexuality 88–9, 92
'horse phase' in girls' development 130–1
housework 88
humour, use of 37, 88, 125, 135, 141–52,
    172–4, 200, 204

imagined communities 165
'indirects' 43–4, 51, 55–6, 182
Instagram 5, 7, 10, 21, 28–9, 58,
    85, 110, 129, 207

intimate photographs 50–1
irony and ironic humour 143, 151, 200

jam-making· 84
jewellery, display of 23
journalism 201
journals about social media 1–2
j'ouvert 165
Junior Queens 159

Keightley, E. 8
Kermit the Frog 182
Khan, A. 116

'laddish' behaviour 78, 80
legs, images of 139
leisure wear 98
'liking' 120
'liming' 96, 114, 161, 163, 178–80

Macfarlane, Alan 203
make-up 46
male machismo 22
Marley, Bob 118
masculinity 74–83, 88–91, 105
masquerade bands 157–8
Mead, M. 7
memes 7, 10, 17, 41–4, 56, 70, 77, 89, 93–4,
    99, 105–7, 123, 142–3, 170–7, 180,
    182, 195–9, 206
'messy eater' shots 62–3
middle-class sensibility and middle-
    ground attitudes 134, 146,
        180, 204
Miller, Daniel (co-author) 1–5, 115, 136–8,
    152–3, 167, 183, 188, 202, 206
mirror selfies 50
mixed heritage 119–21
mixed-sex groups 39–40, 52
modesty 22, 24, 59, 83, 125, 135,
    140, 149, 152
Montana, Hannah 110
moralising and moral positions 44–5, 55,
    188–90
mothers and motherhood 34, 53–4,
    57, 61, 64, 95, 135–7, 205
Murray, Jenni 58
music festivals 20–1, 74
MySpace 206

Naipaul, V.S. 108–9
nakedness 198
narcissism 28
nationalism 55, 171–3
'nigga', use of the word 109, 117
normativity 188, 193–5, 200

Old Year's Night 155
Organo Gold coffee 176–7

parenting 53–4, 57, 60
    outside marriage 34
    parallels with keeping pets 128, 203
    see also fathers and fatherhood;
        mothers and motherhood
party pictures 14, 17, 19

peer engagement 17
Pentecostalism 171
pets 125–32, 193, 203
photographs
  editing of 32
  number taken 13–14
photography
  aims of 207
  analogue and *digital* 8, 10
  anthropology of 9
  genres of 8–9
  literature of 9
  quality of 13–14
  role in helping people to have fun 11–19
Pickering, M. 8
'playing mas' 158
political posting 148
Poole, D. 8
popular culture 112
Port of Spain 113, 186–7
posing for photographs 11–19, 25–6, 36–9,
    158–9, 190
postings 14–24, 47–8, 55–6, 61–2,
    66–78, 83–8, 95–6, 140, 154, 164–7,
    170–3, 176, 182, 185, 188–92,
    196–201, 206–7
  about gender relations 198
  by adults 68–74
  daily number of 10
  reasons for 196–7
  serious 146–8, 171, 173
  varied responses to 199
pretentiousness 182, 190, 194–5
privacy, protection of 7, 152
pulling faces 50
puns 142–3
putting people down 190–2

qualitative research 5

racial epithets 109, 117–18
Rastafarian culture 118
'real talk' (#reltalk) 44–5, 55
religion and religious images 145,
    147, 170, 173–7, 195, 202
'revenge porn' 166
rites of passage 52
romantic relationships 107
roots, re-construction of 202
Rose, G. 8
Rotaract group 177–80

Sarvas, R. 8, 10
schooling
  ending of 26–7, 40
  start of 39
self-confidence 17
self-consciousness 37–40
self-deprecation 24, 125, 149–52, 200
self-effacement 24, 125, 135–41,
    149–51, 204
'selfie girls' 23, 29–30, 57, 139
selfies 6, 8, 28–30, 48–52, 96, 191–2, 206
  'no make-up' type 58–60, 138
  purposes of 28–9
  taken by adults 57

sensationalism 167–8
sentimental messages 92–3
sexualised images 188–9
sexuality 88–9, 166, 202
Shifman, L. 10
shoes *see* footwear
Sinanan, Jolynna (co-author) 2–3, 166,
    186, 188
Singapore 109
Singh, K. 108
Slater, D. 8
slavery 203
'sleepy' selfies 50–1
Snapchat 10, 18, 58, 207
social class *see* class distinctions
social housing, people living in 90–3
social media 1, 3, 7–11, 35, 39, 43, 47,
    56, 58, 90, 95, 110, 116–17, 152–6,
    167, 183, 200, 206–7
'social' aspect of 19–22
social values, roles and norms 55–6, 83
social structures 123
socialisation into norms 202
socialising with other people 98
sofas, sitting on 26
Sontag, S. 7
sophisticated images 112
special occasions 35
spontaneity in images 11–12, 15, 35–6,
    162–3
sports-related images 27–8, 42–3, 47–9,
    77–9, 85, 104
stush behaviour 109, 194
style icons 110
suburbia and the suburban ethos 125, 132–5,
    146, 154, 203–4
'sweet man' image 190–1

tagged pictures 24–5
tattoos 92, 94
themes in postings 55
Thomas, Keith 203
'toilet humour' 141
Tolkien, J.R.R. 134
tongue sticking out 12–13, 15, 75–6
transcendence 55, 124–5, 153–5, 167–8,
    171–2, 176, 180–4, 195, 203
  values of 167–8, 172, 182–3
transience 124–5, 153–67, 176–80, 183–4,
    195, 202–3
  and Carnival 155–67
travel images 110–11
Trinidad and Trinidadian culture 1–2, 7,
    31, 40, 42, 45, 55–6, 66, 116–17,
    123–45, 153–5, 161, 166–7,
    171–4, 178, 182–4, 186–90,
    195–6
'twining' (dance style) 160–1
Twitter 5, 28, 58, 207

ultrasound images 61

Van Dijck, J. 10
visual communication, concern with 56,
    154–5, 162, 184, 201
vocational interests 173–80

walks in the countryside 134
Wang, X. 121
weather as a subject for posting 75
wedding photographs 26, 69, 71
WhatsApp 10, 18
wine, appreciation of 85–6, 146
'wining' (dance style) 53, 189

work-based postings 95–6, 123
work clothing 96–8
work-related events 57, 104–6

Yelvington, K. 95
youth, culture of 55
YouTube 109–10

Lightning Source UK Ltd.
Milton Keynes UK
UKOW06f1646280217
295542UK00004B/22/P